Criminal Litigation and Sentencing

Criminal Litigation and Sentencing

The City Law School
CITY UNIVERSITY LONDON

Authors

Professor Peter Hungerford-Welch, Barrister, Assistant Dean, The City Law School
Robert McPeake, Barrister, Principal Lecturer, The City Law School
Simone Start, Barrister, Senior Lecturer, The City Law School
Nikki Walsh, Solicitor, Senior Lecturer, The City Law School

Editor

Robert McPeake, Barrister, Principal Lecturer, The City Law School

Series Editor

Julie Browne, Barrister, Senior Lecturer, The City Law School

OXFORD
UNIVERSITY PRESS

OXFORD
UNIVERSITY PRESS

Great Clarendon Street, Oxford, OX2 6DP,
United Kingdom

Oxford University Press is a department of the University of Oxford.
It furthers the University's objective of excellence in research, scholarship,
and education by publishing worldwide. Oxford is a registered trade mark of
Oxford University Press in the UK and in certain other countries

Twenty-fourth edition 2012
Twenty-fifth edition 2013
Twenty-sixth edition 2014

Impression: 1

Published in the United States of America by Oxford University Press
198 Madison Avenue, New York, NY 10016, United States of America

British Library Cataloguing in Publication Data
Data available

ISBN 978–0–19–873570–0

Printed in Great Britain by
Ashford Colour Press Ltd, Gosport, Hampshire

FOREWORD

These manuals have been written by a combination of practitioners and members of staff of the City Law School (formerly the Inns of Court School of Law), and are designed primarily to support training on the Bar Professional Training Course (BPTC), wherever it is taught. They provide an extremely useful resource to assist in acquiring the skills and knowledge that practising barristers need. They are updated regularly and are supported by an Online Resource Centre, which can be used by readers to keep up to date throughout the academic year.

This series of manuals exemplifies the practical and professional approach that is central to the BPTC. I congratulate the authors on the excellent standard of the manuals and I am grateful to Oxford University Press for their ongoing and enthusiastic support.

Professor Peter Hungerford-Welch
Barrister
Assistant Dean (Professional Programmes)
The City Law School
City University London
2015

PREFACE

It is essential that practitioners in the criminal courts have mastered the rules of criminal procedure and sentencing. However, such rules never stand still and practitioners must frequently update their knowledge of the relevant statutory provisions and case law. This task has grown increasingly onerous over the last two decades, not least because of the steady stream of legislation in this field.

This manual endeavours to provide a clear guide to the law and rules which govern practice in the magistrates' courts, youth courts, the Crown Court and appellate courts. This edition has been updated to include all relevant developments in the law to April 2015. As ever, though, criminal justice does not stand still. Significant developments will be dealt with on the series' Online Resource Centre, which we hope is a valuable additional resource for readers of the manual. The website is available at www.oxfordtextbooks.co.uk/orc/barmanuals/.

16 April 2015

GUIDE TO USING THIS BOOK

The Bar Manual series includes a range of tools and features to aid your learning. This guide will outline the approach to using this book, and help you to make the most out of each of the features within.

Examples

Examples of indictments are provided to show where there may be issues when dealing with the following situations: when a separate charge cannot be made because of restrictions of another indictment, when there is sufficient evidence to change or add an indictment and when there is a lack of evidence. There are also a number of excerpts from Acts, including the Bail Act 1976 and Magistrates' Courts Act 1980.

Pedagogical features

Tables, flow charts and diagrams offer visual representations of more complex subjects. In particular, flow charts are provided to outline the procedure in the youth court and illustrate the structure and relationship of courts to help you to organise the procedures outlined within the book.

Online Resource Centre updates

For further material and updates to selected manuals in this series please visit the Online Resource Centre at www.oxfordtextbooks.co.uk/orc/barmanuals/.

OUTLINE CONTENTS

DETAILED CONTENTS

TABLE OF CASES

TABLE OF PRIMARY LEGISLATION

UK statutes

International and European legislation

TABLE OF SECONDARY LEGISLATION

Statutory instruments

Directions

Codes

Circulars

1

Introduction

1.1 Introduction to criminal litigation

1.1.1 Aims of the course

The main intention of those responsible for designing the Criminal Litigation element of the Bar Professional Training Course (BPTC), and this manual, has been to make the subject both real and practical. Your Criminal Litigation course should instil you with the knowledge of how the criminal justice system actually works; then give you the opportunity to demonstrate that you have assimilated such knowledge and are able to make the decisions which a barrister could find himself or herself making in practice.

1.1.2 Objectives and structure of the course

By the end of the course, and having read this manual, you should be:

(a) familiar with the progress of a case through the criminal courts, understanding the various stages and what each stage involves;

(b) able to prepare for a hearing in the magistrates' court or Crown Court, knowing what the procedure will be in court and what matters will need to be covered;

(c) capable of taking informed decisions (and, if necessary, advising your client on how to act) with regard to the various different paths that a case can take, both as to its final resolution and the intermediate hearings;

(d) able to decide whether or not a decision taken in criminal proceedings merits an appeal—whether it be in relation to conviction, sentence or some procedural matter;

(e) able to prepare properly for an appeal and advise your client which is the most suitable method of appeal (where a choice exists).

This manual starts at the beginning of the process (eg an individual being charged with an offence) and works its way through to the possible endings—acquittal, conviction and sentence, appeal. This seems to be the best way to promote an understanding of the various practices and procedures that govern the passage of a case through the criminal courts. The manual begins with preliminary matters, such as powers of arrest, then the commencement of criminal proceedings against an accused person. Having dealt with the subject of bail, the manual then looks at what happens when an accused person first appears in court and how a decision is made on which court should try the accused. The usual way of disposing of a case is summary trial by magistrates, so that is next on the list. The manual then examines the treatment of juveniles in the criminal justice system, in particular trial venues and procedures. Our focus then shifts to the Crown Court—how a case may get there (sent for trial or committed for sentence or on appeal from a decision of the magistrates) and then pre-trial issues (eg disclosure, drafting an indictment and entering a plea). This leads us on to consideration of the trial in the Crown Court and then the possibility of further proceedings in the Court of Appeal and Supreme Court. Finally, we look at sentencing powers and procedures in each of the three types of trial court—magistrates' courts, youth courts and Crown Court.

1.1.3 Sources of information

1.1.3.1 Practitioner works

Throughout the text of this manual, you can find references to other sources, in particular law reports and statutes, but there are also references to relevant passages in the main practitioner works. These are:

- *Archbold, Criminal Pleading, Evidence and Practice*, Sweet & Maxwell;
- *Blackstone's Criminal Practice*, OUP;
- *Stones' Justice's Manual*, Butterworths.

Other practitioner works for the criminal barrister include specialist sources such as *Wilkinson's Road Traffic Offences* and more general works such as *Archbold Magistrates' Courts Criminal Practice* (both Sweet & Maxwell).

You are strongly advised to read further about criminal litigation topics in any of these books. In addition, there are excellent books aimed more specifically at readers who are at the BPTC stage. These include:

- John Sprack, *A Practical Approach to Criminal Procedure*, 14th edn, OUP;
- Peter Hungerford-Welch, *Criminal Litigation & Sentencing*, 8th edn, Routledge.

You should also look at journals such as the *Criminal Law Review* which carries both articles and case commentaries. Articles relevant to the criminal practitioner often appear in *Criminal Law and Justice Weekly* (previously *Justice of the Peace*) and *Legal Action* (the magazine of the Legal Action Group), amongst others.

1.1.3.2 Websites

Increasingly, information about the criminal justice system can be found online. There are portals with links to other sources. Examples include:

- <http://www.venables.co.uk>—a portal designed and run by Delia Venables with many useful links;
- <http://www.bailii.org>—the website of the British and Irish Legal Information Institute;
- <http://city.lawbore.net>—the website of the City Law School, City University, London;
- <http://www.kent.ac.uk/lawlinks>—the website for law at the University of Kent.

There are also many websites where you can access information directly. Examples include, in no particular order:

- <http://www.legislation.gov.uk>—a website run by the National Archive on behalf of the Ministry of Justice, where you can find Acts of Parliament, Statutory Instruments and their accompanying Explanatory Notes (this replaces the old website of the Office of Public Sector Information or OPSI);
- <http://lawcommission.justice.gov.uk/>—the website of the Law Commission (where you can find not only proposals for law reform but also the research that underpins them);
- <http://www.justice.gov.uk>—the website of the Ministry of Justice which combines the former roles in the criminal justice system of the Home Office and the Department for Constitutional Affairs;
- <http://www.judiciary.gov.uk>—the website of the judiciary of England and Wales and the Judicial College. On this website, you can find the Crown Court and Equal Treatment Bench Books (the former provides, amongst much valuable information, assistance for judges preparing to direct a jury as well as systematic approaches to sentencing);

- Daily court listings can be found at <http://www.justice.gov.uk/courts/court-lists>;
- <https://www.gov.uk/browse/justice>—material on criminal procedure can be found on the gov.uk website, including publications from the Ministry of Justice;
- <http://sentencingcouncil.judiciary.gov.uk>—the website for the Sentencing Council, which provides guidance for sentencers (the Sentencing Council replaced the Sentencing Guidelines Council in 2010 but some of the older guidelines on the website still refer to the SGC);
- <http://www.cps.gov.uk>—the website of the Crown Prosecution Service, which contains a lot of helpful information, not least the legal guidance that Crown Prosecutors use, as well as statistics on the work of the CPS.

1.1.3.3 The manual (and other BPTC manuals)

This manual is designed primarily for use in conjunction with the Criminal Litigation course on the BPTC. It should prepare you to deal with a particular topic as well as supporting specific classes through the material it contains. It is also designed to stand alone as a practical and sensible guide to legal practice in the criminal courts of England and Wales. It contains most of the 'bare bones' of what anyone needs to know when starting on a career in the criminal courts; it devotes rather less space to the remoter world of the Court of Appeal and the Supreme Court.

The manual does not contain the totality of information on the criminal justice system and that is not its aim. It is intended to deal primarily with matters of significance to the junior practitioner and supplies the level of information which should be 'at the ready' when that practitioner finds himself or herself in court. It is not intended to supplant the excellent practitioner works mentioned in **1.1.3.1** and we would recommend that you should always regard those sources as the best place to research legal issues (in addition to the primary sources—legislation and case law).

Remember that there are other BPTC manuals as well, which may contain information and guidance which is relevant to work in the criminal justice system. These include:

- the ***Advocacy*** manual (with how-to-do-it guides on bail applications, submissions of no case and witness handling, for example);
- the ***Drafting*** manual (with guidance on writing a skeleton argument to support an application, for example);
- the ***Evidence*** manual (to check on admissibility points, for example);
- the ***Opinion Writing and Case Preparation*** manual (to get tips on how to research the law for your case and manage the facts);
- the ***Professional Ethics*** manual (to make sure that you don't do something you shouldn't, or vice versa).

You may find it useful to pull together guidance from a number of the manuals to help you see the complete picture.

Note: In some chapters of ***Criminal Litigation and Sentencing***, statistical tables are reproduced with the kind permission of the Home Office Statistics Department. Owing to different recording procedures in some areas of the country and some incomplete data, the figures in these tables should be taken only as a guide.

1.2 Introduction to the criminal justice system

1.2.1 The Criminal Procedure Rules

1.2.1.1 Generally

The Criminal Procedure Rules (the Rules) set out case management powers for the magistrates' courts and the Crown Court and, perhaps most significantly, an overriding objective for criminal justice. This is an echo of the insertion of an overriding objective into civil litigation via the Civil Procedure Rules in 1998 and is intended to be equally important for the conduct of criminal litigation.

Rule 1.2 states that those involved in the conduct of a case must act in accordance with the Rules (and Practice Directions) and inform the court at once of any significant non-compliance.

Reference will be made to the Rules, where appropriate, in the manual.

1.2.1.2 The overriding objective

The overriding objective is set out in r 1.1 and is as follows:

(1) The overriding objective of this new code is that criminal cases be dealt with justly.

(2) Dealing with a criminal case justly includes—

(a) acquitting the innocent and convicting the guilty;

(b) dealing with the prosecution and the defence fairly;

(c) recognising the rights of a defendant, particularly those under Article 6 of the European Convention on Human Rights;

(d) respecting the interests of witnesses, victims and jurors and keeping them informed of the progress of the case;

(e) dealing with the case efficiently and expeditiously;

(f) ensuring that appropriate information is available to the court when bail and sentence are considered; and

(g) dealing with the case in ways that take into account—

(i) the gravity of the offence alleged,

(ii) the complexity of what is in issue,

(iii) the severity of the consequences for the defendant and others affected, and

(iv) the needs of other cases.

1.2.1.3 Case management powers

Under Part 3 of the Rules, courts are given significant powers to manage cases through the criminal justice system efficiently and effectively. These powers apply to all cases in the magistrates' courts and Crown Court. The principle behind them is to facilitate the overriding objective through enabling courts to engage in active case management. Appropriate directions are to be given in each case as early as possible and the parties are to actively assist the court, where necessary by applying for directions. This is promoted through the appointment, for every case, of an individual—the case progression officer (cpo)—to be responsible for progressing the case. Prosecution, defence and court must each have a cpo and their contact details must be exchanged.

In actively managing a case, a number of objectives are identified (in r 3.2):

- identifying the real issues at an early stage;
- identifying the needs of witnesses at an early stage;
- setting a timetable for the progress of the case, and deciding what must be done, by whom and by when;
- monitoring case progress and compliance with any directions;
- ensuring that evidence is presented in the most succinct and clear way;
- avoiding unnecessary hearings;
- encouraging cooperation;
- using technology.

In particular, applications for directions, representations and any resultant hearings may take place via letters, telephone or electronic communications (presumably this includes e-mails). Alternatively, the court may give a direction without a hearing and can specify 'the consequences' of failure to comply with a direction (r 3.5(2)). Directions must be given at every hearing, to enable the case to conclude at the next hearing, if possible, or as soon as is possible thereafter. The punitive sanction alluded to in r 3.5(2) appears again in r 3.9—'where a direction has not been complied with, [the court is to] find out why, identify who was responsible, and take appropriate action'. Each party must ensure that their case is ready for trial and, as part of this process, the court may require a party to identify those witnesses which he intends to call to give oral evidence, the order in which they will be called, any arrangements for facilitating the giving of evidence and to identify what other material he intends to make available to the court (see rr 3.10 and 3.11). Concerns that Part 3 did not provide for any appropriate sanction and thus was toothless led to the amendment of r 3.5 (see *R (Kelly) v Warley Magistrates' Court* [2007] EWHC 1836 (Admin)). Rule 3.5(6) was added, to specify that failure to comply with a rule or direction may lead to changes to a hearing (it may be fixed, postponed, extended or cancelled), a costs order may be made to penalise the defaulting party or 'the court may impose such other sanction as may be appropriate'.

The improvements in case management have also developed in other ways. For example, cases which are tried summarily in the magistrates' court will require completion of a case progression form (entitled 'Preparation for trial in a Magistrates' Court' and see **Appendix 2**). This form, together with its guidance notes, sets out a case progression timetable for effective preparation of the case; it includes a comprehensive set of standard case preparation time limits (see also the *Criminal Practice Directions*). Where a case is committed or sent to Crown Court for trial, case management will be furthered initially by completion of a 'Magistrates' Court: Directions' form and then a plea and case management hearing (PCMH) will be scheduled; Crim PR, r 3.13 specifies that in order to prepare for a trial in the Crown Court, the Crown Court must conduct a PCMH unless the circumstances make it unnecessary. The PCMH should take place within about 14 weeks after sending the case for trial if the defendant is in custody (or about 17 weeks if he is on bail). According to the *Criminal Practice Directions*, a PCMH 'should reduce the number of ineffective and cracked trials and delays during the trial to resolve legal issues'. Where possible, courts should fix the dates of cases so that the trial advocates are also able to attend the PCMH. See further **Chapters 2** and **4**.

1.2.2 Structure and relationship of the courts

All cases begin in the magistrates' court. A youth court is a type of magistrates' court which deals exclusively with juveniles. The vast majority of criminal cases will be tried in the magistrates' court and will end there (unless either the accused is committed to the Crown Court for sentence, or he appeals to either the Crown Court or the High Court). The remaining cases will begin in the magistrates' court but be sent for trial to the Crown Court with the possibility of an appeal to the Court of Appeal. From both the Court of Appeal and the High Court it is possible, though rare, to appeal to the Supreme Court of the United Kingdom on matters of law. The inter-relationship of the courts is set out in **Figure 1.1**.

Whatever powers the magistrates' court has are given to it by Acts of Parliament—it has no inherent jurisdiction. Numerous Acts establish the jurisdiction of magistrates to deal with a considerable variety of work. It is appropriate to note that the magistrates' court has a civil jurisdiction, in addition to its criminal work. Perhaps the most significant aspects of magistrates' work, for a barrister, are their jurisdiction over family and domestic proceedings and their role in licensing matters. This may change as more civil matters are determined by magistrates despite the apparently criminal nature of such matters, for example granting anti-social behaviour orders.

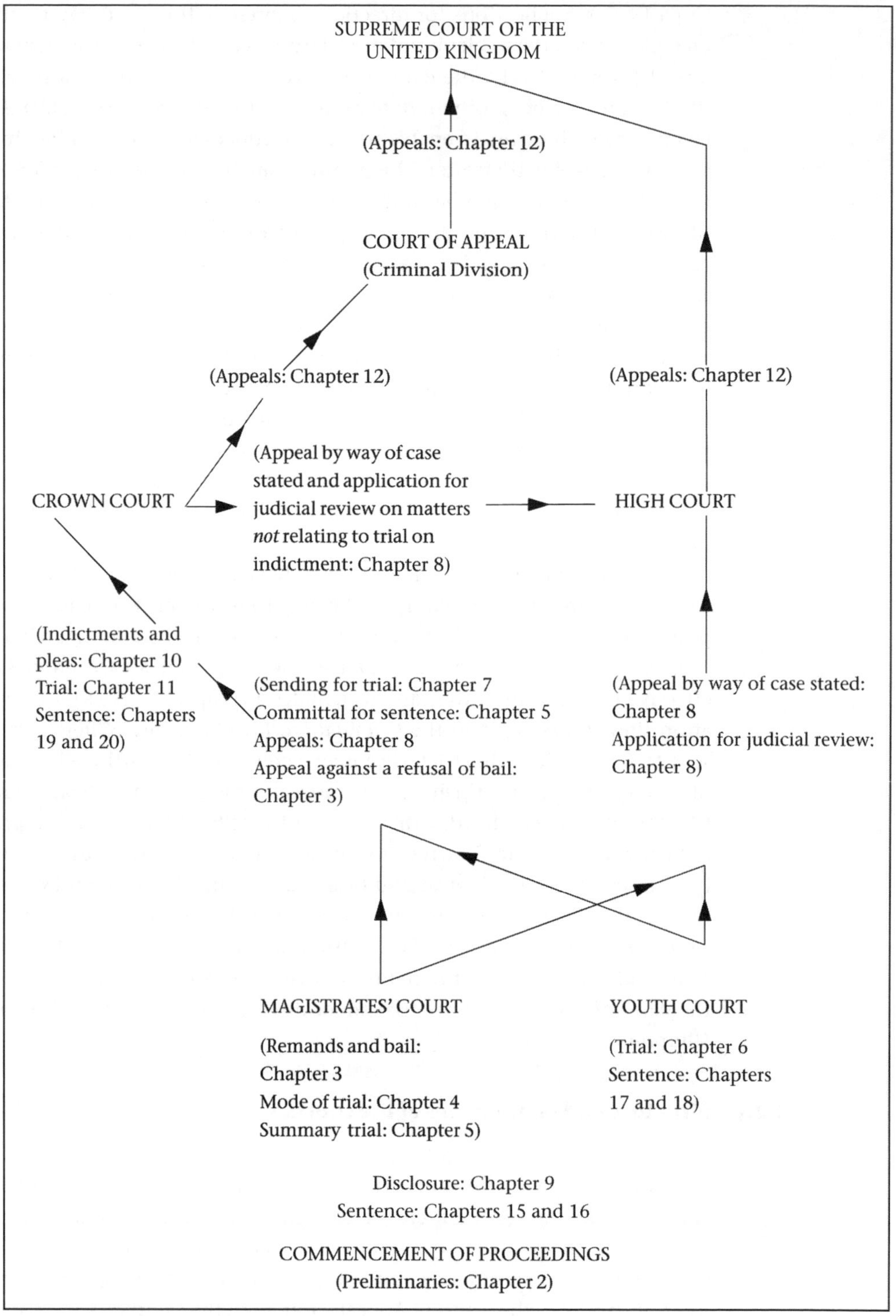

Figure 1.1 Structure and relationship of the courts

1.3 Abbreviations

Abbreviations are often used in the text. Some are probably familiar, for example *Archbold*, *Stone's*, WLR for Weekly Law Reports. Others will become familiar in time. The following list of common abbreviations should help:

AsBCPA 2014 (Anti-social Behaviour, Crime and Policing Act 2014);

BA 1976 (Bail Act 1976);

CAA 1968 or 1995 (Criminal Appeal Act, either 1968 or 1995);

C&JA 2009 (Coroners and Justice Act 2009)
C&SA 2010 (Crime and Security Act 2010);
CCA 2013 (Crime and Courts Act 2013);
CDSA 2006 (Criminal Defence Service Act 2006);
CICB (Criminal Injuries Compensation Board);
CJA (Criminal Justice Act, various years but most notably 2003);
CJCA 2015 (Criminal Justice and Courts Act 2015);
CJCSA 2000 (Criminal Justice and Court Services Act 2000);
CJIA 2008 (Criminal Justice and Immigration Act 2008);
CJPOA 1994 (Criminal Justice and Public Order Act 1994);
CLA (Criminal Law Act, various years);
CPIA 1996 (Criminal Procedure and Investigations Act 1996);
CPS (Crown Prosecution Service);
Cr App R (Criminal Appeal Reports. A specialist series, reporting cases from the Divisional Court of the Queen's Bench Division, Court of Appeal (Criminal Division) and the House of Lords/Supreme Court);
Cr App R (S) (Criminal Appeal Reports (Sentencing). A companion to the Cr App R but concentrating on sentencing decisions);
Crim LR (Criminal Law Review. A monthly publication with brief, up-to-date reports of cases and useful articles);
C(S)A 1997 (Crime (Sentences) Act 1997);
CYPA 1933 or 1969 (Children and Young Persons Act, either 1933 or 1969);
DTO (Detention and Training Orders);
DTTO (Drug Testing and Treatment Orders);
DVCVA 2004 (Domestic Violence, Crime and Victims Act 2004);
EAH (early administrative hearings);
ECHR (European Convention on Human Rights and Fundamental Freedoms);
HRA 1998 (Human Rights Act 1998);
JA 1974 (Juries Act 1974);
LASPO 2012 (Legal Aid, Sentencing and Punishment of Offenders Act 2012);
MCA 1980 (Magistrates' Courts Act 1980);
MHA 1983 (Mental Health Act 1983);
PACE 1984 (Police and Criminal Evidence Act 1984);
PCC(S)A 2000 (Powers of Criminal Courts (Sentencing) Act 2000);
PCMH (plea and case management hearing)
PDBA 2011 (Police (Detention and Bail) Act 2011);
PJA 2006 (Police and Justice Act 2006);
PoFA 2012 (Protection of Freedoms Act 2012);
ROA 1974 (Rehabilitation of Offenders Act 1974);
SCA 1981 (Senior Courts Act 1981, previously the Supreme Court Act);
SOCPA 2005 (Serious Organised Crime and Police Act 2005);
TIC (taken into consideration);
YJCEA 1999 (Youth Justice and Criminal Evidence Act 1999).

2

Preliminaries

2.1 Introduction

This chapter considers the first steps in a criminal case. We will look at police powers to arrest and detain suspects, the three methods of commencing a prosecution if there is sufficient evidence to take the case on to court and, finally, collateral matters, such as case management, costs and funding.

2.1.1 Jurisdiction and immunity: who may be prosecuted?

English courts accept jurisdiction to try an accused for an offence committed in England and Wales, regardless of the nationality of the offender (Courts Act 2003, s 2). In addition, English courts have jurisdiction over some offences committed abroad in certain circumstances, such as offences of murder and manslaughter where the accused is a British subject, and offences of hijacking regardless of the nationality of the accused. For a complete list of such offences, see *Archbold* and *Blackstone's Criminal Practice*.

Certain persons are entitled to immunity from prosecution. The Queen is immune, as are foreign sovereigns and heads of state, their families and personal servants. Diplomatic agents, their staff and families are also immune. For a complete list of those immune from prosecution, see *Archbold* and *Blackstone's Criminal Practice*.

2.1.2 The right to prosecute

The Crown Prosecution Service (CPS) was created by the Prosecution of Offences Act 1985. It is a national prosecution service with the Director of Public Prosecutions (DPP) at its head, and under the 'superintendence' of the Attorney-General. The main duty of the CPS is to conduct all criminal proceedings commenced by the police. This includes the power to discontinue proceedings or to change or amend any charges originally preferred.

The right of an individual, and of certain statutory bodies such as Her Majesty's Revenue and Customs, to institute and conduct criminal proceedings, is expressly preserved by the Act. However, under s 6(2), the DPP has an unfettered discretion to intervene in any proceedings, and conduct them on his or her own behalf.

2.2 Police powers to arrest and detain a suspect

Most police powers of arrest, interviewing and charging a suspect are contained in the Police and Criminal Evidence Act 1984 (PACE 1984) and the Codes of Practice created thereunder. In general terms, the Act provides the overall framework, and the Codes provide the fine detail. There are eight major Codes of Practice, namely:

- Code A: Code of Practice for the Exercise by Police Officers of Statutory Powers of Stop and Search.

- Code B: Code of Practice for the Searching of Premises by Police Officers and the Seizure of Property found by Police Officers on Persons and Premises.
- Code C: Code of Practice for the Detention, Treatment and Questioning of Persons by Police Officers.
- Code D: Code of Practice for the Identification of Persons by Police Officers.
- Code E: Code of Practice on Tape Recording.
- Code F: Code of Practice for the Visual Recording with Sound of Interviews with Suspects.
- Code G: Code of Practice for the Statutory Power of Arrest by Police Officers.
- Code H: Code of Practice in connection with the detention and questioning by police officers of persons under s 41 and Sch 8 of the Terrorism Act 2000.

The Codes contain detailed regulations on the exercise of police powers, and 'notes for guidance'. The notes for guidance are not provisions of the Codes, but are guidance to police officers and others about their application and interpretation.

The Codes of Practice apply to:

- police officers (PACE 1984, s 67(8) and (10)); and
- persons 'other than police officers who are charged with the duty of investigating offences or charging offenders' (PACE 1984, s 67(9)). This includes local authority officials, post office investigators, officers of the Serious Fraud Office, customs officers and store detectives. Whether a body or person conducting an enquiry is subject to s 67(9) is a question of fact in each case (*R v Seelig* [1992] 1 WLR 148).

The Codes of Practice have undergone a number of revisions, and since CJA 2003, s 11 these may be brought into effect by the Home Secretary without the requirement to publish a draft code for consultation. Students are advised to consult the Codes in detail for their full terms and effect (see <https://www.gov.uk/police-and-criminal-evidence-act-1984-pace-codes-of-practice>).

While students should be familiar with all Codes, this manual is mainly concerned with Code C, and any reference to 'the Code' should be understood accordingly. Students should consult practitioner texts for a full discussion of this area (note: Code H applies only to terrorism cases).

2.2.1 Powers of arrest without warrant

The term 'arrest' is not defined by statute. In *Christie v Leachinsky* [1947] AC 573, it was referred to as 'the beginning of imprisonment'. It is a restraint on the liberty of the person within the law. In *R v Inwood* (1973) 57 Cr App R 529, it was said that there is no magic formula, but only an obligation to make it plain to the suspect that he is no longer a free man. There must be:

(a) a power of arrest; and

(b) a properly carried out arrest.

A police officer has a number of powers of arrest, the most important of which are contained in PACE 1984, s 24 and s 24A as amended.

Essentially there are two elements:

(a) there must be actual, suspected or attempted involvement in a criminal offence by the person; and

(b) *reasonable* grounds for believing that the arrest is *necessary*.

Arrest by a police officer is covered by PACE Code G for the Statutory Powers of Arrest by Police Officers. Note in particular:

1.2 The right to liberty is a key principle of the Human Rights Act 1998. The exercise of the power of arrest represents an obvious and significant interference with that right.

1.3 The use of the power must be fully justified and officers exercising the power should consider if the necessary objectives can be met by other, less intrusive means. Arrest must never be used simply because it can be used. Absence of justification for exercising the powers of arrest may lead to challenges should the case proceed to court. When the power of arrest is exercised it is essential that it is exercised in a non-discriminatory and proportionate manner.

PACE 1984, s 24 Arrest without warrant: constables

(1) A constable may arrest without a warrant:

(a) anyone who is about to commit an offence;

(b) anyone who is in the act of committing an offence;

(c) anyone whom he has reasonable grounds for suspecting to be about to commit an offence;

(d) anyone whom he has reasonable grounds for suspecting to be committing an offence.

(2) If a constable has reasonable grounds for suspecting that an offence has been committed, he may arrest without a warrant anyone whom he has reasonable grounds to suspect of being guilty of it.

(3) If an offence has been committed, a constable may arrest without a warrant:

(a) anyone who is guilty of the offence;

(b) anyone whom he has reasonable grounds for suspecting to be guilty of it.

[See *R v Olden* [2007] EWCA Crim 726 as to the arresting officer's reasonable suspicion.]

(4) But the power of summary arrest conferred by subsection (1), (2), or (3) is exercisable only if the constable has reasonable grounds for believing that for any of the reasons mentioned in subsection (5) it is necessary to arrest the person in question.

(5) The reasons are:

(a) to enable the name of the person in question to be ascertained (in the case where the constable does not know, and cannot readily ascertain, the person's name, or has reasonable grounds for doubting whether a name given by the person as his name is his real name);

(b) correspondingly as regards the person's address;

(c) to prevent the person in question:

(i) causing physical injury to himself or any other person;

(ii) suffering physical injury;

(iii) causing loss of or damage to property;

(iv) committing an offence against public decency (subject to subsection (6)); or

(v) causing an unlawful obstruction of the highway;

(d) to protect a child or other vulnerable person from the person in question;

(e) to allow the prompt and effective investigation of the offence or of the conduct of the person in question;

(f) to prevent any prosecution for the offence from being hindered by the disappearance of the person in question.

(6) Subsection (5)(c)(iv) applies only where members of the public going about their normal business cannot reasonably be expected to avoid the person in question.

Section 24A provides for the arrest of a person by another—a citizen's arrest. For this to be lawful, the arrestee must be in the process of committing the offence, the offence must be an indictable offence (one which must or may be tried in the Crown Court) and there is no provision for arresting on suspicion. Retail security guards dealing with shoplifters, and nightclub doormen dealing with disorderly customers, use citizen's arrest to detain until the police arrive, at which point the suspect is arrested by the police under s 24.

2.2.2 Effecting the arrest: reasons for arrest and conveying to a police station

See PACE Code G. A person is arrested by:

- being informed by a police officer that he or she is under arrest; or
- being physically seized by a police officer, in which case he or she must be informed that he or she is under arrest as soon as is practicable after the arrest (PACE 1984, s 28(1)); or

- a combination of words and conduct which makes it clear that the officer will, if necessary, use force to prevent the person from leaving (*Murray v Ministry of Defence* [1988] 1 WLR 692).

The arrested person must be told the reason for the arrest, even if it is obvious (s 28(3) and (4)). This must also be recorded in the officer's notes. The ECHR, Article 5(2) also provides that an arrested person should be told promptly and in language which he understands of the reason for his arrest and any charge against him.

Section 28(3) reflects the common law: *Taylor v Chief Constable of Thames Valley Police* [2004] 1 WLR 3155. The underlying reason is that a person is entitled to know why he is being arrested, and be given the opportunity of explaining any misunderstanding or calling attention to others for whom he may have been mistaken.

If the reason given renders the arrest unlawful, it is irrelevant that there was a valid reason for the arrest if it was not communicated to the arrested person at the time (*Christie v Leachinsky* [1947] AC 573; *Abassy v Commissioner of Police of the Metropolis* [1990] 1 WLR 385).

It is not a requirement of s 28 that the arresting officer supply the reason for the arrest, as long as a reason is provided as soon as practicable thereafter (*Dhesi v Chief Constable of the West Midlands, The Times,* 9 May 2000, where the defendant was arrested by one officer and directed towards another nearby who supplied the reason). By virtue of Code C, para 10.5, the person who is arrested should also be cautioned. See **2.2.8** for a discussion of the caution.

A police officer effecting the arrest of a person may search him or her, if he has reasonable grounds for believing that the person may present a danger to himself or to others, by virtue of PACE 1984, s 32(1). Other powers of search after arrest are also contained in s 32.

The arrested person must be taken to a police station as soon as is practicable, unless it is reasonable to carry out other investigations first, for example search of the arrested person and/or certain premises (PACE 1984, s 30(1), (10) and (10A) and *Dallison v Caffery* [1965] 1 QB 348), or released on street bail (see **2.2.3**). Police officers should not abuse the provisions of s 30 in order to ask questions to avoid the provisions of the Codes of Practice (*R v Khan* [1993] Crim LR 54 and *R v Raphaie* [1996] Crim LR 812).

In each police area, certain police stations are designated as being suitable for the detention of arrested persons (PACE 1984, s 35(1)). If it is anticipated that the detention will exceed six hours, the arrested person must be detained in a designated police station (s 30(2) and (3)).

There is nothing improper in arresting a suspect on a holding charge provided there are reasonable grounds for arresting that person on that charge. It makes no difference, if the arrest is proper, that the motive is to investigate other and more serious offences (*R v Chalkley and Jeffries* [1998] QB 848). But if the arresting officer knows that there is no possibility of a charge being brought, the arrest will be improper even if there are in fact reasonable grounds for suspecting that an offence has been committed (*Holgate-Mohammed v Duke* [1984] AC 437).

Powers of arrest are also governed by ECHR, Article 5, to which students are referred. Article 5 is construed narrowly, and sets out an exhaustive list of the circumstances in which a person may properly be detained. UK domestic law has been held to be formulated with 'the degree of precision required by the Convention' (*Steel v UK* (1988) 28 EHRR 602).

2.2.3 Street bail

The arresting officer has an alternative to taking the suspect immediately to a designated police station: street bail (PACE 1984, s 30A, as inserted by the CJA 2003). This empowers the officer to immediately release the suspect on bail, requiring him to attend at a police station at a future date and time. Conditions may be attached to the street bail (s 30C) to secure surrender, prevent further offences or prevent interference with witnesses. The purpose of street bail is to give the police officer the discretion to remain on the streets rather than return to the police station, particularly when the case is relatively minor. According to PACE Code G:

Having determined that the necessity criteria have been met and having made the arrest, the officer can then consider the use of street bail on the basis of the effective and efficient progress of the investigation of the offence in question. It gives the officer discretion to compel the person to attend a police station at a date/time that best suits the overall needs of the particular investigation. Its use is not confined to dealing with child care issues or allowing officers to attend to more urgent operational duties and granting street bail does not retrospectively negate the need to arrest.

The arresting officer must give the street bailed person a notice, specifying the offence for which he was arrested, the ground(s) on which he was arrested and any street bail conditions. If the bailed person fails to attend as required, he may be arrested (s 30D). If he wishes to vary his bail conditions he can apply at a police station or magistrates' court. There is no statutory limit to the period for which street bail may be granted but six weeks maximum was recommended in Home Office guidance.

2.2.4 At the police station: the detention clock

A suspect under arrest can be generally detained in police custody for a maximum of 24 hours. This is subject to certain extensions that will be explained later in the chapter. Within that 24-hour period, the police are required to follow a strict timetable of detention when dealing with a suspect in custody (PACE 1984, ss 34–46).

Note that a 'volunteer' is a person who attends a police station voluntarily, not on police bail and not under arrest. A volunteer is entitled to leave the station at any time, and he should be informed of this. If the police wish to prevent a volunteer from leaving, they must arrest him or her.

The following provisions involve understanding that police ranks are, in ascending rank, constable, sergeant, inspector and superintendent.

Stage 1: Arrival at the police station and authorisation of detention
On arrival at the police station, the suspect must be taken before the custody officer. He or she holds at least the rank of sergeant and must not, except in exceptional circumstances, be an officer involved in the investigation. The custody officer has several duties, including:

(a) To inform the suspect of his or her rights to consult a solicitor, to have someone informed, and to examine the Codes of Practice and provide him with a written notice of his rights (see **2.2.7**).

(b) To determine whether the suspect:

   (i) is in need of medical treatment or attention (see **2.2.5**);

   (ii) requires either an appropriate adult, help to check documentation, or an interpreter;

   and to record the decision.

(c) To maintain a custody record, being a complete record of the suspect's detention, including such matters as times of meals, interviews, the caution, if given, and the charge. A solicitor or appropriate adult must be permitted to consult a suspect's custody record as soon as practicable after the suspect's arrival at the police station and at any other time during the suspect's detention (Code C, para 2.4).

(d) To ascertain and record everything which the suspect has with him when detaining him. Prior to the CJA 2003, every item in the suspect's possession was individually recorded. This was useful to the defence solicitor in that it may reveal other reasons behind the suspect's arrest. It also protected the police themselves from allegations of tampering with the possessions. Recording possessions, however, was also seen as time-consuming and unnecessary. The CJA 2003, s 8 therefore provides that though the custody officer will still have to ascertain everything that the detained person has with him, he will no longer have to record it on the custody record. Any record that is made does not have to be part of the custody record under s 54(2A), but the suspect must be allowed the opportunity to check and sign it as correct.

   It is a matter for the custody officer to decide whether a record should be made and that if the record is not on the custody record, the custody officer should record where the record exists. Home Office guidance advises the custody officer should have regard to:

- the circumstances of the case, for example whether the property could be the proceeds of crime, could have been used in the commission of crime or could be relevant evidence;
- the nature and volume of the property—drugs, money and property of substantial value should always be recorded;
- the wishes of the suspect—he should be asked if there are any items he wants to be recorded and his wishes should, 'within reason and if practicable', be complied with;
- the facilities for securing property—detailed records may not be necessary if placed in a sealed bag in the presence of the suspect.

(e) To oversee the whole of the suspect's detention. As the custody officer is unconnected with the investigation, he or she can take a more detached view when assessing whether the suspect should be released or detained, or whether there is sufficient evidence to charge the suspect. Any dispute between the custody officer and the investigating officer should be referred to the station superintendent, but otherwise the custody officer has the last word.

(f) To order the release of the suspect, or his or her charge, unless continued detention without charge is necessary:

(i) to secure or preserve evidence relating to the offence; or

(ii) to obtain such evidence by questioning the suspect.

As a mid-way point between release without charge and continued detention, the suspect may be released on bail to return to the police station at a later date, when further enquiries have been made (PACE 1984, s 47(3)(b)).

Fingerprint and non-intimate samples (usually a mouth swab) to obtain DNA are now taken as a matter of routine for all suspects arrested for a recordable offence (CJA 2003, ss 9 and 10 amending PACE 1984, s 61). These samples are subjected to speculative searches against unsolved crime scenes. The Protection of Freedoms Act 2012 sets out the regime for how long fingerprint and biometric data can be subsequently retained. This depends upon a variety of factors, including whether the person is arrested but not charged, and the age of the suspect (ie whether adult or juvenile).

Suspects over the age of 18 may also be required by the police to undergo compulsory drug-testing (PACE 1984, s 63B) if the suspect is under arrest for a trigger offence. These are, broadly, offences under the Theft Act 1968 and the Misuse of Drugs Act 1971. The police must first have reasonable grounds to suspect that the offender's offending is contributed to or caused by his drug habit. Once a sample has been taken, it can be used to inform decisions in relation to bail and sentencing, and guides supervision while in detention. Refusal to comply may be a separate criminal offence.

Stage 2: Review of detention after six hours

If the suspect is still being held six hours after his detention has been authorised, a review must be held by a review officer who is at least the rank of inspector and not directly involved in the investigation. She or he must be satisfied that the custody officer's reasons for authorising detention are still necessary (ie to secure or preserve evidence or to obtain such evidence by questioning the suspect).

The review officer must give the opportunity to the suspect, his solicitor (if available) or an appropriate adult (if available) to make representations about the detention.

Stage 3: Subsequent review of detention every nine hours

After the first review at the six-hour mark, the ongoing need for detention must be reviewed every nine hours thereafter, ie at 15 hours, and 24 hours. According to *Roberts v Chief Constable of the Cheshire Constabulary* [1999] 1 WLR 662, failure to review renders a previously lawful detention unlawful, and amounts to the tort of false imprisonment.

Generally, the review inspector is present at the police station holding the suspect but the reviews of detention may be conducted by telephone (CJA 2003, s 6). The decision to conduct the review by telephone 'must always take full account of the needs of the person in custody' (revised Code C, para 15.3C), including factors such as the suspect's vulnerability by virtue of, for example, being a juvenile, mentally disordered or having health issues.

Stage 4: The 24-hour limit

After a maximum of 24 hours after arrival at the police station, the police have three options: charge the suspect; release him without charge (ie the matter is dropped); or obtain permission from a superintendent to detain the suspect for up to a further 12 hours, to a total maximum of 36 hours.

For this third option to apply, these conditions must be satisfied:

(a) The continued detention is authorised by an officer of at least the rank of superintendent.
(b) The suspect is under arrest in connection with an indictable offence.
(c) The authorising officer has reasonable grounds for believing that the suspect's continued detention is necessary to:
  (i) secure or preserve evidence relating to the offence; or
  (ii) obtain such evidence by questioning the suspect.
(d) The authorising officer has reasonable grounds for believing that the investigation is being conducted diligently and expeditiously.

Again, the suspect or his or her solicitor must be given the opportunity to make representations.

The Code states (para 15.2A) that in the case of a juvenile or mentally vulnerable person detention beyond 24 hours will be dependent upon the circumstances of the case and with regard to the person's:

(a) special vulnerability;
(b) the legal obligation to provide an opportunity for representations to be made prior to a decision about extending detention;
(c) the need to consult and consider the views of any appropriate adult; and
(d) any alternatives to police custody.

Home Office guidance (Circular 60/2003) provided that the power to detain beyond 24 hours:

- should be used sparingly and only where there is full justification;
- should only be used where the authorising officer is satisfied that alternatives to continued detention, such as bail or restorative justice, have been considered and determined to be inappropriate.

Stage 5: The 36-hour point: warrant of further detention from a magistrates' court

At 36 hours, the police have exhausted their own powers to detain the suspect. Any further detention can only be authorised by the courts. At this point, the suspect must be charged, or released without charge, unless a warrant of further detention had been issued by a magistrates' court *before* the 36 hours expired. This requires the police to plan ahead, and list the application before the court whilst it is sitting.

A magistrates' court may authorise detention for a further 36 hours (ie to a total of 72 hours) if:

(a) the court comprises at least two lay magistrates (or a single district judge);
(b) the application for the warrant is made on oath and supported by written information which is also supplied to the suspect;
(c) the suspect is present in court;

(d) the suspect is detained in connection with an indictable offence;

(e) the court is satisfied of the matters in paras (c) and (d) of Stage 4 above.

Stage 6: 72 hours: another warrant of further detention

Before the expiry of 72 hours, the police may repeat the application and bring the suspect back to court for another warrant of further detention. The process is as above, requiring the conditions of Stage 5 to be satisfied. This further detention is for a maximum of 36 hours, bringing the overall detention total to 96 hours.

Stage 7: 96 hours: charge or release without charge

This is the absolute upper limit for the police investigation. At the expiry of 96 hours, the police must charge or release without charge, as the court has no power to authorise detention beyond 96 hours. (Note these time limits do not apply to those who are detained under the Terrorism Act 2000. See further Code H.) A person who is released without charge can expect that to be the end of the matter. He may not be re-arrested without a warrant for this particular allegation unless new evidence justifying a further arrest has come to light (PACE 1984, s 41(9)).

See Table 2.1 for a summary of the detention periods.

Table 2.1 **Detention periods**

Time	Offence	Authorisation
Up to 24 hours	Any	Custody sergeant
Up to 36 hours	Indictable offences	An officer of at least the rank of superintendent
Up to 72 hours	Indictable offences	Magistrates' court
Up to 96 hours	Indictable offences	Magistrates' court

2.2.5 The risk assessment

When the suspect arrives at the police station, the custody officer must initiate a risk assessment (Code, paras 3.6–3.10) to determine whether the suspect may present a specific risk to custody staff or to himself or herself. Considerations include (HO Circular 32/2000):

(a) The requirement to carry out a risk assessment applies to all persons entering into police custody, and all persons must be asked the questions set out in (b) below.

(b) The questions include whether the suspect has any injury or illness, whether they are taking any medication, whether they are suffering from any mental health problems or depression and whether they have ever tried to harm themselves.

(c) The result of the risk assessment must be entered into the custody record, indicating whether any risks have been identified and the answers to the questions.

(d) Risk assessment is an ongoing process and must be reviewed if circumstances change.

(e) Risk categories include medical or mental conditions, medication issued, special needs, violence, escape risk, suicide or self-harm, injuries, vulnerability and any force, restraint or spray used.

(f) It is the responsibility of the custody officer to decide on the appropriate response to any risk identified.

(g) If the suspect is to be transferred from a police station, a Prisoner Escort Record must be completed setting out the details of the risk assessment.

The custody officer may require the suspect to be examined by a health care professional to determine his fitness to be detained, fitness to be interviewed and whether an appropriate adult may be required (see later). The health care professional's determination and any advice should be made in writing and form part of the custody record (Code, Annex G, para 7).

2.2.6 Persons at risk

Certain categories of detainee may be prone in certain circumstances to provide information that may be unreliable, misleading or self-incriminating. Special care should always be taken when questioning such a person, and an appropriate adult may be required to attend the police station to protect their interests when they are in detention, and especially in interview. The support and assistance that the suspect receives from the appropriate adult is in addition to the legal advice he or she receives from the solicitor. If there is any doubt in the custody officer's mind about a person's age or mental state or capacity, he or she should err on the side of caution and appoint an appropriate adult.

2.2.6.1 Juveniles

All juveniles, by virtue of their age, are automatically appointed with an appropriate adult.

2.2.6.2 Mentally vulnerable adults

Mentally vulnerable adults will also require an appropriate adult. The term 'mentally vulnerable' applies to those who 'because of their mental state or capacity, may not understand the significance of what is said, of questions or of their replies' (para 1G of the Code Notes for Guidance). This will apply to an adult with a mental disorder, defined by the Mental Health Act 1983, s 1(2) as 'any disorder or disability of the mind', but could potentially include those whose mental state is adversely affected by drink or drugs. When a custody officer is in doubt, he should treat the detainee as mentally vulnerable and call an appropriate adult.

2.2.6.3 The role of the appropriate adult

When considering who should act as the appropriate adult, the custody officer must consider the following hierarchy:

(i) First, to contact the parent or guardian of a juvenile, or the guardian of the person who is mentally disordered. An estranged parent, however, is not a suitable appropriate adult, where the juvenile specifically objects to their presence: see *R v Morse* [1991] Crim LR 195 and *DPP v Blake* (1989) 89 Cr App R 179; nor is someone who is suspected of involvement in the offence, or the victim or a witness, even if they are a parent.

(ii) If no one in the above category is available, then the police will ask a social worker from the local authority to act.

(iii) If no one in either category is available, then the police will contact another responsible adult who is aged 18 or over who is not connected with the police.

Police officers, persons connected to the victim or anyone to whom the suspect has made prior admissions should not act as appropriate adults. A solicitor should never act as an appropriate adult.

A juvenile or person who is mentally vulnerable should not be interviewed regarding their involvement or suspected involvement in a criminal offence or asked to provide a statement under caution except in the presence of an appropriate adult.

The appropriate adult should be informed by the interviewing police officer of his or her role in protecting the interest of the vulnerable suspect, namely:

- he or she is not expected to act simply as an observer; and
- the purpose of his or her presence is to:
  - advise the person being interviewed;
  - observe whether the interview is being conducted properly and fairly; and
  - facilitate communication with the person being interviewed.

An appropriate adult must be 'appropriate' both in the sense of being capable of understanding what is happening and in the sense of being someone the person at risk wishes to have present. Where an appropriate adult cannot be found, however, a person at risk may be interviewed without delay (Code, para 11.18) if an officer of not less than the rank of superintendent is satisfied that the interview would not significantly harm the person's physical or mental state, and considers that delay would be likely to:

- lead to interference with or harm to evidence connected with an offence;
- lead to interference with or physical harm to other people or serious loss or damage to property;
- lead to the alerting of other people suspected of committing an offence but not yet arrested for it; or
- hinder the recovery of property obtained in consequence of the commission of an offence.

This provision also applies to:

- any person other than persons at risk who at the time of the interview appears to be unable to:
  - — appreciate the significance of questions and their answers; or
  - — understand what is happening because of the effects of drink, drugs or any illness, ailment or condition;
- a person who has difficulty understanding English or has a hearing disability if at the time of the interview an interpreter is not present.

2.2.7 The rights of the suspect

The suspect has three important rights in the police station.

2.2.7.1 The right to see a solicitor

A person who has been arrested and is being held in custody is entitled, upon request, to consult privately with a solicitor at any time (PACE 1984, s 58(1)). The suspect must be informed of this right by the custody officer on arrival at the police station. If he or she declines legal advice (known as waiver of legal advice), the suspect must be asked why, and his reasons should be recorded on the custody or interview record. Nothing must be said or done by police officers with the intention of dissuading a suspect from obtaining legal advice (para 6.4).

Note that PACE 1984, s 58 gives the suspect the right to consult a solicitor as soon as is practicable but not specifically the right to have the solicitor present during the interview. However, the Code provides that a detainee shall be entitled on request to have the solicitor present when they are interviewed (para 6.8) unless one of the exceptions in para 6.6 applies.

If the suspect commences the interview having waived legal advice, but asks for it during the interview, there should be no further questioning until he has had the opportunity to speak with the solicitor (para 6.6).

If the suspect has requested legal advice, and the solicitor is on his or her way or about to set off, the interview should normally await his or her arrival (para 6A).

Access to a solicitor, for a suspect who wants one, can never be entirely denied, but may be delayed in limited circumstances under PACE, s 58(6) and (8). The suspect must be told why access to a solicitor has been delayed, and the reason must be entered in the custody record. The suspect's right can be delayed only for as long as the grounds exist, and in no case for longer than 36 hours. Wrongful delay of access to a solicitor may lead to a confession made without having taken legal advice being excluded at any subsequent trial. See, for example, *R v Samuel* [1988] 1 WLR 920 and *R v Alladice* (1988) 87 Cr App R 380.

The applicable grounds for delay are where:

(a) the suspect is in police detention in connection with an indictable offence, and has not yet been charged with an offence;

(b) an officer of not less than the rank of superintendent authorises the delay; and

(c) that officer has reasonable grounds for believing that the exercise of the right at the present time will lead to:

— interference with, or harm to, evidence connected with an indictable offence; or
— interference with, or physical harm to, other people; or
— lead to the alerting of other people suspected of having committed an indictable offence but not yet arrested for it; or
— hinder the recovery of property obtained in consequence of the commission of such an offence.

Alternatively, delay may be authorised if an officer of superintendent rank or above has reasonable grounds to believe that:

- the suspect has benefited from criminal conduct within the meaning of the Proceeds of Crime Act 2002; and
- the recovery of property constituting the benefit will be hindered by exercise of the right (see PACE, s 58(8A) and Code C, Annex B, para 2).

Once a suspect has requested legal advice, he or she may not be interviewed without it (or an interview continued):

(a) unless delaying access to a solicitor has been properly authorised (as above); or
(b) a solicitor, including a duty solicitor, has been contacted and has agreed to attend, awaiting their arrival would cause unreasonable delay to the process of investigation; or
(c) the solicitor that the suspect has nominated or selected from a list cannot be contacted, has previously indicated that he or she does not wish to be contacted, or declines to attend and the suspect has declined to ask for the duty solicitor having been advised about the Duty Solicitor Scheme; or
(d) the detainee has changed his or her mind about wanting legal advice and consented to the interview beginning (or continuing).

See Code C, para 6.6.

The suspect has the right to consult *privately* with a solicitor at any time (PACE 1984, s 58 and para 6 of the Code). Defence solicitors have complained that these consultations have on occasion been the subject of covert surveillance. No provisions are included in the Code to prevent or control such surveillance. In *McE v Prison Service of Northern Ireland* [2009] UKHL 15, it was held that the Regulation of Investigatory Powers Act 2000 can permit covert surveillance of communications between lawyers and their clients which are covered by legal professional privilege, notwithstanding any statutory right of a person in custody to consult privately with his lawyer.

2.2.7.2 The right to have someone informed

The suspect has the right to have a friend or relative, or some other person who is known to him or her, or who is likely to take an interest in his or her welfare, told of the arrest (PACE 1984, s 56(1)). The request must be complied with as soon as is practicable. This right may be delayed in circumstances similar to the circumstances permitting the delay of access to legal advice. In addition, the suspect must be given writing materials on request and allowed to make one phone call for a reasonable time, unless the above circumstances apply.

2.2.7.3 The right to consult the Codes

The suspect has the right to consult all the Codes of Practice. This does not entitle him or her to delay unreasonably any investigation or administrative action while this is done (Code C, paras 3.1 and 3D).

2.2.8 The caution

Where there are 'grounds to suspect' a person of an offence, he or she must be cautioned before questioning about that offence (Code, para 10.1).

The caution is:

You do not have to say anything. But it may harm your defence if you do not mention, when questioned, something which you later rely on in court. Anything you do say may be given in evidence.

Provided that the sense of the caution is preserved, minor deviations from the stated form do not constitute a breach of the Code.

The wording of the caution arises from the provisions of the CJPOA 1994, s 34. Section 34 provides that a court 'may draw such inferences as appear proper' if evidence is given that the suspect:

(a) at any time before he was charged with the offence, on being questioned under caution by a constable trying to discover whether or by whom the offence had been committed, failed to mention any fact relied on in his defence in those proceedings; or

(b) on being charged with the offence or officially informed that he might be prosecuted for it, failed to mention any such fact, being a fact which, in the circumstances existing at the time, the accused could reasonably have been expected to mention when so questioned, charged or informed, as the case may be.

The caution places the suspect on notice of three things; that he does not have to answer questions, and may remain silent; that if he wishes to rely on a fact at trial (eg a defence such as self-defence) failure to mention this in police interview may allow the jury to draw inferences; and, finally, his answers or silence are admissible at trial.

The caution should be re-administered after a break in questioning, but see *R v Oni* [1992] Crim LR 183, where it was held to be unnecessary after a break of only two minutes. It should always be re-administered, however, if there is any doubt as to whether or not it is necessary.

In addition to being administered prior to questioning, the caution must be given on arrest unless the suspect has already been cautioned immediately prior to arrest, or because it is impracticable to administer the caution by reason of the suspect's behaviour at the time. Finally, a suspect should also be cautioned when charged with an offence.

The importance of the caution was stressed by the Court of Appeal in *Charles v CPS* [2009] EWHC 3521 (Admin):

These provisions are not a mere rigmarole to be recited like a mantra and then ignored. The provisions of the Police and Criminal Evidence Act and the Code relating to caution, are designed to protect a detainee. They are important protections. They impose significant disciplines upon the police as to how they are to behave. If they can secure a serious conviction in breach of those provisions that is an important matter which undermines the protection of a detainee in the police station. That is not to say, by any means, that every breach will lead to the exclusion of the evidence obtained in consequence of that breach; far from it. It is merely to emphasise the general importance of the breaches when exercising the judgment in s 78.

The traditional caution applies in the majority of cases. However, as no inferences may be drawn where the suspect is questioned but has not been given the opportunity to obtain legal advice (s 58 of the Youth Justice and Criminal Evidence Act 1999 (YJCEA 1999) amending the CJPOA 1994), the caution should be tailored as followed:

You do not have to say anything, but anything you do say may be given in evidence.

The caution need not be given where the questions are merely preliminary, for example to establish identity or ownership, in furtherance of a proper and effective search or to obtain verification of any written record of comments made outside the context of an interview. There can be a fine line between the police asking only preliminary questions and conducting an interview. See, for example, *R v Senior* (2004) 148 SJ 300 and *Ridehalgh v DPP* [2005] EWHC 1100 (Admin). The evidential consequences of the caution are more fully discussed in the *Evidence* manual.

2.2.9 Interviews

An interview is defined as:

the questioning of a person regarding their involvement or suspected involvement in a criminal offence or offences which . . . must be carried out under caution.

(*Code C, para 11.1A*)

The arrested person must not be interviewed except at a police station, unless any delay would be likely to lead to interfere with evidence, harm to persons, the alerting of suspects or the hindering of the recovery of property (para 11.1).

Any interview at a police station should take place in an adequately lit, heated and ventilated interview room. At the beginning of the interview, the interviewing officer must identify himself or herself and any other officer present. The suspect must not be required to stand during the interview, and should be given breaks at recognised mealtimes. In addition, there should be short breaks for refreshment every two hours. The Code specifically provides that in any period of 24 hours, the suspect should be allowed a continuous period of eight hours' sleep without interruption, normally at night.

The suspect must be fit for interview. An interview should not be held in relation to a person who appears to be unable to:

(a) appreciate the significance of questions put to him or her, or their answers;

(b) understand what is happening because of drink, drugs, any illness, ailment or condition.

The custody officer, often in conjunction with the health care professional, determines if a suspect is fit to be interviewed (see earlier on Risk Assessments). The custody officer must consider if:

- conducting the interview could significantly harm the detainee's physical or mental state;
- anything the detainee says in the interview about his or her involvement or suspected involvement in the offence about which he or she is being interviewed might be considered unreliable in subsequent court proceedings because of his or her physical or mental state. (Annex G, para 2)

For example, a suspect arrested for drink driving may be fit to be detained (eg he has no health issues preventing him from being held in a police station), but, due to his drunkenness, he may not be fit for interview. The usual approach is to hold the suspect until he has sobered up, and has become fit for interview.

All interviews with persons cautioned in respect of an indictable offence, or where questions are put to, or a statement of another person is shown to, a person who has been charged, should be tape-recorded. Tapes need not be made if it is not reasonably practicable to do so for reasons such as the failure of the equipment, and the custody officer considers that the interview should not be delayed. For detailed provisions relating to tape-recording, see Code E.

Problems occasionally arise where a brief conversation or 'exchange' takes place between police officers and a suspect outside a police station, for example after a speeding or stolen car has been stopped. If the exchange goes beyond a mere request for information and the suspect is, in effect, questioned about his or her involvement in an offence, then the exchange has become an interview. It is the nature of the questioning rather than the length which is relevant (*R v Ward* (1994) 98 Crim App R 337). If the questioning has become an interview, then the defendant is immediately protected by the provisions of the Code, including the requirement to caution, and any breaches will be taken into account by the court at any subsequent trial in determining the reliability of any confession that may have been made (see, eg, *R v Cox* (1993) 96 Cr App R 464).

If a person confesses, or makes a 'significant statement' to a police officer outside of the interview (eg on their way to the police station), Code C, para 11.4 requires that *'at the beginning of an interview the interviewer, after cautioning the suspect ... shall put to them any significant statement or silence which occurred in the presence and hearing of a police officer or other police staff before the start of the interview ... The interviewer shall ask the suspect whether they confirm or deny that earlier statement or silence and if they want to add anything.'*

There has been some debate about the point at which an interview must cease. See *R v Pointer* [1997] Crim LR 676; *R v Gayle* [1999] Crim LR 502; *R v McGuinness* [1999] Crim LR 318; *R v Elliott* [2002] EWCA Crim 931; and *R v Howell* [2003] EWCA Crim 1.

The interview or further interview of a person about an offence with which that person has not been charged or for which they have not been informed they may be prosecuted, must cease when:

> *(a) the officer in charge of the investigation is satisfied all the questions they consider relevant to obtaining accurate and reliable information about the offence have been put to the suspect, this includes allowing the suspect an opportunity to give an innocent explanation, and asking questions to test if the explanation is accurate and reliable eg to clear up ambiguities or clarify what the suspect said;*
>
> *(b) the officer in charge of the investigation has taken account of any other available evidence; and*
>
> *(c) the officer in charge of the investigation, or in the case of a detained suspect, the custody officer . . . reasonably believes there is sufficient evidence to provide a realistic prospect of conviction for that offence.*
>
> *(Code C. 11.6)*

This paragraph does not prevent officers in revenue cases or acting under the confiscation provisions of the Criminal Justice Act 1988 or the Drug Trafficking Act 1994 from inviting suspects to complete a formal question and answer record after the interview is concluded.

2.2.10 The charge

The decision of whether or not to charge a suspect was generally determined by the police, namely the custody sergeant, until 2002, when the primary responsibility for charging was transferred to the CPS. The position has been reviewed and to an extent reversed in 2013, with the issuance of a revised Code for Crown Prosecutors in January 2013 and a *Director's Guidance on Charging* in May. The new Code can be found at <http://www.cps.gov.uk/publications/docs/code_2013_accessible_english.pdf> and the new Guidance at <http://www.cps.gov.uk/publications/directors_guidance/dpp_guidance_5.html>. The Guidance stipulates that:

> The police may charge:
>
> (i) any Summary Only offence (including criminal damage where the value of the loss or damage is less than £5000) irrespective of plea;
>
> (ii) any offence of retail theft (shoplifting) or attempted retail theft irrespective of plea provided it is suitable for sentence in the magistrates' court; and
>
> (iii) any either-way offence anticipated as a guilty plea and suitable for sentence in a magistrates' court.

However, the police cannot charge any case: requiring the consent to prosecute of the DPP or Law Officer; involving a death; connected with terrorist activity or official secrets; classified as Hate Crime or Domestic Violence under CPS Policies; of Violent Disorder or Affray; of causing Grievous Bodily Harm or Wounding, or Actual Bodily Harm; involving a Sexual Offences Act offence committed by or upon a person under 18; an offence under the Licensing Act 2003.

Prosecutors will make the charging decision in all other cases. The custody officer may either hold the suspect (subject to the normal time limits on detention) and seek an expedited CPS decision on charge, or may bail the suspect to return to the police station at a future date, pending the charging decision.

The prosecutor must apply a two-part test (the Full Code Test) to decide whether or not a person should be charged. They will consider:

(i) if there is sufficient evidence to provide a realistic prospect of conviction; and

(ii) if so, whether a prosecution is in the public interest, or whether the matter should be dealt with any other way, for example by way of a caution (see later).

Once the suspect has been charged with the offence, he or she should not be asked any further questions, except in exceptional circumstances as provided by Code C, para 16.5. These include:

- preventing harm or loss to some other person or to the public;
- clearing up an ambiguity in a previous statement or answer;
- it is in the interests of justice for the suspect to be given an opportunity to comment on information about the offence that has come to light since he or she was charged (or was informed that he or she may be prosecuted).

2.2.11 The decision to release

There are two points at which the release of the suspect is to be considered—before and after charge.

2.2.11.1 Before charge

Once the reason or reasons for detention have lapsed (eg interview, taking of samples and fingerprints etc) the custody sergeant must ascertain whether to charge or release the suspect. Before taking a decision to charge (as above), the police may wish to make further enquiries, or to seek advice from the CPS, and so have the power to bail the suspect under PACE 1984, Part IV. If so bailed, he or she must return to the police station at a future date and time when the case will be progressed further (eg he or she may be interviewed on any new evidence) or he or she may be charged, or the proceedings may be discontinued altogether (known as NFA: no further action).

Conditions can be attached to police bail that 'appear necessary' to prevent the person from: failing to surrender to custody; committing an offence while on bail; interfering with witnesses or otherwise obstructing the course of justice, whether in relation to the bailed person or any other person; and/or for his or her own protection (or for a person aged 16 or under, for his or her own welfare or in his or her own interests). The bailed person can apply either to the court or the police to vary the conditions.

If there is no prospect of any criminal proceedings, the police can simply decide to take no further action or 'NFA' and the suspect can be released without bail and without any obligation to return. See further PACE 1984, s 37(2) and (7).

2.2.11.2 After charge

Once the suspect has been charged, and the matter will be put before a court, the custody sergeant must decide whether the charged person should be released to attend court on bail (which may be with or without conditions) or detained and brought to court in police custody.

(i) The grant of police bail to attend court

If the suspect is to be released after charge, he or she is likely to be bailed to attend at the appropriate magistrates' court to answer to the charge on a specified day. The CJPOA 1994, s 27 provides that s 3 of the Bail Act 1976 (BA 1976) (power of the court to impose conditions on bail) shall apply with certain modifications (see later) to bail granted by the police.

The bail decision is taken by the custody officer, who may not impose conditions on the grant of bail unless it appears, under s 3A(5) of the BA 1976 (inserted by s 27 of the CJPOA 1994) that it is necessary to do so for the purposes of preventing the bailed person from:

- failing to surrender to custody; or
- committing an offence while on bail; or
- interfering with witnesses or otherwise obstructing the course of justice, whether in relation to the bailed person or any other person.

The bailed person can apply either to the court or the police to vary the conditions.

The main differences between conditions imposed by police and those imposed by the court are as follows:

(a) The court, but not the police, has the power to order that reports be compiled on the bailed person (BA 1976, s 3A(3), as inserted by the CJPOA 1994, s 27(3)).
(b) The court, but not the police, may require the bailed person to reside in a bail hostel (BA 1976, s 3A(2), as inserted by the CJPOA 1994, s 27(3)).
(c) Where the custody officer has granted bail, either the custody officer or another officer serving at the same police station may vary the conditions of bail, at the request of the bailed person (BA 1976, s 3A(4), inserted by the CJPOA 1994, s 27(3)). Further, the bailed person may apply to a magistrates' court to have conditions of bail varied, but should bear in mind that the court has the power to impose more onerous conditions (MCA 1980, s 43B, inserted by the CJPOA 1994, Sch 3, para 3).

(ii) Refusal of police bail after charge

The custody officer must order the suspect's release from custody under PACE 1984, s 38(1) unless one of the situations contained in s 38(1)(a), as amended by s 28 of the CJPOA 1994, applies:

(a) The suspect's name or address cannot be ascertained.
(b) The custody officer has reasonable grounds for doubting whether the name and address supplied are genuine.
(c) The custody officer has reasonable grounds for believing that:
  (i) the suspect will not surrender to bail; or
  (ii) (imprisonable offences) the detention is necessary to prevent the suspect from committing an offence; or
  (iii) where the person has attained the age of 18, the detention is necessary for a sample to be taken;
  (iv) (non-imprisonable offences) the detention is necessary to prevent the suspect from causing physical injury to any other person or loss or damage to property; or
  (v) the detention is necessary to prevent the suspect from interfering with the administration of justice or with the investigation of any offence or offences; or
  (vi) the detention is necessary for the suspect's own protection.

If the suspect is detained after charge, he or she must be brought before a magistrates' court as soon as is practicable, and in any event not later than the first sitting after he or she has been charged with an offence. If no suitable court is sitting, the clerk of the court must be informed, and a special sitting will be arranged. See generally PACE 1984, s 46.

2.2.12 Alternatives to charge

As an alternative to charge and prosecution of the suspect or his or her release without charge, the suspect may be dealt with in one of the following ways.

2.2.12.1 An informal warning

Such informal warnings may be appropriate for minor matters, particularly minor public order matters. Such a warning will not appear on the person's list of previous convictions.

2.2.12.2 A formal caution

The regime for juveniles (10 to 17-year-olds) is different than for adults. See **6.6** for the system of youth cautions. For adults (persons who are 18 and over), a caution is a very common way of dealing with offenders, particularly first-time offenders and in particular it may be given to offenders who are elderly, the ill or those suffering from acute distress.

The caution is usually administered by an officer of at least the rank of inspector and the offender must sign a form acknowledging the offence and his or her guilt.

The caution may only be given if the following conditions are fulfilled:

(a) there is sufficient evidence to justify a prosecution;

(b) the offender must admit his or her guilt; note that the offender must admit guilt to all the requisite elements of the offence: *R (on the application of Wyman) v Chief Constable of Hampshire Constabulary* [2006] EWHC 1904 (Admin);

(c) the offender agrees to the caution, knowing that the caution may be referred to in court in the event of a future conviction.

In fact, it would be unusual for the caution to be subsequently referred to, unless the offender is now convicted of the same type of offence for which he or she was cautioned.

Two cases illustrate the use of the formal caution. In the first, *R v Chief Constable of Hampshire Constabulary* [2006] EWHC 1904 (Admin), the defendant agreed to a formal caution but he successfully applied for the caution to be quashed on the grounds that the proper procedure had not been followed and he could not properly be said to have admitted all elements of the offence.

In *Jones v Whalley* [2006] UKHL 41, the defendant accepted a formal caution, on the express assurance by the police officer that he would not have to go before a criminal court in connection with the offence. The complainant, however, brought a private prosecution. The House of Lords decided that, in view of the formal caution, the private prosecution was an abuse of process but did not decide whether a private prosecution could or should survive the implementation of a formal caution.

Guidance as to the use of informal and formal cautions is given in HO Circular 16/2008.

2.2.12.3 Conditional cautions

CJA 2003, ss 22–27 introduced the conditional caution. These sections allow an adult offender to be released subject to being cautioned, but unlike other cautions, the conditional caution is 'a caution which is given in respect of an offence committed by the offender and which has conditions attached to it with which the offender must comply' (s 22(2)). Failure to comply may result in the offender being prosecuted for the offence. See <http://www.cps.gov.uk/publications/directors_guidance/adult_conditional_cautions.html>.

Guidance on the giving of conditional cautions states that:

> A conditional caution may be appropriate where a Crown Prosecutor considers that while the public interest justifies a prosecution, the interests of the person, victim or community may be better served by the person complying with certain conditions aimed at rehabilitation or reparation which may include restorative processes.

The person giving the conditional caution is known as the 'authorised person' and is either a constable, an investigating officer or a person authorised by a relevant prosecutor, a group of people including the Attorney-General, the Director of Public Prosecutions, the director of the Serious Fraud Office and the Commissioners of Customs and Excise.

Before the conditional caution may be given, five conditions must be complied with, namely:

(a) the authorised person has evidence that the offender committed an offence;

(b) the authorised person decides that there is sufficient evidence to charge the offender and that a conditional caution should be given;

(c) the offender admits the offence;

(d) the authorised person explains the effect of the conditional caution to the offender and warns him that failure to comply with the conditions may result in his prosecution for the offence;

(e) the offender signs a document setting out:

  (i) the details of the offence;

  (ii) an admission by him that he committed the offence;

  (iii) his consent to the giving of a conditional caution;

  (iv) the conditions attached to the caution.

The conditions which are imposed have the following objects, under s 22(3):

(a) facilitating the rehabilitation of the offender;

(b) ensuring that he makes reparation for the offence;

(c) punishing the offender (inserted by the Police and Justice Act 2006, s 17).

The Conditional Cautioning Code of Practice states that the conditions must be:

- *Proportionate* to the offence—it should not be more onerous than the punishment that would be likely to be imposed if the offender were prosecuted.
- *Achievable* within a reasonable time—having particular regard to any limitations on prosecution if the offender breaches the conditions.
- *Appropriate*—any conditions should be relevant to the offence or the offender.

Failure without reasonable cause to comply with any of the conditions renders the person liable to prosecution for the offence and the document referred to above is admissible as evidence: s 24(1) and (2).

The authorised person may seek the advice and assistance of the National Probation Service in deciding whether a conditional caution should be given and, if one is given, the conditions that should be attached (s 26).

If the offender fails to comply with the conditions he may be prosecuted for the original offence. In such proceedings, the notice which the offender signed is admissible (s 24). Examples of offences for which conditional cautions have been given include: criminal damage; offences contrary to the Public Order Act 1986, s 4 and s 5; affray; common assault; theft; burglary and possessing controlled drugs. Examples of conditions which have been attached as part of a conditional caution include: compensation; a fine; taking part in a restorative justice programme; providing a face-to-face apology to the victim and attending alcohol intervention sessions; and/or a condition that the offender attend at a specified place at specified times for up to 20 hours.

There are a number of disadvantages to the offender of accepting a conditional caution. The caution is an admission of guilt which will stay on his record, and be disclosable should he subsequently apply for certain types of employment. Further, a subsequent caution for an offence is very unlikely, any fingerprints taken will be retained and if the caution was given for a sexual offence, the offender will be placed on the sex offenders register.

Where a conditional caution is quashed, it will not ordinarily amount to an abuse of process to prosecute for the offence in question. Such a course of action will generally be in the public interest (*R (on the application of Guest) v DPP* [2009] EWHC 594 (Admin)).

2.3 The issue of process other than being charged after arrest

The majority of criminal cases are commenced by way of an arrest and charge at a police station, as outlined previously. For more minor offences (eg motoring offences that do not give the police any power of arrest) the method of securing the presence of the accused at the magistrates' court typically involves a different process. Prior to the CJA 2003, the method for commencing criminal proceedings for these minor matters was by way of laying an information and issue of summons by a magistrates' court. The CJA 2003 replaced this with the present system of written requisition and charge. The information and summons is intended to survive only for prosecutions brought by private individuals, and where the public prosecutor is required to lay an information for the purposes of obtaining the issue of a warrant (s 40(4)).

2.3.1 Written charge and requisition

Under s 29, the proceedings are started by issuing a document, called a 'written charge', charging the suspect with an offence. At the same time, a document called a 'requisition' is issued requiring the suspect to appear before the magistrates' court to answer the written charge. These documents are issued by a person referred to as a 'public prosecutor' (defined below), and served on the person charged and on the court.

The 'public prosecutor' is defined in the CJA 2003, s 29(5) as:

(a) *A police force or person authorised by a police force to institute criminal proceedings.*

(b) *The director of the Serious Fraud Office, the Director of Public Prosecutions, the Attorney-General, or a Secretary of State or any person authorised by any one of them to institute criminal proceedings.*

(c) *The Commissioners of the Inland Revenue or of Customs and Excise, or any person authorised by either of them to institute criminal proceedings.*

(d) *A person specified in an order made by the Secretary of State for the purposes of this section, or a person authorised by such a person to institute criminal proceedings.*

There is no requirement that either the written charge or the requisition should be substantiated on oath: s 31(1).

The advantage of the written charge and requisition procedure is that, unlike the process of laying of an information and obtaining a summons, the prosecutor may instigate proceedings against a person without the court having a say in it.

The written charge and requisition procedure should, more importantly, speed up the process of securing the presence of the accused in a court, as the matter does not need to first go before a clerk or justice for consideration.

Under s 30(5) all references in previous statutes referring to information and summonses are to be interpreted as referring to written charges and requisitions, respectively. Also, much of the earlier case law involving an information, and the summons in particular, will apply to written charge and requisition.

2.3.2 Information and summons

The pre-2003 method of information and summons has survived for:

(i) any private prosecutions; or

(ii) public prosecutions for the purposes of obtaining the issue of a warrant: s 30(4), CJA 2003.

Much is similar to the written charge and requisition procedure. The information sets out the allegation. The summons requires the accused to attend court. However, the main difference is that the information must be laid before the magistrates who then decide whether to issue the summons; therefore, a *summons* is a judicial, not merely an administrative, process (*Gateshead Justices, ex p Tesco Stores Ltd* [1981] QB 470). A justice or clerk must apply his or her mind to the information upon which the summons is sought by the prosecutor, and may refuse it, although this is rare.

2.3.3 Amendment

The court has wide powers to amend the original charge. Further, the MCA 1980, s 123 provides that defects in the written charge (or information), or any variations between that document and the evidence subsequently adduced, are not grounds upon which objection may be taken.

The discretion to amend should ordinarily be exercised in favour of amendment, unless to do so would result in injustice (*DPP v Short* (2002) 166 JP 474).

It has been held that if the defect or variation was trivial, and the accused was not in fact misled, any subsequent conviction will be upheld. See, for example, *R v Sandwell Justices, ex p West Midlands Passenger Transport Board* [1979] Crim LR 56. On the other hand, if the defect or variation is substantial, the prosecution should seek to amend the information. The magistrates will then consider whether the accused has been misled by the defect, and if so, offer an adjournment so that he or she can prepare for, and meet the case now put forward by the prosecution. Failure either to amend, or adjourn, in these circumstances is likely to lead to any subsequent conviction being quashed. See, for example, *Wright v Nicholson* [1970] 1 WLR 142.

A written charge (or information) may be amended, even to allege a different offence, including a purely summary offence, more than six months after it was issued, provided that the offence arose from the same incident as the offence originally charged, and the amendment was in the interests of justice: *R v Scunthorpe Justices, ex p M, The Times*, 10 March 1998, where an information alleging robbery was amended to common assault, a purely summary offence.

2.3.4 Duplicity

A written charge or information is said to be *duplicitous* when two offences are charged within it. In such a situation, the prosecution may elect which charge to proceed with. Students are referred to **Chapter 10** for a full discussion of duplicity.

2.3.5 Trying two or more written charges

Where one accused stands charged with several matters, or several accused stand charged of related offences, then they may be tried together. If an objection is made, the magistrates may order separate trials unless they are of the opinion that the offences are so connected that the interests of justice would be best served by a single trial. See *Chief Constable of Norfolk v Clayton* [1983] 2 AC 473.

If the magistrates decide against a single trial, it would seem those magistrates are debarred from hearing the case at all, as they are supposed to be unaware of any charges outstanding against an accused (see *R v Liverpool City justices, ex p Topping* [1983] 1 WLR 119). In these circumstances, each case may have to be heard by a different bench. In *R v Gough* [1993] AC 646, the House of Lords held that the test in all cases of apparent bias is: Was there a real danger of bias?

See also *Porter v Magill* [2002] AC 357. The proper formulation was held to be: Would a fair-minded and informed observer conclude that there was a real possibility, or real danger (the two being the same) that the tribunal was biased? This formulation is consistent with the approach of the ECtHR in *Sanders v UK* [2000] Crim LR 767.

2.4 Issue of a warrant

2.4.1 Information in a warrant

Instead of using a requisition (or summons), application may be made to a magistrate to issue a warrant for the arrest of the person named therein. A warrant should contain the following information:

- the name of the court;
- the name and address of the accused;
- the offence alleged;
- the signature of the magistrate (the signature of the clerk is insufficient);
- if the warrant is to be backed for bail, any conditions of bail imposed by the magistrate (see **3.7**).

2.4.2 Conditions for the issue of a warrant

Before the warrant can be issued the following conditions must be met:

- The information must be in writing. The former condition that the information should be supported by sworn evidence was removed by the CJA 2003, s 31.
- The offence must be imprisonable (or the accused is a juvenile or resides at an unknown address).
- The proceedings must take place before a magistrate, not a clerk.

2.4.3 Warrants 'backed for bail'

In most cases, a warrant will not be necessary. A less serious offence is likely to be commenced by the issue of a requisition (or summons), and more serious offences are arrestable in any event. However, the warrant is important where the accused fails to appear in answer to the requisition or summons, or fails to surrender to bail. A warrant issued in these circumstances is often referred to as a 'bench warrant'.

If the magistrates think that the accused's absence is due to an error, they *may* order that the warrant be 'backed for bail', that is, the conditions of bail upon which the accused may be released once arrested are endorsed on the back of the warrant. After arrest, the accused must be released once the conditions are complied with (see also **Chapter 3**).

2.5 Criminal case management

2.5.1 The Criminal Procedure Rules

The Criminal Procedure Rules came into force in 2005, with subsequent revised versions. The most recent set are the Criminal Procedure Rules 2014, with some amendments made in 2015. The Rules are supplemented by the *Criminal Practice Directions*. Both the Rules and the *Criminal Practice Directions* can be found at <http://www.justice.gov.uk/courts/procedure-rules/criminal> . These govern the correct procedures for the life of a criminal case. Students should familiarise themselves with both the Rules and the Practice Directions, which underpin the whole litigation process.

Part 1 establishes the overriding objective of the Rules as follows:

1.1 (1) The overriding objective of this new code is that criminal cases be dealt with justly.

(2) Dealing with a criminal case justly includes—

(a) acquitting the innocent and convicting the guilty;

(b) dealing with the prosecution and the defence fairly;

(c) recognising the rights of a defendant, particularly those under Article 6 of the European Convention on Human Rights;

(d) respecting the interests of witnesses, victims and jurors and keeping them informed of the progress of the case;

(e) dealing with the case efficiently and expeditiously;

(f) ensuring that appropriate information is available to the court when bail and sentence are considered; and

(g) dealing with the case in ways that take into account—

(i) the gravity of the offence alleged,

(ii) the complexity of what is in issue,

(iii) the severity of the consequences for the defendant and others affected, and

(iv) the needs of other cases.

The court itself must further the overriding objective, in particular, under r 1.3, when:

(a) exercising any power given to it by legislation (including these Rules);

(b) applying any practice direction; or

(c) interpreting any rule or practice direction.

2.5.2 Active case management

Rule 3 imposes a duty on the court to further the overriding objective by active case management. This includes (Crim PR, r 3.2(2)):

(a) the early identification of the real issues;

(b) the early identification of the needs of witnesses;

(c) *achieving certainty as to what must be done, by whom, and when, in particular by the early setting of a timetable for the progress of the case;*

(d) *monitoring the progress of the case and compliance with directions;*

(e) *ensuring that evidence, whether disputed or not, is presented in the shortest and clearest way;*

(f) *discouraging delay, dealing with as many aspects of the case as possible on the same occasion, and avoiding unnecessary hearings;*

(g) *encouraging the participants to co-operate in the progression of the case; and*

(h) *making use of technology.*

In addition, the court must actively manage the case by giving any direction appropriate to the needs of that case as early as possible.

2.5.2.1 Duties of participants

Under r 1.2(1) the duties of the participants in a criminal case are set out. For the purposes of this rule, anyone involved in any way with a criminal case is a participant in its conduct. The duties of the participants in a criminal case include:

(a) *prepare and conduct the case in accordance with the overriding objective;*

(b) *comply with these Rules, practice directions and directions made by the court; and*

(c) *at once inform the court and all parties of any significant failure (whether or not that participant is responsible for that failure) to take any procedural step required by these Rules, any practice direction or any direction of the court. A failure is significant if it might hinder the court in furthering the overriding objective.*

2.5.2.2 Progressing the case

In addition, all parties must be accountable for the progression of the case. Rule 3.4 provides:

(1) *At the beginning of the case each party must, unless the court otherwise directs—*

  (a) *nominate an individual responsible for progressing that case; and*

  (b) *tell other parties and the court who he is and how to contact him.*

(2) *In fulfilling its duty under rule 3.2, the court must where appropriate—*

  (a) *nominate a court officer responsible for progressing the case; and*

  (b) *make sure the parties know who he is and how to contact him.*

(3) *In this Part a person nominated under this rule is called a case progression officer.*

(4) *A case progression officer must—*

  (a) *monitor compliance with directions;*

  (b) *make sure that the court is kept informed of events that may affect the progress of that case;*

  (c) *make sure that he can be contacted promptly about the case during ordinary business hours;*

  (d) *act promptly and reasonably in response to communications about the case; and*

  (e) *if he will be unavailable, appoint a substitute to fulfill his duties and inform the other case progression officers.*

An example of the approach ushered in by the Criminal Procedure Rules can be found in *Malcolm v Director of Public Prosecutions* [2007] EWHC 363 (Admin), a case on whether the magistrates could receive further evidence after they had retired to consider their verdict. The court stated:

Criminal trials are no longer to be treated as a game, in which each move is final and any omission by the prosecution leads to its failure...That duty is implicit in rule 3.3 of the Criminal Procedure Rules, which requires the parties actively to assist the exercise by the court of its case management power... it is the duty of the defence to make the real issues clear at the latest before the prosecution closes its case.

In *R (on the application of the DPP) v Chorley Justices* [2006] EWHC 1795 (Admin), Thomas LJ said:

[T]he Criminal Procedure Rules . . . have effected a sea change in the way in which cases should be conducted. The days of ambushing and taking last-minute technical points are gone. They are not consistent with the overriding objective of deciding cases justly, acquitting the innocent and convicting the guilty.

For a further discussion of this area in connection with procedural failures at trial, see **Chapter 12**.

2.5.2.3 Sanctions

The court's ability to impose sanctions upon a party for non-compliance is broad; Crim PR, r 3.5(6) permits 'such other sanction as may be appropriate'. Lawyers may be placed in difficulty if, for example, the rules are not complied with because of problems created by the client, such as a late change of instructions.

2.5.3 Streamlining justice

Various other government initiatives have been implemented to streamline and harmonise the criminal court processes. In 2007, 'Criminal Justice: Simple, Speedy, Summary' (CJSSS) was rolled out in England and Wales primarily to improve the speed and effectiveness of magistrates' and youth courts via two main aims:

- reducing the number of hearings from an average of five or six to just one for guilty pleas and two for contested cases; and
- reducing the average time taken from charge to disposal to six weeks or less.

The CJSSS initiative was based on the following principles:

(i) Pre-court—the aim is to ensure:
   1. That the prosecution case is sufficiently ready to help ensure the first hearing is effective and proportionate to that end;
   2. That the level of information is appropriate and sufficient for the type of charge, expectation of plea and decisions required by the court; and
   3. That all appropriate information has been provided to the defence and court, the defence to ensure that the defence case is sufficiently ready to help ensure the first hearing is effective.

(ii) At first hearing:
   1. Court is to ensure that issues are identified;
   2. Defendant to enter a plea;
   3. Where a guilty plea is entered, sentence will take place on the same day where possible; where a not guilty plea is entered, an effective trial date will be fixed within six weeks, where possible.

(iii) From first hearing to trial—to ensure:
   1. The case management regime is appropriate to the seriousness of the case;
   2. Pre-trial reviews to be by exception;
   3. Case progression to take place outside of the courtroom—interim hearings only to take place where necessary;
   4. Trials proceed where appropriate on the appointed day in the absence of the defendant where there is a failure to appear.

The Criminal Procedure Rules 2014 require that a standard form be completed by the parties where there will be a magistrates' court trial: see <http://www.justice.gov.uk/courts/procedure-rules/criminal/docs/2014/part3-magistrates-courts-trial-preparation-form.pdf>.

This form requires the *defence* to provide significant information about the issues in the case at the earliest opportunity, including answering Yes, No or N/A to a range of questions such as whether the defendant took part in the alleged conduct, was present at the scene, was lawfully arrested, disputes fingerprint or DNA evidence (and if so, what is disputed), whether the record of police interview is accurate. The defence is also asked to identify all other agreed facts and issues, as well as any further points of dispute. As noted earlier, these disclosure requirements can cause problems where defence lawyers need to maintain client confidentiality but the client does not sanction disclosure of important information. They also raise interesting questions about the burden of proof and the presumption of innocence.

Where the prosecutor anticipates a not guilty plea, he must complete the relevant parts of the form and serve it on the defence prior to the *first* court hearing. The defence is to complete the relevant sections *before that hearing or, if the court permits, whilst it is taking place*; one might consider the pressure on a defence lawyer and whether she or he can really do their best for their client in this situation. The notes for guidance acknowledge that a defendant might not be legally represented at this hearing; if so, 'it may be necessary for the court to assist him or her to answer such questions'. The Crim PR have equivalent standard forms to be completed in the Crown Court, including specific forms for multi-handed cases depending on the number of co-defendants. For example, there are different forms if there are between two and five co-defendants, or six or more.

2.5.4 Powers that do not require a full court

The Crime and Disorder Act 1998 (CDA 1998) introduced a number of provisions designed to reduce delay in the criminal process. These included empowering a single lay justice (as opposed to the full court of three lay justices) to exercise the powers of a full magistrates' court, such as extending bail, imposing or varying bail conditions and dismissing an information (now replaced by the written charge, of course). The Criminal Procedure Rules also enable a justices' clerk (legal adviser) to make a number of administrative (as opposed to judicial) decisions without the lay justices. These measures were introduced in order to reduce the delays inherent in a system which requires the decision of three people, and to attempt to achieve continuity in the handling of a case, particularly prior to trial.

2.5.5 Early Administrative Hearings (EAHs)

The defendant's first appearance at court is now usually dealt with by way of early administrative hearing, or EAH (CDA 1998, s 50). The EAH may be before a court consisting of a single lay justice. At this hearing, the accused shall be asked if he or she wishes to receive publicly funded legal representation (ie legal aid); and, if he or she does, the Legal Aid Agency decide whether or not to grant it. The hearing may need to be adjourned to enable that decision to be made.

In addition, the single justice may exercise any of the usual powers available to a single justice, (see CDA 1998, s 49), as he or she thinks fit, including remanding the accused in custody or on bail. As the EAH deals mainly with administrative matters, the powers of the single justice may also be exercised by a justices' clerk (legal adviser). The only exception is that the justices' clerk has no power to remand the accused in custody or remand the accused on bail on conditions other than any previously imposed.

2.6 Public funding for legal representation and advice

2.6.1 The present position

Those arrested for or charged with criminal offences can, of course, choose to pay privately for legal representation at the police station and/or at court.

Those without the means to pay privately may seek publicly-funded representation (or what is often called 'legal aid') from the Legal Aid Agency. The provisions on criminal legal aid are complex and prone to significant changes. More up-to-date information is available on the Bar Council's website <http://www.barcouncil.org.uk/> and the Legal Aid Agency website <https://www.gov.uk/government/organisations/legal-aid-agency>.

2.6.2 Representation for criminal proceedings

The decision whether an individual qualifies for legal aid depends on two criteria (LASPO 2012, s 17(1)):

- a means test (s 21); and
- the interests of justice.

Section 17(2) sets out the basis of the 'interests of justice' test:

In deciding what the interests of justice consist of for the purposes of such a determination, the following factors must be taken into account—

(a) whether, if any matter arising in the proceedings is decided against the individual, the individual would be likely to lose his or her liberty or livelihood or to suffer serious damage to his or her reputation,

(b) whether the determination of any matter arising in the proceedings may involve consideration of a substantial question of law,

(c) whether the individual may be unable to understand the proceedings or to state his or her own case,

(d) whether the proceedings may involve the tracing, interviewing or expert cross-examination of witnesses on behalf of the individual, and

(e) whether it is in the interests of another person.

Even if the defendant meets the interests of justice test, he must also pass the means test. This could mean he has a meritorious case, but may be excluded from legal aid if his income exceeds the limit set by the Legal Aid Agency. It is vital that counsel checks the Legal Aid Agency website to know the current position. A calculator is available for practitioners at <https://www.gov.uk/criminal-legal-aid-means-testing>.

2.7 Costs

The law on costs can be found principally in two sources: the Prosecution of Offences Act 1985 and the *Practice Direction (Costs in Criminal Proceedings)* [2013] EWCA Crim 1632. The 1985 Act empowers the court to make a number of different costs orders.

2.7.1 Defendant's costs order (s 16)

A defendant who is acquitted (or whose appeal against conviction succeeds) may have his costs paid from central funds. Costs which have been covered through legal aid are excluded.

The *Practice Direction* says that a defendant's costs order 'should normally be made unless there are positive reasons for not doing so, for example, where the defendant's own conduct has brought suspicion on himself and has misled the prosecution into thinking that the case against him was stronger than it was'.

Under s 16A(2)–(5), corporate defendants cannot recover their legal costs; individuals can recover their legal costs in respect of proceedings in a magistrates' court but not in respect of Crown Court proceedings (unless those costs relate to an appeal against conviction and/or sentence from the magistrates' court). This means that legal costs incurred in the context of a trial on indictment can no longer be recovered.

For these purposes, legal costs are defined as 'fees, charges, disbursements and other amounts payable in respect of advocacy services or litigation services including, in particular, expert witness costs' (s 16A(10)).

2.7.2 Prosecution costs to be paid from central funds

Section 17 enables private prosecutors (but not public prosecutors, such as the Crown Prosecution Service) to obtain their costs from central funds. According to the *Practice Direction*, an order should be made save where there is good reason for not doing so, for example where proceedings have been instituted or continued without good cause.

2.7.3 Defendant to pay prosecution costs

Where a defendant is convicted, the court may order that he pays some or all of the prosecution costs (s 18). The *Practice Direction* says that an order should be made where the court is satisfied that the defendant has the means and the ability to pay. It follows that the court must take account of the defendant's means when deciding whether to make an order and, if so, the amount.

In *Northallerton Magistrates' Court, ex p Dove* (1999) 163 JP 657, Lord Bingham CJ set out a number of propositions:

> (1) *An order to pay costs to the prosecutor should never exceed the sum which, having regard to the defendant's means and any other financial order imposed upon him, the defendant is able to pay and which it is reasonable to order the defendant to pay.*
>
> (2) *Such an order should never exceed the sum which the prosecutor has actually and reasonably incurred.*
>
> (3) *The purpose of such an order is to compensate the prosecutor and not to punish the defendant. Where the defendant has by his conduct put the prosecutor to avoidable expense he may, subject to his means, be ordered to pay some or all of that sum to the prosecutor. But he is not to be punished for exercising a constitutional right to defend himself ...*
>
> (4) *While there is no requirement that any sum ordered ... to be paid to a prosecutor by way of costs should stand in any arithmetical relationship to any fine imposed, the costs ordered to be paid should not in the ordinary way be grossly disproportionate to the fine ...*
>
> (5) *It is for the defendant facing a financial penalty by way of fine or an order to pay costs to a prosecutor to disclose to [the court] such data relevant to his financial position as will enable [the court] to assess what he can reasonably afford to pay. In the absence of such disclosure [the court] may draw reasonable inferences as to the defendant's means from evidence they have heard and from all the circumstances of the case ...*
>
> (6) *It is incumbent on any court which proposes to make any financial order against a defendant, whether by way of fine or costs, to give the defendant a fair opportunity to adduce any relevant financial information and make any appropriate submissions ...*

2.7.4 Wasted costs order

A court may make a costs order where the court is satisfied that one party to criminal proceedings has incurred costs as a result of an unnecessary or improper act or omission by, or on behalf of, another party to the proceedings (s 19).

2.7.5 Costs against legal representatives (s 19A)

A wasted costs order can also be made against a party's legal representative (s 19A). That means you! There are two key cases on this. The first is *Re A Barrister (Wasted Costs Order) (No 1 of 1991)* [1993] QB 293, where it was said that:

> *A three-stage test or approach is recommended when a wasted costs order is contemplated.*
>
> (i) *'Has there been an improper, unreasonable or negligent act or omission?*
>
> (ii) *As a result have any costs been incurred by a party?*
>
> (iii) *If the answers to (i) and (ii) are "Yes," should the court exercise its discretion to disallow or order the representative to meet the whole or any part of the relevant costs, and if so what specific sum is involved?';*

The second case is *Re P (A Barrister)* [2001] EWCA Crim 1728; [2002] 1 Cr App R 207, where it was said that 'a mere mistake is not sufficient to justify an order. There must be a more serious error.'

2.7.6 Costs against third parties

A costs order may be made against someone who is not a party to the proceedings if there has been serious misconduct by the third party, and the court considers it appropriate, having regard to that misconduct, to make a third party costs order against him (s 19B).

3 Bail

3.1 Bail—practice and procedure

3.1.1 Introduction to bail

Breaking the cycle, para 179, December 2010:

> In order to make best use of prison to punish serious and dangerous offenders, we also need to rethink how we use it for remand. When it is used properly, remand in custody helps to keep the public safe, and bail legislation has rightly been strengthened recently to reflect that priority better. Clearly the courts must be able to remand defendants in custody in serious cases, and where there is a risk of reoffending of a sort that would cause injury. However, each year several thousand people are remanded in custody awaiting trial for offences for which they would be unlikely to receive a custodial sentence if they were convicted, because the offence of which they are accused is not serious enough to warrant it. In these cases custodial remand achieves little. There are limits to what the criminal justice system can properly do with unconvicted prisoners. The Government therefore intends to remove the option of remand in custody for defendants who would be unlikely to receive a custodial sentence. This will not impede justice. If a defendant fails to attend, the trial will proceed in their absence, unless there is good reason why it should not.

Breaking the cycle was a Government Green Paper, looking mainly at issues around sentencing. However, the paragraph quoted above indicated that a profound re-think of the purposes of pre-trial custody, and therefore bail, was quite likely in the near future. This was accomplished through changes made to the bail system by the Legal Aid, Sentencing and Punishment of Offenders Act 2012.

Bail is an enormously important issue for many defendants within the criminal justice system. The potential loss of liberty may have serious effects on them, regardless of the outcome of the proceedings. A period spent remanded in custody will feel like a prison sentence, especially for someone of good character or even someone who has never spent any time in custody before. Time spent as a remand prisoner could exceed the length of any custodial sentence passed on the defendant; indeed, the eventual sentence may be non-custodial (as *Breaking the Cycle* acknowledged). In the meantime, the defendant is prevented from doing his or her job, if he or she has one, resulting in probable loss of income and perhaps a lost job. The financial consequences may spill over, for example, into an inability to pay rent or mortgage leading to the loss of one's home.

The Criminal Justice Statistics September 2013 show for the preceding year, just under 40,000 people were remanded in custody by magistrates, quite a drop from 2010 when some 67,000 people were remanded in custody (although that figure was perhaps exceptionally high). In 2012–13, more than 7,500 defendants who had spent at least some time remanded in custody were eventually acquitted by magistrates (or the case was not proceeded with). Of the defendants who were tried in the Crown Court, who pleaded not guilty and were remanded in custody for at least a part of the time, 12 per cent were eventually acquitted or their case was not proceeded with in the Crown Court (more than 4,000 people). Again, statistics show that in 2012–13, almost one-third of all defendants who were remanded in custody eventually had a custodial sentence (immediate or suspended) passed upon them by a magistrates' court. As the rest of this chapter will show, the reasons for deciding to remand a defendant in custody are quite separate from issues of guilt or innocence, or the appropriate sentence for the crime, but the possible consequences of this decision (particularly for an unconvicted defendant) require courts to exercise great care before taking it.

The main statute here is the Bail Act 1976. The Criminal Procedure Rules 2014 deal with bail in both the magistrates' court and Crown Court, in Part 19. See also the *Criminal Practice Directions*, Part III.

3.1.2 Bail Act 1976, s 4—the general right to bail

(1) A person to whom this section applies shall be granted bail except as provided in Schedule 1 to this Act.

(2) This section applies to a person who is accused of an offence when—

(a) he appears or is brought before a magistrates' court or the Crown Court in the course of or in connection with proceedings for the offence, or

(b) he applies to a court for bail in connection with the proceedings.

This subsection does not apply as respects proceedings on or against a person's conviction of the offence.

[(2A) and (2B) relate to extradition and are omitted]

(3) This section also applies to a person who, having been convicted of an offence, appears or is brought before a magistrates' court or the Crown Court to be dealt with under—

(za) Schedule 1 to the Powers of the Criminal Courts (Sentencing) Act 2000 (referral orders; referral back to appropriate court),

(zb) Schedule 8 to that Act (breach of reparation order),

(a) Schedule 2 to the Criminal Justice and Immigration Act 2008 (breach, revocation or amendment of youth rehabilitation orders),

(b) Part 2 of Schedule 8 to the Criminal Justice Act 2003 (breach of requirement of community order), or

(c) the Schedule to the Street Offences Act 1959 (breach of orders under section 1(2A) of that Act).

(4) This section also applies to a person who has been convicted of an offence and whose case is adjourned by the court for the purpose of enabling inquiries or a report to be made to assist the court in dealing with him for the offence.

(5) Schedule 1 to this Act also has effect as respects conditions of bail for a person to whom this section applies.

(6) In Schedule 1 to this Act "the defendant" means a person to whom this section applies and any reference to a defendant whose case is adjourned for inquiries or a report is a reference to a person to whom this section applies by virtue of subsection (4) above.

(7) This section is subject to [section 41 of the Magistrates' Courts Act 1980] (restriction of bail by magistrates' court in cases of treason) [and section 115(1) of the Coroners and Justice Act 2009 (bail decisions in murder cases to be made by Crown Court judge)].

[(8) This section is subject to section 25 of the Criminal Justice and Public Order Act 1994 (exclusion of bail in cases of homicide and rape).]

[(9) In taking any decisions required by Part I or II of Schedule 1 to this Act, the considerations to which the court is to have regard include, so far as relevant, any misuse of controlled drugs by the defendant ("controlled drugs" and "misuse" having the same meanings as in the Misuse of Drugs Act 1971).]

Section 4 is shown in its current form, as amended.

Any question of bail being granted which is not governed by s 4 of the BA 1976 (or some other statutory provision) is at the discretion of the court. See, for example, *Burgess v Governor of Maidstone Prison* [2000] All ER (D) 1688; *Criminal Practice Directions*, Part III 19G.2.

3.1.3 'Unconditional' bail—the duty to surrender to custody

The question of whether to release a defendant on bail or keep him or her in custody arises whenever a case is remanded (see **3.15**). If a defendant is granted bail, this means that he or she is released from court subject to a primary duty to attend the next court hearing in the case. This is known as the duty to surrender to custody. (See BA 1976, s 3(1).) Failure to appear at the appointed place, time and date is itself a criminal offence leading to a fine or imprisonment (BA 1976, s 6—see **3.9**).

In the past, it has appeared that, for the magistrates' court, a defendant surrenders to custody by:

- turning up at the court where he or she was due to appear;
- on the due date;
- at the appointed time (usually 10 am); and
- reporting to the appropriate person.

See *DPP v Richards* [1988] QB 701.

The defendant is then allowed to remain *apparently* at liberty, by staying in the public areas of the court building. Strictly, though, he or she is in custody until the case comes up in court. It follows that the defendant is under an implied obligation not to leave the building without first obtaining permission to do so (where departure is thought to be necessary, permission should be sought from the court or someone acting on its behalf). If the defendant leaves without consent, the court may issue a warrant for his or her arrest. See BA 1976, s 7(2); *DPP v Richards*; confirmed in *R v Central Criminal Court, ex p Guney* [1995] 1 WLR 376.

The position is different in the Crown Court, according to *R v Evans* [2011] EWCA Crim 2842. Here, the Court of Appeal observed that in Crown Courts:

> the almost universal practice is to require those who surrender to enter the dock and place themselves in the custody of the custody officers . . . It seems to us that—general practice also accords with principle. Surrender means surrender to custody section 2(2) of the Bail Act. Whatever may be the position in courts such as the magistrates' courts where there is no physical movement into an identifiable place of custody and perhaps no custody officers in the courtroom, in the great majority of Crown Courts the dock is such a place and it is staffed for the purpose by uniformed custody officers. Next, once a defendant has surrendered he must by definition be under the control of the court and he must be the responsibility of the court. The plain threshold for such control and responsibility in the ordinary case is placing oneself in the dock. If simply reporting one's presence to the usher were to constitute surrender, the defendant could not then go off into conference with his lawyer without express permission and indeed arguably without a fresh grant of bail for the purpose. He certainly could not leave the building for lunch even if he was told that his case would not be reached until after 3 o'clock, unless there were a fresh grant of bail . . . Accordingly, as it seems to us, the general practice of accepting surrender by way of entry into the dock accords not only with common experience and general practice, but also with principle.

So, we were left with two different points in time when a defendant might be said to have surrendered to custody—either when they have 'booked in' with a court official or when they physically appear before the court. The consequences of the defendant subsequently leaving the building would differ according to which approach was used by the individual courthouse. This has been recognised as undesirable, and in 2014 the Justices' Clerks' Society (JCS) recommended that a single common practice should be adopted—namely, that a defendant only surrenders to custody when he or she appears in court. The JCS suggested that all courts could have a single time (say, 10.30 am) when all the cases where defendants are absent are called on in court. At that moment, where they have been called upon to surrender and have failed to do so, then the Bail Act offence is made out.

Remember that some defendants are released on police bail subject to a duty to surrender to custody at a police station. This occurs, typically, where enquiries are being pursued and the individual has not been charged with an offence. See also 'street bail' (**2.2.3** and **3.1.4.2**). Release on bail 'freezes' the detention clock; it will not resume until the suspect re-enters police detention in those proceedings. See Police (Detention and Bail) Act 2011.

The primary duty may be accompanied by secondary duties imposed on the defendant—for example, to keep a curfew within certain hours; to report to the local police station once a week; to surrender one's passport. These secondary duties are often described as 'conditions of bail' (see **3.7**). A defendant who is released on bail, subject only to the primary duty to surrender to bail at the next court hearing, is often described as being released on 'unconditional' bail.

The text of the BA 1976, s 3(1), is as follows:

Incidents of bail in criminal proceedings

(1) A person granted bail in criminal proceedings shall be under a duty to surrender to custody, and that duty is enforceable in accordance with section 6 of this Act.

3.1.4 Where there is no right to bail

3.1.4.1 Generally

It is important to realise that the 'right' to bail under the BA 1976 *usually* applies only prior to conviction. It also only applies when a defendant appears in court (see BA 1976, s 4). So there is *no* right to bail in the following situations:

(a) when being arrested;

(b) when being charged with an offence;

(c) when a warrant for the arrest of an accused person is issued;

(d) after conviction for an offence *unless*:

  (i) the case is adjourned so that enquiries or reports can be made to assist the court when passing sentence (BA 1976, s 4(4)); or

  (ii) the defendant is subsequently brought before a court to be dealt with for breach of a youth rehabilitation order, or breach of a requirement of a community order (BA 1976, s 4(3) as amended);

(e) if the accused is charged with murder, manslaughter, rape or a number of other serious sexual offences (or an attempt to commit the offence, where appropriate), and he or she has a previous conviction for any one of these offences, the court may only grant bail if there are 'exceptional circumstances which justify it'. (See the Criminal Justice and Public Order Act 1994 (CJPOA), s 25, as amended; and **3.1.5**.) A previous conviction for manslaughter will only qualify if the accused was sentenced to custody for it;

(f) if the accused appears in court charged with an indictable offence, or one triable either way, and it appears to the court that he or she was already on bail at the time of the present offence, the court 'need not' grant bail under the BA 1976, s 4. The court continues to have discretion to release such a 'bail bandit' on bail again. (See BA 1976, Sch 1, Part I, para 2A.)

3.1.4.2 Street bail

As noted in **3.1.4.1(a)**, there is no right to bail when arrested without a warrant. Under PACE 1984, s 30, an arresting officer is required to take the person arrested 'to a police station as soon as practicable after the arrest'. That requirement is subject to two exceptions.

The first is where, on the way to a police station, the arresting officer is satisfied that there are no grounds for either keeping the person under arrest or releasing him on bail; in this situation (probably quite unlikely), the person must be released.

The second, and much more significant, exception is 'street bail', pursuant to PACE 1984, s 30A. This enables a police officer to release a person on bail following their arrest but prior to their arrival at a police station. The person so bailed is then under the duty to attend at a police station. The location, date and time of that attendance ought to be specified in a notice given by the officer using street bail to the person released on bail. Failure to attend is enforceable by arrest without warrant. For an interesting critique of 'street bail', see the article by Anthea Hucklesby [2004] Crim LR 803 (see also 2.2.3).

3.1.5 The right to bail—a human right?

The Bail Act 1976, s 4 gives a 'general right to bail' (sic) for defendants in criminal litigation. However, s 4 does not apply to *all* defendants in the criminal justice system, nor does it apply at all stages of the system (see **3.1.2** and **3.1.4**). Furthermore, even those defendants to whom BA 1976, s 4 applies cannot demand to be released on bail automatically. There is a presumption, but no more, that such a defendant will be released on bail if a case is remanded. Section 4(1) says that a person to whom s 4 applies shall be granted bail (this is the 'right'), *except* as provided in the BA 1976, Sch 1. When Sch 1 applies, bail will be denied, and the defendant will be remanded in custody (see **3.4**).

In addition to the 'general right' to bail in the BA 1976, s 4, Article 5 of the European Convention on Human Rights provides a right to liberty and security. This is clearly relevant to bail.

Relevant provisions in Article 5 include:

> 1. *Everyone has the right to liberty and security of person. No one shall be deprived of his liberty save in the following cases and in accordance with a procedure prescribed by law:*
>
> . . .
>
> (c) *the lawful arrest or detention of a person effected for the purpose of bringing him before the competent legal authority on reasonable suspicion of having committed an offence or when it is reasonably considered necessary to prevent his committing an offence or fleeing after having done so;*
>
> (d) *. . . lawful detention [of a minor] for the purpose of bringing him before the competent legal authority;*
>
> 3. *Everyone arrested or detained in accordance with the provisions of paragraph 1(c) of this article shall be brought properly before a judge or other officer authorised by law to exercise judicial power and shall be entitled to trial within a reasonable time or to release pending trial. Release may be conditioned by guarantees to appear at trial.*
>
> 4. *Everyone who is deprived of his liberty by arrest or detention shall be entitled to take proceedings by which the lawfulness of his detention shall be decided speedily by a court and his release ordered if the detention is not lawful.*
>
> 5. *Everyone who has been the victim of arrest or detention in contravention of the provisions of this article shall have an enforceable right to compensation.*

The impact of human rights on bail generally is seen in the Law Commission Report (No 269) in 2001, *Bail and the Human Rights Act 1998*. This Report made several recommendations about legislative changes, some of which have since been implemented.

Article 5 has already been used to assess the legality of an English bail provision—CJPOA 1994, s 25. In its original form, this provision required courts to deny bail to a defendant accused of a serious offence (listed in s 25(2)) if he or she had previously been convicted of such an offence. In several cases, notably *Caballero v UK* (2000) 30 EHRR 643, the European Court of Human Rights found s 25 to contravene Article 5. In consequence, s 25 was amended so that courts are now allowed to release a defendant who is accused of his second serious offence if there are 'exceptional circumstances which justify it'. See CDA 1998, s 56.

One offence covered by s 25 is murder. The grant of bail for this offence was considered by the Ministry of Justice during 2008–9. In part, this review was stimulated by the killing of a woman by her son-in-law, a police officer who had already been charged with murdering his wife but who was released on bail by a Crown Court judge. The Consultation Paper (CP11/08) disclosed the quite surprising information that in January 2008, 13 per cent of defendants charged with murder were on bail (60 people), while 85 per cent of those charged with manslaughter were on bail (35 people). Following the consultation, the law was amended so that a defendant accused of murder may not be granted bail unless the court is of the opinion that there is no significant risk that he would commit an offence that would cause an injury; see now BA 1976, Sch 1, Part 1, para 6ZA. The onus would be on the prosecution to show that the risk existed. Any decision to grant bail to a defendant charged with murder would be taken only by a judge of the Crown Court. See now the Coroners and Justice Act 2009, ss 114 and 115.

In 2001, the Law Commission Report (No 269) concluded that there were no provisions in either the BA 1976 or the CJPOA 1994 which were *incapable* of being interpreted and applied compatibly with Convention rights. The Report nevertheless recommended reform of some legislative provisions. Subsequent changes to conditional bail in the BA 1976, s 3(6), reflect this sort of concern. The amended version of s 25 was considered by the House of Lords in *R (on the application of O) v Harrow Crown Court* [2007] 1 AC 249. The House of Lords agreed with the view of Hooper LJ in the Court of Appeal that s 25 (if read literally) clearly imposed the burden of proof on the defendant to show exceptional circumstances. This was contrary to Article 5(3) (and see *Hutchison Reid v UK* (2003) 37 EHRR 9) and therefore s 25 should be 'read down' to impose only an evidential burden on the defendant—'the burden remains upon the prosecution to satisfy the court that bail should not be granted'. Subsequently, the European Court of Human Rights found there had been no breach of Article 5(3); see *O'Dowd v UK*, 21 September 2010, Application no 7390/07.

In situations where there is no right to bail, the defendant may still be released on bail. The court, if it remands such a case, usually has a *discretion* to grant bail. This discretion is unfettered by the need to satisfy the BA 1976, Sch 1, if bail is to be refused—in other words, the court has more freedom to refuse bail in such circumstances. On the grant of bail at the police station following charge, see PACE 1984, s 38 (see **2.2.11**).

3.1.6 Custody time limits

There are certain limits on the length of time that a defendant can be kept on remand in custody, under the Prosecution of Offences Act 1985. See the Prosecution of Offences (Custody Time Limits) Regulations 1987 (SI 1987/299) as amended. That there should be limits on the time to be spent in custody awaiting trial cannot be doubted. As Lord Bingham CJ declared in *R v Manchester Crown Court, ex p McDonald* [1999] 1 WLR 841, to proceed without time limits:

> . . . would manifestly afford inadequate protection to unconvicted defendants, since a person could, if the Bail Act conditions were satisfied, be held in prison awaiting trial indefinitely, and there would be no obligation on the prosecuting authority to bring him to trial as soon as reasonably possible.

The regulations impose deadlines within which the proceedings must reach a specified stage. For example, where a defendant is sent for trial to the Crown Court on an indictable-only or triable either-way offence and he is kept in custody, he can only be kept in custody for a maximum 182 days following the date that he was sent for trial (see reg 5(6B)). If the deadline is not met, the defendant *must* be released on bail. There are also deadlines which apply generally, regardless of whether or not the defendant is in custody. These are sometimes referred to as *statutory time limits* and originate in the Prosecution of Offences Act 1985, s 22. Non-compliance results in the proceedings being stayed. In certain circumstances, the case may be re-started later. See also the CDA 1998, ss 43 and 45, on statutory time limits. The prosecution can apply for a deadline to be extended. It must show (on a balance of probabilities) that there is good and sufficient cause for the extension and that it has acted with all due diligence and expedition (POA 1985, s 22(3)). Even where the prosecution has failed to show that it has acted with all due diligence, so that an application to extend the custody time limit fails, some defendants may nevertheless continue to be remanded in custody as the right to be released on bail is subject to CJPOA 1994, s 25 (no bail for defendants who are charged with or convicted of homicide or rape after a previous conviction for such an offence): see *R (O) v Crown Court at Harrow* [2007] 1 AC 249 and **3.1.5**.

When a defendant is freed on bail following the expiry of a custody time limit, his or her bail should only have conditions attached to it that he or she can comply with *after* release (eg reporting to a police station or a condition to reside at a specified address). Conditions which must be complied with *prior* to release (eg providing a financial surety) cannot be imposed. The significance of this can be seen in *Re Ofili* [1995] Crim LR 880, where O was originally granted bail, subject to providing a surety of £4,000. O could find no one to stand surety in that sum, so he remained in custody. When he challenged this, the Divisional Court held that on expiry of the custody time limit, he was entitled to be freed on bail, subject only to reporting or residence conditions.

In a magistrates' court the maximum length of time that a defendant should spend in custody where he is charged with an either-way offence is 70 days. This period should be calculated as follows:

- 70 days from first court appearance to the start of summary trial (for either-way offences);
- 70 days from first court appearance to being sent for trial (for either-way offences).

Where the defendant is charged with a summary offence, the custody time limit becomes 56 (not 70) days, starting with the first appearance and ending with the summary trial. Where the defendant is charged with an indictable-only offence, he will be sent for trial 'forthwith' on his first appearance in the magistrates' court (see CDA 1998, s 51).

Once an offence is sent to the Crown Court for trial, the *maximum* length of time that a defendant should spend in custody prior to his or her trial is 182 days, beginning with the date that he or she was sent for trial by the magistrates and expiring with the date of his or her arraignment (ie being asked in Crown Court to plead either guilty or not guilty). Any days spent in the custody of the magistrates' court prior to being sent for trial must be deducted from the 182-day maximum.

This period can be extended, but any use of a 'sham' arraignment simply to defeat the purpose of the custody time limit will be struck down. See, for example, *R v Maidstone Crown Court, ex p Hollstein* [1995] 3 All ER 503.

If the 182-day period expires, the CPS should either apply for an extension or bring the defendant back to court to be released on bail. A prison governor has no power to release the defendant without an order from the court. If the defendant continues to be detained in the absence of a court order for release, the appropriate remedies are either to apply to the Crown Court for bail or to seek *habeas corpus* or judicial review. No action will lie against the Home Office for false imprisonment, nor will the CPS be liable for breach of statutory duty if it fails to return the defendant to court after expiry of a custody time limit. See *Olotu v Home Office and Another* [1997] 1 WLR 328.

The precise length of the custody time limits is subject to the HRA 1998 and Article 5(3) of the ECHR which provides that everyone detained 'shall be entitled to trial within a reasonable time or to release pending trial'. The relationship between these provisions was considered by Lord Bingham CJ in *R v Manchester Crown Court, ex p McDonald* [1999] 1 WLR 841. He reviewed the ECHR case law on the subject and stated that:

> We do not . . . find anything in these European cases which in any way throws doubt on the English law . . . It would indeed appear that the term of 112 days [as it then was] prescribed by the regulations imposes what is, by international standards, an exacting standard.

3.2 Taking a decision on bail—when and how

3.2.1 When is the decision taken?

Usually, the question of bail or custody is decided at the end of each day's proceedings in the case, immediately prior to adjourning it to another day. If a case is being heard in court in the morning, and will continue in the afternoon, the court should determine whether the accused will take lunch in the cells (custody) or in the restaurant of his or her choice (bail), immediately before breaking for lunch. Sometimes, though, the question of bail is the sole reason for a case appearing in court. Examples are:

- The defendant, sent in custody to the Crown Court for trial or sentence, who applies to the Crown Court for bail pending his first appearance in the Crown Court (see **3.11.1**).
- The defendant who has been refused bail by magistrates and appeals to a Crown Court judge (see **3.11.1**).

3.2.2 How is the decision taken?

The court must decide for itself whether or not to grant bail. It may be addressed by representatives of both prosecution and defence if the grant of bail is opposed, but the decision is one for the court. If the court is minded to refuse bail, it should always allow the defence the opportunity to make representations before making its final decision: *R v Evans* [2011] EWCA Crim 2842. Lay magistrates will often retire briefly to consider whether to grant bail if release on bail is opposed by the prosecution. District and Crown Court judges will normally decide in court, straight after counsel have finished their submissions. If the release of the defendant on bail is unopposed by the prosecution (and especially if the defendant is already on bail in the current proceedings), the decision to grant bail is usually a formality but defendants cannot successfully raise an argument of legitimate expectations if they are remanded in custody following an unopposed application; see *R (on the application of Burns) v Woolwich Crown Court* [2010] EWHC 129 (Admin).

3.2.3 Records, reasons, certificates and rights

3.2.3.1 Records

There are two common situations when a record must be kept of a decision on bail. Pursuant to the BA 1976, s 5(1), these are:

- whenever bail is granted (either by the police or a court);
- whenever a defendant with the right to bail under the BA 1976, s 4 is remanded in custody by a court.

Also, if an application is made to a court either:

- to attach conditions to a grant of bail which was hitherto unconditional; or
- to vary any extant conditions of bail,

the court must make a record of its decision.

If the defendant asks for a copy of the record, he or she must be given one (BA 1976, s 5). In some of the situations set out at **3.2.3.2**, the defendant must be given a copy of the record even if one is not requested.

3.2.3.2 Reasons

Reasons for refusing to grant bail, etc. If a defendant has a right to bail under the BA 1976, s 4, then if a court:

- refuses to grant bail; or
- grants bail subject to conditions; or
- on application for the purpose, imposes or varies conditions in respect of bail,

the court shall give reasons for its decision (BA 1976, s 5(3)).

These reasons shall be entered on the s 5 record and a copy must be given to the defendant (s 5(4)). However, if the decision is taken by the Crown Court, the defendant is legally represented in court, and the representative does not request a copy, a copy need not be given (BA 1976, s 5(5)). The purpose of giving reasons in these situations is to enable the defendant to make an informed decision about applying to another court about bail.

As well as the specific obligations imposed by the BA 1976, s 5(3), there is a more general obligation to provide reasons when refusing bail. Case law decided under the ECHR establishes that a court must:

> . . . examine all the facts arguing for or against the existence of a genuine requirement of public interest justifying, with due regard to the principle of the presumption of innocence, a departure from the rule of respect for individual liberty and set them out in their decisions on applications for release.

See *Letellier v France* (1992) 14 EHRR 83.

Reasons for granting bail. Where a court grants bail notwithstanding that the prosecution has opposed it, the court must state its reasons for granting bail, and these should be entered on the s 5 record. See BA 1976, s 5(2A).

3.2.3.3 Certificates of full argument

Under the BA 1976, s 5(6A), if magistrates withhold bail after hearing a fully argued application for bail, they must issue a certificate stating that they heard full argument. The first application in court is usually rather under-cooked and so typically the magistrates will not issue the certificate then but will allow the defence to make a second application, probably based on the same facts but a little more organised, a week later. If this fails, then the certificate will definitely be issued. After two unsuccessful bail applications in a case, if the magistrates allow the defendant to make a third application (which is unsuccessful), they should issue a certificate indicating the change in circumstances or new consideration that persuaded them to hear the third application. See BA 1976, s 5(6A) and (6B); also BA 1976, Sch 1, Part IIA (inserted by the CJA 1988, s 154). See further **3.10** and **3.11**. Note that some barristers, and some defendants, don't want to wait for a week to make a second application to the magistrates, so they ask for a certificate of full argument immediately after the first application has failed. This lets them go straight away to a Crown Court judge to apply for bail.

3.2.3.4 Right to appeal a refusal of bail

When magistrates issue a certificate of 'full argument', they must tell the defendant that he or she may now apply to a Crown Court judge for bail; the position is the same when magistrates send a case to Crown Court for trial. See BA 1976, s 5(6). On appeals generally, see **3.11**.

3.3 Applying for bail—what happens in court?

The procedure for determining whether a defendant is to be released on bail does not really vary from court to court, either between courts on the same level of the court system or between courts on different levels. Some defendants have a right to bail under the BA 1976, s 4. Others can only seek the exercise of the court's discretion in their favour. In practice it is always incumbent on the defendant to apply for bail notwithstanding the duty of the court to consider it (BA 1976, Sch 1, Part IIA).

3.3.1 The first step—dealing with the opposition

When a court hearing is adjourned and the defendant is to be remanded, the defendant (or defence counsel) is asked whether he or she seeks release on bail. If the answer is yes, the prosecution will be asked if there are any objections to bail (see **3.4** and **3.5**).

Usually, defence counsel will seek out the prosecution *before* the case is called into court and ask whether there are any objections to bail. If there are none, the application will be unopposed and is likely to succeed (see **3.3.2**). If there are objections, defence counsel may ask what these are and then think about what bail conditions might overcome them. If defence counsel can get his client's agreement to such conditions, the approval of the prosecution may then be sought. If this is obtained, the defence can apply to the court for bail and offer the 'agreed' terms. As the application is now unopposed in effect, success (with the agreed conditions) is likely.

3.3.2 The unopposed application for bail

In this situation, the defence having indicated that bail is sought, the prosecution offer no objection. Although the court could try to investigate whether there are reasons why it should withhold bail from the accused, it is unlikely to do so—largely because the prosecution is its normal source of information which is critical of the accused. If prosecuting counsel sees no reason to object, the court is unlikely to discover such a reason from that source for itself.

3.3.3 The bail application which is opposed

If no agreement on bail has been reached between defence and prosecution prior to coming into court (see **3.3.1**) the prosecution objections are set before the court. The strict rules of evidence do not apply to bail applications but the defence is entitled to cross-examine any witness that the prosecution calls. The defendant may also testify. See *R (on the application of DPP) v Havering Magistrates' Court* [2001] 3 All ER 997. Defence counsel then makes oral submissions dealing with the objections to bail. Counsel may suggest that the objections are groundless and/or propose any conditions which might be attached to bail to overcome the objections (see further **3.6** and **3.7.5**). The defence may call potential sureties into the witness box in an attempt to persuade the court that the defendant is unlikely to abscond. Finally, the court takes its decision to remand either on bail or in custody.

(See further Chapter 38 in the *Advocacy* manual for a checklist and flow chart on bail applications.)

3.4 Objections to a release on bail

As previously mentioned, the prosecution may object to the defendant being freed on bail. In practice, any objections will correspond to one or more of the reasons for refusing bail to a 's 4' defendant, found in the BA 1976, Sch 1. These will be substantiated with information provided to the court by the prosecutor. Examples are:

(a) 'The accused is likely to fail to surrender to bail': he failed to turn up last time and we had to get a warrant; he has three convictions for this sort of thing already and faces a long spell in prison; he has no permanent address.

(b) 'The accused is likely to commit offences if freed': he was already on bail for an offence when he was arrested for this lot; he's done it in the past; he makes his living from crime.

(c) 'The accused must be remanded in custody for his own protection': he is on 12 charges of burglary, all from houses on the estate where he lives. Some of the residents have told the police that he's a dead man if he shows his face round there.

3.5 Refusing to release a defendant on bail

3.5.1 If the offence is imprisonable

3.5.1.1 The general principle

If a defendant has the right to bail under the BA 1976, s 4, and asks to be released, then the court can only withhold bail where the offence is indictable and imprisonable if one (or more) of the following criteria is present in the case:

(a) The court is satisfied that there are substantial grounds for believing that the defendant would:

   (i) fail to surrender to custody*;

   (ii) commit an offence whilst on bail*;

   (iii) interfere with witnesses* or otherwise obstruct the course of justice.

(b) The court is satisfied that there are substantial grounds for believing that the defendant would commit an offence through conduct which would, or would be likely to, cause physical or mental injury to an 'associated' person, or cause them to fear such injury. This aims at preventing domestic violence. 'Associated' people are defined in the Family Law Act 1996, s 62, and include a spouse, civil partner, cohabitee, someone D agreed to marry and people who have had an intimate personal relationship with D of significant duration. So it is quite a broad definition.

(c) The defendant is charged with an offence triable either way and it appears to the court that he or she was already on bail at the time of the present offence.*

(d) The court is satisfied that the defendant must be kept in custody for his or her own protection (or welfare, if the accused is a child or young person—see **Chapter 6** for definitions of these terms).

(e) The defendant is currently serving a custodial sentence imposed for a previous offence.

(f) If this is the first time that the case has been in the court and the court is satisfied it has not been practicable to obtain all the information necessary for a proper decision on bail to be made.

(g) If the defendant has already failed to surrender to bail in the current case (or has broken the conditions attached to the grant of bail)* and has been arrested for this.

(h) If, after conviction, the case is adjourned for enquiries or reports and it appears to the court that it would be impracticable to complete the enquiries or report without keeping the defendant in custody.

(See BA 1976, Sch 1, Part I.)

LASPO 2012 inserted Sch 1, Part 1, para 1A. This states that where:

- the defendant is aged 18 or above;
- is not charged in extradition proceedings;
- has not been convicted of an offence in the present proceedings; and
- it appears to the court that there is *no real prospect* that the defendant will be sentenced to a custodial sentence in the proceedings,

then the court cannot refuse him bail using any of the five criteria marked in the list above with a *. As these include the 'big three' of failing to surrender, committing an offence and interfering with a witness, you can see that this is intended to mark a significant change to bail decisions.

3.5.1.2 Exceptions to the general principle

(a) In 2007, the CJA 2003, ss 14 and 15 came into **limited** effect. This remains the position. The result is that a court is required to **refuse** bail to a person accused of an offence which is punishable with life imprisonment (eg rape or robbery) in two situations:

- If he or she was already on bail in a different case at the date of the new offence. The new offence must have been committed on or after 1 January 2007. This requirement may be defeated if the court can be satisfied that there is no significant risk of the accused committing an offence if released.
- If he or she has previously failed to surrender to custody in the present proceedings. The failure to surrender must have occurred on or after 1 January 2007. Again, the requirement to refuse bail may be overcome by satisfying the court that there is no significant risk that the accused will abscond again if released now.

If the accused is aged under 18, these requirements are relaxed slightly, so that the factors which 'trigger' the refusal 'shall be given particular weight' when deciding whether there are substantial grounds for believing that he would commit offences or abscond, if released.

(b) We should also note that the courts may deny bail to a defendant who is a Class A drug user. See BA 1976, Sch 1, Part I, paras 6A–6C. It is a little more complicated than that, of course. There are several criteria to consider:

- the defendant must be aged 18 or over; and
- he or she must have tested positive for the presence of Class A drugs in his or her system (such testing is now permitted after arrest, under PACE 1984, s 63B); and
- either:
  — the current proceedings relate to possession or the supply of Class A drugs; or
  — the court believes that the defendant's misuse of a Class A drug caused or contributed to the current offence; or
  — the court believes that the current offence was motivated by the defendant's intended misuse of a Class A drug; and
- either:
  — the defendant has refused to undergo an assessment of his or her dependency on (or propensity to misuse) Class A drugs; or
  — the defendant has had a positive assessment and refused the offer of such further assessment or assistance or treatment as the original assessor considered appropriate.

If, in the case of such a defendant, he or she is willing to undergo an assessment, or have the suggested follow-up, and the court decides to release the defendant on bail, it must make it a condition of bail that the defendant has the assessment or participates in the follow-up.

(c) The Criminal Justice and Immigration Act 2008 inserted BA 1976, Sch 1, Part IA. This restricts the grounds on which bail may be refused to a defendant charged with either a *summary* imprisonable offence or with 'summary-only' *low-value criminal damage* offence. These changes came into force in 2008. A defendant facing one of these charges need not be granted bail if one of seven grounds is satisfied:

(i) It appears to the court that he has previously failed to surrender to custody (in any criminal proceedings) and the court believes that, taking account of that failure, he would not surrender if released now.*

(ii) He was already on bail at the time of the current offence and the court is satisfied that substantial grounds exist to believe that he would commit an offence if released now.*

(iii) The court is satisfied that there are substantial grounds to believe that he would commit an offence by engaging in conduct which would, or would be likely to, cause physical or mental injury to someone who is 'associated' with them (eg spouses, civil partners, cohabitants, children), or would cause a person to fear such injury.

(iv) The court is satisfied that the defendant should be kept in custody for his own protection (or welfare, if he is a juvenile).

(v) The defendant is already in custody, serving a sentence.

(vi) The defendant has been released on bail in the current proceedings but has now been arrested under BA 1976, s 7, and the court is satisfied that there are substantial grounds to believe that he would fail to surrender, commit an offence, interfere with witnesses or otherwise obstruct the course of justice, if released on bail again.*

(vii) There has been insufficient time to obtain the information needed to make a proper decision on bail.

(See BA 1976, Sch 1, Part IA (inserted by CJIA 2008, s 52 and Sch 12).)

LASPO has significantly altered this scheme. If a defendant to whom Sch 1, Part 1A applies, is aged 18 or above, and has not been convicted of an offence in the present proceedings, and it appears to the court that there is *no real prospect* that the defendant will be sentenced to a custodial sentence in the proceedings, then the court cannot refuse him bail using any of the three criteria marked in the list above with a *.

Schedule 1, Part IA also applies to juvenile defendants. In the case of a juvenile charged with a low-value criminal damage offence, this is achieved by the inclusion of a new section, s 9A, into the BA 1976. The usual mode of trial provisions do not apply to juveniles, of course, so s 9A empowers magistrates to make an assessment of the value of criminal damage, in order to determine whether an application for bail by the juvenile should be decided under Sch 1, Part I or Part IA.

3.5.2 Considerations for the court

When a court is considering whether one of the reasons for refusing bail (referred to in **3.5.1 (a)**) is satisfied, it should take account of:

(a) The nature and seriousness of the offence (and probable sentence).
(b) The character, antecedents, associations and community ties of the accused.
(c) The defendant's record of fulfilling bail requirements in the past.
(d) The strength of the case against the accused (unless adjourning for reports or enquiries before passing sentence).
(e) If the court is satisfied that there are substantial grounds for believing that the defendant, if released on bail, would commit an offence whilst on bail, the risk that the defendant may do so through conduct which would, or would be likely to, cause injury to another person,

as well as to any others which appear to be relevant.

See Sch 1 to the BA 1976 (at Part I, para 9). With regard to (b), the disclosure of D's *antecedents* means that the magistrates learn of his or her criminal record, if any. There are several points to note about this:

- evidence of any criminal record should be tendered in writing, not orally (*R v Dyson* (1944) 29 Cr App R 104);
- the press *should not* report any convictions which are publicised at that time (*R v Fletcher* (1949) 113 JP 365) (note that there is no direct power to coerce the media, although note the Contempt of Court Act 1981, s 4(2));
- any magistrate who sits on a bail application hearing and learns of previous convictions is disqualified from subsequently trying D's guilt/innocence in that case (MCA 1980, s 42).

Also on 'associations and community ties', see the suggestions in *Stone's Justices' Manual*, 2013 edn, para 1–481. The phrase covers:

- name, age, nationality and (if applicable) length of residence in the UK;
- family circumstances (married? dependent children? does he or she live with wife/parents/other relatives?);
- residence (type of accommodation; recent addresses and length of stay);
- employment (recent record; present job—location and income);
- possible sureties, any relative, friend, employer in court . . .;
- anything else that the defendant wants to put forward, for example medical problems, difficulties with job or home if remanded in custody.

With regard to any other considerations 'which appear relevant', the C&JA 2009 imposes an obligation on courts to consider the risk of injury posed by a defendant, if released on bail.

This arises in two specific ways. First, where the accused is charged with murder, he or she may only be released on bail by a Crown Court judge (C&JA 2009, s 115) and he or she may not be released on bail unless the judge takes the view that there is no significant risk of him committing an offence which is likely to cause injury (see BA 1976, Sch 1, Part 1, para 6ZA, inserted by C&JA 2009, s 114(2)). Secondly, where an accused is charged with an indictable offence punishable with imprisonment (this is virtually all indictable offences), if the court is satisfied that there are substantial grounds to believe that he or she would commit offences if released on bail, it must go on to consider the risk that these offences would be likely to cause injury to any person (BA 1976, Sch 1, Part 1, para 9(e)).

One should also note the BA 1976, s 4(9), which states that a court may have regard to any misuse of controlled drugs by the defendant, where it is relevant to the court's decision on bail. Section 4(9) was inserted by the Criminal Justice and Court Services Act 2000 (CJCSA), s 58; to support this move, the CJCSA 2000 provides that samples of urine or a non-intimate sample may be taken from an adult defendant charged with a 'trigger offence' (as well as in some other circumstances) for the purpose of ascertaining whether he or she has any specified Class A drug in his or her body (see s 57). Failure to provide a sample is an imprisonable offence; information obtained from a sample may be disclosed for the purpose of informing any decision about granting bail in criminal proceedings to that defendant. Trigger offences include typical drug crimes (possession and possession with intent to supply); also most of the offences in the Theft Act 1968 (see CJCSA 2000, Sch 6).

Special considerations apply to bail decisions concerning *juvenile* defendants who are charged with offences punishable with life imprisonment (strictly, detention during Her Majesty's pleasure or custody for life):

(a) when deciding whether it is satisfied that there are substantial grounds for believing that the defendant would commit offences if released on bail, the court shall give particular weight to the fact that he was already on bail at the date of the present offence (BA 1976, Sch 1, Part I, para 9AA, inserted by the CJA 2003, s 14(2));

(b) when deciding whether it is satisfied that there are substantial grounds for believing that the defendant would fail to surrender to custody if released, the court shall give particular weight to the fact that, having been released on bail in the present proceedings, he subsequently failed to surrender to custody without reasonable cause (BA 1976, Sch 1, Part I, para 9AB, inserted by the CJA 2003, s 15(2)).

These two provisions were intended to have general application to juvenile defendants whatever offence they were charged with but they have only ever been brought into force for these most serious crimes. See SI 2006/3217.

Finally, remember, if a court withholds bail from a 's 4' defendant, it must give its *reasons* in open court and on the record (BA 1976, s 5(3); see **3.2.3**).

3.5.3 If the offence is non-imprisonable

The grounds for refusing bail set out in **3.5.1** are applied only to defendants charged with crimes for which they can be sent to prison, if convicted. The Bail Act 1976, Sch 1, Part II covers bail for non-imprisonable offences and is more liberal in allowing bail. The grounds for withholding bail now are:

- the defendant is a child or young person;
- the defendant has been convicted in the proceedings;
- for the protection of the defendant;
- where the defendant is already serving a custodial sentence;
- where the defendant has been arrested for a bail offence in connection with this case (see **3.9**);
- where the defendant has previously failed to surrender to bail and, in the light of that failure, the court is satisfied he or she would not surrender to bail if released now.

There is no power to remand a defendant in custody for the purpose of preparing medical/psychiatric reports if the offence is non-imprisonable.

It may seem rather odd that a defendant could be denied bail simply because of his age; see above and Sch 1, Part II, para 2(za), inserted by LASPO 2012. The Explanatory Notes that accompany LASPO state that this is to ensure that the child or young person is not simply released on bail but has 'looked after' status from the local authority. This in turn means that they are assessed by the local authority and should receive 'appropriate assistance and supervision'.

The detailed provisions which govern the imposition of bail conditions are to be found in the BA 1976, Sch 1, Part I, para 8. Part I applies to defendants 'accused or convicted of *imprisonable* offences' (emphasis added). There is no corresponding text in Sch 1, Part II, which deals with *non-imprisonable* offences, nor in Sch 1, Part IA, which deals with summary or low-value criminal offences. It might be thought, then, that the BA 1976 makes no provision for attaching conditions to a grant of bail where a defendant is accused or convicted of a non-imprisonable offence. In fact, it has been decided that the basic power to attach conditions to a grant of bail (found in BA 1976, s 3) applies to both imprisonable and non-imprisonable offences (see *R v Bournemouth Magistrates' Court, ex p Cross* (1989) 89 Cr App R 90).

This decision can produce a rather odd result by virtue of the different criteria which now apply to non-imprisonable offences when (a) refusing bail and (b) imposing conditions. The BA 1976, s 3(6) and Sch 1, Part I, para 8 both allow a court to attach conditions to a grant of bail if it appears necessary to do so in order to ensure that the defendant surrenders to custody; but Sch 1, Part II, does not allow a court to withhold bail on the grounds that it believes the defendant will not surrender to custody. So if the court fears that a Sch 1, Part II defendant will abscond, it may attach conditions to his or her bail but if there are no conditions that will allay such fears, it seems that they must release him or her on bail anyway.

3.6 Overcoming objections to bail—the power of imagination

It was mentioned earlier (in **3.3.3**) that if the prosecution is objecting to the release of the defendant on bail, defence counsel can suggest that certain conditions be attached to the grant of bail. These suggestions can be made to the prosecutor before going into court or once the prosecutor states the objections in court. Additionally, defence counsel can make (or repeat) these suggestions in his or her final submissions to the court. Apart from some qualifications on the power of the courts to attach conditions to a grant of bail, the conditions which can be used to overcome the fears of the prosecution or court are almost limitless. See, for example, *R (on the application of Ellison) v Teesside Magistrates' Court* [2001] EWHC Admin 12 which records that a defendant charged with attempted rape was released on bail by a Crown Court judge subject to a number of conditions, one of which was that he was not to consume alcohol.

3.6.1 Keeping one's imagination within reasonable bounds

There are some very common conditions (see **3.7**) which will be suggested by the defence almost as an automatic reaction to certain objections. Nevertheless, one should not be afraid to put forward novel solutions to allay any objections, subject only to two observations. First, that one should always get the defendant's consent before putting a suggestion forward. Apart from the ethical problem of arguing a case with no instructions from the lay client to do so, there is a practical problem—to get your client released on bail, subject to conditions which he or she will not or cannot accept, is effectively not getting bail. Secondly, remember that the everyday bail conditions are used so often because they are workable and answer a particular objection sensibly. Do not invent new ones which fail to satisfy those criteria. One should seek only to improve the commonplace conditions to deal with novel situations when they arise.

3.7 Attaching conditions to release on bail

3.7.1 Generally

As regards a person granted bail, the BA 1976, s 3, provides that:

Incidents of bail in criminal proceedings

(1) A person granted bail in criminal proceedings shall be under a duty to surrender to custody, and that duty is enforceable in accordance with section 6 of this Act.

(2) No recognizance for his surrender to custody shall be taken from him.

(3) Except as provided by this section—

(a) no security for his surrender to custody shall be taken from him,

(b) he shall not be required to provide a surety or sureties for his surrender to custody, and

(c) no other requirement shall be imposed on him as a condition of bail.

(4) He may be required, before release on bail, to provide a surety or sureties to secure his surrender to custody.

(5) He may be required, before release on bail, to give security for his surrender to custody. The security may be given by him or on his behalf.

(6) He may be required to comply, before release on bail or later, with such requirements as appear to the court to be necessary—

(a) to secure that he surrenders to custody,

(b) to secure that he does not commit an offence while on bail,

(c) to secure that he does not interfere with witnesses or otherwise obstruct the course of justice whether in relation to himself or any other person,

(ca) for his own protection or, if he is a child or young person, for his own welfare or in his own interests,

(d) to secure that he makes himself available for the purpose of enabling inquiries or a report to be made to assist the court in dealing with him for the offence, and, in any Act, 'the normal powers to impose conditions of bail' means the powers to impose conditions under paragraph (a), (b) (c) or (ca) above,

(e) to secure that before the time appointed for him to surrender to custody, he attends an interview with a person who, for the purposes of the Legal Services Act 2007, is an authorised person in relation to an activity which constitutes the exercise of a right of audience or the conduct of litigation . . .

In **3.1.3**, it was said that any grant of bail was subject to a primary duty—to surrender to bail at the appointed time, date and place—but also that secondary duties (known as 'conditions of bail') could sometimes be imposed on a defendant. The BA 1976 originally specified two forms of bail condition—the surety and security (see the BA 1976, s 3(3) and (4)). The police were originally limited to these two conditions (but see now **3.7.7**), while the courts had more choice due to the BA 1976, s 3(6), which allowed a court to impose any condition that they thought necessary to secure certain objectives.

3.7.2 The surety

If the court (or police, following an arrest or charge) considers it is necessary to ensure that the defendant surrenders to custody, the defendant may be required to provide sureties to guarantee his or her surrender (BA 1976, s 8). If no sureties are forthcoming, the defendant stays in custody, although technically bail has been granted. A surety is a person—usually a friend, relative or employer—who agrees to ensure that the defendant attends court at the next hearing. The surety acknowledges that, should the defendant fail to surrender, the surety is liable to forfeit a specified sum of money to the court. See also **3.9.6** on forfeiture. A person may stand as a surety either in the courtroom or in any of the situations covered by the BA 1976, s 8(4) (eg, at the police station after the accused is charged; by the gaoler at court if the surety arrived too late to appear in court; at the prison holding the defendant).

3.7.3 The surety in court

Before starting the final submissions to the court, defence counsel should call any proposed sureties into the witness box. The 'surety' will take an oath and defence counsel should then explain the obligation to ensure the defendant's surrender to bail and the possibility of the surety losing money should this not happen. He or she should then be asked if he or she is still willing to be a surety. If so, counsel will enquire what sum of money he or she is prepared to run the risk of forfeiting and how this will be paid if required by the court to do so. The court will examine the surety's financial resources, character and any criminal record, and relationship to the defendant (kinship, geographical, etc).

If the procedure outlined is followed, there should be no problems about lack of resources if the surety is subsequently called on to forfeit his or her recognisance. The issue of the surety's ability to pay was considered by the Divisional Court in *R v Birmingham Crown Court, ex p Ali and another* [1999] Crim LR 504. The court declared that a qualified lawyer, or legal executive, should not put someone forward as a possible surety unless he or she has reasonable grounds for believing that the surety would, if necessary, be able to meet the financial undertaking. Failure to observe this requirement is irresponsible and possibly a matter for consideration by a professional disciplinary body. Furthermore, a court should conduct appropriate enquiries with an individual before accepting that person as a surety. It might be necessary to require evidence of the assets that the would-be surety claims to have. How far that enquiry would go depends upon all of the circumstances, the most important of which is the amount of money at stake. (See **3.9.6**; also the *Advocacy* manual, Chapter 38.)

3.7.4 Security

The defendant may be required to provide security for his or her surrender (BA 1976, s 3(5) as amended by the CDA 1998, s 54(1)). This may take the form of money or other valuables (BA 1976, s 5(9)) and may be demanded from the defendant personally, unlike a surety. It will be deposited with the court and, if the defendant fails to surrender to custody, it may be forfeited by court order, either totally or in part. The monetary amount of the security should be assessed with reference to the defendant, his assets and his relationship with the person who is to provide the security: *Mangouras v Spain* [2011] Crim LR 481; [2010] ECHR, Application no 12050/04, a decision of the European Court of Human Rights.

The obligation to pay a security, if it is held forfeit, is that of the defendant alone. If a third party actually supplies the funds to deposit with the court, he or she should note that the court is under no obligation to ascertain his or her ability to pay the money. Further, the third party's position need not be considered by the court when it imposes (or varies) bail conditions. Such a third party has far less protection here than when standing as a surety for a defendant: see *R v Maidstone Crown Court, ex p Jodka* (1997) 161 JP 638.

3.7.5 Other bail conditions

A court can impose any conditions it (or defence counsel) can think of, but they must be considered to be necessary to ensure that the defendant either:

- surrenders to custody; or
- does not commit offences while on bail; or
- does not interfere with witnesses; or
- does not obstruct the course of justice; or
- is for his own protection (or for his own welfare or in his own interests, if he is a juvenile); or
- is available for enquiries or reports to be completed; or
- attends an interview with a legal representative.

(See BA 1976, s 3(6).)

See *Stone's Justices' Manual*, at para 1–468.

3.7.6 Common conditions

3.7.6.1 Reporting to a police station

A defendant may be ordered to do this in order to ensure that he or she stays within the vicinity. This may be strictly enforced—for example, 'daily at 7 am and 7 pm'—or be a quite loose check—for example, 'every Thursday'. The purpose of this is to ensure the defendant is around to surrender to custody on the appointed date.

Now that the police are able to be more creative in attaching conditions to bail, there is room for confusion here. The police could always release a suspect on bail, subject to a requirement that he attend subsequently at the police station for further enquiries—that was not conditional bail as the attendance was a primary obligation on the accused. Nowadays, the police may also require a suspect to report to the police station if they are concerned that he or she may abscond—this would be a secondary obligation (he or she is not being required to surrender to custody) and if the suspect failed to report as required he or she would only be in breach of a bail condition; he or she would not have committed an offence under the BA 1976, s 6 (see **3.9.1**).

3.7.6.2 Keeping curfew

Originally a medieval rule requiring fires to be extinguished at a certain hour at night, this now means the obligation to stay indoors between certain hours (usually at night). This condition is often used where a number of crimes have allegedly occurred at roughly the same time of day—for example, five houses have been burgled in the early hours of the morning: curfew to be kept between 11 pm and 6 am. It is commonly used for juvenile defendants.

Under the CJA 2003, s 240A, if a defendant is released on bail subject to (a) a daily curfew of at least nine hours and (b) electronic tagging, half of the days spent like this will count towards serving any custodial sentence which is eventually imposed in the proceedings. However, for the reduction to be applied, the sentencer must make an order to this effect; for a complaint about this condition, see *R v Irving* [2010] EWCA Crim 189. For a review of the case law on s 240A, see *R v Monaghan* [2009] EWCA Crim 2699 and the commentary at [2010] Crim LR 322.

3.7.6.3 Staying out of/in a certain area

These are separate conditions. The first aims to separate the accused from temptation—the woman who has been charged with shoplifting from four West End stores in London may be ordered not to go within a two-mile radius of Oxford Circus. (As precise measurement of this is virtually impossible for the average citizen, it is wiser not to tempt fate!) The second condition is intended to prevent the defendant either absconding or, occasionally, from contacting prosecution witnesses. Compliance with both conditions may be very difficult to check but, if a breach does come to the attention of a police officer, the defendant may be re-arrested. In a novel twist on this common condition, it was reported in the press in May 1994 that the Marquis of Blandford had a bail condition that he must not use taxi-cabs unless accompanied by his solicitor; at the time, he was charged with, inter alia, using taxis and dishonestly not paying the fares.

3.7.6.4 Electronic monitoring

BA 1976, s 3 now makes it clear that a court can impose a condition of electronic monitoring of the defendant's compliance with bail conditions, or 'tagging'; see BA 1976, s 3(6ZAA) and (6ZAB). Electronic tagging can be used for juveniles and for adult defendants, although slightly different requirements apply depending on whether or not the defendant is aged under 17. The use of electronic monitoring as a bail condition is regulated by BA 1976, ss 3AA–AC.

3.7.6.5 Contact details

In order to ensure that cases go ahead as planned whenever possible, for some time now magistrates' courts have been requiring defendants to supply their mobile telephone number or e-mail address so that the court can remind them of an upcoming court appearance. Reluctance to give this information might result in the magistrates making it a condition of bail. Now, in the 'Magistrates' Court: Preparation for trial' form, the defendant is explicitly asked to provide details of phone, mobile and e-mail address. See **Appendix 2**.

3.7.7 Conditional police bail

The 'normal powers to impose conditions of bail' are available to a custody officer at a police station (see PACE 1984, s 47(1A)). The main limitations now are that any conditions must appear to be necessary to ensure that the defendant either:

- surrenders to custody; or
- does not offend whilst on bail; or
- does not interfere with witnesses or otherwise obstruct the course of justice; or
- is for his own protection (or welfare or otherwise in his own interests, if he is a juvenile).

See the BA 1976, s 3A(5), as amended by the CJA 2003, s 13(2). In addition, the police cannot use some specific bail conditions—residence in a bail hostel (see the BA 1976, s 3A(2)) or in connection with medical reports for defendants accused of murder (see the BA 1976, s 3A(3)).

When considering the use of bail conditions, the police are unlikely to be influenced by representations from defence counsel since barristers do not usually attend a police station. The ability of either a duty solicitor or the defendant's own choice of solicitor to suggest or influence bail conditions at the police station remains the subject of speculation. See further on this, Ede and Edwards, *Criminal Defence: Good Practice in the Criminal Courts,* 2008, 3rd edn, Law Society.

3.8 Changing bail conditions

If circumstances change, so that the original conditions are no longer appropriate, the defence can apply to the court to alter or remove them. In exceptional situations, the prosecution can apply for existing conditions to be altered (presumably to strengthen them), or for conditions to be attached to an unconditional grant of bail.

Such application is made under the BA 1976, s 3(8), either to the magistrates' court which is dealing with the case or, if the case has been sent to the Crown Court, to a Crown Court judge. Where a defendant has been sent to the Crown Court for trial but has not yet been required to surrender to custody at the Crown Court, then the magistrates' court which sent him for trial has concurrent jurisdiction with the Crown Court to hear any application for variation of bail conditions (see *R v Lincoln Magistrates' Court, ex p Mawer* [1995] Crim LR 878). Once the defendant has surrendered to custody at the Crown Court, the magistrates cease to have any jurisdiction over the matter. See also the BA 1976, s 3(8A)—this extends the Crown Court's jurisdiction to cover applications made in serious fraud cases which go to Crown Court on a notice of transfer. (For notices of transfer, see **Chapter 11**.) See *Blackstone's Criminal Practice,* 2014 edn, paras D7.67 and D7.84 for the basic procedure on bail applications to the magistrates' court and Crown Court respectively.

Under the Criminal Procedure Rules 2014, Part 19, there is a requirement for a defendant to give advance notice of an application to vary bail conditions in the magistrates' court or Crown Court. Notice must be given not less than 24 hours in advance of the application; it should specify the variation sought and the reasons for it. Where it is proposed that a defendant be released subject to a condition of residence at a specified address, CPR, r 19.11 requires the defendant to notify the prosecution of that address as soon as practicable after proceedings have begun against him. The prosecution is under an obligation to help the court to assess the suitability of that address. This requirement flows from concerns about the lack of information available to magistrates when assessing the suitability of an address proposed for a residence requirement, in the aftermath of a murder committed by Anthony Leon Peart on a London bus in 2005, whilst on bail.

It should be noted that if a defendant is released by the police on conditional bail, he or she may apply to a custody officer to vary those conditions (see the BA 1976, s 3A(4)). The custody officer may impose different conditions and may even make them more onerous than before. Counsel is very unlikely to be involved in such an application. However, the defendant may choose to apply to the magistrates' court and counsel may then be briefed (see the MCA 1980, s 43B).

3.9 What happens if the defendant disobeys?

3.9.1 Failure to surrender to custody

It seems that around 10–15 per cent of all defendants who are remanded on bail by magistrates subsequently fail to surrender to custody. The proportion does not vary much whether one looks at indictable offences or summary offences; see **Table 3.1**. The court will usually issue a warrant for the arrest of the accused unless, perhaps, defence counsel is able to offer an explanation for the absence. Such warrants are known as *bench warrants*. When the warrant is executed and the accused is brought before the court, the court is very likely to remand the accused into custody. Note that, even though the accused may have had a general right to bail hitherto (under BA 1976, s 4), they have it no longer (BA 1976, Sch 1). There are at least three possible courses of action that the court may take following a non-appearance by the defendant:

- punish the defendant for the s 6 offence;
- remand the defendant in custody or release subject to more severe conditions;
- try the defendant in his absence.

Clearly, these are not mutually exclusive and a defendant may eventually find that all three actions have been taken in his or her case.

Table 3.1 **Persons directed to appear at magistrates' courts[1] by type of offence, how directed to appear and outcome, 2007**

England and Wales	Number of persons (thousands)			
		Outcome		
How directed to appear	Total	Dealt with by magistrates[2]	Committed for trial	Failed to appear[3]
Indictable offences				
Summoned	48	35	4	9
Arrested and bailed	351	239	56	56
Arrested and held in custody	76	47	24	5
Total	475	321	84	70
Summary offences (other than motoring)				
Summoned	387	380	*[4]	6
Arrested and bailed	215	195	*[4]	20
Arrested and held in custody	25	23	*[4]	1
Total	627	598	*[4]	27
Summary motoring offences				
Summoned	615	590	*[4]	25
Arrested and bailed	139	130	*[4]	9
Arrested and held in custody	9	9	*[4]	0
Total	763	729	*[4]	34
All offences				
Summoned	1,049	1,005	4	40
Arrested and bailed	705	564	56	85
Arrested and held in custody	110	79	24	6
Total	1,864	1,648	84	131

(1) The number of persons directed to appear includes those who failed to appear to a summons or to bail, who are excluded from the proceedings figures given in other chapters of this volume.
(2) Including those committed to the Crown Court for sentence.
(3) At any stage before final disposal by magistrates' court.
(4) Not applicable, because summary offences committed for trial will not be counted as principal offences as they must accompany an indictable-only or triable-either-way offence.

It is the norm in both magistrates' courts and the Crown Court, when granting bail, to give the defendant both an oral warning and a printed card to the effect that if he or she does not attend the trial, the court may well proceed in his or her absence. If a defendant has had adequate notice, the courts are unlikely to be reluctant to proceed in his or her absence even where the charge is a very serious one (see *O'Hare* [2006] EWCA Crim 471; but also *Criminal Practice Directions*, Part III 19E). Accessing credit databases has helped in tracing people who were subject to 'FTA' warrants (ie Failure To Appear).

If the defence counsel is able to put before the court some prima facie good reason for the absence of their client, the bench warrant may be *backed for bail*. In this situation, the warrant is executed by arresting the defendant and taking them to a police station. The defendant will then be re-released from the police station on (court) bail, subject to whatever conditions have been endorsed on the bench warrant, and will not then be produced in court but be under a duty to surrender to the court on a date to be notified. For obvious reasons, it is unusual for a bench warrant to be backed for bail.

3.9.2 Non-compliance with other conditions

No separate offence is committed in this situation but the accused is at risk of arrest (without warrant) by a police officer who has reasonable grounds for believing that a bail condition has been broken. Indeed, a police officer can arrest a defendant when he or she has reasonable grounds for believing that the defendant is *likely* to break a bail condition (see the BA 1976, s 7(3)). Once arrested, the defendant must be produced in the magistrates' court within 24 hours. The defendant should not be produced in the Crown Court, even if on Crown Court bail, nor may the magistrates commit the defendant to the Crown Court for a decision to be made on bail. See *R v Marshall* (1995) 159 JP 688; *R (on the application of Ellison) v Teesside Magistrates' Court* [2001] EWHC Admin 12.

When the defendant is produced in the magistrates' court, the magistrates have to make a two-stage determination (see the BA 1976, s 7(5); *R (on the application of DPP) v Havering Magistrates' Court* [2001] 2 Cr App R 2). The first stage is to decide whether the defendant has broken (or is likely to break) a condition of his or her bail. The hearing is quite informal; usually, a police officer attends the court and states the grounds for his or her belief that a bail condition has been (or was likely to be) broken. In so doing, the officer may rely on hearsay evidence. There is no need to call other witnesses to testify for the prosecution but the defendant may cross-examine any who are called. The defendant is then entitled to give evidence, if he or she wishes to do so. The defendant must be given a full and fair opportunity to comment on, and respond to, the material put forward by the prosecution but where the defendant asserts that a reasonable excuse existed for a breach, that matter is irrelevant at this stage (see *R (on the application of Vickers) v West London Magistrates' Court* [2003] EWHC Admin 1809). The prosecution may succeed even though they offer *only* hearsay evidence, as in *R (on the application of Thomas) v Greenwich Magistrates' Court* [2009] EWHC 1180 (Admin). The two-stage process outlined may be completed by the court without allowing further representations.

If the magistrates determine that the defendant has broken a bail condition, the second stage is to consider bail for the future of this case. The defendant may be remanded into custody, or released on bail again. Bail may be subject to the same or different conditions (BA 1976, s 7(5)). The breach of bail that was established in stage one is one factor relevant to the magistrates' decision now; another relevant factor would be any suggestion by the defendant that there was a reasonable excuse for the breach. See also *R v Liverpool City Magistrates' Court, ex p DPP* [1993] QB 233; and the commentary at [2004] Crim LR 64. An important change was made by LASPO 2012: the magistrates' court may not remand a defendant into custody under s 7(5) if he is an adult (18 or over), not charged in extradition proceedings, not yet convicted in the present proceedings and it appears to the court that there is *no real prospect* of the defendant being sentenced to a custodial sentence in the proceedings (BA 1976, s 7(5A)).

3.9.3 Prosecutions for failure to surrender

Under the BA 1976, s 6, it is an offence for a defendant to fail to surrender to custody at the appointed time and place. This offence is often referred to by courts, and counsel, as 'absconding'.

It is otherwise commonly referred to, particularly by defendants, as 'doing a runner' (see also *Marku v National Crime Agency* [2014] EWHC 4507 (Admin). It is punishable by imprisonment or a fine (see **3.9.5**) and any security or sureties will be liable to forfeiture by order of the court (see **3.9.6**). Although the BA 1976, s 6, creates a single offence of failure to surrender to custody, there are some distinctions to observe in the commencement of proceedings (this is an area that is currently dealt with in the *Criminal Practice Directions* at Part III 19C.7).

(a) *Where the defendant fails to surrender to court, having been bailed by police*

It is for the police or prosecutor to decide whether to initiate proceedings for the s 6 offence. If proceedings do go ahead, they should be dealt with on the defendant's first court appearance following arrest. The offence is summary and usually such offences have a six-month time limit on the commencement of proceedings, starting with the date of absence. However, if the defendant remains absent for a longer period, that will not defeat proceedings under s 6. CJA 2003, s 15(3) provides that proceedings may be instituted within three months of the date when the defendant eventually surrenders to custody, or is arrested in connection with the offence for which bail was granted, or appears in court in respect of that offence; see further *Criminal Practice Directions*, Part III 19C.1–3. Proceedings will be commenced by the new procedure of written charge and requisition (CJA 2003, s 29).

(b) *Where the defendant fails to surrender, having been bailed by a court*

It is for the court to initiate proceedings by its own motion, although the prosecutor may invite them to do so (see *Criminal Practice Directions*, Part III 19C.4). The defendant should be produced at the court dealing with the proceedings for which bail was granted previously—that may be the Crown Court, of course, if the defendant had been sent there for trial or sentence.

In either situation, the bail offence should be dealt with as soon as practicable: *Criminal Practice Directions*, Part III 19C.5. It is not good practice to postpone its consideration until the conclusion of the proceedings for the main offence.

3.9.4 The hearing of a s 6 offence

The court is entitled to adopt a relatively informal procedure (*R v Hourigan* [2003] EWCA Crim 2306). The hearing usually begins with the court asking the defendant if he admits the breach of bail. The defendant should always be given the opportunity to explain his absence, and defence counsel should be invited to address the court, if appropriate (see *R v Davis (Seaton Roy)* (1986) 8 Cr App R (S) 64; *R v Boyle* [1993] Crim LR 40; *Hourigan*). The defendant bears the burden of proving a reasonable excuse for non-attendance, on the balance of probabilities. A court should be careful not to tie the hands of a later court (which might deal with the s 6 offence) or the CPS by expressing a premature view of leniency or indicating that no proceedings need be taken—see *France v Dewsbury Magistrates' Court* [1988] Crim LR 295. See *Criminal Practice Directions*, Part III 19C.7.

3.9.5 Penalties for failure to surrender

Following conviction by magistrates for absconding, there is a maximum penalty of three months' imprisonment and/or a fine of up to £5,000 (this will increase to £15,000 when the amendment made by the CJA 2003 to Level 5 on the standard scale of fines takes effect, and be an unlimited amount when LASPO 2012, s 85 comes into force; see BA 1976, s 6(7)). However, the magistrates may instead commit the defendant to the Crown Court for sentence if they think greater punishment is required or if they are sending him to the Crown Court for trial on another offence and feel that it is appropriate for the Crown Court to deal with him for both offences (see BA 1976, s 6(6)). In the Crown Court, the absconder faces a maximum term of 12 months' imprisonment and/or an unlimited fine.

There are definitive guidelines for punishing a failure to surrender to bail (see the Sentencing Council website). These guidelines address both the defendant's culpability and the harm which resulted from the absence. The same principles should apply whether the offence is contrary to BA 1976, s 6(1) (no excuse for failure) or s 6(2) (initial reasonable excuse then a failure to surrender as soon as possible thereafter). However, the degree of harm is likely to be less in the latter situation and so it will normally be seen as a less serious offence. Where the failure is to surrender to a police station, the degree of harm is likely to be less (compared to a court) and it may be seen as a less serious offence in the circumstances.

The punishment may be severe if it is thought necessary to deter others. Sentences of six or nine months are not unknown although an absence of 22 years only resulted in a ten-month sentence, in a case described by the Court of Appeal as meriting a sentence 'very much at the top end of the bracket' (see *Clarke* [2000] 1 Cr App R (S) 224; *Igbebion* [2004] EWCA Crim 2724; *McKendrick* [2005] 2 Cr App R (S) 68, respectively). Where the defendant receives custodial sentences for both the original offence and the BA offence, the sentences should usually be consecutive, subject to the aggregate sentence remaining proportionate to the combined seriousness of the offences (see SGC guidelines, para 33 and, eg, *Lastauskas* [2015] EWCA Crim 262). It has been said that the responsibility for their absence is unaffected by whether or not they were eventually acquitted or convicted of the original offence (see *Clarke* again). For example, in *R v Neve* (1986) 8 Cr App R (S) 270, the defendant had been acquitted at his eventual trial for the main offence but was nevertheless sentenced to six months' imprisonment and ordered to forfeit a security of £10,000 for going to Spain in an attempt to avoid trial. This principle was confirmed in the Sentencing Council guidelines—see para 13: the culpability and harm are the same, regardless of the outcome of the original charge.

It is perhaps necessary to balance these cases with some statistics published by the Sentencing Advisory Panel in 2006. In 2004, some 98 per cent of all defendants who were sentenced for a *principal* Bail Act offence were dealt with by magistrates. Of these, the majority were fined and only 10 per cent received a custodial sentence for their failure to surrender. Conversely, in the Crown Court only 600 defendants were sentenced for a principal Bail Act offence but just under 50 per cent of them were sentenced to immediate custody for it. The most common length of custodial sentence was less than 15 days (magistrates' courts) and 15 days to one month (Crown Court). Whilst there is no clear trend in the Crown Court, it is clear that from 1999 to 2004, the size of fines increased whilst custodial sentences shrank in the magistrates' courts. Where the Bail Act offence was a *subsidiary* one (approximately two in every three such cases), again the overwhelming majority were disposed of by magistrates (96 per cent). There was a three-way tie between fines, community orders and custody as punishments. In the Crown Court, 58 per cent of these offenders were sentenced to custody whilst only 1 per cent were fined. In these statistics, 'principal offence' meant that either the BA offence was the only one being sentenced or was the offence which attracted the greater sentence.

The Sentencing Council (SC) guidelines identify aggravating and mitigating factors:

1. Aggravating factors include:
   - Leaving the jurisdiction;
   - Repeat offending;
   - Causing a lengthy delay to the administration of justice;
   - Making a determined effort to avoid the court proceedings.

2. Mitigating factors include:
   - Prompt voluntary surrender where it is initiated by D;
   - Misunderstanding, where it does not amount to a defence (the SC distinguishes this from a mistake by D, for which D must take responsibility); for example, where D has literacy or language difficulties which were not identified or addressed satisfactorily when bail was granted;
   - Being the sole or primary carer of dependent relatives, if this is the reason for the failure to surrender.

The guidelines state that the fact that a defendant has a 'disorganised or chaotic lifestyle', possibly due to a dependency on drink or drugs, will not reduce the seriousness of the offence. This description may apply to many defendants, of course. However, it may be seen as personal mitigation.

The SC says that it is a key principle that a Bail Act offender should be dealt with as soon as is practicable (echoed by the *Criminal Practice Directions* at Part II 19C.5). A decision on whether a Bail Act offence has been committed is important when deciding whether to grant bail again and, if so, on what conditions. Once the defendant's guilt is determined, the sentence is to be imposed as soon as is practicable. As the guidelines make clear, a crucial factor in determining the appropriate sentence is whether proceedings for the original offence are being adjourned and, if so, whether the remand is on bail or in custody. In the latter situation, there is little possibility of a non-custodial sentence for the BA offence. Where the defendant is released on bail, however, the court may wish to consider a community order, possibly with an electronically monitored curfew requirement and a supervision requirement. In a more serious situation which crosses the custody threshold, a suspended sentence order may have the same impact.

The SC guidelines indicate that for a first-time offender who pleads not guilty, the worst cases could fall into the range of community order (medium) to 40 weeks' custody in the Crown Court or community order (low) to 10 weeks' custody in the magistrates' court. Where a defendant surrenders late but on the correct day and the proceedings can go ahead as planned, a fine is appropriate; however, the guidelines note that magistrates' courts retain the power to impose a penalty of one day's detention where appropriate (see MCA 1980, s 135).

One of the less obvious possible penalties for absconding is when the court decides to try the defendant for the original offence, in his absence. This can happen in the magistrates' court (see MCA 1980, s 11 and **5.1.1**) but it can also happen in the Crown Court once the defendant has been arraigned on the indictment (for guidance on when to proceed in the absence of the defendant, see the speech of Lord Bingham in *R v Jones* [2003] AC 1). Any such trial must be fair, of course. The SC guidelines note the 'encouragement' given to such action in the old *Consolidated Criminal Practice Direction*; that is slightly less apparent now in the *Criminal Practice Directions* at Part II 19E.3—proceeding in the absence of the accused 'is a step which ought normally to be taken only if it is unavoidable'. But the SC guidelines reflect that taking swift action to run with the trial as scheduled may reduce the harm occasioned by the absence, although not the culpability of the defendant.

3.9.6 Forfeiture of a surety

If a defendant was granted bail subject to providing a surety, then a failure by the defendant to surrender to custody puts the surety in jeopardy of losing the sum which he or she guaranteed by his or her oath to the court.

In the past, forfeiture was likely to occur, usually for the whole sum. The test was that the whole sum had to be paid, unless it was fair and just to forfeit a lesser amount or nothing at all. Forfeiture provisions were tightened by the CDA 1998, s 55. When a defendant fails to surrender, the court is required to declare any surety to be forfeit *automatically*. It shall then require the surety (if present in court) to explain why he or she should not have to pay the whole sum. The court retains its discretion to demand payment of a lesser sum. If the surety is absent from court, or the court allows him or her time to produce evidence of his or her lack of culpability, it will issue a summons requiring his or her appearance at a later date.

There is a heavy onus on the surety to prove why he or she should not forfeit the full amount. This should be done either by showing a lack of means to meet the forfeiture or by establishing that he or she acted responsibly. The surety has a duty to maintain contact with the defendant and to keep informed as to the conditions of bail in order to ensure the defendant's surrender to custody. The Court of Appeal has pointed out that any reduction in the amount ordered to be forfeited, following a defendant absconding, 'must be the exception not the rule and be granted only in really deserving cases'. Lack of culpability by a surety is a factor to consider but in *R v Maidstone Crown Court, ex p Lever* [1995] 1 WLR 928, two sureties who were found to be blameless for the absconding nevertheless were ordered to forfeit 85 per cent of their total surety of £59,000. Hoffmann LJ (as he then was) observed that 'in one sense the system has unfairness built into it. It may result in persons entirely innocent having to suffer on account of the wrongdoing of another.' One might contrast the decision of the Chief Metropolitan Magistrate to order forfeiture of £93,500 on original sureties of £140,000 in the case of Julian Assange, the Wikileaks founder. The judge said that the sureties had acted in good faith:

> I accept that they trusted Mr Assange to surrender himself as required. I accept that they followed the proceedings and made necessary arrangements to remain in contact with him, However, they failed in their basic duty, to ensure his surrender.

If the initial enquiry into the surety's means was conducted properly (see **3.7.3**), the surety should have no problem finding the money to pay the forfeit. However, where the enquiry was inadequate, or the surety's means have changed, the sum which the surety is ordered to forfeit should be such as is within his or her actual means. So, in a case where a surety of £25,000 was forfeited but the surety had originally provided an extremely exaggerated account of his assets, the magistrates' court ordered him to pay the forfeit at £12 per fortnight. The matter was then considered by the Divisional Court who observed that it would be correct in any normal case for the court to think of a sum which the surety could be reasonably expected to pay in full within two or three years (not 80 years as here). The matter was remitted to the magistrates for a re-hearing. See *R v Bristol Magistrates' Court, ex p Davies* [1999] Crim LR 504.

Usually, the obligation of a surety will end when the defendant is arraigned on the charges as this is when trial normally commences. At this moment, the defendant is understood to have surrendered to the custody of the court and the surety has done all that the court required. This is subject to exceptions, though, and a surety should remain well-informed as to the exact status of the defendant and the view of the court as to whether the surety's obligation is at an end or continues. The penalty for being ill-informed is seen in *R v Central Criminal Court, ex p Guney* [1994] 1 WLR 438, where a surety for Asil Nadir was ordered to forfeit £650,000 following Mr Nadir's departure to Northern Cyprus. It could have been worse, as originally he stood surety for £1 million; in fact, it got even better for Mr Guney, as the Court of Appeal later quashed the forfeiture completely (see [1995] 1 WLR 376 and [1996] AC 616). Nadir eventually returned to the UK in 2010.

See also MCA 1980, s 120; Criminal Procedure Rules 2014, Part 19.15.

3.10 Renewing an application for bail (or 'If at first you don't succeed, try again—but only once!')

3.10.1 Obligation to consider bail

See the BA 1976, Sch 1, Part IIA:

1. *If the court decides not to grant the defendant bail, it is the court's duty to consider, at each subsequent hearing while the defendant is a person to whom s 4 above applies and remains in custody, whether he ought to be granted bail.*
2. *At the first hearing after that at which the court decided not to grant the defendant bail, he may support an application for bail with any argument as to fact or law that he desires (whether or not advanced previously).*
3. *At subsequent hearings the court need not hear arguments as to fact or law which it has heard previously.*

According to the BA 1976, Sch 1, Part IIA (inserted by the CJA 1988, s 154), at every hearing of a case (when the defendant is in custody) the magistrates' court is obliged to consider whether he or she should be released on bail. The defence is allowed to make up to two applications for bail at which the same arguments may be used. If the accused is still in custody after this, the court may consider the matter of bail no longer open to argument from the defence.

Although the court is under a duty (CJA 1988, s 154) to consider bail at subsequent hearings in the case, these will be formalities. The defence may only re-open the issue of bail by raising fresh circumstances or arguments. Section 154 represents the statutory embodiment of a common law rule which was first reported in *R v Nottingham Justices, ex p Davies* [1981] QB 38.

Several cases have considered what constitutes a 'change in circumstances'. It seems to be a question of fact in each case, although the Queen's Bench Divisional Court has stated that the change need not be major. *R v Blyth Juvenile Court, ex p G* [1991] Crim LR 693 offers an illustration. Where there has been no application for bail by a defendant on the first appearance of a case at court and he or she has been remanded in custody, it seems that he or she has a right to apply for bail at a later hearing of the case (see *R v Dover and East Kent Justices, ex p Dean* [1992] Crim LR 33).

It seems possible that, with the advent of the HRA 1998 and the need to comply with decisions already made under the ECHR, a slight amendment to English law may be needed. It has usually been the position in English case law that simple effluxion of time does not give rise to a change in circumstances. However, in *Neumeister v Austria (No 1)* (1979–80) 1 EHRR 91, the European Court declared that a person should be released at the point when it is no longer reasonable to continue his or her detention. So, as time passes, the prisoner who is held in custody on remand should be able to seek review by the court of the decision to detain. This is clearly relevant to a prisoner held on remand under lengthy custody time limits. According to the European Court of Human Rights:

> . . . the nature of detention on remand calls for short intervals [between bail reviews]; there is an assumption in the Convention that detention on remand is to be of strictly limited duration . . . because its raison d'être is essentially related to the requirements of an investigation which is to be conducted with expedition. In the present case an interval of one month is not unreasonable.

See *Bezicheri v Italy* (1989) 12 EHRR 210.

In its 1999 Consultation Paper (CP No 157) the Law Commission felt that it was adequate that bail should be reconsidered by magistrates at least every 28 days (see **3.16.2**) but was concerned that the possibility of a renewed application for bail might be denied by operation of Sch 1, Part IIA. It pointed out that para 3 only says the court '*need not* hear arguments as to fact or law which it has heard previously' and thus has a discretion to hear such arguments. However, in practice, courts seem to be reluctant to do so and also rarely accept that there has been a change in circumstances. The Law Commission noted reports which asserted that if the accused found a job, sureties or a fixed address, these were seldom sufficient to show a 'change in circumstances'. In its final Report on the matter (No 269, 2001), the Law Commission maintained that a review of bail at least every 28 days complied with Article 5(4), but felt that courts should only have to consider whether the lapse of time has resulted in a change of circumstances. A defendant should not be able to insist on a full re-hearing of bail arguments every 28 days even though there had been no material change in the circumstances. See paras 12.9–12.24 of the Report.

3.10.2 The magistrates' certificate

Under the BA 1976, s 5(6A), if magistrates withhold bail after hearing a fully argued application for bail, they must issue a certificate stating that they heard full argument. After two unsuccessful bail applications in a case, if the magistrates allow the defendant a third application (which is unsuccessful), they should issue a certificate indicating the change in circumstances or new consideration that persuaded them to hear that third application. See BA 1976, s 5(6A) and (6B); also BA 1976, Sch 1, Part IIA (inserted by the CJA 1988, s 154).

3.11 Appealing against a bail decision

3.11.1 Appeals to a Crown Court judge by a defendant

A defendant can apply to the Crown Court for bail, as provided for in the Senior Courts Act 1981, s 81 (as amended), in particular:

- where a magistrates' court has sent the defendant to the Crown Court in custody on an offence triable either way (either for trial or committed for sentence); or
- where a magistrates' court has sent the defendant to the Crown Court for trial on an indictable-only offence (under the CDA 1998, s 51); or

- where the defendant has been convicted by a magistrates' court, given a custodial sentence and been refused bail pending an appeal to the Crown Court (against either conviction or sentence); or
- where a case is proceeding in a magistrates' court, the magistrates have heard a fully argued application for bail and refused it.

In this last instance, the defendant can appeal against the refusal to release on bail by producing a certificate issued under the BA 1976, s 5(6A) (see **3.2.3** and **3.10.2**). This appeal will be heard at the nearest location of the Crown Court dealing with Class 4 (low-grade) crimes. The appeal will usually be heard by a judge sitting 'in chambers'. This means that counsel need not wear a wig or gown, even though the hearing often takes place in a courtroom. This is not the same as a hearing in open court. If a defendant wishes to have the hearing in open court with the public able to attend, then that should happen unless the judge finds that the interests of justice require the application to be heard 'in chambers': see *R (Malik) v Central Criminal Court* [2007] 1 WLR 2455. The defendant will not usually be present at the hearing, although the Crown Court has the power to permit this. Compare the position on a prosecution appeal against the grant of bail: the European Court of Human Rights has said that a refusal to allow the accused to attend the court hearing of such an appeal would usually be an infringement of Article 5(4). See *Allen v United Kingdom* (2010) ECHR, Application no 18837/06.

The SCA 1981, s 81 only deals with defendants who are in custody. The CJA 2003, s 16 makes provision for defendants who wish to appeal against the conditions subject to which they have been released. The CJA 2003, s 16 only allows appeals against certain conditions:

- residence (either at a specified address, other than a bail hostel, or *not* at a specified address or area);
- any surety;
- provision of a security;
- curfew;
- electronic monitoring ('tagging');
- not to contact a specific person.

Furthermore, there must already have been a hearing at which the magistrates were asked to vary the bail conditions (see **3.8**).

3.11.2 Appeal to the High Court by a defendant

The High Court can only hear bail appeals:

- where a magistrates' court has stated a case for the opinion of the High Court (under the MCA 1980, s 111) and has refused bail; or
- where a defendant seeks judicial review of his conviction or sentence imposed in the magistrates' court and wants to be released on bail; or
- where a Crown Court judge has refused bail to a defendant in the course of proceedings there.

Therefore, a defendant who has been refused bail by magistrates should usually appeal to the Crown Court and no alternative or further appeal to the High Court is possible except as indicated above. A defendant who is denied bail during Crown Court proceedings will find it tough to appeal that refusal. A refusal of bail, at least at an early stage of proceedings, does not 'relate to a trial on indictment' and thus the High Court will have a supervisory role (cf Senior Courts Act 1981, s 29 and **8.3**). Historically, the High Court refused judicial review of such refusals because there was an alternative appeal route of going to a High Court judge in chambers. This route no longer exists (courtesy of the CJA 2003, s 17), and it seems that the option of judicial review has become more available. This change was recognised in *M v Isleworth Crown Court* [2005] EWHC 363 (Admin), although Maurice Kay LJ observed there that this is a jurisdiction that should be exercised 'very sparingly indeed. It would be ironic and retrograde if, having abolished a relatively short and simple remedy on the basis that it amounted to wasteful duplication, Parliament has, by a side wind, created a more protracted and expensive remedy of common application.' See more recently *R (on the application of Rojas) v Snaresbrook Crown Court* [2011] EWHC 3569 (Admin): 'a stream of authorities clearly establishes that in certain limited circumstances this court can still, within judicial review, set aside a decision in relation to bail . . .'. The test is one of *Wednesbury* unreasonableness. See further the Law Commission Report No 324, 2010.

3.11.3 Appeals by the Crown Prosecution Service

3.11.3.1 Appeal to the Crown Court

Under the Bail (Amendment) Act 1993, s 1(1), the prosecution can appeal to the Crown Court when a defendant—charged with (or convicted of) any imprisonable offence—is released on bail by a magistrates' court.

The prosecution may appeal if the defendant was granted bail despite objections from the prosecution *and* the prosecution is being conducted by the Crown Prosecution Service. If the CPS decides to appeal, it must say so (give oral notice of appeal) *before* the defendant is released from custody. Written notice of appeal must follow, within two hours, and must be served on the court and the defendant. Non-compliance with this two-hour period *may* be fatal to the appeal. That was the decision in *R v Middlesex Crown Court, ex p Okoli* [2000] Crim LR 921 but it has since been held that as long as the prosecutor uses due diligence in service, a few minutes' lateness in serving the defendant may be excused (see *R (on the application of Jeffrey) v Warwick Crown Court* [2002] EWHC 2469 (Admin)).

The appeal must be heard within 48 hours (excluding weekends and bank holidays). The defendant will be kept in custody until the appeal is determined. If the appeal succeeds, the Crown Court judge may remand the defendant in custody or release him or her on bail with conditions. The defendant is normally entitled to attend the appeal hearing; see *Allen v UK* (2010) ECHR, Application no 18837/06.

3.11.3.2 Appeal to the High Court

Where a Crown Court judge grants bail to a defendant, the prosecution may now appeal against that decision to the High Court (B(A)A 1993, s 1(1B)) (inserted by LASPO 2012). The procedure is the same as that for an appeal against the grant of bail by the magistrates' court. The prosecution cannot use this provision to appeal against a Crown Court judge's decision to grant bail consequent on a prosecution appeal from the magistrates' court under B(A)A 1993, s 1(1).

3.11.3.3 Reconsideration by the magistrates' court

The prosecution has a limited ability to ask for 'reconsideration' of a decision to release a defendant on bail. The BA 1976, s 5B, enables a prosecutor to apply to a magistrates' court to reconsider such a decision, whether it was originally taken by the court or by a custody officer. Having reconsidered, the magistrates may attach conditions to unconditional bail, vary the current conditions or withhold bail (BA 1976, s 5B(1)) or, presumably, preserve the status quo. Reconsiderations may only be sought where the defendant is on bail for an offence which must or may be tried on indictment; the application must be based upon information which was not available to the magistrates (or custody officer) when the original decision was taken.

3.12 Juvenile bail

Present government policy is that juveniles should spend as little time as possible awaiting final disposal of their cases. The provisions of the BA 1976 apply to juveniles in basically the same manner as they do to adult defendants. That is, juveniles may be remanded on bail or in custody when proceedings in court are adjourned. While awaiting disposal of their cases, most juveniles will be on bail.

In its 2011 response to the Green Paper *Breaking the Cycle*, the Government announced that it would reform *secure* remands for young people, so that everyone aged under 18 would be treated in the same way, and not as adults. The aim would be to make the UK compliant with the UN Convention on the Rights of the Child. All young people remanded to secure accommodation would be 'looked after' by an appropriate local authority. See Cm 8070, 2011.

This situation was achieved under LASPO 2012. Section 91 applies where a court deals with a child who has been charged with or convicted of an offence and the child has *not* been released on bail. Note that 'child' here means anyone under the age of 18 (s 91(6)). Note also that BA 1976, Sch 1, Part II provides that a court 'need not' grant bail to a child or young person (anyone under 18) charged with a non-imprisonable offence.

Under s 91, the court that orders a remand in custody must remand the 'child' either to local authority accommodation or youth detention accommodation. The local authority will be the one which already is looking after that child or, if none is, the authority where the child habitually resides. Conditions can be attached to this remand, in the same manner as bail conditions (s 93), but if it does so, the court must explain the conditions to the child in open court and using ordinary language. In certain circumstances, the court can require the child to wear an electronic tag (ss 94–96). If conditions are imposed and a police officer reasonably suspects that there has been a breach, the child may be arrested and taken before a court.

A remand into youth detention accommodation can only be ordered for children aged 12 or over. There are two *alternative* ways to order this type of remand. First, under s 98, the child must be charged with a violent or sexual offence or one which carries at least 14 years' imprisonment in the case of an adult offender. The court must be of the opinion that a remand to youth detention accommodation is necessary to protect the public from death or serious injury caused by further offending by the child or to prevent the child from committing imprisonable offences (the 'necessity' condition). Second, under s 99, the child must be charged with an imprisonable offence and there must be a real prospect that a custodial sentence will be imposed. Further, a 'history' condition must be satisfied. Either:

- the child has a history of absconding from a custodial remand and the present offence is alleged to have been committed whilst the child was remanded to local authority accommodation or youth detention accommodation; or
- the current offence(s), plus any other imprisonable offences for which the child has been convicted, amount to a recent history of committing imprisonable offences whilst on bail or on a custodial remand.

Finally, the same 'necessity' condition (as in s 98) must be satisfied, regarding public protection and the prevention of further offending. To use either route into youth detention accommodation, the child must be legally represented at court or have had at least the opportunity to be so represented. When a child is remanded into youth detention accommodation, the Secretary of State will direct that he goes to either a secure children's home, a secure training centre, a young offender institution or other specified accommodation (s 102). For an interesting review of the obligations imposed upon juvenile detention in England and Wales by international treaties, such as the UN Convention on the Rights of the Child, see *R (on the application of BG) v The Chief Constable of the West Midlands Constabulary and anor* [2014] EWHC 4374 (Admin).

3.13 Remands

Put in very simple terms, a remand is the name for the decision taken whenever criminal proceedings are left unconcluded and the court has to take a decision whether to release the defendant on bail or remand in custody until the next hearing in those proceedings. The case itself is adjourned. That adjournment may be to an open date (or date to be fixed), or it may be to a specific date. Thus, the parties to the proceedings may know when they are due back in court when they leave the courtroom today or they may need to wait for notification from the court of the next hearing date. Any time that a case has to be put off to another court session (either on the same day or a different day), it can be said to be adjourned. It is only in certain circumstances that the court will need to take a decision about remanding the defendant at the same time. See **3.14**.

3.14 When will a case be remanded?

If a criminal case before a court in England and Wales is not disposed of conclusively on one day, it will have to carry over into another day. For an analysis of how many cases are concluded on the first appearance in court, see **Table 3.2**, column 5.

Examples of such 'carry over' are:

(a) a trial which is too long to finish in a single day;

(b) a trial which has finished in a single day but the court wants more information on the offender before passing sentence (eg getting a pre-sentence report);

(c) a case which has been listed for a preliminary matter only to be determined (eg which court will try a defendant charged with an offence triable either way);

(d) a case which has been listed for trial but either party (or perhaps the court, if it has insufficient time that day) is unable to proceed with the case there and then;

(e) a case which has finished in one court but is going to another—on appeal or committal.

Note that, with regard to (a) above, a part-heard trial in the Crown Court continues on the next day. A part-heard case in the magistrates' court may continue the next day or may resume in several weeks' time (depending upon the availability of the courtroom and of the district judge or justices of the peace who are trying the case).

Whenever magistrates adjourn a case, they may remand the defendant. The MCA 1980 provides several situations where, on an adjournment, a magistrates' court *must* remand a defendant and then consider the alternatives of bail and custody. See **Figure 3.1**, which is based upon the MCA 1980, s 10.

If the defendant is remanded, he or she will either:

- be kept in custody—that is, stay locked up until produced by the (police, prison or other) authorities for the next court appearance; or
- be freed on bail. Being released on bail imposes a duty on a defendant to return to court at the appointed date, place and time (often called 'surrendering to custody'). Failure to attend the next hearing is itself a crime (BA 1976, s 6; see also **3.9**).

1. When D first appeared in the court, was he on bail or in custody?
   If YES—he must now be remanded (on bail or in custody).
   If NO—
2. Has D been remanded at any time during the proceedings for this offence?
   If YES—he must now be remanded (on bail or in custody).
   If NO—
3. The magistrates have a choice to remand or simply adjourn the case.

Figure 3.1 Will the adjournment be a remand?

Table 3.2 **Defendants proceeded against at magistrates' courts—average time for criminal cases by offence type and stage of proceedings, percentage dealt with on first appearance, average number of times case listed and average length of adjournments(1), 2003–2007**

England and Wales

Offence type	Average number of days: From offence to completion	From offence to charge or laying of information	From charge or laying of information to first listing	From first listing to completion	Percentage of defendants dealt with on first court appearance	Average number of times case listed in court	Average length of adjournments in days	Percentage of defendants pleading: Guilty(2)	Not guilty(2)	Number of defendants in sample (thousands)
Indictable offences (including triable either way)										
2003	111	47	8	56	30	3.2	26	55	23	33.1
2004	118	54	9	55	30	3.1	26	55	23	28.5
2005	122	59	10	54	31	3.1	26	56	22	28.1
2006(3)	123	61	10	52	30	3.1	25	58	22	27.7
2007(4)	118	61	10	47	32	3.0	23	59	22	28.8
Summary non-motoring offences										
2003	142	88	33	21	72	1.7	29	35	13	18.5
2004	140	82	33	26	69	1.8	30	39	14	17.5
2005	148	90	34	24	70	1.8	31	38	13	18.8
2006(3)	146	85	37	24	71	1.8	31	37	16	19.0
2007(4)	144	83	37	24	70	1.8	28	38	16	18.2
Summary motoring offences										
2003	162	97	39	26	61	1.8	31	52	8	31.1
2004	166	101	39	26	62	1.8	31	54	9	32.1
2005	162	99	39	24	63	1.8	31	56	9	29.5
2006(3)	160	94	41	25	63	1.8	33	57	10	26.7
2007(4)	162	96	41	25	65	1.8	33	57	10	26.4

Source: Time Intervals Surveys for Criminal Proceedings in magistrates' courts—Ministry of Justice.

(1) Results based on proceedings in one sample week in March, June, September and December for indictable offences and March and September only for summary offences.

(2) Defendants entering an initial guilty or not guilty plea, as a proportion of those proceeded against in sample weeks.

(3) In the June 2006 survey—North Yorkshire data were unavailable.

(4) From June 2007, changes were made to the way adult data was collected. As a consequence, any changes in results could be due to the changed data-collection process, and care should be taken when interpreting the results.

3.14.1 Situations where remand is required

(a) *Magistrates dealing with an offence triable either way*. If, before or during the summary trial of such an offence, an adjournment is needed, then usually the defendant must be remanded on bail or in custody. See **Figure 3.1**.

(b) *Magistrates determining which court will try an 'either-way' offence*. If the magistrates adjourn a case while determining whether the defendant will be tried by the magistrates or a jury, they must usually remand the defendant on bail or in custody (MCA 1980, s 18(4)). See **Figure 3.1**.

(c) *Magistrates sending a defendant to the Crown Court for trial*. Following a decision to send the defendant to the Crown Court for trial, if the defendant is currently remanded in custody, the magistrates may either order that he or she be kept in custody pending his or her trial or release him or her on bail with a direction that he or she appear before the Crown Court for trial (MCA 1980, s 8(1); CDA 1998, ss 51 and 52).

There are two other situations to be aware of:

(d) *Magistrates dealing with a summary offence*. Prior to deciding whether a defendant is guilty or innocent in such a case, the magistrates may have to adjourn the proceedings. If they do so, they have a choice—either to remand the defendant or simply to adjourn (MCA 1980, s 10(4)). If the defendant fails to appear at court on the next appointed date, the magistrates may proceed to try the case in the absence of the defendant or, in some circumstances, issue a warrant for arrest (MCA 1980, ss 11 and 13). See **Chapter 5**.

(e) *Magistrates deferring sentence*. Where a magistrates' court defers sentence on a convicted defendant (for up to six months) under the PCC(S)A 2000, s 1, this is not a remand, and the defendant, although released subject to a duty to return to court, is not on bail. (See *R v Ross* (1988) 86 Cr App R 337.)

3.14.2 The use of remands and adjournments by magistrates

For an analysis of the use of remands and adjournments by magistrates, see **Table 3.3**.

3.15 Who can remand a case?

3.15.1 Remands in the magistrates' court

It might seem, from what you have just read, that only magistrates can remand a criminal case. This is not the whole story. The vast majority of remands occur in the magistrates' court simply because that is where the bulk of criminal litigation takes place, particularly when you realise that almost all hearings in a case prior to trial will occur in the magistrates' court.

3.15.2 Remands in the Crown Court

The question of a simple adjournment never seems to arise in the Crown Court. A defendant who is committed to the Crown Court (whether for trial or sentence) will be remanded either on bail or in custody. Once there, the Crown Court judge has the power to grant bail for the period before the matter is dealt with (see the Senior Courts Act 1981, s 81, as amended).

Table 3.3 **Defendants proceeded against by court type, type of remand and outcome of proceedings, 12 months ending September 2013**

England and Wales — Defendants (thousands) and percentages

	Magistrates' courts			The Crown Court[1]		
	Not remanded	Bailed	Remanded in custody[2]	Not remanded	Bailed	Remanded in custody[2]
			Defendants (thousands)			
Acquitted or not proceeded etc	156.0	75.4	7.6	0.1	11.6	4.3
Convicted:						
Discharge	60.5	20.0	1.0	0.2	1.0	0.1
Fine	763.0	34.5	1.9	0.7	1.1	0.1
Community sentence[3]	47.0	63.6	3.5	2.8	7.3	1.6
Suspended sentence	5.4	14.1	2.1	4.5	13.8	2.3
Immediate custody[4]	20.2	12.1	10.6	9.1	12.6	26.3
Otherwise dealt with[5]	11.8	11.4	1.6	0.6	0.5	0.7
Total offenders sentenced	908.0	155.5	20.8	17.9	36.3	31.1
Committed for sentence	14.0	4.4	2.2	*	*	*
Committed for trial	56.5	23.6	7.8	*	*	*
Failed to appear	49.1	23.4	1.0	0.5	1.3	0.8
Total	1,183.6	282.4	39.4	18.5	49.1	36.3
			Percentages			
Acquitted or not proceeded etc	13.2	26.7	19.3	0.8	23.5	12.0
Convicted:						
Discharge	5.1	7.1	2.6	1.2	2.0	0.4
Fine	64.5	12.2	4.9	3.5	2.3	0.4
Community sentence[3]	4.0	22.5	9.0	15.2	15.0	4.4
Suspended sentence	0.5	5.0	5.3	24.2	28.0	6.3
Immediate custody[4]	1.7	4.3	26.9	49.3	25.6	72.5
Otherwise dealt with[5]	1.0	4.0	4.1	3.5	1.0	1.8
Total offenders sentenced	76.7	55.1	52.7	96.8	4.4	85.8
Committed for sentence	1.2	1.6	5.5	*	*	*
Committed for trial	4.8	8.4	19.9	*	*	*
Failed to appear	4.2	8.3	2.6	2.4	2.6	2.3
Total	100.0	100.0	100.0	100.0	100.0	100.0

* = Not applicable —committals for trial or sentence apply only to magistrates' courts cases.
(1) Crown Court cases are not necessarily concluded in the same year as the committal.
(2) Including those remanded in custody at any stage of proceedings at the Crown Court who may also have been given bail at some stage of those proceedings. Remand status of defendants shown is based on decisions made during proceedings at the Crown Court which may be different to that recorded in Table Q3.4, A3.1, A3.6, A3.7, A3.8, A3.9. A3.10 and A3.11.
(3) Community rehabilitation orders, supervision orders, community punishment orders, attendance centre orders, community punishment and rehabilitation orders, curfew orders, reparation orders, action plan orders and drug treatment and testing orders.
(4) Includes detention in a young offender institution, detention and training orders and unsuspended imprisonment.
(5) Includes one day in police cells, disqualification order, restraining order, confiscation order, travel restriction order, disqualification from driving, recommendation for deportation and other miscellaneous disposals.
Note: Some figures may not sum due to rounding.
Source: Table Q3a, Criminal justice statistics quarterly: September 2013, Ministry of Justice (February 2014).

Once a Crown Court trial has started, the judge will remand the defendant either in custody or on bail during any lunch or overnight breaks in the trial. Whether or not to release on bail is usually regarded as a matter solely within the power and discretion of the trial judge; see the observation by Peter Gibson LJ in *R v Central Criminal Court, ex p Guney* [1995] 1 WLR 376 that from 'the commencement of a [Crown Court] trial it is for the court conducting the trial to decide whether the defendant should be in custody or on bail'. See also the *Criminal Practice Directions* at Part III 19G.2.

3.16 Duration of remands

3.16.1 General examples

There are various maximum periods for a remand by magistrates in different circumstances.

Before conviction

(a) Three clear days in police custody (MCA 1980, s 128(7)).

(b) Eight clear days in prison custody (MCA 1980, s 128(6)). (Exception: if an 'either-way' offence is to be tried by the magistrates but they cannot convene in time, remand to whenever they can convene the court.)

(c) Twenty-eight clear days in prison custody if the defendant is in court, and has previously been remanded in custody for this offence. (See **3.16.2**.)

(d) Twenty-eight clear days in prison custody if the defendant has at least that long still to serve on a current custodial sentence (MCA 1980, s 131(1)).

(e) Any period to which both the prosecution and defence agree on bail (MCA 1980, s 128(6)).

After conviction

(f) Three weeks in custody for enquiries or reports for sentencing.

(g) Four weeks on bail for enquiries, etc.

Each of these periods is the maximum duration for a *single* remand. At its conclusion, the defendant will be produced before the magistrates once more. At that time, and subject to the custody time limits (see **3.1.6**), the magistrates may again remand him or her either on bail or in custody for a further period. Once a defendant is sent to the Crown Court, either for trial or sentence to be passed, he or she is remanded on bail or in custody until such time as the case is listed for hearing (again, subject to the custody time limits).

3.16.2 Avoiding weekly remands

A very large number of prisoners are held on remand in custody at any time in England and Wales. Typically, the prisoner has been remanded in custody by a court, prior to his or her trial, and is therefore usually subject to eight-day remands (see **3.16.1(b)**). The need to produce all of these prisoners at court, every week, would impose a tremendous burden on the Prison Service and its subcontractors, in terms of both administration and logistical arrangements. This effort would in large measure be wasted if the only reason for the court appearance was that eight days had passed. In order to minimise wasted costs, magistrates' courts have the power either to remand prisoners in their absence or to extend the remand period beyond the eight-day norm.

A magistrates' court can remand a defendant in custody, in his or her absence, on up to three occasions. To do so, the defendant must have legal representation and have consented to this procedure. (See the MCA 1980, s 128(3A).) This can effectively extend the remand period up to four weeks, although the case is still listed every eight days and the defendant is formerly remanded in his or her absence.

An alternative procedure is simply to remand the defendant for up to 28 clear days. Magistrates' courts are able to do this if:

(a) the accused has been remanded in custody already in the case; and
(b) the accused is present in court when the extended remand is ordered; and
(c) the court has fixed a date when the next stage in the proceedings will take place.

The power to do so derives from the MCA 1980, s 128A. Clearly, it is more straightforward than the alternative under the MCA 1980, s 128(3A) and is the usual method of remanding a prisoner in custody for periods exceeding eight days.

In addition to the above powers, there may also be the opportunity to conduct proceedings via a live television link between the magistrates' court and the prison where a defendant is being held. This power derives from the Crime and Disorder Act 1998, s 57, which provides that a court may treat the defendant as being present for pre-trial hearings where he or she is in custody but is able to see and hear the court (and be seen and heard by the court) via a live television link or other means. This procedure is being applied nationally to both magistrates' courts and the Crown Court.

3.16.3 Remands in the Crown Court

Neither s 128 nor s 128A MCA 1980 apply to the Crown Court. However, where the Crown Court hears an appeal against a bail decision made by magistrates, any consequent remand in custody ought to be made in a manner consistent with those provisions. Thus, a defendant ought not to be remanded in custody to reappear in the magistrates' court more than eight days later unless the requirements of s 128A are satisfied. See *Remice v Governor of Belmarsh Prison* [2007] Crim LR 796.

3.17 What are the alternatives to remanding a case?

Alternatives to remanding a case have been mentioned already but, in brief, the court may:

(a) *Try the case anyway*. If a case is ready for summary trial and the defendant does not appear, the magistrates may well go ahead and try the case in his or her absence, having entered a formal plea of not guilty. (See **5.2.1** and the MCA 1980, s 11(1).) The power to hold a summary trial in the absence of the accused has historically been used sparingly. One reason for reluctance is the 'statutory declaration' (see MCA 1980, s 14). This refers to the ability of a person convicted in his or her absence to declare that he or she did not know of the proceedings or summons which resulted in his or her conviction. Once the declaration is made, and served on the clerk to the justices, then the summons and all subsequent proceedings (eg a summary trial and guilty verdict) are void (see the MCA 1980, s 14(1)(b)). There may also be concerns about ensuring the defendant has a fair trial; see further the Human Rights Act 1998, Sch 1, Art 6. However, trial is much more likely to happen now; the 'Magistrates' Courts: Preparation for trial' form specifically asks—'Does the defendant understand . . . the trial can go ahead even if he or she does not attend?' See also Crim PR, r 37.11; **5.2.1.1**.

This power to try absent defendants does not exist in the Crown Court—the accused must be present at the start of a jury trial to enter a plea to the indictment personally. However, once the plea has been entered, typically at a plea and case management hearing, if the accused chooses to absent himself from subsequent proceedings, the court *may* try him in his absence. See the guidance on this subject given by Lord Bingham in *R v Jones* [2003] AC 1; *Criminal Practice Directions*, Part III 19E.3.

(b) *Adjourn to another date*. A case may be simply adjourned to another date and the prosecution and accused told to be at court on that date. No penal sanction exists in this situation to compel attendance at the adjourned hearing. The defence may seek an adjournment in order, for example, to instruct an expert witness to appear as a witness for the defendant. (See *R v Sunderland Justices, ex p Dryden, The Times*, 18 May 1994.)

(c) *Adjourn indefinitely and issue a warrant for arrest.* If the defendant does not appear at court, the outcome will often be the issue of a warrant for his or her arrest (sometimes called a 'bench' warrant) (see the MCA 1980, s 13). When the defendant is arrested on a bench warrant, he or she will usually stay in custody until a court hearing can be arranged. Exceptionally, if the magistrates suspect there might be a reasonable excuse for the defendant's non-attendance, they can issue the warrant *and* release the defendant on bail without requiring a court hearing upon arrest. The effect of this combination is that the defendant will be arrested and taken to a police station (this constitutes execution of the warrant); at the police station, he or she is then released on bail to attend the magistrates' court at a later date. Such a warrant is usually described as being 'backed for bail'. Crown Court judges can also issue a bench warrant if a defendant is absent from court without permission. (See also **2.4** and **3.9**.) The warrant may be issued once the court is satisfied that the information against the accused has been supported on oath, that the accused is aware of the hearing and the offence is imprisonable. Warrants may be issued for non-imprisonable offences if the first two criteria are satisfied *and* the court proposes to impose a disqualification on the defendant.

(d) *Dismiss the case.* If the prosecution is not ready to proceed with a summary trial, it is possible that the magistrates will dismiss the charge if there has been a long delay between the commission of the alleged offence and the court hearing. See, for example, *R v Oxford City Justices, ex p Smith* (1982) 75 Cr App R 200; cf *R v Barnet Magistrates' Court, ex p DPP* (1994) 158 JP 1060. See also **2.3.1**.

4 Classification of offences and mode of trial

4.1 Classification of offences

All offences fall into one of the following categories:

- summary offences, ie those which must be tried in the magistrates' court;
- offences triable only on indictment, ie those which must be tried in the Crown Court;
- offences which are triable either way, ie those which may be tried in either the magistrates' court or the Crown Court.

Note that the term 'indictable offence' means an offence which 'is triable on indictment, whether it is exclusively so triable or triable either way' (Interpretation Act 1978, s 1(a)). It therefore includes both 'either-way' and 'indictable-only' offences.

4.1.1 Summary offences

Summary trial, ie trial by magistrates' court, is a creature of statute, and all summary offences, similarly, are created by statute. The statute usually does this by providing a maximum penalty for summary conviction, with no alternative penalty for conviction on indictment.

4.1.2 Offences triable only on indictment

All common law offences (eg murder and manslaughter) are triable only on indictment, ie by a judge and jury in the Crown Court. Other offences in this category are created by statute, where the statute provides for a maximum penalty for conviction on indictment, with no alternative penalty on summary conviction. Where the defendant is charged with an indictable-only offence, the first court appearance will be in the magistrates' court, but the defendant will be sent to the Crown Court for trial.

4.1.3 Offences which are triable either way

Offences which are triable either way are technically 'indictable' but may be tried in the magistrates' court if both the magistrates and the defendant agree. See **4.2** for details. Offences are shown to be triable either way by either:

- the statute which created them providing for alternative penalties on summary conviction or conviction on indictment; or
- being contained in Sch 1 to the Magistrates' Courts Act 1980 (MCA).

4.1.4 Classification of individual offences

The quickest way to find out whether a particular offence is summary-only, triable either way or indictable-only, is to look up the particular offence in *Blackstone's Criminal Practice*, in section B.

4.2 Either-way offences: procedure for determining mode of trial

Where the offence is triable either way (ie one which may be tried in *either* the magistrates' court *or* the Crown Court), it must first be determined which court should try the case.

The procedure is governed by the MCA 1980.

4.2.1 The standard procedure

The procedure for determining mode of trial applies where a defendant who has attained the age of 18 is charged with an offence which is triable either way.

The procedure may be presided over by a lay justice sitting alone, though it is more usual to have two or more lay magistrates.

The procedure is in two stages. The first stage is to ascertain the defendant's intended plea. This stage is often known as 'plea before venue'. If the defendant pleads guilty, the court will move to the sentencing stage. If the defendant indicates a not guilty plea, the court will move to the second stage, to determine the court of trial.

The standard procedure is as follows:

4.2.1.1 Plea before venue

(a) The charge is written down, if it has not already been written down, and read to the defendant.

(b) The court explains that the defendant may indicate whether he or she intends to plead guilty or not guilty should the case proceed to trial. The court should also explain that if the defendant indicates a plea of guilty, the court will:

  (i) proceed as if the proceedings had constituted a summary trial from the outset;

  (ii) proceed as if the defendant had in fact pleaded guilty to the charge;

  (iii) warn the defendant of the possibility of committal to the Crown Court for sentence if the magistrates consider that their powers of punishment are inadequate.

(c) The court then asks the defendant whether, if the case were to proceed to trial, he or she intends to plead guilty or not guilty.

(d) The defendant then indicates a plea of guilty, a plea of not guilty or gives no indication as to plea.

  (i) *Indication of a plea of guilty.* This allows the defendant the earliest opportunity to record a plea of guilty, and gain the maximum credit for having done so (see **Chapter 14** for guidance on reduction in sentence for a guilty plea). It should be noted that the indication is not the plea itself, but an indication of what the plea would be in the event of a trial. By virtue of MCA 1980, s 17A(6), however, the court proceeds as if the hearing had constituted a summary trial from the beginning, and treats the indication of plea as if it were, in fact, a plea of guilty. No further pleas are taken, and the court proceeds to the sentencing stage.

  (ii) *Indication of a plea of not guilty.* Where the defendant indicates a plea of not guilty, the court proceeds to determine the mode of trial as set out below.

  (iii) *No indication of plea.* A defendant who fails to indicate a plea is taken to have indicated a plea of not guilty (MCA 1980, s 17B(3) as amended).

4.2.1.2 Determining the mode of trial

The prosecution and defence have the opportunity to make representations as to whether summary trial or trial on indictment would be more suitable (s 19(2)(b)). At that stage, the prosecution must also be given the opportunity of informing the magistrates of any previous convictions recorded against the accused (s 19(2)(a)), since the existence of relevant previous convictions would affect the appropriate sentence.

If the defendant wishes to be tried on indictment, representations are generally unnecessary as, whatever the decision of the magistrates, the defendant can decline to consent to summary trial. The only time that representations in these circumstances may be valuable is if the defendant fears being penalised in costs in the Crown Court for electing trial on indictment for a relatively simple offence, which may be avoided if it is the choice of the magistrates.

(e) The court then makes the decision as to whether summary trial or trial on indictment is more suitable (s 19(1)). Section 19(3) provides that the court, when deciding which mode of trial is more suitable, has to consider whether the sentence which a magistrates' court would have power to impose for the offence would be adequate, any representations made by the prosecution or the defendant and any allocation guidelines issued by the Sentencing Council as definitive guidelines under s 122(2) of the Coroners and Justice Act 2009. The Allocation Guideline issued by the Sentencing Council states that:

> It is important to ensure that all cases are tried at the appropriate level. In general, either-way offences should be tried summarily unless it is likely that the court's sentencing powers will be insufficient. Its powers will generally be insufficient if the outcome is likely to result in a sentence in excess of six months' imprisonment for a single offence. The court should assess the likely sentence in the light of the facts alleged by the prosecution case, taking into account all aspects of the case including those advanced by the defence.

When assessing the likely sentence for the offence, the court should, of course, refer to any sentencing guidelines relevant to that particular offence.

The Allocation Guideline also makes the point that, because the magistrates' court is able, by virtue of s 3 of the Powers of Criminal Courts (Sentencing) Act 2000, to commit the defendant to the Crown Court for sentence following summary conviction, where the court decides that the case is suitable to be dealt with in the magistrates' court, 'it should remind the defendant that all sentencing options remain open, including committal to the Crown Court for sentence at the time it informs the defendant of this decision'.

Joint Guidance from the Senior District Judge (Magistrates' Courts) and the Justices' Clerks' Society was issued in March 2015, pending review of the Allocation Guideline by the Sentencing Council. This interim guidance to magistrates' courts on the allocation decision emphasises that jurisdiction to commit an offender to the Crown Court for sentence under the PCC(S)A 2000, s. 3, is not dependent on information being received which shows the offence(s) to be more serious than originally thought to be when the decision to accept summary jurisdiction was made. The guidance refers to Sir Brian Leveson's *Review of Efficiency in Criminal Proceedings* (January 2015) recommendation (at para 78), that:

> Magistrates' Courts must be encouraged to be far more robust in their application of the allocation guideline which mandates that either-way offences should be tried summarily unless it is likely that the court's sentencing powers will be insufficient. The word 'likely' does not mean 'possible' and permits the court to take account of potential mitigation and guilty plea, so can encompass cases where the discount for a guilty plea is the feature that brings the case into the Magistrates' jurisdiction. It is important to underline that, provided the option to commit for sentence is publicly identified, the decision to retain jurisdiction does not fetter discretion to commit for sentence even after requesting a pre-sentence report.

The *Criminal Practice Directions*, Part II 9A.2, makes the point that, where cases involve complex questions of fact or difficult questions of law, including difficult issues of disclosure of sensitive material, the court should consider sending for trial. Paragraph 9A.3 goes on to say that the court should never make its decision on the grounds of convenience or expedition; also, the fact that the offences are alleged to be specimens is a relevant consideration, but the fact that the defendant will be asking for other offences to be taken into consideration, if convicted, is not.

Rule 9.2(6)(a) of the Criminal Procedure Rules provides that, where the court is dealing on the same occasion with two or more accused who are charged jointly with an offence that can be tried in the Crown Court, the court must explain that, if one of them is sent to the Crown Court for trial, then the other(s) must also be sent for trial in the Crown Court for the offence that is jointly charged and for any other offence which the court decides is related to that offence. This is so even if the court by then has decided that the case against the other accused is suitable for summary trial. To prevent having to repeat the procedure where the case has been found suitable for summary trial in respect of one accused but a co-accused then elects Crown Court trial, r 9.2(6)(b) states that the court may ask the accused questions to help it decide in what order to deal with them (this would include questions about intention to elect Crown Court trial). In any event, by virtue of r 9.2(7), if the court is dealing on the same occasion with two or more accused who are jointly charged and it accepts jurisdiction in respect of one of them but another is then sent for Crown Court trial (this would be as a result of that accused electing Crown Court trial), the court must deal again with the accused in respect of whom it has accepted jurisdiction (sending him instead to the Crown Court for trial). This has the effect of reversing the decision of the House of Lords in *Brentwood Justices, ex p Nicholls* [1992] 1 AC 1, where it had been held that a case remained suitable for summary trial even if a co-accused had elected Crown Court trial.

Where summary trial appears more suitable

(f) If the court decides that summary trial is more suitable, the court will explain to the defendant that:

  (i) it appears to the court more suitable for the case to be tried summarily; and
  (ii) that the defendant can consent to be so tried or may instead choose to be tried on indictment; and;
  (iii) that if the defendant consents to summary trial and is found guilty, and the magistrates consider that greater punishment should be imposed than they have power to inflict, they may send the defendant to the Crown Court to be sentenced.

(g) At that point, the defendant may request an indication from the magistrates of whether, if the plea were to be one of guilty at that stage, the sentence would be custodial or non-custodial (s 20(3)). The magistrates are not obliged to give such an indication (s 20(4)). If the court does give an indication of sentence, it must ask whether the defendant wishes, on the basis of the indication, to reconsider the indication of plea which was given (s 20(5)). If the defendant does wish to do so, the court has to ask for a fresh indication of intended plea, and so the 'plea before venue' stage is repeated (s 20(6)). A defendant who indicates an intention to plead guilty following an indication of sentence will be regarded as having entered a guilty plea (s 20(7)), and the magistrates' court will proceed to sentence (if necessary adjourning for a pre-sentence report); in such a case, a custodial sentence will be available only if such a sentence was indicated by the court (s 20A(1)). Where an indication of sentence is given and the defendant does not choose to plead guilty on the basis of it, the sentence indication is not binding on the magistrates who later try the case summarily, or on the Crown Court if the defendant subsequently elects trial on indictment (s 20A(3)).

If the court does not give an indication of sentence (either because the defendant does not seek one or the court declines to give one), or if the defendant seeks and receives an indication of sentence but does not then indicate an intention to plead guilty, the court asks whether the defendant consents to summary trial (s 20(8), (9)).

If the defendant agrees to summary trial, the case proceeds in the magistrates' court. If the defendant elects trial on indictment, the case is sent to the Crown Court for trial under s 51 of the Crime and Disorder Act 1998.

Where trial on indictment appears more suitable

(h) If the court decides that the offence appears more suitable for trial on indictment, the court simply tells defendant of its decision and the case is sent to the Crown Court for trial under s 51 of the Crime and Disorder Act 1998. The defendant's consent is not required.

4.2.2 Presence of the defendant

The MCA 1980, s 17A(2) and s 18(2), provide that the defendant must be present during the plea before venue and mode of trial hearings.

However, under s 17B(1), the court will conduct the plea before venue hearing in the defendant's absence if: (a) the defendant is represented by a legal representative; (b) the court considers that by reason of the defendant's disorderly conduct before the court it is not practicable for the plea before venue hearing to be conducted in the defendant's presence; and (c) the court considers that it should proceed in the absence of the defendant. In such a case, the legal representation is asked to give an indication on behalf of the defendant.

Section 18(3) goes on to set out the circumstances in which the mode of trial hearing may take place in the absence of the defendant, namely if the court considers that, by reason of the defendant's disorderly conduct before the court, it is not practicable for the proceedings to be conducted in his defendant's presence. It should be noted that, for the mode of trial hearing to take place in the absence of the defendant, the defendant does not have to be legally represented (as is the case if the court wishes, as a result of the defendant's disorderly conduct, to conduct the plea before venue hearing in the defendant's absence).

Additionally, by virtue of the MCA 1980, s 23(1), the court may hold the mode of trial hearing in the absence of the defendant if: (a) the defendant is legally represented; (b) the representative signifies to the court that the defendant has consented to the mode of trial proceedings being conducted in their absence; and (c) the court is satisfied that there is 'good reason' for proceeding in the absence of the defendant (eg that the defendant is ill).

It should also be noted that a defendant will not be present in court for the plea before venue or mode of trial hearings where that defendant is in custody and the court has decided to use a live TV link, having been satisfied that appropriate facilities exist (Crime and Disorder Act 1998, s 57B).

4.2.3 Failure to comply with the procedure

The mode of trial set out in the MCA 1980 is obligatory, and any deviation from it is likely to render the whole proceedings null and void. The defendant then has the option of applying for judicial review to quash any eventual conviction. For example, in *R v Kent Justices, ex p Machin* [1952] 2 QB 355, the magistrates failed to tell the defendant of the possibility of a committal for sentence, and the conviction and subsequent committal were quashed. In *R v Ashton* [2007] 1 WLR 181, the Court of Appeal said that, where there is a procedural irregularity, the court should ask itself whether Parliament intended the subsequent proceedings to be invalid; if it concluded that Parliament did not, then the court should ask itself whether there was a real possibility that either party would suffer prejudice. The Court of Appeal suggested that cases such as *Machin* should be therefore reconsidered. However, in *R (Rahmdezfouli) v Wood Green Crown Court* [2013] EWHC 2998 (Admin), it was held that Parliament must have intended that, where a magistrates' court fails to follow the requirements of the statutory mode of trial procedure, it is acting without jurisdiction (and so those proceedings, and any subsequent proceedings based on them, must be invalid).

It is open to the prosecution to seek judicial review of the magistrates' decision to accept jurisdiction, although such proceedings are rare, and are unlikely to be successful. However, for a case where the Divisional Court did overrule the magistrates, see *R v Northampton Magistrates' Court, ex p Commissioners for Customs and Excise* [1994] Crim LR 598 (judicial review of the magistrates' decision to accept jurisdiction in a VAT fraud case concerning nearly £200,000).

4.2.4 Changing the mode of trial

Variation of the mode of trial decision is governed by s 25 of the MCA 1980, which enables the prosecution to make an application to the magistrates to reconsider their acceptance of summary jurisdiction. This application must be made before the summary trial begins and must be dealt with by the court before any other application or issue in relation to the summary trial is dealt with (s 25(2A)). Under s 25(2B), the court may accede to the application only if satisfied that the sentence which a magistrates' court would have power to impose for the offence(s) would be inadequate. If the court accedes to the prosecution application, the case is sent to the Crown Court for trial under s 51 of the Crime and Disorder Act 1998.

4.3 Special cases

4.3.1 Criminal damage

Under the MCA 1980, s 22, where the defendant is charged with criminal damage (other than where the damage was caused by fire) and the value of the damage does not exceed £5,000, the magistrates must proceed *as if* the offence were summary only. The court is only proceeding *as if* the offence is summary, but it is not summary for all purposes. In *R v Alden* [2002] 2 Cr App R (S) 326, for example, the Court of Appeal confirmed that if the Crown Court is dealing with criminal damage (other than under a provision such as CJA 1988, s 40), the maximum sentence of ten years is available.

4.3.2 Special procedure in criminal damage cases

Under s 22, before embarking on the normal procedure for determining the mode of trial as set out in **4.2**, the procedure set out here must be followed:

(a) The court must, having regard to any representations made by the prosecution or defence, consider the value of the damaged property. There is no appeal on the basis that the value was mistaken (s 22(8)).

When determining the value of the damage where the property is damaged beyond repair, the value is the market value of the property at the material time. The court is not concerned with determining consequential loss. See *R v Colchester Justices, ex p Abbott, The Times*, 13 March 2001, where the value of damaged genetically modified crops was their market value, and not the consequential loss of lost research.

(b) If the value is:

- (i) £5,000 or less, the court proceeds to summary trial. The defendant has no right to trial on indictment, and (in the event of conviction) cannot be committed for sentence (MCA 1980, s 17D(2)(b)). The maximum sentence in this case is three months' imprisonment or a £2,500 fine;
- (ii) more than £5,000, the offence is triable either way, and the court follows the usual procedure to determine the mode of trial. If the offence is tried summarily the maximum penalty is six months' imprisonment and/or a £5,000 fine. The magistrates may commit the defendant to Crown Court for sentence;
- (iii) uncertain, the lower penalty and absence of any power to commit for sentence continue to apply. The court will ask whether the defendant consents to summary trial. If consent is given, then the court proceeds to summary trial. If not, the court will follow the procedure for determining the mode of trial set out in **4.2**. See s 22(4)–(6).

4.3.3 A series of offences

If the defendant is charged with two or more offences of criminal damage which appear to the court to be a series of offences of the same or a similar character, then the court has regard to the aggregate value in determining the mode of trial. Thus, if the value of all items damaged totals £5,000 or less, then the magistrates must proceed as if the offences are all summary, regardless of the number of offences (see s 22(11)).

4.3.4 Burglary

Where the defendant has been convicted of a third offence of 'domestic' burglary since 1999, the Powers of Criminal Court (Sentencing) Act 2000, s 111 requires the imposition of a custodial sentence of at least three years, unless there are circumstances which would make it unjust to impose such a sentence. This sentence is in excess of the magistrates' sentencing powers, and the magistrates have no alternative but to treat the offence as triable only on indictment and send the matter to the Crown Court under the Crime and Disorder Act 1998, s 51 (s 111(4) of the 2000 Act).

4.3.5 Low-value shoplifting

Where a defendant appears in the magistrates' court charged with theft of goods from a shop (or other trading location, eg a market stall) and it is alleged that the stolen goods were for sale for a price of £200 or less, and the defendant was posing as a customer (or potential customer) of the business, then the offence shall be summary only. See the Magistrates' Courts Act 1980, s 22A (inserted by the Anti-social Behaviour, Crime and Police Act 2014, s 176). However, the court must give the defendant the choice to have jury trial and, if he so chooses, it must send him to the Crown Court for trial by jury.

4.4 Linked summary and indictable offences

The CJA 1988, s 40, allows certain summary offences to be included in an indictment.

Under s 40, there are three conditions that must be fulfilled:

(a) the summary offence must be one that is specified in s 40: common assault, taking a motor vehicle without consent, driving whilst disqualified or criminal damage within the MCA 1980, s 22; and
(b) the summary offence must either be founded on the same facts as an offence on the indictment or form part of a series of offences of the same or a similar character as an offence on the indictment; and
(c) evidence of the summary offence must be disclosed in the evidence which formed the basis on which the case was sent to the Crown Court for trial.

At the Crown Court, the summary offence is included on the indictment, and the defendant is tried on it in the usual way. Section 40 applies whether the 'main' offence is triable either way or triable only on indictment.

The decision to add the summary offence(s) to the indictment is taken by the prosecution (the magistrates are not involved). If the defendant is convicted of the summary offence, the powers of the Crown Court are limited to those of the magistrates.

In *R v Lewis* [2013] EWCA Crim 2596; [2014] 1 Cr App R 25, the defendant was sent to the Crown Court for trial on a charge of attempted theft. Two charges of common assault, which were founded on the same facts as the attempted theft, were joined in the indictment pursuant to s 40 of the Criminal Justice Act 1988. The prosecution subsequently offered no evidence on the attempted theft (and so the defendant stood acquitted of that offence). The defendant was then tried for the two summary offences, and found guilty by the jury. McCombe LJ, at [15], said:

> Section 40 is relevant to the stage at which an indictment is drawn up. Once the indictment is preferred, it remains the indictment before the court. The loss of one charge by reason of an acquittal, either by a jury verdict at the conclusion of the trial, or on earlier judicial direction, or on the entry of a formal verdict on the offering of no evidence on that charge at whatever stage, does not remove the count from the indictment. It remains in the indictment on which the defendant is charged and tried.

It followed that the Crown Court retained jurisdiction to try the summary offences, even though the either-way offence was no longer before the court.

4.5 Advantages and disadvantages of each mode of trial

There are many matters to be taken into account in advising a defendant on the most appropriate forum:

(a) *Speed*. Whether a case in the magistrates' court is likely to be heard more quickly than if it had been listed for hearing in the Crown Court depends on local waiting lists. However, the case itself is likely to take less time in the magistrates' court.

(b) *Expense*. Proceedings in the magistrates' court are much less expensive than in the Crown Court—a very important consideration if the defendant is not legally aided.

(c) *Informality*. Proceedings in the magistrates' court are much more informal than in the Crown Court. The Crown Court can be daunting to someone who has little experience of criminal courts.

(d) *Sentence*. The magistrates' powers of sentence are limited to six months' imprisonment for one either-way offence (an aggregate maximum of 12 months for two or more either-way offences). However, this limit is effectively nullified by the fact that they have the power to commit to the Crown Court for sentence if they take the view that their sentencing powers are inadequate, and so cannot properly be regarded as an advantage of summary trial. See **Chapters 15** and **16** for details of the magistrates' powers of sentence.

(e) *Division between the tribunals of fact and law*. In the magistrates' court, the tribunals of fact and law are the same, so that they will first have to hear evidence before deciding on any question of admissibility, and then, if inadmissible, endeavour to forget it. In the Crown Court this problem simply does not arise, since the judge alone will decide on admissibility, and evidence will only go before the jury if it is admissible. In the magistrates' court there is a procedure whereby one bench can give a pre-trial ruling on admissibility which binds the bench which eventually tries the case (under the MCA 1980, ss 8A–8C); however, the effectiveness of this provision depends on there being an opportunity for a pre-trial hearing to take place.

(f) *Legal submissions*. Despite the fact that lay magistrates are advised by a qualified court legal adviser, any submissions on the law are made to lay people. (The case may eventually be heard by a district judge, but this would not be known when determining the mode of trial.) In the Crown Court, the same submission would be made to a professional lawyer.

(g) *Appeals*. Appeals from the magistrates' court may be made without leave (see **Chapter 8**), whereas appeals from the Crown Court always require leave (see **Chapter 12**).

(h) *The benefit of the doubt*. It is generally assumed that a jury are more likely to give the defendant the benefit of the doubt than magistrates. In any event, if the case involves a substantial attack on police evidence, the defendant is likely to find a jury more sympathetic than magistrates.

4.6 Summary: 'plea before venue' and mode of trial

The main stages of the 'plea before venue' and mode of trial (or 'allocation') procedure for either-way offences are as follows:

1. D is asked to indicate plea.
2. If D indicates a 'guilty' plea, the court proceeds to the sentencing stage: the magistrates pass sentence (after an adjournment if necessary) or, if their sentencing powers are inadequate, commit D to the Crown Court for sentence.
3. If D indicates a 'not guilty' plea, the court proceeds with the mode of trial hearing.

4. The prosecution (and sometimes the defence) make representations about whether or not the case is suitable for summary trial.
5. The magistrates decide whether the case is suitable for summary trial (this depends principally on whether their sentencing powers are sufficient).
6. If the magistrates reject jurisdiction, D is sent to the Crown Court for trial.
7. If the magistrates accept jurisdiction, D is asked to choose between trial in the magistrates' court and trial in the Crown Court.
8. Before doing so, D may request an indication as to whether, if he were to plead guilty at this stage, the sentence would be custodial or non-custodial. If an indication is given, D is given an opportunity to change the indication of plea from 'not guilty' to 'guilty'.
9. If D consents to summary trial, the trial takes place in the magistrates' court.
10. If D does not consent to summary trial (ie D chooses Crown Court trial), D is sent to the Crown Court for trial.

5

Summary trial

5.1 Procedure at trial

The vast majority of criminal cases are tried in magistrates' courts. The procedure is the same, whether the offence is triable only summarily, or triable either way, though if the offence is triable either way, the magistrates must first determine the mode of trial (see **Chapter 4**).

5.1.1 Case management in the magistrates' court

The Criminal Procedure Rules, Part 3, requires active case management by the courts, and requires the parties to assist in this active case management. Guidance on how this is to be achieved is set out in *Essential Case Management: Applying the Criminal Procedure Rules*, a document issued in December 2009 by the then Senior Presiding Judge, Leveson LJ.

In particular:

1. The plea should be taken at the first hearing (if the plea cannot be taken, the court must find out what the plea is likely to be).
2. If the plea is 'guilty', the court should (unless committing for sentence) pass sentence on the same day, if at all possible.
3. If the plea is 'not guilty', the parties must identify the disputed issues and inform the court. There is now a detailed case management form to facilitate the identification and notification of disputed issues.

In *R (Firth) v Epping Magistrates Court* [2011] EWHC 388 (Admin), the Divisional Court held that the contents of such case management forms could be relied upon by the prosecution if they contain admissions by the accused. However, in *R v Newell* [2012] EWCA Crim 650, the Court of Appeal had to consider the same question in respect of a Plea and Case Management Hearing form in the Crown Court. Giving the judgment of the Court of Appeal, Sir John Thomas P considered the position in magistrates' courts and (at [31]) said:

> The Trial Preparation Form . . . provides for the making of admissions or the acknowledgement that matters are not in issue. Where admissions are made in that way they will be admissible at the trial. Where statements are made on the form which are not made under the section relating to admissions, such statements should be made without the risk that they would be used at trial as statements of the defendant admissible in evidence against the defendant, provided the advocate follows the letter and the spirit of the Criminal Procedure Rules.

The effect of this ruling is that it will only be in exceptional cases that the prosecution will be able to rely on admissions made by the accused in case management forms unless those admissions effectively count as 'formal admissions' (under s 10 of the Criminal Justice Act 1967) or where the accused is attempting to 'ambush' the prosecution.

The importance of active case management in magistrates' court was emphasised by the Divisional Court in *Drinkwater v Solihull Magistrates' Court* [2012] EWHC 765 (Admin). Sir John Thomas P said (at [47]) that it is 'self-evident that proceedings in the Magistrates' Courts ought to be simple, speedy and summary. That requires close attention to the Criminal Procedure Rules and active case management before and during the trial'. His Lordship went on to say (at [50]–[52]) that:

> In setting the timetable, the court should scrutinise the reasons why it is said a witness is necessary and the time examination and cross-examination would take. It is also important in setting a timetable to have regard to the nature of the issues and the fact that the trial is a summary trial; any estimate of more than a day in the magistrates' courts should be scrutinised with the utmost rigour. Parties must realise that a summary trial requires a proportionate approach. If a timetable for the trial is not set, it is difficult to have any real confidence that the estimate is accurate.
>
> At the commencement of the trial, the magistrates' court should check with the parties that the timetable and the estimates remain valid. If there is any variation which lengthens the estimate, the court should make every effort to see if the trial can still be accommodated that day by sitting late or otherwise.
>
> Once the trial has started, the court must actively manage the trial, keeping an eye on progress in relation to the timetable . . .

5.1.2 Pre-trial hearings

It may be necessary for one or more pre-trial hearings to take place. The MCA 1980, s 8A, provides that, where the accused is to be tried summarily and has pleaded not guilty, a pre-trial hearing may take place. At such a hearing, the court may, if it is in the interests of justice to do so, make a ruling on the admissibility of any evidence and on any other question of law relating to the case. Before such a ruling can be made, the court must give the parties an opportunity to be heard and an unrepresented accused must be given an opportunity to apply for legal aid if he or she wishes to do so. A ruling can be made following an application by a party, or on the initiative of the court itself. By virtue of s 8B, any ruling given at a pre-trial hearing remains binding until the case against the accused is concluded. This means that the ruling is binding on the magistrates who eventually try the case. However, an application may be made for a pre-trial ruling to be varied or discharged. Such an application may be made only if there has been a 'material change of circumstances' since the original ruling was made. In *R (CPS) v Gloucester Justices* (2008) 172 JP 506, MacKay J (at para 12) said that there had to be a 'compelling reason, such as changed circumstances or fresh evidence' to justify invoking s 8B, and that it would not be 'in the interests of justice for one bench to set aside a previous bench's ruling previously because on the same material it thought it would reach a different conclusion'.

5.2 The trial

5.2.1 The absence of the defendant

Although the defendant will usually be present in court for the hearing, the magistrates have the power to proceed in the absence of the defendant.

5.2.1.1 Where the defendant fails to attend

Under the Magistrates' Courts Act 1980 (MCA), s 11(1), the magistrates must, if the defendant is over the age of 18, hear the case in the defendant's absence if he or she fails to attend court (where the defendant is under the age of 18, the court *may* proceed in the absence of the defendant), unless it appears to the court to be contrary to the interests of justice to do so. If the offence is triable either way, the trial can only proceed if the defendant was present at a previous hearing and consented to summary trial (since the defendant normally has to be present during mode of trial proceedings).

If the proceedings were commenced by means of a written charge and requisition (or, in the case of a private prosecution, by the laying of an information and service of a summons), the prosecution have to prove that the requisition (or summons) was served in accordance with the Criminal Procedure Rules, r 4.7. They can do so simply by establishing that, for example, it was sent by first-class post to the defendant's last known address (they do not have to prove that the defendant received it). If the proceedings started with the defendant being arrested and charged, the defendant will be aware of the date of the hearing from the charge sheet (if the present hearing is the first hearing) or from being present at the previous hearing when the date of the current hearing was fixed. Under the MCA 1980, s 14, a defendant who did not, in fact, know of the proceedings, may make a 'statutory declaration' of this fact within 21 days of finding out about them; if such declaration is made, the trial and conviction are rendered void. In such a case there is likely to be a retrial.

Where the court decides to proceed in the absence of the defendant, a plea of not guilty will be entered on the defendant's behalf and the prosecution evidence will be called. Such hearings often end in the conviction of the defendant, as none of the prosecution evidence will have been tested by cross-examination, and the magistrates will not have heard the defence case.

The MCA 1980, s 11(2A), provides that the court 'shall not proceed in the absence of the accused if it considers that there is an acceptable reason for his failure to appear'. However, subs (6) goes on to state that 'nothing in [s 11] requires the court to enquire into the reasons for the accused's failure to appear before deciding whether to proceed in his absence'. This means that if there is no explanation for the absence of the defendant, the court must (if the defendant is an adult) proceed with the trial in accordance with s 11(1) unless it would be contrary to the interests of justice to do so. The requirement to consider the interests of justice means that, despite the statutory presumption in favour of trying an absent defendant, the power to do so must be exercised with some care. In *Drinkwater v Solihull Magistrates' Court* [2012] EWHC 765 (Admin), Beatson J (at [35]) referred to the decision of the House of Lords in *R v Jones* [2002] UKHL 5, and quoted from the speech of Lord Bingham, who had said (at [6]) that the discretion to proceed in the absence of a defendant is 'to be exercised with great caution and with close regard to the overall fairness of the proceedings'. Beatson J also cited the case of *R v Armouchi* [2007] EWCA Crim 3019, where Hughes LJ (at [10]) had stated that proceeding in the absence of a defendant 'is a step which ought normally to be taken only if it is unavoidable'.

The *Criminal Practice Directions,* Part III 19E.2, says that the court must exercise its discretion to proceed in the absence of the defendant with due regard for the interests of justice, adding that the overriding concern must be to ensure that such a trial is as fair as circumstances permit and leads to a just outcome. In particular, if the defendant's absence is due to involuntary illness or incapacity it would 'very rarely, if ever, be right to exercise the discretion in favour of commencing or continuing the trial'.

In *Killick v West London Magistrates' Court* [2012] EWHC 3864 (Admin), Sharp J summarised the principles which are relevant where it is suggested that the defendant is unfit to attend court:

1. The overriding principle is that the court should not proceed to hear a case in the defendant's absence without satisfying itself that the claim for an adjournment may properly be rejected and that no unfairness will thereby be done . . .
2. The discretion to commence a trial in the absence of a defendant should be exercised with the utmost care and caution. Where a defendant to a criminal charge wishes to resist it and is shown by medical evidence to be unfit to attend court to do so, either as a result of involuntary illness or incapacity, it would be very rarely, if indeed ever, right for the court to exercise its discretion in favour of commencing the trial, or to proceed to hear the case in his absence, at any rate unless the defendant is represented and asks that the trial should begin . . .
3. If a court asked for an adjournment on medical grounds, suspects the grounds to be spurious or believes them to be inadequate, the court should ordinarily express its doubts and thereby give the defendant an opportunity to resolve those doubts . . .

4. A court considering an application to adjourn will need carefully to distinguish between genuine reasons for the defendant not being present and those reasons which are spuriously advanced or designed to frustrate the process. However, if the court comes to the conclusion that either of the latter is the case, it should say so. It cannot simply be inferred that a court has come to that conclusion unless that is clearly stated by the magistrates . . .
5. If a conclusion is open to the court reasonably on the material before it either to the effect that an excuse given is spurious or there is a truly compelling and exceptional reason for proceeding notwithstanding a good excuse for non-attendance, the court has the power to do so. This however will be an exceptional case . . .

It should be noted that the presumption in s 11 in favour of trying an absent defendant is replaced by a power to do so where the defendant is under the age of 18. In *Dewsbury Magistrates' Court, ex p K, The Times*, 16 March 1994, the Divisional Court quashed the conviction in his absence of a 16-year-old, for burglary of a dwelling-house, holding that the convenience of the court in processing the case could not possibly outweigh the facts that he was 16, on a very serious charge entailing the risk of a custodial sentence if convicted and had no record of non-attendance.

5.2.1.2 The disorderly defendant

If the defendant's behaviour is so disruptive that the proceedings cannot continue, the defendant may be removed from the courtroom, and the trial may proceed nonetheless.

5.2.1.3 Presence through representation

A defendant who is represented is deemed to be present *unless* their presence is expressly required by statute (MCA 1980, s 122(2)). An example of where the defendant's presence *is* so required is where the defendant is on bail (and so under a duty to attend court).

5.2.1.4 Pleading guilty by post

Under the MCA 1980, s 12, a defendant may plead guilty by sending a letter to court. This can be done if:

- the offence is summary; and
- proceedings have been started by the service of a summons (or written charge and requisition).

In such circumstances the procedure is as follows:

(a) The prosecution serves on the defendant:
   (i) the summons (or written charge and requisition);
   (ii) a brief statement of the facts upon which the prosecution proposes to rely or copies of witness statements complying with the Criminal Justice Act 1967 (CJA), s 9;
   (iii) any information relating to the accused which will or may be placed before the court; and
   (iv) a notice explaining the procedure.

   The prosecution informs the court that the documents have been served.

(b) A defendant who wishes to plead guilty notifies the court of this fact and may enclose a statement setting out any mitigation. Subsequently, the defendant may withdraw this plea, and the case then proceeds as if it were a not guilty plea.

(c) Neither the prosecution nor the defence is represented or appears at court, and the court proceeds on the basis of the statements which are read out in court. Failure to do so will lead to the conviction being quashed, as in *R v Epping and Ongar Justices, ex p Breach* [1987] RTR 233 where the defendant's statement in mitigation was not read out. The magistrates may refuse to accept the plea of guilty if the statement in mitigation discloses information which amounts to a defence.

(d) The magistrates, if content to accept the plea, may pass sentence, or adjourn for the accused to be present. The magistrates may not impose a custodial sentence or disqualification from driving in the absence of the defendant, and so have to adjourn in order for the defendant to attend if they are minded to impose such penalties.

Section 12A of the MCA 1980 deals with the situation where the defendant actually appears in court. Two situations may occur:

- The defendant, having expressed a wish that the case should proceed under s 12, nevertheless appears in court at the appointed time. The court may proceed to deal with the matter as if the defendant were absent, provided that the defendant consents to the court so doing: s 12A(1).
- The court has not received notification that the defendant wishes the case to proceed under s 12, and the defendant appears at the appointed time. If the defendant indicates an intention to plead guilty, and consents, the court may proceed to deal with the matter as if the defendant were absent (s 12A(2)).

In either case, the court must afford the defendant an opportunity to make oral submissions with a view to mitigation of sentence (s 12(5)(c)).

5.2.1.5 Trial on the papers by a single justice

Section 16A of the Magistrates' Courts Act 1980 (inserted by the Criminal Justice and Courts Act 2015 (CJCA)) enables a single justice to try certain cases on the papers. This procedure is limited to cases where a person who has attained the age of 18 is charged with a summary offence that does not carry imprisonment, and does not apply where the accused serves a written notice indicating a desire either to plead not guilty or not to be tried under s 16A.

Where s 16A applies, the court hears no oral evidence but considers only the documents served on the court by the prosecution and the accused. The court may disregard a written submission if it has not been served within 21 days of the service of the prosecution documents (Crim PR, r 37.9(4)).

The court is not required to conduct any part of the proceedings in open court, and tries the charge in the absence of the parties; if a party appears, the court must proceed as if the party were absent. Where s 16A applies, the court (which may be composed of a single justice) tries the charge as if the accused had pleaded guilty.

Under s 16B, if the court decides, before the accused is convicted of the offence, that it is not appropriate to proceed under s 16A, the trial will (if it has begun) be adjourned, and a summons will be issued requiring the accused to appear before a magistrates' court for the trial.

Similarly, under s 16C, if the court decides, after the accused has been convicted of the offence, that it is not appropriate to proceed under s 16A, the court must adjourn the case and issue a summons requiring the accused to appear before a magistrates' court to be dealt with. Under s 16C(2), if a magistrates' court which has been proceeding under s 16A, having convicted the accused, proposes to disqualify him from driving, the court must give the accused the opportunity to make representations about the proposed disqualification; if the accused indicates a wish to make such representations, the court may not continue to proceed under s 16A (and so must adjourn and issue a summons requiring the attendance of the offender).

Where a case has been adjourned under s 16B or s 16C, the court which hears the case when it resumes will be composed in the usual way (namely, at least two lay justices, as required by s 121(1) of the MCA 1980 or a District Judge (Magistrates' Courts)).

Where the case is being dealt with under s 16A, the powers of the court as regards sentence are limited by s 121(5A) of the MCA 1980 (inserted by CJCA 2015): the court may, for example, discharge the offender (conditionally or absolutely) or impose a fine, and may make a number of ancillary orders (eg compensation and disqualification from driving), but cannot impose a community order or a custodial sentence.

5.2.2 Absence of the prosecution

Under the MCA 1980, s 15, if the prosecution fails to appear at the time and place fixed for the summary trial, the magistrates may adjourn the case or dismiss the case. Where the magistrates act unreasonably in dismissing a case, their decision may be challenged by way of judicial review (*R v Hendon Justices, ex p DPP* [1994] QB 167) (see **8.3.1.1**). In *DPP v Jarman* (2014) 178 JP 89, the prosecutor failed to attend and the magistrates dismissed the case for want of prosecution under MCA 1980, s 15. The prosecution appealed by case stated. On the appeal, Griffith Williams J (at [20] and [36]) said that:

> On the facts, the magistrates were told a prosecutor was on his or her way to court. Had they waited they would have found out the extent of any further delay to allow the prosecutor time to read the papers. There were four hours put aside for the trial and so it was bound to be part heard into the afternoon and there was a prospect of the trial being concluded in the day. While I sympathize with magistrates who are kept waiting due to the inefficiency of a party, a balanced approach is needed in such circumstances, and balancing includes a consideration of the right of the complainant who was there wanting to give evidence . . .
>
> While the overriding objective [in the Crim PR, Part 1] includes . . . the requirement to deal with cases efficiently and expeditiously, the . . . power to dismiss proceedings pursuant to s 15 of the Act must not . . . be used, save in the most exceptional cases, to, in effect, punish the prosecution for its inefficiency.

5.2.3 Representations in private

A decision to hear representations in private is within the magistrates' discretion, but careful consideration should always be given to whether such a step is appropriate. In order to guard against injustice, steps must be taken to ensure that all parties are notified of the hearing and are represented, with a contemporaneous note being taken, normally by the clerk (see *R v Nottingham Magistrates' Court, ex p Furnell* (1996) 160 JP 201). See Crim PR, r 37.2.

5.2.4 Taking the plea

The defendant must plead unequivocally, that is, clearly and unambiguously, 'guilty' or 'not guilty'. Where the offence is triable either way, the plea will already have been taken at the 'plea before venue' stage.

Rule 37.7 deals with cases where the defendant pleads guilty. Provided that the court is 'satisfied that the plea represents a clear acknowledgement of guilt', it may 'convict the defendant without receiving evidence'.

5.2.4.1 Change of plea

Change of plea from 'guilty' to 'not guilty'. The court may permit a change of plea from 'guilty' to 'not guilty' at any time before sentence has been passed (see *S (an infant) v Recorder of Manchester* [1971] AC 481). Allowing a change of plea is entirely within the discretion of the magistrates. If they take the view that the defendant understood the charge, the consequence of pleading guilty and had intended to plead guilty, they will be unlikely to allow a change. See generally, *R v McNally* [1954] 1 WLR 933 and *Revitt and Others v DPP* [2006] EWHC 2266 (Admin).

Where the magistrates have allowed a change of plea from guilty to not guilty, they should also allow the defendant to reconsider the question of consent to summary trial (*R v Bow Street Magistrates' Court, ex p Welcome* (1992) 156 JP 609). Under the Criminal Procedure Rules, r 37.10, a defendant who wishes to withdraw a guilty plea must apply to do so as soon as practicable after becoming aware of the reasons for doing so. Unless the court otherwise directs, the application must be in writing and must explain why it would be unjust not to allow the defendant to withdraw the guilty plea and must identify any witness that the defendant wants to call, and any other proposed evidence.

Change of plea from 'not guilty' to 'guilty'. A defendant who has pleaded not guilty may, with leave of the court, change that plea to guilty at any time before the justices retire to consider the verdict.

5.2.4.2 'Equivocal' pleas

The defendant's plea may be regarded as 'equivocal' in three situations:

(a) The defendant, when pleading guilty, immediately qualifies that plea with words which amount to a defence. See, for example, *R v Emery* (1943) 29 Cr App R 47, where the defendant entered a plea of guilty but immediately added that he had been acting in self-defence. In such a case, the magistrates should explain the law and the defendant will be asked to plead again. If the plea is still equivocal, the magistrates must record a plea of not guilty and proceed to trial. If they make no enquiry into the plea, the defendant may later challenge the validity of the plea on appeal.

(b) The defendant unequivocally pleads guilty, but the plea is subsequently rendered equivocal by information given to the magistrates before sentence (see, eg, *R v Durham Justices, ex p Virgo* [1952] 2 QB 1, where the defendant unequivocally pleaded guilty but, in the course of mitigation, said that he had taken the goods he was alleged to have stolen in mistake for goods he had permission to take). In *P Foster (Haulage) Ltd v Roberts* [1978] 2 All ER 751, it was said that this is essentially a situation in which the magistrates have a discretion to allow a change of plea.

(c) The defendant unequivocally pleads guilty and no further information is given to the court casting doubt on the correctness of the plea. However, if the defendant argues that the plea was made under duress, the Crown Court may (on appeal) treat it as an equivocal plea, as in *R v Huntingdon Crown Court, ex p Jordan* [1981] QB 857, where the defendant, who had pleaded guilty to theft, said that she had committed the offence under the coercion of her husband and that she had been threatened by her husband that he would physically ill-treat her if she did not plead guilty.

So far as the first two situations are concerned, the magistrates should always ensure that the defendant, particularly if unrepresented, understands the offence and the consequences of pleading guilty. If a defendant wishes to argue that their guilty plea was equivocal, they may appeal to the Crown Court; if the Crown Court decides that the plea was equivocal, it should remit the case to the magistrates with an order that they enter a plea of not guilty and proceed to trial (*R v Plymouth Justices, ex p Hart* [1986] QB 950).

5.3 The stages of a summary trial

Rule 37.3(3) of the Criminal Procedure Rules sets out the sequence of events in a summary trial:

> *(a) the prosecutor may summarise the prosecution case, identifying the relevant law and facts;*
>
> *(b) the prosecutor must introduce the evidence on which the prosecution case relies;*
>
> *(c) at the conclusion of the prosecution case, on the defendant's application or on its own initiative, the court—*
>
> *(i) may acquit on the ground that the prosecution evidence is insufficient for any reasonable court properly to convict, but*
>
> *(ii) must not do so unless the prosecutor has had an opportunity to make representations;*
>
> *(d) the justices' legal adviser or the court must explain, in terms the defendant can understand (with help, if necessary)—*
>
> *(i) the right to give evidence, and*
>
> *(ii) the potential effect of not doing so at all, or of refusing to answer a question while doing so;*
>
> *(e) the defendant may introduce evidence;*
>
> *(f) a party may introduce further evidence if it is then admissible (for example, because it is in rebuttal of evidence already introduced);*
>
> *(g) the prosecutor may make final representations in support of the prosecution case, where—*
>
> *(i) the defendant is represented by a legal representative, or*

(ii) *whether represented or not, the defendant has introduced evidence other than his or her own; and*

(h) *the defendant may make final representations in support of the defence case.*

Rule 37.4(2)(a) says that a witness waiting to give evidence must wait outside the courtroom unless he or she is a party to the case or an expert witness. A witness's address must not be announced unless it is relevant to an issue in the case (sub-rule (c)).

We will now examine some of those stages in greater detail.

5.3.1 The prosecution opening speech

Magistrates will be familiar with the cases that frequently come before them, so that, although the prosecution has the right to an opening speech, it is usually brief and is often not made.

In *L and B v DPP* [1998] 2 Cr App R 69, the case was adjourned for a month after hearing the prosecution witnesses. The defendants appealed against their convictions as the prosecution had made a second speech on the resumed hearing, at the magistrates' request, to remind them of the evidence given at the earlier hearing. It was held that there was nothing unfair in that, subject to the safeguard that the defence should always be asked to address the court in reply to correct any errors or draw attention to differences of recollection.

5.3.2 The prosecution evidence

The prosecution calls the evidence upon which it relies. This will take the form of 'live' witnesses and (where appropriate) the reading of written statements admitted with the consent of the defendant under the CJA 1967, s 9 (and sometimes hearsay evidence admitted without the consent of the defendant under the CJA 2003, ss 114 and 116). Some evidence may be given by way of video link.

Rule 37.5 deals with evidence being adduced in the form of a written statement of a witness: the party introducing the statement must read or summarise aloud those parts that are relevant to the issues in the case.

As to the defence knowledge of the prosecution case, see **Chapter 9**.

In the Crown Court, the trial judge is the tribunal of law and the jury are the tribunal of fact. In the magistrates' court, however, the magistrates are both tribunal of law and tribunal of fact. The question as to whether the magistrates, having heard evidence and decided that it is inadmissible, should then recuse themselves was considered in *R (on the application of the DPP v Acton Youth Court* [2001] 1 WLR 1828. Lord Woolf CJ (at para 30) said that: 'Justices and district judges from time to time have to make rulings on the admissibility of evidence and thereafter have to continue the trial. Interlocutory rulings do not in the ordinary way (unless there is special reason) deprive the district judge or the justices from continuing with the hearing.' The power of magistrates to make binding pre-trial rulings (MCA 1980, s 8A) is, of course, relevant in this context.

5.3.3 The submission of no case to answer

The Criminal Procedure Rules, r 37.3(3)(c), provides that, at the conclusion of the prosecution case, the court (either at the request of the defence or on its own initiative) may acquit the defendant 'on the ground that the prosecution evidence is insufficient for any reasonable court properly to convict'. Before doing so, the court must give the prosecution an opportunity to make representations.

A submission of no case is likely to succeed where the prosecution have failed to adduce evidence of an essential ingredient of the offence, or where the prosecution evidence has been thoroughly discredited in cross-examination. However, in the case of the first of those situations, the court may, instead of acquitting the defendant, allow the prosecution to re-open their case in order to supply the missing evidence. In *Tuck v Vehicle Inspectorate* [2004] EWHC 728 (Admin), the Divisional Court said that the discretion to allow the prosecution to re-open their case 'will only be exercised on the rarest of occasions'; moreover, of 'particular significance is the consideration of whether there is any risk of prejudice to the accused' (per MacKay J at [15]). However, in *R (CPS) v Norwich Magistrates' Court* [2011] EWHC 82 (Admin), the prosecution had opened the case (a charge of assault) by stating that identification was not in dispute (the section of the case management form completed by the defence raised the issue of self-defence). At the close of the prosecution case, the defence made a submission of no case based on the lack of adequate identification. The prosecution sought to call additional evidence, but the magistrates refused to allow this. The Divisional Court said that the decision of the magistrates was wrong. Richards LJ said (at [22]):

> . . . if the defence was going to take a positive point on identification, it was incumbent on it to flag the point at an early stage, not to wait until the close of the prosecution case before raising it for the first time in a submission of no case. It should have been expressed during the case management process and included in terms in the trial information form . . . Even if there had been an omission to deal with it at that earlier stage, it ought to have been raised very clearly when the prosecuting advocate opened the case by telling the magistrates that there was no issue over identification. It was not appropriate . . . simply to sit tight and to raise it at the end of the prosecution case by way of a submission of no case.

His Lordship concluded, at [25], that 'the decision to refuse the prosecution application to re-open ran counter to the overriding objective of the Criminal Procedure Rules, was plainly contrary to the interests of justice and lacked any reasonable basis'.

There is no obligation on justices to give reasons for rejecting a submission of no case to answer (*Moran v DPP* [2002] EWHC 89 (Admin)).

5.3.4 The defence case

Assuming no submission of no case to answer is made, or is made but fails, the defence may present its case. The justices' legal adviser (or the court) must explain that the defendant has the right to give evidence, and must also explain the potential effect of not doing so at all, or of refusing to answer a question while doing so (namely adverse inferences, under the Criminal Justice and Public Order Act 1994, s 35). The Criminal Procedure Rules make no provision for an opening speech by the defence, and so the defence usually begins to call its evidence straight away. The defendant, if going to be called to testify, should do so before any other defence witnesses (PACE 1984, s 79).

5.3.5 Evidence in rebuttal

Rule 37.3(3)(f) provides that, after the defence evidence has been adduced, either party 'may introduce further evidence if it is then admissible (for example, because it is in rebuttal of evidence already introduced)'. As the defence evidence will have just been given, it is likely to be the prosecution who seek to take advantage of this provision. In *Khatibi v DPP* (2004) 168 JP 361, Nelson J said (at paras 17 and 18) that the discretion to admit evidence after the close of the prosecution case must be exercised with great caution. The magistrates should bear in mind that the normal order of events, namely the cases for the prosecution and the defence being presented consecutively in their entirety, should not be departed from substantially unless justice really demands such a course of action. In deciding whether to exercise their discretion to permit the calling of evidence after the close of the prosecution case, the magistrates must look carefully at the interests of justice overall and, in particular, the risk of any prejudice to the defendant.

5.3.6 Closing speeches

After the evidence has been called, the prosecutor may make 'final representations in support of the prosecution case'; however, the prosecutor is entitled to do so only if the defendant is legally represented or if the defence have called evidence from anyone other than the defendant. After any closing speech by the prosecution, the defence 'may make final representations in support of the defence case'.

5.3.7 The verdict

Lay magistrates usually retire to consider their verdict. The court legal adviser (clerk to the justices) must not retire with them as this may create the impression that the adviser may somehow influence the decision.

The verdict is a majority decision, and the chairman has no casting vote. Therefore, if an evenly numbered court is equally divided, it must adjourn for a fresh hearing before a new bench (*R v Redbridge Justices, ex p Ram* [1992] QB 384).

District judges rarely retire, usually announcing their decision immediately after the defence closing speech.

In reaching their decision, the magistrates may rely on any local knowledge that they have, but both prosecution and defence should have been informed of this during the trial so that they have an opportunity to comment upon that knowledge (*Norbrook Laboratories (GB) Ltd v Health and Safety Executive, The Times*, 23 February 1998). See also *Gibbons v DPP* (2001) 165 JP 812, where the district judge hearing a trial visited the place of the offence after closing speeches and checked whether an eye-witness's view could have been obstructed. The Divisional Court held that, given the importance of such matters, the district judge should, at the very least, have informed the parties beforehand so that they could make submissions, if they chose, as to the witness's actual position. The convictions were quashed and a retrial ordered.

If the magistrates convict the defendant, they are required to give 'sufficient reasons' to explain their decision (r 37.3(5)). The justices do not have to give their reasons in an elaborate form (*McKerry v Teesdale & Wear Valley Justices* (2000) 164 JP 355, per Lord Bingham, at para 23). In *R (McGowan) v Brent Justices* (2002) 166 JP 29, Tuckey LJ (at para 18), said that 'the essence of the exercise in a criminal case such as this is to inform the defendant why he has been found guilty. That can usually be done in a few simple sentences'.

If the court acquits the accused, it may (but is not required to) give an explanation of its decision (r 37.3(6)).

It should be noted that the provisions of the Criminal Law Act 1967 (CLA), s 6(3), do not apply in magistrates' courts. Thus, the magistrates have no power to find the defendant guilty of an alternative offence not specifically charged: *Lawrence v Same* [1968] 2 QB 93. To this rule there are certain statutory exceptions (eg under the Road Traffic Offenders Act 1988, s 24(3) and (4), a defendant charged with dangerous driving may be found guilty of careless driving; under the Theft Act 1968, s 12A(5), a defendant who has been charged with aggravated vehicle taking may be found guilty of simple taking).

However, it would be open to the magistrates to ask for a charge alleging the alternative offence to be preferred immediately and then to proceed to deal with it at once, as an alternative to an acquittal where the defendant is clearly guilty. In addition, the prosecution may, at the outset, prefer two charges in the alternative, in which case the magistrates have the opportunity to dismiss the more serious charge and convict on the less serious one. Where charges are in the alternative but the magistrates decide that the defendant is guilty of both, they should not convict the defendant of both, since that would be 'unfair and disproportionate' (per Laws LJ, in *R (Dyer) v Watford Magistrates' Court* [2013] EWHC 547 (Admin), at [11]). In such a case, the magistrates should adjourn the lesser charge at the end of the trial but before conviction (so that if an appeal succeeded against conviction on the greater charge, a conviction on the lesser offence might thereafter properly be recorded against the accused): thus, the court gives no verdict on the lesser charge, instead adjourning it *sine die* under the MCA 1980, s 10 (ibid per Hickinbottom J at [14]).

5.3.8 Sentence

If the magistrates find the case proved, they will proceed to sentence, after an adjournment if necessary. A detailed analysis of the procedure prior to sentence is found in **Chapter 13**, but in brief is as follows:

- the prosecution gives details of the defendant's character and antecedents;
- any pre-sentence or other reports are placed before the court;

- the defence puts forward a plea in mitigation;
- the court passes sentence.

The magistrates' sentencing powers are discussed in full in **Chapters 15** and **16**. However, in brief, the magistrates may sentence a person over the age of 21 to a maximum period of six months' imprisonment on each offence, or the statutory maximum for the offence, whichever is the less. Where the person is convicted of two or more either-way offences, the sentences may be made to run consecutively to a maximum aggregate of 12 months. A magistrates' court may also impose a fine. In the case of a summary offence, the maximum fine depends on the level of maximum fine specified for the particular offence; if the offence is triable either way, the fine is unlimited.

5.4 Power to rectify mistakes

Under the MCA 1980, s 142(2), where a person has been convicted by a magistrates' court and it subsequently appears to the court that it would be in the interests of justice that the case should be heard again by different justices, the court may so direct. An application under s 142 can be considered by the same magistrates who convicted the defendant or by a different bench. The magistrates may re-open a case under s 142(2) regardless of whether the defendant pleaded guilty or not guilty. If the conviction is set aside, the case is reheard by different magistrates from those who convicted the defendant.

An application under s 142(2) may be appropriate if, for example, the magistrates made an error of law or there was a defect in the procedure which led to the conviction. In *R v Croydon Youth Court, ex p DPP* [1997] 2 Cr App R 411, McCowan LJ (at 416) said that the purpose of s 142(2) is best described as a 'power to rectify mistakes'. Similarly, in *Zykin v CPS* (2009) 173 JP 361, Bean J referred to *Holme v Liverpool City Justices* [2004] EWHC 3131 (Admin); (2005) 169 JP 306, and said (at para 16) that s 142 'does not confer a wide and general power on a magistrates' court to re-open a previous decision on the grounds that it is in the interests of justice to do so'; rather, it is 'a power to be used in a relatively limited situation, namely one which is akin to mistake or the slip rule'. The limited scope of s 142(2) was emphasised in *R (Williamson) v City of Westminster Magistrates' Court* [2012] EWHC 1444 (Admin), where Burnett J said (at [31]) that the power under s 142 'remains rooted in the concept of correcting mistakes and errors. It is not a power equivalent to an appeal to the Crown Court or the High Court, nor is it a general power of review'. Similarly, in *DPP v Chajed* [2013] EWHC 188 (Admin), Hickinbottom J, with whom Laws LJ agreed, said (at [26]) that where there has been a simple mistake (or something akin to such), s 142 enables a magistrates' court to rectify it, if necessary by directing the case be reheard by different justices. However, once a guilty verdict has been pronounced by magistrates, it does not enable a convicted defendant to make further submissions with a view to persuading the bench to change its mind and substitute a not guilty verdict. If the magistrates have reached the wrong decision on the merits of submissions which have been made to them, the appropriate course for the accused is to appeal to the Crown Court or by way of case stated to the High Court.

Section 142 may also be invoked where a magistrates' court wrongly proceeds in the absence of the defendant. For example, in *R (Killick) v West London Magistrates' Court* [2012] EWHC 3864 (Admin), it was held that a magistrates' court erred in refusing to set aside a conviction under s 142 where the accused had been tried in his absence despite medical evidence which suggested that he was unfit to attend court.

Under s 142(1), a magistrates' court may vary or rescind a sentence or other order imposed or made by it, if it appears to the court to be in the interests of justice to do so. Use of this power is appropriate where, for example, the magistrates made an error of law when passing the original sentence. In *R (Trigger) v Northampton Magistrates' Court* (2011) 175 JP 101, Ramsey J, at para 30, said that it is appropriate to use the power conferred by s 142 'where the mistake is quickly identified and [it] is accepted on all sides that a mistake had been made'. His Lordship added (at para 33) that the 'wide power and absence of any time limit in s 142 must . . . be exercised taking account of the principle of finality of sentencing' and that 'it must be borne in mind that it would not usually be in the interests of justice to increase a sentence imposed earlier unless the power is exercised speedily after the date of the original sentence'.

The power to rescind under s 142(1) only applies where the defendant has been found guilty or pleaded guilty, not where he has been acquitted or the prosecution have withdrawn the charge (see *Coles v DPP* (1998) 162 JP 687, which concerned a costs order).

There is no time limit to the re-opening of the case under s 142. However, delay is a factor which the magistrates are entitled to take into account when considering such an application (*R v Ealing Magistrates' Court, ex p Sahota* (1998) 162 JP 73). The court's right to exercise its powers under s 142 are lost after the case has been appealed to the Crown Court or the High Court by way of case stated, and that court has determined the appeal (s 142(1A) and (2A)).

5.5 The clerk to the justices (court legal adviser)

The clerk to the justices (often known as 'court legal adviser') is a barrister or solicitor of at least five years' standing or has a five year magistrates' court qualification. He or she is usually supported by assistant clerks who often are, but need not be, legally qualified.

Under r 37.15(1), a justices' legal adviser must attend, unless the court includes a district judge. Rule 37.15(2) says, before the hearing starts, the justices' legal adviser must draw the court's attention to what the prosecutor alleges, what the parties say is agreed, what the parties say is in dispute and what the parties say about how each expects to present the case (especially as regards matters affecting the duration of the trial). The justices' legal adviser must also give the court legal advice and, if necessary, attend the members of the court outside the courtroom to give such advice; however, the adviser must inform the parties of any such advice given outside the courtroom.

Rule 37.4(6) says that the justices' legal adviser (or the court) may ask a witness questions and, in particular, where the defendant is not represented, may ask any question that is necessary in the defendant's interests. Rule 37.15(3) says that the justices' legal adviser must also assist the defendant, if unrepresented, and must assist the court by making a note of the substance of any oral evidence or representations and ensuring that an adequate record is kept of the court's decisions and the reasons for them.

By virtue of the *Criminal Practice Directions*, Part VI 37A.5, the legal adviser is responsible for providing the justices with any advice they require properly to perform their functions, whether or not the justices have requested that advice, on:

(a) questions of law;
(b) questions of mixed law and fact;
(c) matters of practice and procedure;
(d) the process to be followed at sentence and the matters to be taken into account, together with the range of penalties and ancillary orders available;
(e) any relevant decisions of the superior courts or other guidelines;
(f) the appropriate decision-making structure to be applied in any given case; and
(g) other issues relevant to the matter before the court.

In addition to advising the justices, the legal adviser is also responsible for assisting the magistrates, where necessary, by reminding them of the evidence and with the formulation of reasons for their decisions. However, the legal adviser must not play any part in making findings of fact (Part VI 37A.12 of the *Criminal Practice Directions*).

Where the justices request their adviser to join them in the retiring room, this request should be made in the presence of the parties in court. Any legal advice given to the justices other than in open court should be clearly stated to be provisional, and the adviser should subsequently repeat the substance of that advice in open court and give the parties the opportunity to make any representations they wish on that provisional advice. The legal adviser should then state in open court whether the provisional advice is confirmed or, if it is varied, the nature of the variation (para 37A.15).

5.6 Committal to the Crown Court for sentence

In certain circumstances, a defendant who pleads guilty or who is found guilty in the magistrates' court may be committed to the Crown Court for sentence. The main powers of committal are as follows.

5.6.1 Committal for sentence under PCC(S)A 2000, s 3

Section 3 of the Powers of Criminal Courts (Sentencing) Act 2000 applies where a defendant aged over 18 has been convicted in a magistrates' court of an either-way offence. In those circumstances, the magistrates may commit for sentence if the offence is so serious that they have insufficient powers of sentence. Normally this will be the case where the magistrates think that a sentence in excess of six months' imprisonment (or an aggregate total of 12 months, if the court is dealing with two or more either-way offences) would be inadequate. However, committal under s 3 is also permissible if the magistrates take the view that a fine would be appropriate but that the fine which should be imposed exceeds their powers, currently limited to £5,000 per offence (*North Essex Justices, ex p Lloyd* (2001) 165 JP 117).

In *North Sefton Magistrates' Court, ex p Marsh* (1994) 159 JP 1, the Divisional Court ruled that the decision to commit for sentence under s 3 does not have to be based on information received by the court after the decision to try the accused summarily. However, the court did stress that magistrates should think carefully when deciding to accept jurisdiction because normally an offender should be able to conclude that, once jurisdiction had been accepted, he would not on the same facts be committed for sentence. It follows that magistrates should not normally commit an offender for sentence under s 3 unless new information has come to light since the mode of trial decision was taken but, if they do commit for sentence on the basis of information which was already known to the court when the decision to try the case was reached, judicial review will not be granted since the magistrates have not acted beyond their powers.

The discretion of the magistrates to commit for sentence is subject to the general principle that an offender who has been led to believe, whether expressly or by implication, that sentence will be passed by the magistrates, should not subsequently be committed for sentence, whether by the same or a differently constituted bench. In *Nottingham Magistrates' Court, ex p Davidson* [2000] 1 Cr App R (S) 167, at 169, Lord Bingham CJ identified the key question as being whether the defendant had a 'legitimate expectation' that he would (or would not) be sentenced in a particular way. It follows that a defendant who received an indication, when the case was adjourned for a pre-sentence report, that there would be no committal for sentence, should not subsequently be committed for sentence (*Wirral Magistrates' Court, ex p Jermyn* [2001] 1 Cr App R (S) 137). However, the expectation must be a legitimate one (*R (Harrington) v Bromley Magistrates' Court* [2007] EWHC 2896 (Admin)).

The PCC(S)A, s 5(1), provides that a defendant who has been committed for sentence under s 3 may be dealt with by the Crown Court 'in any way in which it could deal with him if he had just been convicted of the offence on indictment'. In other words, the Crown Court is not limited to the sentencing powers of the magistrates.

5.6.2 Committal for sentence under PCC(S)A 2000, s 4

A defendant who has been sent for *trial* on an indictable offence, may also be committed for *sentence* on any other, related, either-way offences to which the defendant has indicated a guilty plea (see PCC(S)A 2000, s 4). In this situation, the Crown Court may sentence a 's 4' offence as if the defendant had just been convicted of the offence on indictment (see PCC(S)A 2000, s 5(1)), provided that either (a) the defendant is convicted of the offence which was sent to the Crown Court for trial, or (b) the magistrates stated that the 's 4' offence was one that they would have committed for sentence anyway under s 3. If neither condition is met, the Crown Court is limited to the sentencing powers of the magistrates' court (see

PCC(S)A 2000, ss 4(4) and 5). To avoid inadvertently fettering the powers of the Crown Court, the magistrates should commit under s 3 if they take the view that their sentencing powers are inadequate, even if they could also have committed under s 4.

5.6.3 Committal under the PCC(S)A 2000, s 6

Section 6 provides that, where the magistrates exercise what may be termed a 'primary' power of committal for sentence (eg under s 3), they may also commit the defendant to the Crown Court to be dealt with for any other matter that the magistrates' court would otherwise be dealing with.

For example, under s 6, the magistrates may commit to the Crown Court summary offences which could not otherwise be committed for sentence. This enables the Crown Court to deal with the defendant for all outstanding offences, avoiding the otherwise inconvenient result of the magistrates' court dealing with the summary offences and the Crown Court dealing with everything else.

The purpose of s 6 is convenience, and to ensure consistency of sentencing. In these circumstances, the powers of the Crown Court when dealing with a defendant for offences committed under s 6 are limited to those of the magistrates.

Note also the power to commit a defendant under the Proceeds of Crime Act 2002, s 70, for a confiscation order to be made.

Sometimes the basis of a committal for sentence is misdescribed by the magistrates' court. In *R v Ayhan* [2011] EWCA Crim 3184; [2012] 1 WLR 1775, Lord Judge CJ said (at [22]):

> ... provided the power of the magistrates' court to commit for sentence was properly exercised in respect of one or more either way offences in accordance with section 3 of the 2000 Act, a mistake in recording the statutory basis for a committal of summary only offences does not invalidate the committal. The principle is that thereafter the Crown Court must abide by the sentencing powers available to the magistrates' court in relation to the summary only offences. If that principle is not followed, then the sentences must be reduced to sentences which fall within the jurisdiction of the magistrates.

5.6.4 Breach of a Crown Court order

A defendant who has been convicted of an offence which constitutes a breach of a Crown Court order may be committed to the Crown Court (see **19.3** for further details). The most important orders are:

(a) A suspended sentence. If the defendant is convicted of an imprisonable offence committed while subject to a Crown Court suspended sentence, the magistrates may either commit for sentence or simply notify the Crown Court of the breach (CJA 2003, Sch 12, para 11(2)).

(b) A community order or conditional discharge. A defendant who is in breach of a Crown Court community order or conditional discharge may be committed to the Crown Court to be dealt with (CJA 2003, Sch 8, para 9(6), and PCC(S)A 2000, s 13(5), respectively).

5.6.5 Challenging committal for sentence

A defendant who wishes to appeal against a committal for sentence may apply for judicial review (see **8.3**); however, the application would succeed only if the defendant could show that the committal was *Wednesbury* unreasonable. An appeal to the Crown Court is not possible, as a committal is neither a conviction nor a sentence (see **8.1**); appeal by way of case stated is not available as the case has not yet finished (see **8.2.1**).

Similarly, the prosecution may apply for judicial review of the magistrates' refusal to commit, but again they would have to show that the decision of the magistrates was *Wednesbury* unreasonable.

5.7 Summary: outline of procedure for a trial in the magistrates' court

The main stages of a trial in the magistrates' court are as follows:

1. The prosecutor may make an opening speech.
2. The prosecution evidence is then called.
3. The defence may make a submission of no case to answer. Unless the magistrates are minded to rule that there is a case to answer, they must give the prosecution a chance to respond to the defence submission before making their decision. The magistrates may indicate that they are minded to dismiss the case at this stage without the defence inviting them to do so, but the prosecution must be given the opportunity to make representations first.
4. The court (usually through the clerk) must inform the defendant of the right to give evidence and must warn the defendant of the risk of adverse inferences being drawn (under s 35 of the Criminal Justice and Public Order Act 1994) if the defendant does not testify (or refuses to answer questions while testifying).
5. The defendant may then testify and call any supporting witnesses.
6. Either party may call further evidence, for example evidence in rebuttal. The calling of rebuttal evidence should be regarded as an exceptional course of action.
7. The prosecution may make a closing speech (unless the defendant is unrepresented or called no witnesses other than his own testimony).
8. The defence may make a closing speech.
9. The magistrates decide their verdict.
10. If the defendant is found guilty, the magistrates proceed to the sentencing stage (which may include committal to the Crown Court for sentence).

6

Youth court trials

6.1 Introduction

For most people charged with a criminal offence, there is only one court that they need to know about—the magistrates' court. For those who are charged with an indictable offence there is also the Crown Court. And of course cases can go *on appeal* to the Divisional Court or Court of Appeal and then to the Supreme Court.

For juveniles there is another court—the youth court. This court is a special type of magistrates' court. To avoid confusion, the ordinary magistrates' court will be referred to in this chapter as the *adult* magistrates' court.

Since Parliament passed the Children and Young Persons Act 1933 (CYPA), courts have had a statutory duty to have regard to the welfare of juveniles when dealing with them. The youth justice system of England and Wales has been subjected to considerable scrutiny over recent years and has undergone major change over the last 15 years. It may be helpful to review, briefly, some of the history and objectives that lay behind the root-and-branch reforms that began in 1998 and have continued up to the present. For a longer-term retrospective, see 'Youth justice? Half a century of responses to youth offending' by Caroline Ball [2004] Crim LR 167.

In a 1996 report, *Misspent Youth*, the Audit Commission said that:

> The current system for dealing with youth crime is inefficient and expensive, while little is done to deal effectively with juvenile nuisance. The present arrangements are failing the young people who are not being guided away from offending to constructive activities. They are also failing victims . . . and they lead to waste in a variety of forms, including lost time, as public servants process the same young offenders through the courts time and again . . .

In 1997, the Home Office published a seminal White Paper on youth justice—*No More Excuses—A New Approach to Tackling Youth Crime in England and Wales*. It expressed concern that too much effort went into merely 'processing' juveniles and very little was directed to the prevention of crime or providing a service to victims, offenders and witnesses. Earlier intervention—nipping crime in the bud—was the preferred option. A 'fundamental change of approach' was required for the youth courts, looking beyond simple questions of 'guilt or innocence'. Courts were to enquire more widely into the circumstances of the offending behaviour, leading on to action being taken to change that behaviour.

One apparent problem was the confusion caused by the conflict between the statutory duty imposed by the CYPA 1933 to look to the juvenile's welfare and the aims of protecting the public and preventing offending. Clarification of the correct approach came in the Crime and Disorder Act 1998, s 37:

> (a) *It shall be the principal aim of the youth justice system to prevent offending by children and young persons.*
>
> (b) *In addition to any other duty to which they are subject, it shall be the duty of all persons and bodies carrying out functions in relation to the youth justice system to have regard to that aim.*

So, when considering how best to prevent offending, it would be sensible to identify the most common factors associated with criminal behaviour and address them. Research quoted in *No More Excuses* identified the following key factors as relevant to youth criminality:

- being male;
- being brought up by a criminal parent or parents;
- living in a family with multiple problems;
- experiencing poor parenting and lack of supervision;
- poor discipline in the family and at school;
- playing truant or being excluded from school;
- associating with delinquent friends; and
- having siblings who offend.

The 'single most important factor in explaining criminality is the quality of a young person's home life, including parental supervision' (*No More Excuses*, ch 1). So, youth courts were given the power to refer first-time offenders, who show contrition, to youth offender panels (YOPs). The YOP will draw up a contract, regulating the juvenile's future behaviour. The police now have the power to give a caution to a juvenile (ie rather than prosecute); this can be a conditional caution—see **6.6**. The police can also refer a juvenile to rehabilitation programmes, run by youth offending teams (YOTs). YOTs are multi-agency bodies, created by local authorities, in cooperation with the local chief officer of police, probation service and health authority, under the CDA 1998, s 39. Amongst their tasks, YOTs are to:

> tackle the issues identified in the White Paper—from poor parental supervision and domestic violence or abuse to peer group pressure, from truancy and school exclusion to substance misuse or mental health problems—which can place young people at risk of becoming involved in crime.

With these reforms, new sentences were introduced in 1998 including reparation orders, detention and training orders and parenting orders. Juvenile offenders may be confronted by the victims of their crimes and required to make a direct apology (reparation orders); children and parents may have to attend family counselling sessions (parenting orders). In an attempt to stop offending before it starts ('nipping crime in the bud') powers were given to courts and local authorities to make child safety orders and impose local child curfews on children under ten years. The former are targeted at individual children who are seen to be at risk of being drawn into crime; a court can require a child to be at home at specific times or stay away from specific places or people, and specific conduct may be forbidden (eg truanting from school). The latter aim to minimise the risk that peer pressure and the absence of responsible adult role models in a community will foster anti-social behaviour; local authorities are empowered to bar all children under ten years from a specified public area after a certain time (not to be earlier than 9 pm). According to the latest information from the Youth Justice Board, no local child curfew had actually been imposed by March 2011.

As noted earlier, the Audit Commission's 1996 report was very useful in encouraging change. In 2004, the Commission reviewed the results (see *Youth Justice*, 2004). Its bottom line conclusion was that 'the new system is a considerable improvement on the old one'. For example, young offenders were being dealt with faster (on average, twice as quickly compared to 1997). Young offenders were more likely to make amends for their actions (in 2002–3, nearly one in three young offenders received either a referral order or reparation order as their sentence). Reconviction rates, where the young offender had received a final warning or reprimand, were between 7 and 10 per cent lower than had been predicted. Nevertheless, the report identified some continuing problems—for example, low public confidence in the youth justice system (apparently, three out of four people had not heard of YOTs); also, young offenders from black and ethnic minority backgrounds were much more likely to be remanded in custody or receive a custodial sentence than those from white backgrounds (1 in

12 and 1 in 10 given custodial sentences, compared to 1 in 40). Perhaps the most significant observation in the Report is this:

> Many young offenders who end up in custody have a history of professionals failing to listen, assessments not being followed by action and nobody being in charge. If effective early intervention had been provided for just one-in-ten of these young people, annual savings in excess of £100 million could have been made . . . [E]arly intervention programmes can be effective if they are properly co-ordinated . . . [B]etter still, mainstream agencies, such as schools and health services, should take full responsibility for preventing offending by young people.

In its response, the Labour Government accepted the point about early and effective intervention, noting that it aimed to establish 2,500 Children's Centres by 2008 and highlighting the reforms evolving from its 2003 Green Paper, *Every Child Matters,* and the Children Act 2004. The response also indicated that the Government aimed to make much greater use of Final Warnings and reprimands (replaced by youth cautions and youth conditional cautions in 2013). The aim was for courts to focus on the more serious offences and persistent young offenders.

In 2003, Parliament introduced the *Youth Community Sentence*. This was intended to replace the eight existing community sentences for juveniles. It would have a 'menu of interventions' and operate in a similar fashion to the adult community order which was introduced in the CJA 2003, s 177; see **15.4**. Its implementation was postponed on several occasions and in 2009 a different sentence—the *Youth Rehabilitation Order* (YRO)—came into force (introduced by the Criminal Justice and Immigration Act 2008). As the Explanatory Notes to the CJIA state, the Youth Rehabilitation Order is a:

> new generic community sentence for children and young people. It sets out the requirements that may be attached to a YRO, makes provision for their enforcement . . . and abolishes certain existing community sentences which are to be replaced by the YRO . . . When imposing a YRO, the court will be able to choose from a 'menu' of different requirements that the offender must comply with.

The sentences which are abolished (or 'combined' in the new YRO) are—curfew orders, attendance centre orders, exclusion orders, supervision orders and action plan orders. See further, **Chapter 17**.

In its 2004 report, *Youth Justice*, the Audit Commission observed that:

> given the scope of the reforms and the relatively short space of time in which they have been up and running, it would be unwise to embark on further wholesale change.

This suggestion seems to have gone unheeded.

Information published by the Youth Justice Board can now be found on the gov.uk website.

6.2 Juveniles and criminal responsibility

6.2.1 What do we mean by 'juvenile'?

A juvenile is basically anyone under the age of 18 (CJA 1991, s 68). Once an individual has reached his or her eighteenth birthday, he or she must be treated like any other adult defendant. This could lead to problems if the defendant's eighteenth birthday occurs while a case is pending at court (see **6.5.2**). Thus, while for the layman the term 'juvenile' generally means a youth or young person, for the criminal justice system one's youth ends on the eighteenth birthday. However, we must continue to divide this population into different age groups.

6.2.2 The under 10s

Currently, children aged under ten years are irrebuttably presumed to be incapable of committing any crime. Therefore, they do not fall within the criminal jurisdiction of any court (CYPA 1933, s 50). The abolition of the presumption of innocence for children aged 10–13 in 1998, coupled with the introduction of child safety orders and local child curfews for the under-10s (see **6.1**), has led to concern in some places that some under-10s may soon feel criminalised, even if they are not strictly covered by the criminal justice system.

Finally, it should be noted that older children and adults sometimes use children under ten to carry out crimes, knowing that no criminal action can be taken against such innocent pawns. This may result in the conviction of the 'manipulator', usually as the principal offender, with the child being regarded as merely an innocent agent of the other.

6.2.3 Criminal responsibility starts at ten

Historically, a presumption of innocence (or 'incapacity') was applied to juveniles aged 10–13 years. This presumption stated that children were presumed not to know that they were doing wrong, even though they had done an act which constituted a crime. The onus was on the prosecution to rebut this presumption by calling evidence intended to show that the child in question knew that what he or she had done was 'seriously wrong'. The presumption was abolished in 1998 (see CDA 1998, s 34). The rationale for abolition was a concern that the need to call evidence to rebut the presumption 'could lead to real practical difficulties, delaying cases or even making it impossible for the prosecution to proceed' (*No More Excuses*, ch 4; for a contrary perspective, see *Protecting the Rights of Children*, a report by the Howard League for Penal Reform, 1999).

Many other European countries consider their youngsters incapable of bearing criminal responsibility before their fourteenth birthday. The issue of a minimum age was considered by the European Court of Human Rights in *T v UK* (2000) 30 EHRR 121. The Court considered whether the attribution of criminal responsibility for acts done when the defendant was aged ten might amount to inhuman or degrading treatment, contrary to the European Convention on Human Rights, Article 3. The Court said that:

> it did not find that there was any clear common standard amongst the member States of the Council of Europe as to the minimum age of criminal responsibility. While most had adopted an age-limit which was higher than that in force in England and Wales, other States, such as Cyprus, Ireland, Liechtenstein and Switzerland, attributed criminal responsibility from a younger age, and no clear tendency could be ascertained from examination of the relevant international texts and instruments, for example, the United Nations Convention on the Rights of the Child. Even if England and Wales was among the few European jurisdictions to retain a low age of criminal responsibility, the age of ten could not be said to be so young as to differ disproportionately to the age limit followed by other European States. The attribution of criminal responsibility to the applicants did not, therefore, in itself give rise to a breach of Article 3.

6.2.4 10–17-year-olds

Juveniles between the ages of 10 and 13 inclusive are often described in criminal law statutes as 'children', but this is not a universal usage. Those aged between 14 and 17 years inclusive are usually described as 'young persons'. See the CJA 1991, s 68 and Sch 8. Historically, these two groups have been distinguished for two reasons—sentencing powers, and the presumption of innocence. That presumption has now gone (**6.2.3**) but the question of a juvenile's age remains significant for sentencing purposes.

The sentences applicable to young offenders are considered in **Chapters 17** and **18**. In summary, the range of sentences available to courts when dealing with juveniles differs significantly from those available for adult offenders. Different types of sentence (or different maxima) apply to juveniles at different ages. However, the recent trend has been to toughen the sentences available, even when dealing with the youngest offenders. For example, the power to sentence defendants as young as ten to long-term detention for various grave offences (eg house burglary, some types of arson and criminal damage, and robbery). Another example is the power to make detention and training orders (DTOs). A DTO may be used for 15–17-year-olds who are convicted of any imprisonable offence which is sufficiently serious to cross the custody threshold in the CJA 1991. Twelve to 14-year-olds would be at risk of a DTO when convicted of an imprisonable offence if they are persistent offenders.

6.3 The youth court

6.3.1 Youth court—the usual forum for juvenile defendants

A juvenile accused will make his or her first appearance, following a charge or written requisition, at the level of the magistrates' court. If the juvenile is charged alone, or with other juveniles, then this will be the youth court (the branch of magistrates' court which specialises in juvenile justice). If the juvenile is charged with an adult defendant (either on a single joint charge or on separate but related charges), then the first appearance for both the accused will be in the *adult* magistrates' court. The aim is that juvenile defendants should be dealt with at summary level unless some exceptional circumstance is present, and that the specialist summary court—the youth court—will be the most appropriate forum. See, for example, *R (on the application of P) v Derby Youth Court* [2015] EWHC 573 (Admin); and MCA 1980, s 24(1) as substituted by the CJA 2003, Sch 3, para 9.

It may occasionally be suggested that even the youth court is unsuitable to try the charge against a particular juvenile. This can occur when the juvenile's development is later or slower than normal. It is clear that a juvenile, like any other defendant, is entitled to receive a fair trial but the lack of sufficient development may hamper this.

> In the case of a child, it is essential that he will be dealt with in a manner which takes full account of his age, level of maturity and intellectual and emotional capacities, and that steps are taken to promote his ability to understand and participate in the proceedings, including conducting the hearing in such a way as to reduce as far as possible his feeling of intimidation and inhibition. [However] the trial of a defendant with a mental age of 8 does not necessarily involve a breach of Article 6. What is crucial is whether the tribunal hearing the case . . . is able to adapt its procedures so that the defendant can effectively participate in the proceedings.

Scott Baker LJ in *R (on the application of TP) v West London Youth Court* [2005] EWHC 2583 (Admin), offering his view on the European Court of Human Rights judgment in *SC v UK* (2004) 40 EHRR 10.

Youth courts often use the same buildings and courtrooms that the local adult magistrates' court uses. However, courts have to make arrangements so that young defendants do not associate with adult defendants from other cases whilst awaiting hearing (see CYPA 1933, s 31).

In some places, mainly inner city areas where the scale of juvenile proceedings justifies the cost, special youth courts have been built to deal with the workload. Adult defendants never appear in these courtrooms.

6.3.2 Inside the youth court

6.3.2.1 The magistrates

In a youth court, the court will usually consist of three lay magistrates (or 'justices of the peace'). They will have been selected from a 'youth court panel' of magistrates who are specially qualified to deal with juveniles and who have also had some additional training for this purpose. Normally, there should be at least one male and one female magistrate present for a hearing in the youth court. If all the magistrates in court are of the same sex, they may only hear cases if:

- this situation could not have been foreseen; and
- having heard representations from the parties in open court, the magistrates do not consider it is expedient to adjourn proceedings to see if a mixed-gender bench might be formed.

District judges usually sit in the adult magistrates' court but are also members of the youth court panel by virtue of their office and may deal with cases in the youth court. If they do so, they will usually sit alone, unaccompanied by lay magistrates. In 1997, a Home Office report (*Review of Delay in the Criminal Justice System*, also known as the Narey Report) recommended that district judges should specialise in the management of particularly complex cases which, when they involve children and young persons, 'can be particularly difficult'. This suggestion has been acted upon; see, for example, the 2010 Protocol on the trial of sexual offences in the youth court, which refers to some district judges undergoing specialised training to handle such 'complex and sensitive' cases.

6.3.2.2 The parents of the juvenile

When a juvenile appears in court, accused of a crime, it is understandable that his or her parents may want to be present to support their child. This is not always the attitude of parents, however, and the trial courts have the power to compel parents to attend court. If a juvenile is aged 15 or under, the court *must* order a parent to attend, unless it would be unreasonable to do so. If the juvenile is aged 16 or 17, the court *may* make such an order (see CYPA 1933, s 34A, inserted by the CJA 1991, s 56). When parents attend court, they usually sit next to their child.

Part of the reason for requiring a juvenile's parents to be present in court may be that although '[p]arents of young offenders may not directly be to blame for the crimes of their children, [they] have to be responsible for providing their children with proper care and control' (*No More Excuses*, 1997). Home Office research has shown that inadequate parental supervision is strongly associated with offending; also that the quality of the parent–child relationship is crucial. Bringing the parents to court may bring home to them the need to modify their behaviour as well as that of their child. However, *No More Excuses* also reported that parental firmness was not necessarily the answer: 'We know that parents who are harsh or erratic in disciplining their children are twice as likely to have children who offend.'

Parents may need to be present in court anyway, to represent their own interests. For example, when a court convicts a child or young person, it can make *a parenting order* (see CDA 1998, s 8). This order obliges parents to attend counselling or guidance sessions for a maximum of three months and to comply with any additional requirements for up to one year (eg ensuring full school attendance by their child). Non-compliance, without reasonable excuse, may result in a conviction and a fine of up to £1,000. Parents can also be made responsible for any financial penalty imposed by a court against their children. In 2004, the Court of Appeal considered the appeal of a man against a compensation order for £1,000. The man had been ordered by a judge to pay this sum to the victim of a robbery committed by the man's 16-year-old son. The judge had the power to make the order but it was set aside by the Court of Appeal as the judge had failed to give the man the chance to be heard on the matter and had not considered whether it would be reasonable to order the man to pay compensation. See *R v JJB* [2004] EWCA Crim 14. This power arises under PCC(S)A 2000, s 137. It should not be confused with the 'parental compensation order' which may be made where a child aged under ten (ie below the age of criminal responsibility) takes or damages property in a manner which would be theft or criminal damage if the child were older; see CDA 1998, s 13A, inserted by the Serious Organised Crime and Police Act 2005, but still only in force in certain areas. See SI 2006/1871.

6.3.2.3 The witnesses

As the youth court is a criminal court, all witnesses will usually be kept out of the courtroom until it is their time to give evidence. Once their evidence is concluded, they could stay in the courtroom but in practice there is often nowhere convenient for them to sit.

An adult witness, for example a police officer or store detective, will give their evidence in exactly the same way as they would in any other court proceedings. However, if the witness is a juvenile (perhaps the victim of a mugging), then special provisions become relevant. One simple difference is that the juvenile witness gives a 'promise' to tell the truth, rather than 'swear' to do so. Another difference is that special procedures may be used in order to get the best evidence from the juvenile witness since such witnesses are automatically considered to be vulnerable.

The YJCEA 1999 established a coherent set of provisions to deal with all of the so-called 'special measures' which may be used by courts to protect vulnerable (or intimidated) witnesses. In summary, these are:

- the power to clear the public from the courtroom while the witness gives evidence (in trials involving sexual offences or when it appears that someone is trying to intimidate the witness);
- that the lawyers and the judge may remove their wigs and gowns;
- that a screen may be used in court, to shield the witness from the accused;
- that a pre-recorded video may serve as part or all of the evidence of the witness;
- that the witness may give evidence at the trial from a separate room via a live link.

Some of these provisions existed already, either in statute or more informally. The YJCEA 1999 clarified and strengthened the facilities which are available to aid children (and other vulnerable witnesses) and put the process of making decisions about special measures on to a rational basis. In principle, special measures are available for proceedings in all criminal trial courts. In practice, a court will need notice from the Home Secretary that appropriate facilities are available to it, either permanently or temporarily, before it can consider making a special measures direction (SMD). The special measures most likely to require notice are those involving technology—the live TV link and the equipment to play pre-recorded evidence to the court.

Children under the age of 18 at the time of the trial are presumed to be in need of such help. The procedure for determining which special measure to use for a child witness will depend upon which of three categories the witness falls into:

- children testifying in a case involving a sexual offence;
- children testifying in a case involving an offence of violence, abduction or neglect;
- children giving evidence in all other cases.

For most child witnesses, the YJCEA 1999, s 21, creates a presumption (or 'primary rule'; see s 21(3)) that their evidence will be given by pre-recorded video (for evidence-in-chief) and live link (for all other evidence). Since December 2013, cross-examination by pre-recorded video is permitted under s 28 and is currently the subject of a pilot scheme, following concerns expressed in 2013 about the treatment of child witnesses in court. One example that caught media attention came when one witness was cross-examined by seven different defence barristers over the course of 12 days. The appropriate orders for special measures should be made unless the court decides that the measures would not be likely to maximise the quality of the witness's evidence as far as practicable.

A child testifying in a trial for a sexual offence will give evidence-in-chief through a pre-recorded video. Any cross-examination should also take place at a pre-trial hearing and be recorded for playback at the trial unless the witness tells the court that he or she does not want that protection. Video evidence may be excluded in certain circumstances; in particular if the court is of the opinion, having regard to all the circumstances of the case, that it is not in the interests of justice that the recording be used in evidence (YJCEA 1999, s 27(2)). A child witness in a trial for an offence involving violence, abduction or neglect will have his or her examination-in-chief recorded on video for playback at the trial. Any further evidence (including cross-examination and re-examination) will normally be via a live link. The court is not required to take a decision on whether the special measures are likely to maximise the quality of the evidence.

All of the special measures provisions in the YJCEA are now in force. The final provision was s 28 (cross-examination by pre-recorded video) and this came into effect in December 2013. As Baroness Hale has said,

> Parliament has decided what is to be the norm when child witnesses give evidence. Hence there will have to be a special reason for departing from it. The fact that there is no particular reason to think that [a specific] child will be upset, traumatised or intimidated by giving evidence in court does not make it unjust for her to give it by live link and video if there is one.

See *R (D) v Camberwell Green Youth Court* [2005] 1 WLR 393.

The House of Lords held that SMDs are compatible with the right to a fair trial under ECHR, Article 6. Although they have sometimes been criticised as being too inflexible, Baroness Hale pointed out that several SMDs may be *disapplied* by exercise of the court's discretion and that this may be used where, for example, 'the child was positively anxious to give evidence in the courtroom and the court considered that it would be contrary to the interests of justice to require her to use the live link'.

The SMD regime in the YJCEA 1999 applies only to child witnesses who are not defendants. This exclusion has been criticised by some (see, eg, the commentary in [2000] Crim LR 75) and defended by others (see references in (2005) 69 JoCL 6). In contrast, since 2006 in Scotland child defendants are treated mostly in the same way as any other child witness (see Vulnerable Witnesses (Scotland) Act 2004, s 271F). A change made by the Police and Justice Act 2006 goes some way towards helping the juvenile accused—since 2007 all vulnerable defendants are permitted to give their evidence via a live link instead of from the witness box; see YJCEA 1999, s 33A. This option is available where the juvenile's ability to participate is compromised by his intellectual ability or social functioning and use of the live link would enable more effective participation by him. There is a further provision allowing the juvenile defendant to be questioned via an intermediary where he would otherwise be unable to participate effectively as a witness in the proceedings due to his level of intellectual ability or social functioning; see YJCEA 1999, s 33BA, added by the Coroners and Justice Act 2009. Section 33BA is not yet in force but see *Criminal Practice Directions*, Part I 3F. We should also note YJCEA 1999, s 19(6) which leaves intact any power that courts previously had to make an order 'in relation to a witness who is not a eligible witness . . .'

A witness aged under 18 must not be cross-examined by an unrepresented defendant where the trial involves sexual offences. In such cases, the defendant will be given an opportunity to appoint a lawyer specifically to cross-examine the witness. If he or she does not take that opportunity, the court must decide whether it should appoint a cross-examiner in the interests of justice (YJCEA 1999, s 38).

6.3.2.4 The media

Journalists may attend the youth court. Currently there is a ban on the media reporting any details which may identify any child or young person involved in a case in the youth court (whether as a defendant or as a witness; see CYPA 1933, s 49 as substituted by the CJPOA 1994, s 49 and subsequent legislation). Thus,

> *No matter relating to any child or young person concerned in proceedings to which this section applies shall while he is under the age of 18 be included in any publication if it is likely to lead members of the public to identify him as someone concerned in the proceedings.*

'Publication' has a broad definition. It can apply to online publication, including posting information on social media, as well as the more traditional media. It covers 'any speech, writing, relevant programme or other communication in whatever form, which is addressed to the public at large or any section of the public...' (see YJCEA 1999, s 63). The ban may be lifted in three situations.

(a) The defence may apply to lift the ban. Publicity must be appropriate for the avoidance of injustice to the juvenile accused (eg publicising details of the incident to attract the attention of potential defence witnesses).

(b) The prosecution may apply to lift the ban. Publicity may be necessary here if the juvenile accused is 'unlawfully at large' and publicity may assist in his or her recapture. The offence must be either:

    (i) serious (in that it carries a maximum punishment of 14 years' or more imprisonment for an adult offender); or

    (ii) violent or sexual (as defined in Sch 15, CJA 2003; see **Chapter 20** and *Blackstone's Criminal Practice*, D24.16).

(c) After the juvenile has been convicted, the youth court itself may consider it to be in the public interest to remove the reporting restrictions. Before doing so, the court should allow the parties to make representations on the matter. The aims here are to disclose the outcome of the case, to show that justice has been done and, perhaps, to shame the individual offender.

The CYPA 1933, s 49 applies to proceedings in the youth court and to appeals from the youth court. Criminal courts have a complementary, discretionary, power to make an order prohibiting the media from reporting information which may lead to the identification of a defendant, victim or witness under the age of 18 in *any* proceedings; see YJCEA 1999, s 45. The restrictions imposed by both CYPA 1933, s 49 and YJCEA 1999, s 45 cease to apply once the subject of the restriction reaches 18 years of age. By virtue of a new provision—YJCEA 1999, s 45A (inserted by the Criminal Justice and Courts Act 2015, s 78)—those restrictions may be continued for the lifetime of a victim or witness. The purpose behind such an extension is to ensure the quality of the evidence given by that individual or the level of cooperation they give to any party to the proceedings.

6.3.2.5 Probation officers

It is quite usual to see probation officers or staff from local authority social services sitting in the youth court. It is sometimes the case that the juvenile defendant is in the care of the local authority; more often, the juvenile is already 'known' to these bodies and their personnel may have been involved in preparing a pre-sentence report in a previous hearing or have worked with the juvenile on a supervision order, for example. They may be a helpful source of information for a barrister inexperienced in appearing before the youth court.

6.3.2.6 The public

Youth courts operate rather differently from other courts, in that there is no general right to enter a youth courtroom. Attendance is governed by the CYPA 1933, s 47(2), as amended, so that no person shall be present at any sitting of a youth court except:

- the juvenile, his or her parents, the parties' legal representatives and the magistrate(s);
- court officers (the clerk, ushers);
- bona fide media reporters (but not to take photographs or to film);
- witnesses (both during and after giving their evidence);
- anyone else directly concerned in that case (probation officers, social workers, etc);
- such other persons as the court may specially authorise to be present.

In the past, these restrictions on access have usually been enforced strictly. The reason for this limited access was, in part, a desire to protect the juvenile from being (or feeling) stigmatised as a criminal. The effect was to exclude the general public and, not infrequently, the victim of the offence. The victim would enter the courtroom only when and if needed as a witness, where the juvenile pleaded not guilty. In the late 1990s this led to criticism of the youth court system as a 'secret garden', where proceedings took place in private and young offenders were not encouraged to face the consequences of their actions and take steps to change their behaviour. It was suggested that the practice placed too great an emphasis on protecting the identity of young offenders at the expense of victims and the community. In 1998, the former Home Office Minister Alun Michael observed that youth courts:

> . . . have wide discretion about who can attend [their] proceedings . . . We believe that justice is best served in an open court where the criminal process can be scrutinised and the offender cannot hide behind a cloak of anonymity.

Subsequently, the Home Office and Lord Chancellor's Department issued a joint circular which included the following recommendations:

- all victims of juvenile crime should have the opportunity to attend the youth court (for the trial or preceding hearings) unless to do so would not be in the interests of justice;

- greater access should be allowed for the public to attend proceedings in the youth court (an example being a case where the offender's conduct has had an impact on the local community generally).

6.3.2.7 The layout of the youth court

There will not usually be seating provided for members of the public in dedicated youth courtrooms. These courtrooms provide seating only for those people who are specifically allowed to be present during the proceedings (see CYPA 1933, s 47(2)). The magistrates do not sit up on a raised platform, but often are on ordinary chairs behind plain tables. Since the court clerk, lawyers, probation officers and social workers also sit on ordinary chairs behind desks, it is not as obvious as in other courtrooms where one should sit.

As a rule of thumb, the chairs in the centre of the room will be reserved for the juvenile defendant(s) and parents. These chairs will face the desk where the magistrates sit (and the Royal Coat of Arms may be on the wall behind the magistrates). The clerk's desk will be at the side of the one used by the magistrates and, usually, the lawyers' seats and desks will be on the same side of the room as the clerk. These dedicated youth courtrooms do not contain docks to hold a prisoner.

In adult magistrates' courts and the Crown Court, public seating is always provided. When an adult courtroom is used as a youth court, typically the public seating will be left empty. Everyone will sit where they normally would, except that no dock will be used even if there is one. In such cases, the juvenile defendant will sit in front of the dock.

6.3.3 Procedure in the youth court

As the youth court is a special type of magistrates' court, most of what happens in a hearing is the same as for adults in the adult magistrates' court. In particular, a juvenile can be tried summarily, sentenced if found guilty and remanded if a case is adjourned for any reason by the youth court. The youth court can also issue a warrant for the arrest of a juvenile defendant who fails to attend the hearing (see BA 1976, s 7; MCA 1980, s 13). There are some semantic differences, however. See **Figure 6.1**.

Name

Juveniles (both defendants and witnesses) are addressed by their first names.

Oath

Juveniles 'promise' to tell the truth. The usual form of oath requires a witness to swear to do so. (Those aged under 14 give evidence unsworn: YJCEA 1999, s 55.)

Guilt

A juvenile is never 'convicted' of an offence; the court will simply record a finding of guilt.

The difference is largely cosmetic, presumably to avoid the trauma of conviction.

Sentence

A juvenile is not sentenced to a punishment after the case has been proved, rather the court makes an order upon a finding of guilt. Again, the distinction is semantic.

Figure 6.1 Terminology in the youth court

The usual method of classifying offences that we saw in **Chapter 4** (summary, indictable-only and triable either way) does not of itself determine the mode of trial for juvenile defendants. Indictable-only crimes, such as robbery and rape, need not be sent to Crown Court for trial where the defendant is a juvenile (the main exception is homicide offences which *must* be sent for trial to Crown Court; see PCC(S)A 2000, s 91, MCA 1980, s 24 and CDA 1998, s 51A). Similarly, just because the juvenile defendant faces a crime which is triable either way, it does not follow that the defendant can choose trial by jury. However, it is quite possible for the youth court to send a juvenile defendant for trial to Crown Court on indictable offences. It is necessary to consider how this may happen.

According to MCA 1980, s 24, when a juvenile appears before the court charged with an indictable offence (note that this includes both indictment-only and either-way offences), he shall be tried summarily, subject to MCA 1980, ss 24A and 24B and also to CDA 1998, ss 51 and 51A. Both ss 51 and 51A are expressed to be subject to ss 24A and 24B. CDA 1998, s 51 applies in the adult magistrates' court and will be considered in **6.4.1** below.

6.3.3.1 Sending a juvenile for trial in Crown Court

Under s 51A, if a juvenile appears before a magistrates' court charged with an offence on the list in s 51A(3), the court shall send him forthwith to the Crown Court to stand trial for that offence. The list includes:

- homicide;
- an offence which, in the case of an adult offender, is punishable with 14 or more years' imprisonment and the court considers that if he is found guilty it should be possible to sentence him to long-term detention under PCC(S)A 2000, s 91(3);
- an offence where a notice has been given under s 51B or s 51C (complex fraud cases or cases involving child witnesses);
- a *specified* offence which may trigger the 'dangerous offender' sentencing provisions.

If the offence is on this list, the court *shall* deal with it in the manner set out in s 51A(3) and not by using any other provision of s 51A or s 51; s 51A(10)(a). At the same time (or later), the court *may* also send the juvenile for trial in the Crown Court for any indictable offence which appears to be related to the one for which he has been sent for trial. The court *may* also send a summary offence for trial, at the same time or later, if it is imprisonable or punishable by disqualification from driving; s 51A(4) and (5). But remember—all of this is subject to MCA 1980, s 24A.

6.3.3.2 Juvenile's intended plea

Under MCA 1980, s 24A, if a juvenile appears before a court charged with an offence (other than one listed in s 51A(12) (mainly homicide offences)), and the court would normally be required by s 51 or s 51A to determine whether or not to send the juvenile forthwith for trial in the Crown Court, *before* doing so it must first follow the procedure in s 24A.

Under s 24A(5), the court must ask the juvenile to indicate their plea to the charge. Thus, a 'plea before venue' stage has been introduced into the procedure. This will work in the same way as it does for adults; see **4.2.2.1**. If the juvenile indicates a guilty plea, then the court will not move on to make any decision under s 51 or 51A; however, the court may commit the juvenile to Crown Court for sentence under the PCC(S)A 2000, s 3A or s 3B. If the juvenile indicates a not guilty plea (or stays silent), then the court must proceed to follow the procedure under either s 51 or s 51A, as applicable.

Section 24A(3) specifies that the juvenile must be present in court throughout this process. However, where the juvenile misbehaves to such an extent that the court considers that it should proceed in his absence, it may do so as long as he is legally represented in court; s 24B. The representative will then be asked to indicate his client's plea at the appropriate time and the court will proceed accordingly.

6.3.4 Sentencing in the youth court

There are many sentences which are used exclusively in relation to juvenile offenders, for example referral orders and detention and training orders. Provisions in the CJA 2003, which were intended to standardise community orders for juvenile offenders with those applicable to adults, have never been brought into effect. Instead, the Criminal Justice and Immigration Act 2008 introduced the Youth Rehabilitation Order and this came into force in 2009. See further **Chapter 17**.

All of the sentences which can be applied to a juvenile offender are available to the youth court (reflecting the notion that this court should be the usual venue for juvenile justice) with the exception of custody for life, long-term detention and custody for 'dangerous' offenders, all of which are reserved for the Crown Court's exclusive use. In the youth court, if a juvenile is charged with an offence which could attract long-term detention under PCC(S)A 2000, s 91 (a 'grave' offence) and he either indicates a guilty plea to it or is convicted of it following a summary trial, then the youth court may commit the juvenile to Crown Court for sentence under PCC(S)A 2000, s 3B (as amended by CJCA 2015, s 53).

Further information on juvenile sentences can be found in **Chapters 17**, **18** and **20**.

We should note that the general purposes of sentencing which are listed in the CJA 2003, s 142, do not apply to offenders who are aged under 18 at the time of conviction. The Criminal Justice and Immigration Act 2008, s 9, will address this apparent vacuum when it comes into force (not as at April 2015). It will insert a new s 142A into the CJA 2003. Under this provision, courts are reminded that the *principal aim* of the youth justice system is to prevent juveniles from offending (CDA 1998, s 37). Secondly, the obligation to have regard for the juvenile offender's welfare (CYPA 1933, s 44) is reiterated—but this is explicitly made subordinate to the principal aim. The purposes of sentencing for juveniles are then specified as:

a. the punishment of offenders,

b. the reform and rehabilitation of offenders,

c. the protection of the public, and

d. the making of reparation by offenders to persons affected by their offences.

6.4 Juveniles in the adult courts

6.4.1 Juvenile defendants in the adult magistrates' court

Where a juvenile is charged with an adult defendant, then the first appearance for both of the accused will be in the adult magistrates' court. There are several possible permutations:

- the juvenile and the adult face a single joint charge;
- the juvenile is charged with aiding and abetting the adult to commit an offence (or vice versa);
- the juvenile is charged with an offence which arises out of circumstances which are the same as, or connected with, those which have resulted in a charge against the adult.

The offence or offences involved may be summary, indictable or a combination.

The usual classification of offences is of little direct assistance in determining which court will try (or sentence) a juvenile defendant. In particular, we should note that a juvenile defendant never has the right to select jury trial in the Crown Court. Which court tries the juvenile will be dependent largely upon what happens to the adult defendant (see **Figure 6.2**). The charge against the adult may be for any one of the usual three types of offence.

6.4.1.1 Summary offence alleged against adult

If the adult faces a summary offence, he or she will simply be asked to enter a plea to the charge. If the adult pleads guilty, obviously there will be no trial of the adult. The juvenile will then be asked to enter a plea to his or her charge. If the juvenile pleads guilty, the next stage is to sentence the juvenile so mode of trial has ceased to be an issue (for sentencing decisions, see **6.4.1.2**). If the juvenile pleads not guilty, then a summary trial is needed. This may take place in the adult magistrates' court but the case may be referred to the youth court for trial there instead. On the other hand, the adult may plead not guilty to the summary offence, thus necessitating a summary trial. Again, the juvenile will then be asked to enter a plea—if it is guilty, then the juvenile will requires only to be sentenced. If the juvenile pleads not guilty, then both juvenile and adult require summary trial. If there is a single joint charge

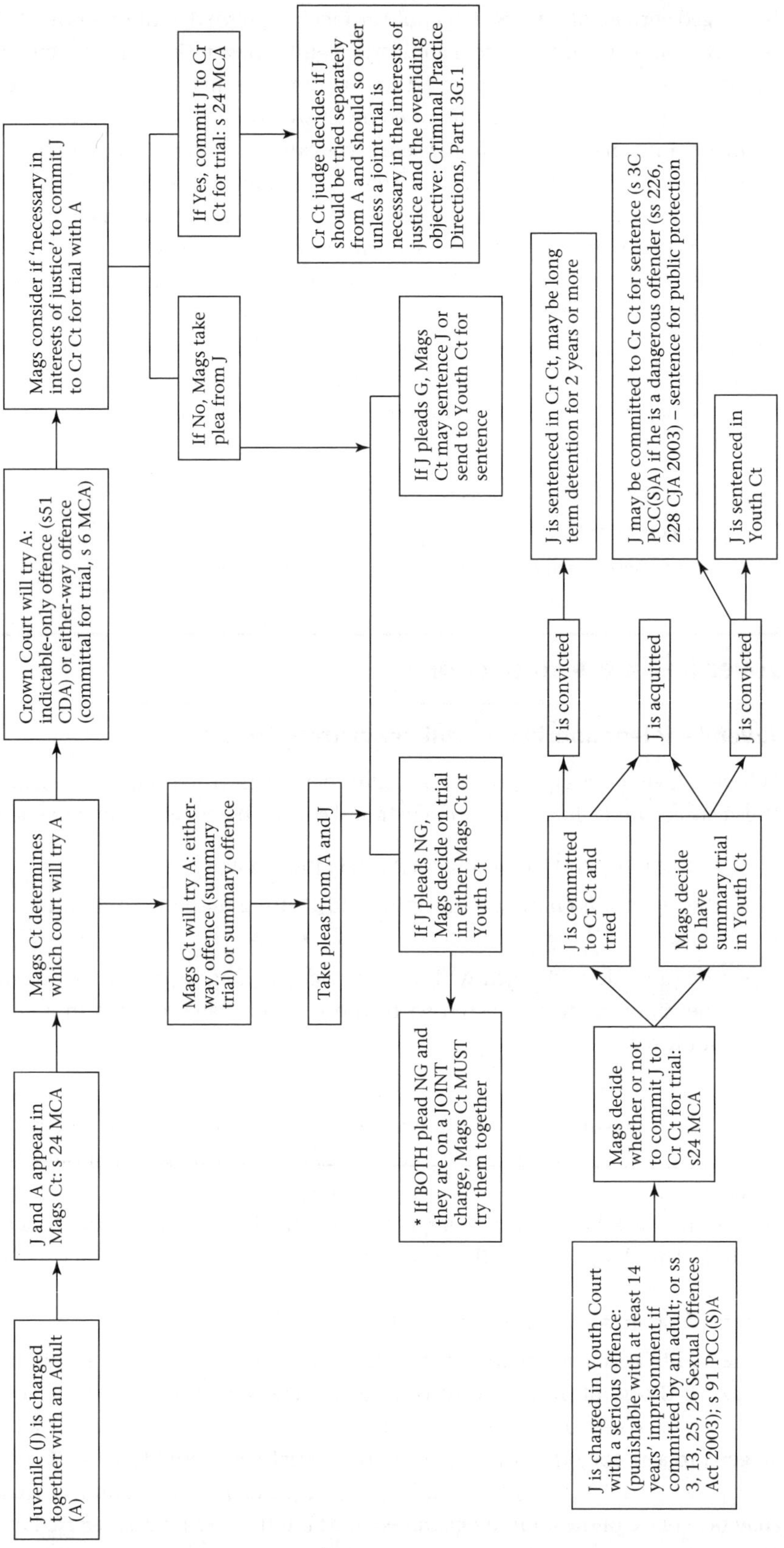

Figure 6.2 Mode of trial and sentencing for juveniles

against them, then they *must* be tried together in the adult magistrates' court. If they are not on a single joint charge but instead face two or more *related* charges, then the justices in the adult magistrates' court must make a decision. Their choice rests between a single trial of both accused (which will take place in the adult court) or to order split trials (with the juvenile being sent to the youth court). If there are close factual connections between the offences and the same witnesses will appear in both trials, the likelihood is that the justices will choose a single summary trial (see also on this point *CPS v South East Surrey Youth Court and Ghanbari* [2005] EWHC 2929 (Admin) at [17(v)]). We should also note here that magistrates are required to consider in a case management hearing whether the juvenile (as a vulnerable defendant) should be tried on his or her own, apart from the adult defendant. The magistrates 'should so order unless of the opinion that a joint trial would be consistent with the overriding objective and is in the interest of justice'. See the *Criminal Practice Directions*, Part I 3G.

6.4.1.2 Indictable offence alleged against adult

We begin again with the adult accused. If the adult is charged with a triable either-way offence, then plea before venue and mode of trial are relevant for *him or her*. If the outcome is an indicated plea of guilty by the adult, the court will proceed with the juvenile in the same fashion as considered earlier (under summary offences; **6.4.1.1**). Likewise, if the adult indicates a not guilty plea and the mode of trial outcome is for a summary trial, the court proceeds with the juvenile in the same way as if it were now handling a summary offence. If the mode of trial outcome is for Crown Court trial, then the magistrates will proceed to send the adult for trial, under CDA 1998, s 51.

If the adult is charged with an indictable-only offence, then he or she must be sent for trial in the Crown Court forthwith, under CDA 1998, s 51 (see **Chapter 7**).

If the adult is sent for trial to the Crown Court, the magistrates must now turn their attention to the juvenile. Under CDA 1998, s 51, if the adult magistrates' court sends an adult for trial to the Crown Court for an indictable offence, then it may also send a child or young person to the Crown Court for trial if they are jointly charged with the same indictable offence (or one which is related to that indictable offence). The court must consider it to be *necessary in the interests of justice* to send the juvenile to the Crown Court for trial. The court can use this power either on the same occasion that it sends the adult for trial or if the juvenile appears on a later occasion; s 51(7). Where the magistrates' court uses this power, it may also send the juvenile for trial on any indictable or summary offence which appears to be related to the indictable offence. A summary offence must be either imprisonable or punishable with disqualification from driving to be caught by s 51.

Whether it is 'necessary' to send the juvenile to Crown Court for trial must be decided on a case-by-case basis and by looking at the individual juvenile defendant in that case. See the CPS website for further guidance on this; also the *Criminal Practice Directions* at Part I 3G. Factors to consider include likely sentence for the juvenile and the respective ages and roles of the adult and juvenile. Prior to taking this step, though, the court will need to work through 'plea before venue' for the juvenile; see **6.3.3** and MCA 1980, s 24A. If the juvenile indicates a guilty plea to the indictable offence, then he will not face trial on it, of course.

Where the juvenile is sent for trial on an indictable offence, using CDA 1998, s 51A, the court may also send him or her to the Crown Court for trial for any other offence (whether triable either way or summary) which appears to the court to be 'related' to the indictable-only offence and, in the case of a related summary offence, is punishable with imprisonment or disqualification from driving.

6.4.2 Crown Court

Trial of juveniles in the Crown Court ought to follow the same basic pattern as the trial of any adult accused (see **Chapter 11**). However, the courts have recognised over recent years that different principles may need to be considered when a juvenile is tried in the Crown Court. This came to a head with the judgment of the European Court of Human Rights in *T v UK* (2000) 30 EHRR 121, the appeal by Robert Thompson and Jon Venables in connection with their murder trial at Preston Crown Court (see further at **6.4.3**). The European Court found that the trial had been defective in many respects. As a result, a Practice Direction was published, setting out guidelines for the trial by jury of juvenile defendants. See now the *Criminal Practice Directions*, Part I 3G.7 onwards.

In particular, it will be desirable:

- for all participants to be on the same (or almost the same) level in the courtroom;
- for the vulnerable defendant to be free to sit with family members or others in a supporting role, whilst being able to communicate easily with his or her lawyer(s);
- to explain to the vulnerable defendant at the outset what is about to take place, in terms he or she can understand, and in the Crown Court to explain the role of the jury;
- to operate a timetable which takes account of any inability to concentrate. 'Frequent and regular breaks will often be appropriate';
- to use simple, clear language to aid understanding;
- not to wear robes and wigs (both lawyers and the judge) unless there is some good reason to do so.

6.4.3 Reporting restrictions in the adult courts

The general principle here is that the media can report court proceedings unless ordered not to. Under the YJCEA 1999, s 45 any criminal court may direct that no matter relating to any person concerned in the proceedings shall, whilst they are under the age of 18, be included in any publication if it is likely to lead to public identification of him as a person concerned in those proceedings. 'Publication' has a broad definition, see YJCEA 1999, s 63 and **6.3.2.4.**

One example of the Crown Court using this type of order (under previous legislation) was at the murder trial at Preston Crown Court of Robert Thompson and Jon Venables in November 1993. The victim was a toddler, James Bulger, who had been abducted, and the case had attracted nationwide publicity. The trial judge ordered that the two juvenile accused be known simply as 'child A' and 'child B'. The fact that the identities of these children were published subsequently illustrates the fact that such a ban may be temporary. Typically, it will last at least until the end of the trial. If the verdict is not guilty, the juvenile is acquitted and the ban will continue in force. If the juvenile is convicted, the ban may be removed. It is thought that the public interest served by naming the juvenile offender may outweigh the consequences of publicity for him or her. However, the court should consider the age of the juvenile and the potential damage that he or she may suffer by being publicly identified as a criminal, before lifting the ban. Where there is a continuing ban on reporting, then that will usually end with the eighteenth birthday of the individual, whether they were the defendant, the victim or a witness; see, for example, *JC and RT v Central Criminal Court and Others* [2014] EWHC 1041(QB). The court may make an order for a lifetime extension of the ban, under YJCEA 1999, s 45A, but this will only apply to victims and witnesses.

Under the *Criminal Practice Directions*, Part I 3G.13, a court may limit the number of reporters allowed into the courtroom (and subject of course to any restrictions it has imposed under the CYPA 1933). Where it does so, arrangements may need to be made to relay the proceedings to another part of the building to enable the media to hear, and possibly see, the proceedings.

6.4.4 Public access to adult courts

Both the Crown Court and magistrates' courts operate their usual policy of being open to the general public when hearing a case, whether or not the case involves a juvenile (either as a witness or defendant). These courts have the power to order the public to be cleared from the courtroom if a juvenile witness is to testify in a trial involving offences of indecency or immorality. The possibility also exists for the court to order that a vulnerable witness may, in certain circumstances, give his or her evidence from behind a screen, or through a live television link, or in the form of a pre-recorded video. Under the *Criminal Practice Directions*, Part I 3G.13, the court may decide to restrict the members of the public allowed into the courtroom in order to further the overriding principle, namely 'to assist a vulnerable defendant to understand and participate in [the] proceedings'. It may be sensible to allow entry only to people with an immediate interest in the proceedings (eg family of victim).

6.5 Young adults

6.5.1 Defendants aged 18 or over at the start of proceedings

The youth court has no jurisdiction over such defendants. If a defendant was aged under 18 when charged with an offence, but is 18 when the case first comes to court, he or she should appear in the adult magistrates' court. Parents will usually be adults; they may be charged with offences such as not sending their child to school. This will be a matter for an adult magistrates' court to hear and to determine the appropriate steps to take to ensure the well-being of the juvenile.

6.5.2 Defendants who reach their eighteenth birthday after their case has begun in the youth court

This situation is governed by the CDA 1998, s 47(1)–(4). This provides a youth court with the discretionary power to remit a defendant to an adult magistrates' court for trial. The power is exercisable if the defendant, having appeared initially before the youth court as a juvenile, subsequently has his or her eighteenth birthday before the start of the trial.

The defendant has no right of appeal against a decision to remit. The adult magistrates' court may proceed as if all previous proceedings relating to the offence had taken place in that court. The intention behind s 47(1) appears to be to enable the courts to deal with young people in the most appropriate way, taking into account their maturity, attitude and offending history.

The youth court has no power to remit a defendant to the Crown Court for trial or sentence simply because he or she is now aged 18 (the decision to commit for sentence does not depend upon D's age). Some defendants who are remitted to the adult magistrates' court will have been awaiting trial for an offence which, for an adult, is triable either way (see **4.1**). It is possible that when a 'remitted' ex-juvenile defendant appears in the adult magistrates' court, he will then have the opportunity to choose Crown Court trial if charged with an either-way offence, although case law on the subject prior to CDA 1998 is unhelpful. It is also possible that a remitted defendant will have only a brief stay in the adult magistrates' court. He or she may be charged with an offence which *must* be tried on indictment, in the case of an adult. That classification was inapplicable whilst the case was in the youth court. Now that the defendant is appearing in the adult magistrates' court, the magistrates should send the defendant to Crown Court for trial forthwith (and see CDA 1998, s 51).

If a defendant reaches the age of 18 before sentence is passed, he or she may be remitted to the adult magistrates' court for sentence (PCC(S)A 2000, s 9). Note that this is *not* a committal for sentence. One effect is to take the offender out of the detention and training order scheme, and make him or her eligible instead for detention in a young offender institution. Also, if the offence is triable either way, the offender may be remitted from the youth court into the adult magistrates' court and may then be committed to the Crown Court for sentence (pursuant to the PCC(S)A 2000, s 3). Alternatively, it appears that the youth court can decide to retain jurisdiction over the 18-year-old and sentence him or her as if still a juvenile (CYPA 1963, s 29).

The Court of Appeal has stated that, where a defendant crosses a relevant age threshold between the date of commission of an offence and the date of conviction, the starting point for the court's sentencing powers is the sentence which the defendant would have been likely to receive if sentenced at the date of commission. In practice, this will mean that a juvenile aged 15, who is not a persistent offender, should not receive a custodial sentence (whether a DTO or long-term detention under PCC(S)A 2000, s 91), if aged 14 at the time of the offence. Likewise, a defendant aged 17 at the time of the offence but 18 when sentenced may expect to receive a custodial sentence of no more than two years, as this is the maximum term DTO that could have been imposed. See *R v LM* [2002] EWCA Crim 3047; [2003] Crim LR 205; *R v Ghafoor (Imran)* [2003] 1 Cr App R (S) 84, respectively. *Ghafoor* was subsequently approved in *Britton* [2007] 1 Cr App R (S) 121 but in *R v Bowker* [2007] EWCA Crim 1608, the Court of Appeal restated that *Ghafoor* is a starting point only. It predates the CJA 2003. That Act set out the principles of sentencing (in s 142) and although those principles do not apply to offenders aged under 18 at the time of conviction, they will apply where the offender has his eighteenth birthday between committing the offence and being convicted of it. One example would be the need for deterrence in a case such as *Bowker* where there was violent disorder between two gangs of youths. The court considered the impact of Article 7 ECHR (no heavier penalty to be imposed than the one which was applicable at the time the offence was committed) but concluded that it was not constrained by Article 7 in any way—there was no change in the law here; all that changed was the penal regime to which the offender would be exposed as the result of his birthday. For a more recent example, see the 2011–12 case of Gary Dobson and David Norris who were convicted of murdering Stephen Lawrence nearly 20 years after the killing occurred. The trial judge noted that both defendants were juveniles at the date of the killing and the sentencing regime then in place was quite different as well (eg no statutory requirement to consider racial motivation as an aggravating factor). The sentences of imprisonment with minimum tariffs of 14 and 15 years reflected the situation more as it was in 1993 at the time of the murder than in 2012 when sentence was passed.

6.6 Alternatives to prosecution

6.6.1 Youth cautions

It has sometimes been suggested that juveniles may be damaged by contact with the criminal justice system. Consequently, a diversionary method was developed whereby a juvenile might be given a *caution*, instead of being prosecuted for an offence. The effect of a caution was believed to be less traumatic for the juvenile since no court appearance was involved. It might be considered that cautions were quite successful in nipping nascent criminal careers in the bud because statistics show that between 70 and 80 per cent of offenders who were cautioned did not re-offend within the next two years. However, there was also a small core of persistent juvenile offenders to whom a caution clearly meant nothing (3 per cent of young offenders were said to be responsible for 25 per cent of crimes, according to a Home Office report published in 1997, *Aspects of Crime Young Offenders 1995*).

In April 2013, a new system of youth cautions was introduced; see LASPO 2012, s 135. Section 135 inserts a new provision—s 66ZA—into the CDA 1998.

Under this provision:

(1) A constable may give a child or young person ("Y") a caution under this section (a "youth caution") if—

(a) the constable decides that there is sufficient evidence to charge Y with an offence,

(b) Y admits to the constable that Y committed the offence, and

(c) the constable does not consider that Y should be prosecuted or given a youth conditional caution in respect of the offence.

(2) A youth caution given to a person under the age of 17 must be given in the presence of an appropriate adult.

(3) If a constable gives a youth caution to a person, the constable must explain the matters referred to in subsection (4) in ordinary language to—

(a) that person, and

(b) where that person is under the age of 17, the appropriate adult.

(4) Those matters are—

(a) the effect of subsections (1) to (3) and (5) to (7) of section 66ZB, and

(b) any guidance issued under subsection (4) of that section.

It is therefore necessary to refer to s 66ZB as well:

66ZB Effect of youth cautions

(1) If a constable gives a youth caution to a person, the constable must as soon as practicable refer the person to a youth offending team.

(2) Subject to subsection (3), on a referral of a person under subsection (1), the youth offending team—

(a) must assess the person, and

(b) unless they consider it inappropriate to do so, must arrange for the person to participate in a rehabilitation programme.

(3) If the person has not previously been referred under subsection (1) and has not previously been given a youth conditional caution, the youth offending team—

(a) may assess the person, and

(b) may arrange for the person to participate in a rehabilitation programme.

(4) The Secretary of State must publish, in such manner as the Secretary of State considers appropriate, guidance as to—

(a) what should be included in a rehabilitation programme arranged for a person under subsection (2) or (3),

(b) the manner in which any failure by a person to participate in a programme is to be recorded, and

(c) the persons to whom any such failure must be notified.

(5) Subsection (6) applies if—

(a) a person who has received two or more youth cautions is convicted of an offence committed within two years beginning with the date of the last of those cautions, or

(b) a person who has received a youth conditional caution followed by a youth caution is convicted of an offence committed within two years beginning with the date of the youth caution.

(6) The court by or before which the person is convicted—

(a) must not make an order under section 12(1)(b) of the Powers of Criminal Courts (Sentencing) Act 2000 (conditional discharge) in respect of the offence unless it is of the opinion that there are exceptional circumstances relating to the offence or the person that justify it doing so, and

(b) where it does so, must state in open court that it is of that opinion and its reasons for that opinion.

(7) There may be cited in criminal proceedings—

(a) a youth caution given to a person, and

(b) a report on a failure by a person to participate in a rehabilitation programme arranged for the person under subsection (2) or (3), in the same circumstances as a conviction of the person may be cited.

(8) In this section "rehabilitation programme" means a programme with the purpose of rehabilitating participants and preventing them from reoffending.

The Explanatory Notes to LASPO 2102 point out that the circumstances in which a police officer can give a youth caution (or a youth conditional caution; see **6.6.2**) to a juvenile are essentially the same as those which applied to the previous Final Warning Scheme. The main difference between the two schemes on this issue is that reprimands and warnings could not have been used when the juvenile had previously been convicted of an offence or had received a youth conditional caution; use of a youth caution is not restricted in this way.

6.6.2 Youth conditional cautions

The Criminal Justice and Immigration Act 2008 extended the application of the conditional caution scheme from only adults (see **2.2.12.3**) to apply also to offenders aged 10–17. As with adults, a failure to comply with the conditions will render the individual liable for prosecution for the original offence. See the Crime and Disorder Act 1998, ss 66A–H (inserted by CJIA 2008, Sch 9). A youth conditional caution can be used even if the juvenile has previously been convicted of an offence, see s 66A. The conditions that can be attached are intended to achieve one or more of the following objectives:

(a) *facilitating the rehabilitation of the offender;*

(b) *ensuring that the offender makes reparation for the offence;*

(c) *punishing the offender,*

and they can include a financial penalty.

No caution other than a youth caution or youth conditional caution may be given to a child or young person; CDA 1998, s 66ZA(6). A youth conditional caution may be given by a police officer or a Crown Prosecution Service prosecutor (or other authorised persons); a police officer cannot use a youth conditional caution for an indictable-only offence unless the CPS confirms it.

7

Sending cases to the Crown Court

7.1 Background

The majority of cases which are dealt with in the Crown Court are dealt with initially by the magistrates' court. That being so, a mechanism of some sort is necessary to remove the matter from the jurisdiction of the magistrates into that of the Crown Court.

The Crime and Disorder Act 1998, s 51, establishes the procedure for making this transition. Section 51A addresses the position for juvenile defendants and was considered in **Chapter 6**. Initially, s 51 applied only to indictable-only offences, so that, for example, someone charged with murder would make a single appearance in the magistrates' court and be sent to the Crown Court for trial there and then. In 2012, the scope of s 51 was extended to deal with *all* indictable offences, by the CJA 2003, Sch 3; however, the principles and procedures that we have already covered in the manual—classification of offences, allocation proceedings, plea before venue—all still apply to those offences as appropriate (see **Chapter 4**). This is important to remember when looking at an offence which is triable either way. References to s 51 in this chapter are references to the CDA 1998, s 51 unless otherwise indicated.

In brief, the situation as regards moving cases to the Crown Court is:

(a) Indictable-only offences are simply and swiftly *sent* to the Crown Court under s 51. See **7.2.1**.

(b) In either-way offences where the defendant has indicated a not guilty plea and *either* the magistrates have decided that it is more suitable for him to be tried on indictment (MCA 1980, s 21) *or* the defendant wishes to be tried on indictment (MCA 1980, s 20(9)), the magistrates' court will then proceed under s 51 and *send* the offence to the Crown Court. See **7.2.2**.

(c) Serious fraud cases and violent or sexual cases involving child witnesses are *sent* to the Crown Court under CDA 1998, ss 51(2)(c) and 51B or 51C. See **7.4**.

(d) Other 'related' offences may also be *sent* for trial at the same hearing as the primary indictable offence is sent, or at a later hearing. So, other either-way offences and even summary offences may be sent for trial in certain circumstances under CDA 1998, s 51(3)(b).

7.2 Sending offences to the Crown Court for trial under CDA 1998, s 51

Section 51 provides as follows:

(1) Where an adult appears or is brought before a magistrates' court ("the court") charged with an offence and any of the conditions mentioned in subsection (2) below is satisfied, the court shall send him forthwith to the Crown Court for trial for the offence.

(2) Those conditions are—

(a) that the offence is an offence triable only on indictment other than one in respect of which notice has been given under section 51B or 51C below;

(b) that the offence is an either-way offence and the court is required under section 20(9)(b), 21, 23(4)(b) or (5) or 25(2D) of the Magistrates' Courts Act 1980 to proceed in relation to the offence in accordance with subsection (1) above;

(c) that notice is given to the court under section 51B or 51C below in respect of the offence.

(3) Where the court sends an adult for trial under subsection (1) above, it shall at the same time send him to the Crown Court for trial for any either-way or summary offence with which he is charged and which—

(a) (if it is an either-way offence) appears to the court to be related to the offence mentioned in subsection (1) above; or

(b) (if it is a summary offence) appears to the court to be related to the offence mentioned in subsection (1) above or to the either-way offence, and which fulfils the requisite condition (as defined in subsection (11) below).

(4) Where an adult who has been sent for trial under subsection (1) above subsequently appears or is brought before a magistrates' court charged with an either-way or summary offence which—

(a) appears to the court to be related to the offence mentioned in subsection (1) above; and

(b) (in the case of a summary offence) fulfils the requisite condition,

the court may send him forthwith to the Crown Court for trial for the either-way or summary offence.

(5) Where—

(a) the court sends an adult ("A") for trial under subsection (1) or (3) above;

(b) another adult appears or is brought before the court on the same or a subsequent occasion charged jointly with A with an either-way offence; and

(c) that offence appears to the court to be related to an offence for which A was sent for trial under subsection (1) or (3) above,

the court shall where it is the same occasion, and may where it is a subsequent occasion, send the other adult forthwith to the Crown Court for trial for the either-way offence.

(6) Where the court sends an adult for trial under subsection (5) above, it shall at the same time send him to the Crown Court for trial for any either-way or summary offence with which he is charged and which—

(a) (if it is an either-way offence) appears to the court to be related to the offence for which he is sent for trial; and

(b) (if it is a summary offence) appears to the court to be related to the offence for which he is sent for trial or to the either-way offence, and which fulfils the requisite condition.

(7) Where—

(a) the court sends an adult ("A") for trial under subsection (1), (3) or (5) above; and

(b) a child or young person appears or is brought before the court on the same or a subsequent occasion charged jointly with A with an indictable offence for which A is sent for trial

under subsection (1), (3) or (5) above, or an indictable offence which appears to the court to be related to that offence,

the court shall, if it considers it necessary in the interests of justice to do so, send the child or young person forthwith to the Crown Court for trial for the indictable offence.

(8) Where the court sends a child or young person for trial under subsection (7) above, it may at the same time send him to the Crown Court for trial for any indictable or summary offence with which he is charged and which—

(a) (if it is an indictable offence) appears to the court to be related to the offence for which he is sent for trial; and

(b) (if it is a summary offence) appears to the court to be related to the offence for which he is sent for trial or to the indictable offence, and which fulfils the requisite condition.

(9) Subsections (7) and (8) above are subject to sections 24A and 24B of the Magistrates' Courts Act 1980 (which provide for certain cases involving children and young persons to be tried summarily).

(10) The trial of the information charging any summary offence for which a person is sent for trial under this section shall be treated as if the court had adjourned it under section 10 of the 1980 Act and had not fixed the time and place for its resumption.

(11) A summary offence fulfils the requisite condition if it is punishable with imprisonment or involves obligatory or discretionary disqualification from driving.

(12) In the case of an adult charged with an offence—

(a) if the offence satisfies paragraph (c) of subsection (2) above, the offence shall be dealt with under subsection (1) above and not under any other provision of this section or section 51A below;

(b) subject to paragraph (a) above, if the offence is one in respect of which the court is required to, or would decide to, send the adult to the Crown Court under—

(i) subsection (5) above; or

(ii) subsection (6) of section 51A below,

the offence shall be dealt with under that subsection and not under any other provision of this section or section 51A below.

(13) The functions of a magistrates' court under this section, and its related functions under section 51D below, may be discharged by a single justice.

7.2.1 Sending indictable-only offences

Since 2001, all indictable-only offences are 'sent' to the Crown Court for trial, without spending any time in the magistrates' court other than the first hearing. This reduces delay in the criminal justice process and is consistent with the active management of the case that the Crown Court now has, through the Plea and Case Management Hearing. See, for example, the case of Ian Huntley, who was charged with the murder of Holly Wells and Jessica Chapman in Soham, Cambridgeshire. Huntley appeared in Peterborough Magistrates' Court for the first time, following charge, on 11 September 2002 and was immediately sent for trial to Peterborough Crown Court (although the case was subsequently moved to the Old Bailey). The trial was not held until November 2003.

Under s 51, where a defendant aged 18 or over appears before the magistrates' court charged with an offence which is triable only on indictment (an 'indictable-only' offence), he *must* be sent to the Crown Court for trial 'forthwith' (s 51(1) and (2)(a)).

7.2.1.1 Sending related offences for trial

In addition to sending the defendant for trial on the primary offence under s 51(1), if he is also charged with:

- a triable either-way offence that is related* to the indictable-only offence; or

- a summary offence that is related* to the indictable-only offence and which is punishable with imprisonment or disqualification from driving,

then the magistrates *must* also send him to Crown Court for trial on those charges (s 51(3)). If the defendant appears on a subsequent occasion in the magistrates' court, charged with an either-way or summary offence which appears to be related to the offence for which he was sent for trial, the magistrates *may* send him for trial on the either-way or summary offence; s 51(4).

7.2.1.2 Sending other defendants for trial

Other defendants who are adults

Where a defendant is sent for trial under s 51(1) and a second defendant appears together with him before the magistrates, and the two are jointly charged with a related either-way offence, then the magistrates *must* send the second defendant to Crown Court for trial on the either-way offence. If the two defendants appear in the magistrates' court on a later occasion, jointly charged with an either-way offence which seems to be related* to the offence which was previously sent for trial, then the magistrates *may* send the second defendant for trial on the either-way offence; see s 51(5). When the magistrates send a second defendant for trial under s 51(5), they must also send him for trial on any related* either-way, or summary offences with which he is then charged; s 51(6). As usual, the summary offence must be punishable with either imprisonment or disqualification from driving.

Other defendants who are juveniles

Where magistrates send an adult defendant for trial on an indictable offence under s 51(1), (3) or (5), and a juvenile defendant appears before the court, either on the same occasion or a subsequent one, jointly charged with that indictable offence or one which appears to be related* to it, then the magistrates shall send the juvenile for trial forthwith, if they consider it to be necessary in the interests of justice to do so; see s 51(7). When a juvenile is sent for trial under s 51(7), the magistrates *may* also send him for trial on any other related indictable offences or summary offences which appear to be related to any of the indictable offences; s 51(8).

*An either-way offence is 'related' to an indictable offence if they could be joined in the same indictment (s 51E(c); and see Criminal Procedure Rules (Crim PR), r 14.3(2)). A summary offence is 'related' to an indictable offence if it arises out of circumstances which are the same as, or are connected with, those giving rise to the indictable offence; s 51E(d).

Note: The magistrates have the power to send a juvenile defendant to Crown Court for trial forthwith, in certain circumstances, regardless of the involvement of an adult defendant. See CDA 1998, s 51A, and **Chapter 6**.

7.2.2 Sending either-way offences

As can be seen in s 51(2)(b), the magistrates shall send an either-way offence for Crown Court trial, where required to do so under various provisions in the MCA 1980. These are essentially:

- where an allocation hearing has resulted in the defendant not consenting to a summary trial;
- where an allocation hearing has resulted in the magistrates deciding that trial on indictment (ie in the Crown Court) appears more suitable;
- where an allocation hearing has resulted in the magistrates deciding that summary trial is more suitable, and the defendant has consented to summary trial *but* the prosecution has made a successful application under the MCA 1980, s 25(2) and (2D). This is an application that the offence be tried instead in the Crown Court. The application must be made before the summary trial begins and the court must deal with it before addressing any other issue or application relating to the summary trial. The magistrates may only grant the application where they are satisfied that the sentence which a magistrates' court would have the power to impose for the offence would be

inadequate. If the defendant is charged with a series of offences of the same or a similar character, then the magistrates should only allow the application if satisfied that the maximum aggregate sentence that they would have the power to impose for the series of offences would be inadequate (s 25(2B)). One may consider that such an application should succeed rarely, since the magistrates would have considered the adequacy of their sentencing powers when making their initial decision on allocation (see Crim PR, r 9.10(2)(e)(i)).

For detail on allocation proceedings, see **4.2**.

Where the magistrates are required to send the either-way offence to Crown Court for trial under s 51, then all of the ancillary provisions concerning sending other related offences and other defendants to Crown Court also apply (see **7.2.1.1** and **7.2.1.2**).

7.2.3 Ancillary decisions

When the magistrates send an offence(s) to the Crown Court for trial, several other decisions may need to be made.

7.2.3.1 Bail

Where a defendant has made a fully argued bail application but has been refused bail in the proceedings and is therefore remanded in custody, he cannot re-apply unless he can show a change of circumstances (see **3.10**). The mere fact that the case has been sent for trial is not in itself a change of circumstances.

7.2.3.2 Disclosure

The prosecution must disclose 'unused' material in its possession, as soon as is reasonably practicable after the prosecution evidence is served on the defendant (Crim PR, r 22).

7.2.3.3 Reporting restrictions

Proceedings will usually take place in open court but there are restrictions on what may be reported in the media, so that any potential juror is not improperly influenced. Under the CDA 1998, s 52A(7), the following details may be reported:

(a) the identity of the court and the names of the justices;

(b) the name, age, home address and occupation of the accused;

(c) the offence or offences, or a summary of them, with which the accused is or are charged;

(d) the names of the legal representatives engaged in the proceedings;

(e) in a serious or complex fraud case, any relevant business information including the name and address of any business in which he was involved at a relevant time;

(f) where the proceedings are adjourned, the date and place to which they are adjourned;

(g) any arrangements as to bail;

(h) whether representation was provided to the accused or any of the accused under Part 1 of LASPO 2012 (ie funded by the Legal Aid Agency).

Reporting restrictions are for the protection of the accused, but they can be removed where the court considers this to be in the interests of justice (or in a case where there is just a single accused, he does not object to their removal). It has previously been said to be unusual, however, to remove restrictions where several defendants are not unanimous in wanting them removed: *R v Wirral District Magistrate, ex p Meikle* [1991] COD 2, DC.

Breach of reporting restrictions is a summary offence: CDA 1998, s 52B(2). Proceedings for breach cannot be instituted other than by or with the consent of the Attorney-General.

Under Crim PR, r 9.2(2), the court may use any power it has to withhold information from the public or to hold the hearing in private.

7.3 Procedure when sending a charge to the Crown Court under s 51

See generally Crim PR, Part 9. Where the court deals with a defendant on the same occasion with more than one offence, under r 9.2(5) it must do so in the following sequence:

1. Any offence where a notice has been served by the prosecution requiring Crown Court trial (serious fraud or certain violent or sexual offences involving a child witness).
2. Any offence which must be sent, without allocation, for trial.
3. Any offence which may be sent, without allocation, for trial.
4. Any offence which must go through an allocation hearing.

The defendant who is charged with an indictable-only offence will not be entitled to have advance disclosure of the prosecution case prior to his appearance in the magistrates' court, since advance disclosure is to assist him in making an appropriate mode of trial decision, and he is not going to make one here (see Crim PR, r 9.15; also r 21: 'details are served . . . after the case is sent for trial'). Nevertheless, the CPS's own legal guidance recommends that 's 51' defendants should be given advance disclosure prior to the first hearing in the magistrates' court 'to ensure equality of arms'. Advance disclosure is plainly a requirement where the defendant faces an either-way charge. See Crim PR, r 10 for advance disclosure.

The defendant will appear in the magistrates' court for the first hearing and, where appropriate, for the allocation hearing.

7.3.1 Crim PR, r 9.7: sending for Crown Court trial without allocation

9.7.—(1) This rule applies where a magistrates' court must, or can, send a defendant to the Crown Court for trial ***without first allocating the case*** *for trial there.* [emphasis added]

(2) The court must read the allegation of the offence to the defendant.

(3) The court must explain, in terms the defendant can understand (with help, if necessary)—

(a) the allegation, unless it is self-explanatory;

(b) that the offence is one for which the court, as appropriate—

(i) must send the defendant to the Crown Court for trial because the offence is one which can only be tried there, or

(ii) may send the defendant to the Crown Court for trial if the magistrates' court decides that the offence is related to one already sent for trial there;

(c) that reporting restrictions apply, which the defendant may ask the court to vary or remove.

(4) In the following sequence, the court must then—

(a) invite the prosecutor to—

(i) identify the court's power to send the defendant to the Crown Court for trial for the offence, and

(ii) make representations about any ancillary matters, including bail and directions for the management of the case in the Crown Court;

(b) invite the defendant to make representations about—

(i) the court's power to send the defendant to the Crown Court, and

(ii) any ancillary matters; and

(c) decide whether or not to send the defendant to the Crown Court for trial.

(5) If the court sends the defendant to the Crown Court for trial, it must—

(a) ask whether the defendant intends to plead guilty in the Crown Court and—

(i) if the answer is 'yes', make arrangements for the Crown Court to take the defendant's plea as soon as possible, or

(ii) *if the defendant does not answer, or the answer is 'no', make arrangements for a case management hearing in the Crown Court; and*

(b) *give any other ancillary directions.*

7.3.2 Crim PR, r 9.14: sending for Crown Court trial following allocation

If the case is one which has required an allocation hearing then, once the decision has been made to send the offence for Crown Court trial, Crim PR, r 9.14 states that:

Allocation and sending for Crown Court trial

9.14.—(1) This rule applies where—

(a) *under rule 9.10 or rule 9.13, the court allocates the case to the Crown Court for trial;*

(b) *under rule 9.11, the defendant does not agree to trial in a magistrates' court; or*

(c) *under rule 9.12, the court grants the prosecutor's application for Crown Court trial.*

(2) *In the following sequence, the court must—*

(a) *invite the prosecutor to make representations about any ancillary matters, including bail and directions for the management of the case in the Crown Court;*

(b) *invite the defendant to make any such representations; and*

(c) *exercise its powers to—*

(i) *send the defendant to the Crown Court for trial, and*

(ii) *give any ancillary directions.*

7.3.3 Crown Court location

The magistrates' court issues a notice under s 51D, specifying the location of the Crown Court where the defendant is to be tried. In practice, this is the most local court and the parties rarely apply for the case to be heard elsewhere, though such an application is possible in appropriate circumstances.

Section 51D(1) provides as follows:

(1) The court shall specify in a notice—

(a) *the offence or offences for which a person sent for trial under section 51 or 51A above: and*

(b) *the place at which he is to be tried . . .*

(4) where the court selects the place of trial . . . it shall have regard to—

(a) *the convenience of the defence, the prosecution and the witnesses;*

(b) *the desirability of expediting the trial; and*

(c) *any directions given by or on behalf of the Lord Chief Justice . . .*

Crim PR, r 9.3(3) adds to these considerations how soon a suitable courtoom will be available.

7.3.4 First hearing at Crown Court following allocation

There are no rules as to when the first appearance at the Crown Court should take place, though both the magistrates' court and the Crown Court have the power to order a preliminary hearing when one is considered necessary. The *Criminal Practice Directions,* Part I 3A provide that a plea and case management hearing should be held within 13 weeks of the defendant being sent for trial if he is in custody, and within 16 weeks if he is not. However, this PCMH may be pre-empted by one or other of two other hearings—the early guilty plea hearing and the preliminary hearing.

Either the magistrates or the Crown Court may order an *early guilty plea hearing,* where such a plea is anticipated. The aim is to allow the Crown Court to deal with the case promptly.

Sentence is likely to be passed at the hearing and the parties should prepare accordingly; for example, obtaining any necessary reports. See *Criminal Practice Directions*, Part I 3A.6–8. If no early guilty plea hearing is ordered, then a *preliminary hearing* may be ordered if:

- there are case management issues which make such a hearing desirable; or
- the trial is likely to last for more than four weeks; or
- an early trial date should be set; or
- the accused is a child or young person.

It is preferable for a preliminary hearing to be listed in the Crown Court for between 14 and 21 days after the date on which it was sent for trial. See *Criminal Practice Directions*, Part I 3A.9.

7.3.5 Applications for dismissal of charge

The defendant may apply to the Crown Court for the case to be dismissed at any time after the date upon which he or she has been served with the prosecution documents and before his arraignment, under the CDA 1998, Sch 3, para (2)(1). The judge in the Crown Court must dismiss any charge, or quash any count if the indictment has already been preferred, if it appears to the judge that the evidence against the defendant would not be sufficient for him to be properly convicted. The application can be made in writing or orally, but in the latter situation no oral evidence will be given at the hearing.

There is no power to challenge the judge's decision by way of judicial review, because it is a matter relating to trial on indictment: *R (Snelgrove) v Woolwich Crown Court* [2005] 1 WLR 3223. If the application is successful, the prosecution may decide to commence proceedings again, with an application for a voluntary bill of indictment (see 7.5).

7.4 Sending offences to Crown Court following a notice

The relevant provisions here are CDA 1998, s 51B and s 51C. Section 51B applies to indictable serious or complex fraud cases; s 51C applies to certain violent or sexual offences involving child witnesses. Under both provisions, once proper notice is given, the magistrates' court must send the case to the Crown Court for trial forthwith; s 51(2).

7.4.1 Serious fraud

Under CDA 1998, s 51B, at any time before a summary trial begins a notice may be given to the magistrates' court which has jurisdiction over the charge. Only certain authorities are designated to give a notice under s 51B, of which the most obvious are the DPP or the Director of the Serious Fraud Office. The notice may be given whenever a defendant is charged with an indictable offence and there is:

(a) sufficient evidence for him to be committed for trial; and

(b) the evidence reveals a case of fraud of such seriousness or complexity that it is appropriate that the management of the case should be taken over by the Crown Court without delay.

Once the notice is given, the magistrates' powers are restricted to decisions relating to bail, legal representation and witness orders.

The defendant may apply to the Crown Court to dismiss the charge, as outlined earlier.

7.4.2 Child witnesses

Similar provisions relate to cases of violence and sexual offences involving child witnesses under CDA 1998, s 51C. For these purposes, a 'child' is either anyone under the age of 17 or someone whose account was recorded when they were aged under 17 with the aim of using the recording as his evidence-in-chief at the trial; s 51C(7).

The decision to use a notice is taken by the DPP who must be satisfied, under s 51C(1):

(a) that the evidence of the offence would be sufficient for the person charged to be put on trial for the offence;

(b) that a child would be called as a witness at the trial; and

(c) that, for the purpose of avoiding any prejudice to the welfare of the child, the case should be taken over and proceeded with without delay by the Crown Court.

The defendant may apply to the Crown Court to dismiss the charge, as outlined earlier.

7.5 Voluntary bills of indictment

Under the Administration of Justice (Miscellaneous Provisions) Act 1933, s 2, as amended by the CJA 2003, a High Court judge has the power to prefer a voluntary bill of indictment, that is, he or she may order that the accused be tried on indictment. In making such an order, the case is not sent to the Crown Court in the usual way.

The preferment of a voluntary bill is exceptional, and consent to the preferment should only be given where 'good reason to depart from the normal procedure is clearly shown, and only where the interests of justice, rather than considerations of administrative convenience, require it': *Criminal Practice Directions*, Part II 14B.

Traditionally, voluntary bills have been sought in two situations:

(a) Where committal proceedings have resulted in the discharge of an accused. These proceedings no longer exist, but an analogous situation would be where a Crown Court judge has dismissed the charge, following an application by the defendant under CDA 1998, Sch 3, para 2(1); see **7.3.5**.

(b) Where the prosecution case is that an offence was committed jointly by two or more persons, and at least one of them has already been sent for trial, and an indictment signed against him or her. In these circumstances, the prosecution will wish to try all the accused together, but may only do so if a second indictment is signed against all the accused. A voluntary bill of indictment will achieve the desired result.

Under Part II 14B.2 of the *Criminal Practice Directions*, applications for a voluntary bill must not only comply with the 1933 Act and the Indictments (Procedure) Rules 1971, but must also be accompanied by:

(a) a copy of any charges on which the defendant has been sent for trial;

(b) a copy of any existing indictment which has been preferred in consequence of his sending;

(c) a summary of the evidence or other document which:

  (i) identifies the counts in the proposed indictment on which he has been sent for trial (or which are substantially the same as charges on which he has been so sent); and

  (ii) in relation to each other count in the proposed indictment, identifies the pages in the accompanying statements and exhibits where the essential evidence said to support that count is to be found;

(d) marginal markings of the relevant passages on the pages of the statements and exhibits identified under (c)(ii) above.

The judge will consider the application and any written submission from the defendant and may seek amplification if necessary. He or she may invite oral submissions from either party or accede to a request for the opportunity to make such oral submissions if he or she considers it necessary or desirable in order to make a sound and fair decision. Any such oral submission should be made on notice to the other party (Part II 14B.8 of the *Criminal Practice Directions*).

There is no requirement under either the 1933 Act or the 1971 Rules that a defendant be notified of the application for a voluntary bill. Paragraph IV.35.5 of the Practice Direction, however, gives guidance to prosecutors on procedures to be adopted in seeking judicial consent, directing prosecutors:

(a) on the making of the application, to notify the defendant of this;

(b) at about the same time, to serve on the defendant a copy of all the documents delivered to the judge;

(c) to inform the defendant of his or her right to make written submissions to the judge within nine working days of giving the notice.

These procedures should be followed unless there are good reasons for not doing so, in which case the prosecutor must inform the judge of this situation, and ask for leave to dispense with all or any of them. The judge will only give leave if good grounds are shown.

A High Court judge's decision to issue a voluntary bill is not subject to judicial review, according to *R v Manchester Crown Court, ex p Williams* (1990) 154 JP 589. However, the decision of a prosecutor to seek a voluntary bill of indictment may be challenged: *R v IRC, ex p Dhesi, The Independent,* 14 August 1995. The nature of the voluntary bill procedure is that the application is made *in the absence of the defendant* (or, as was said in *Dhesi*—'behind the defendant's back') and therefore runs against the normal principles of justice, hence the High Court's powers of judicial review could be exercised in the case of alleged bad faith or personal malice on the part of the prosecutor. The *Criminal Practice Directions* indicate that it is good practice for a prosecutor to give notice to a defendant that an application has been made and that the defendant has nine working days in which to make written submissions to the judge. This practice may be dispensed with if there are good grounds to do so. The *Criminal Practice Directions* says, at Part II 14B.4, that:

> The preferment of a voluntary bill is an exceptional procedure. Consent should only be granted where good reason to depart from the normal procedure is clearly shown and only where the interests of justice, rather than considerations of administrative convenience, require it.

Once the bill of indictment has been preferred, it is an indictment like any other, and capable of amendment under the Indictments Act 1915, s 5 (*R v Wells* (1995) 159 JP 243).

8

Appeals from decisions of magistrates

There are three ways of appealing against the decision of the magistrates:

- appeal to the Crown Court;
- appeal to the High Court by way of case stated;
- application to the High Court for judicial review.

Students should also be aware of the power of the magistrates to rectify mistakes under the Magistrates' Courts Act 1980 (MCA), s 142, discussed at **5.4**. This is often a quick and simple way to correct an error.

8.1 Appeal to the Crown Court

8.1.1 Who can appeal

The defendant may appeal against conviction and/or sentence to the Crown Court. If the defendant has pleaded guilty, he or she may only appeal against sentence (MCA 1980, s 108) unless he or she can argue that the plea was equivocal (see **5.2.4.2**).

Note that the Criminal Cases Review Commission can refer a conviction by the magistrates' court to the Crown Court (Criminal Appeal Act 1995, s 11). Such a reference is treated as if it had been made by the convicted person under s 108, whether or not he or she pleaded guilty. See also Crim PR, Part 63.6.

8.1.2 Procedure for appealing

For appeals under the MCA 1980, s 108, see generally the Criminal Procedure Rules, Part 63.

(a) An appeal notice is given in writing to the magistrates' court officer and to the prosecution within 21 days of sentence. The 21 days run from the date of sentence, even if the appeal is against conviction and the appellant was convicted and sentenced on different days (*unless* sentence was formally deferred; see Crim PR, r 63.2(2)(b)(i)). This time limit may be extended, on application; Crim PR, r 63.9.

(b) The appeal notice must summarise the issues (see Crim PR, r 63.3(b)). In addition, in an appeal against conviction, the appellant must identify those prosecution witnesses he or she will want to question if they are called to give oral evidence, saying how long the summary trial lasted and how long the appeal is likely to last. If the appellant has already asked the magistrates to reconsider the case under s 142, that also should be stated. It has been said that the magistrates' court office is under no duty to provide the appellant with any notes of evidence, but any defence request for these should be viewed sympathetically: *R v Clerk to the Highbury Justices, ex p Hussein* [1986] 1 WLR 1266. Crim PR, r 63(4)(c) also states that the magistrates' court officer must 'provide the Crown Court with any document, object or information' for which the Crown Court asks. It is not necessary to provide the Crown Court with the reasons given by the magistrates for their decision on an appeal against conviction as the matter is heard anew; similarly on an appeal against sentence, the Crown Court will not want to know the reasons given for imposing the original sentence but they will want to know the magistrates' reasons and findings of fact that led to the conviction; *Criminal Practice Directions*, Part X 63A. The magistrates' court must also forward to the Crown Court copies of any reports received by the magistrates for the purpose of sentencing in the case.

(c) All documents are forwarded to the Crown Court, where the listing officer will place the appeal on the list, and send notice of the time and place to the appellant, the prosecution and the magistrates' court.

(d) The appellant may appeal out of time by applying for leave in writing from the Crown Court (Crim PR, r 63.2(3) and r 63.9). Leave is not otherwise required.

8.1.3 Bail

If the appellant is in custody and gives notice of appeal, the magistrates may grant him or her bail, with a duty to appear at the hearing of the appeal (MCA 1980, s 113). If bail is refused, or unacceptable conditions are imposed, the appellant may appeal against that decision to the Crown Court, under the Senior Courts Act 1981 (SCA), s 81. (See further **3.11.**)

The appellant does not have a right to bail under BA 1976, s 4, because he is now convicted, but bail may well be granted if the sentence is likely to have been served before the appeal is heard.

8.1.4 The hearing

At the hearing, the judge (usually a circuit judge or recorder) sits with lay magistrates (usually two but maximum four) who have not been concerned with the case in the magistrates' court; Crim PR, r 63.10. If the appeal is from the youth court, the magistrates should be drawn from the youth court bench and there should be a man and a woman, if possible. If only one magistrate is available (or on a youth court appeal, only magistrates of the same sex are available), the court may proceed nevertheless, if the judge decides that to wait until the court can be properly composed would cause unreasonable delay.

Where the appeal is an appeal against conviction, the hearing itself is a complete re-hearing of the whole case. It is not a review of what happened before the magistrates. Thus, either party may call evidence not called before the magistrates, or omit evidence that was called before the magistrates.

The lay magistrates must accept the law from the judge, but the decision on the appeal itself is a majority decision. Thus, the lay magistrates may outvote the judge. However, if an evenly numbered court is equally divided, the judge has a casting vote.

A Crown Court judge giving the decision of the court must give reasons for its decision, and a refusal to do so might amount to a breach of natural justice. The reasoning required would depend on the circumstances of each case, but should be enough to demonstrate that the court had identified the main contentious issues, and how it had resolved them. An appellant is entitled to know the basis upon which the prosecution case has been accepted by the court. See *R v Harrow Crown Court, ex p Dave* [1994] 1 WLR 98, DC.

Reasons should be given whether the Crown Court accepts or rejects the appeal (*R v Inner London Crown Court, ex p London Borough of Lambeth Council* [2000] Crim LR 303). Failure to do so will usually, but not necessarily, invalidate the decision of the Crown Court. The decision will not be invalidated, for example, if the reasons are obvious: *R v Kingston Crown Court, ex p Bell* (2000) 164 JP 633.

The reasons should enable the appellant: (a) to see the nature of the criminality found to exist by the court; and (b) to consider properly whether there are grounds for a further appeal to the Divisional Court by way of case stated (*R v Snaresbrook Crown Court, ex p Input Management Ltd* (1999) 163 JP 533).

Note: In hearing an appeal, the judge should not act as prosecutor in the absence of the prosecution advocate. This amounts to a procedural irregularity, as the judge is not then sufficiently removed from the proceedings to meet the requirement of justice (*R v Wood Green Crown Court, ex p Taylor* [1995] Crim LR 879).

8.1.5 Appeal against sentence

The defendant may appeal against 'any order made on conviction by a magistrates' court': s 108(3).

The appropriate court to deal with an appeal against sentence is normally the Crown Court, where the case may be appealed by way of a re-hearing. Thus, at the hearing of the appeal, the Crown Court will approach the determination of sentence anew. It will need to be appraised of the facts of the case (unless it has also heard an appeal against conviction in the case), consider any relevant reports and hear a defence plea in mitigation.

8.1.6 Powers of the Crown Court

Under the SCA 1981, s 48, the Crown Court may:

(a) Confirm, reverse or vary *any* part of the decision appealed against. Thus, even though the defendant may have appealed against only a part of the magistrates' decision, the Crown Court is not restricted to reviewing just that part, but may review the whole decision.

(b) Remit the case to the magistrates with its opinion. In cases where it thinks the plea was equivocal, this will usually be a direction to the magistrates to enter a plea of not guilty and hold a trial.

(c) Make any such order as it thinks just. This includes a power to increase sentence up to the maximum sentence which was available to the magistrates. This power is seldom exercised, but its existence is a useful means of discouraging frivolous appeals, bearing in mind that usually no leave to appeal is required.

(d) Where the appeal is unsuccessful, the court may order that the appellant pay the costs of the Crown: Prosecution of Offences Act 1985, s 18(1)(b).

8.2 Appeals to the High Court by way of case stated

Under the MCA 1980, s 111(1):

Any person who was a party to any proceeding before a magistrates' court or is aggrieved by the conviction, order, determination or other proceeding of the court may question the proceeding on the ground that it is wrong in law or in excess of jurisdiction by applying to the justices to state a case for the opinion of the High Court on the question of law or jurisdiction involved . . .

Appeals by way of case stated go to the Administrative Court in the High Court (formerly the Divisional Court of the Queen's Bench Division). The procedure is set down in the Criminal Procedure Rules, Part 64; see also the Civil Procedure Rules, Part 52 and PD 52E.

8.2.1 Subsidiary points on appeals by way of case stated

(a) The magistrates have no power to state a case until they have reached a *final* determination on the matter. Thus, they have no power to state a case during the hearing and must wait until the case is at an end. So, for example, it is not an appropriate method of challenging a committal for sentence because the sentence has not yet been determined and so the case is still 'live'. See generally *Streames v Copping* [1985] QB 920, *Loade v DPP* [1990] 1 QB 1052 and *Gillian v DPP* [2007] EWHC 380 (Admin).

(b) Both the defence and the prosecution have the right to apply for a case to be stated (and so may a third party whose legal rights have been affected by the court's decision). This means that effectively the prosecution can appeal against a defendant's acquittal and, if they are successful, the acquittal will be reversed.

(c) The appellant must show that the decision of the magistrates was either wrong in law or in excess of jurisdiction. Questions raised will therefore be questions of jurisdiction, admissibility of evidence or the like. If the appeal is based on the *facts* of the case, then generally speaking it will be refused (*Oladimeji v DPP* [2006] EWHC 1199 (Admin)). The only exceptions are where the magistrates have made a finding of fact which is totally unsupported by the evidence, or the finding of fact is one which no reasonable tribunal, properly directing itself, could have reached. In either of these two situations, the High Court may treat it as an error of law. In *Oladimeji*, Keene LJ said:

> the function of this court . . . is to determine whether the decision of the justices is 'wrong in law or is in excess of jurisdiction'. . . This court is consequently only concerned with the state of the evidence in so far as it is said that the findings of fact made by them demonstrate an error of law or jurisdiction. The justices should decline to pose questions for this court unless those questions are ones of law . . . The weight to be attached to particular pieces of evidence is a matter for the justices. Only if no reasonable bench could have reached the finding in question will that finding produce an error of law . . . If a defendant believes that the justices have arrived at a finding for which there was evidence but at which he contends they should not have arrived (for example because it was against the weight of the evidence) his remedy lies in an appeal to the Crown Court.

As to where the magistrates are entitled to draw inferences from facts, see *Plowden v DPP* [1991] Crim LR 850.

Where the applicant seeks to raise new matters of fact and law in his appeal by way of case stated, which were not included in the case stated by the justices, the appeal will be dismissed: *Campbell v DPP* [2003] All ER (D) 412.

Appeal by case stated (or judicial review) is not appropriate unless there are clear and substantial reasons for believing that disposal in such a way is in the interests of the defendant. See *Allen v West Yorkshire Probation Service Community Service Organisation* [2001] EWHC Admin 2.

Sentences are rarely wrong in law or in excess of jurisdiction and so they are rarely challenged by way of case stated. Remember that counsel is under a duty to advise the court if it errs in passing sentence; see for example, the obligation imposed on prosecuting counsel by the Farquharson Guidelines, 6.9. So a mistake in sentencing should not be made or, if one is made, it should be spotted, brought to the court's attention swiftly and corrected. Nevertheless, where a sentence is technically correct but falls outside the magistrates' normal discretionary powers, the High Court may be prepared to treat it as being imposed in excess of jurisdiction.

(d) Once an application to state a case to the High Court is made, the right to appeal to the Crown Court is lost (MCA 1980, s 111(4)).

(e) If the same point arises in several cases on the same day, the appellants may apply for a collective case to be stated. For example, the magistrates have clearly misunderstood the test for attaching conditions to bail and have imposed the same inappropriate conditions on every defendant brought before them.

8.2.2 Procedure

(a) The application must be made in writing within 21 days of the decision which is the subject of the appeal, and it should state the point of law upon which the opinion of the High Court is sought.

(b) The application is sent to a court officer of the convicting magistrates' court, and to every other party.

(c) The magistrates may refuse to state a case (MCA 1980, s 111(5)), but this decision is itself reviewable by the High Court on an application for judicial review. For an example of such an application, see *R v Huntingdon Magistrates' Court, ex p Percy* [1994] COD 323. Magistrates may legitimately refuse to state a case in two situations:

(i) They may refuse to state the case if they consider that the application is frivolous. The test is whether the application raises an arguable point of law (*R v North*

West Suffolk (Mildenhall) Magistrates' Court, ex p Forest Heath DC (1997) 161 JP 401 and *R (on the application of Robertson) v South Western Magistrates' Court* [2003] EWHC 63 (Admin)). The magistrates must give the appellant a certificate to that effect, enabling him or her to seek judicial review of their decision not to state a case.

(ii) They may refuse to state the case unless the appellant enters into a recognisance to prosecute the appeal without delay, and to pay such costs as the High Court may award. Such a condition would be imposed if the magistrates think the appellant is likely to abandon the appeal halfway through, having incurred expense and wasted the court's time.

Where the magistrates refuse to state a case, the would-be appellant should immediately apply for permission to seek judicial review. If the magistrates have already given a reasoned judgment, the single judge in the Administrative Court should give permission for judicial review of the original order, assuming there is an arguable point, thus avoiding the need for an appeal by case stated entirely. In any event, the Administrative Court will adopt the shortest, least expensive and swiftest course of action. The same principles apply to the Crown Court when it refuses to state a case. See generally *R v Blackfriars Crown Court, ex p Sunworld Ltd* [2000] 1 WLR 2102.

(d) The statement itself is usually drafted by the magistrates' court officer, but exceptionally it may be drafted by the magistrates themselves (this is more likely to happen if the case was heard by a district judge). If the parties at the original trial were represented by advocates, the court may invite the advocates to submit a first draft indicating any areas of disagreement, as long as, by the time the case is stated, it is in satisfactory form: *Vehicle and Operator Services Agency v George Jenkins Transport Ltd and Others* [2003] EWHC 2879 (Admin).

(e) The draft statement is submitted to the parties for their comments, which must be lodged with the magistrates' court within 21 days. The statement may be adjusted in response. It is a part of the procedure for stating a case that if a properly drafted question is to be altered, the party which framed the original question must be allowed to comment on the changes (*Waldie v DPP* (1995) 159 JP 514).

Where it is adjusted, the Administrative Court will consider only the final statement, and not any earlier variations.

(f) The contents of the statement are:

(i) The names of the parties and of the court.

(ii) The charges.

(iii) The findings of fact, but not the evidence upon which those findings were made, unless the appellant's argument is that, on that evidence, the magistrates could not have come to the conclusion that they did (see *Crompton and Crompton v North Tyneside Metropolitan Borough Council* [1991] COD 52). And see again *Oladimeji v DPP* [2006] EWHC 1199 (Admin).

(iv) The points of law involved, and the authorities relied on. This should include the arguments heard by the justices (*DPP v Kirk* [1993] COD 99).

(v) The decision of the magistrates.

(vi) A request for the opinion of the High Court, posing the question(s) which the appellant wishes the High Court to answer.

(g) Once the final draft is completed, the magistrates sign it and send it to the appellant.

(h) The appellant then has ten days in which to file the appellant's notice at the High Court, together with the case stated and a copy of the decision in respect of which the case has been stated, and a further four days to serve notice on the respondent. See Civil PR, PD 52 at paras 2.2 and 2.4.

Note: All the time limits set out above may be extended *except* the first period of 21 days for making the application, which is statutory and cannot be varied (see MCA 1980, s 111(2), *Michael v Gowland* [1977] 1 WLR 296 and *Reid v DPP* [1993] COD 111, DC, where 'pressure of work' on the part of the solicitor was insufficient reason for extending time).

8.2.3 Bail

Under the MCA 1980, s 113, the appellant may be granted bail pending the outcome of the hearing in the High Court. Bail will be granted on the basis that the appellant returns to the magistrates' court within ten days of the High Court judgment, unless the conviction is quashed.

8.2.4 The hearing

Under the SCA 1981, s 66(3), the court must consist of at least two judges, though there are usually three. The court acts entirely on the basis of the facts as set out in the case, and no new evidence is adduced: *Skipaway Ltd v Environment Agency* [2006] Env LR 41. The hearing therefore consists solely of legal argument by counsel.

If only two judges are sitting, and they cannot agree, the decision of the judge who agrees with the court below prevails, and thus the appeal will fail.

8.2.5 Powers of the High Court

Under the SCA 1981, s 28A, the High Court may affirm, reverse or vary the decision of the court below, make any other order it thinks fit or remit the case to the original court with its opinion. The High Court decision is enforced as if it were the decision of the court below. Thus, if the High Court thinks that an acquittal is incorrect, it can remit to the magistrates with a direction to convict and sentence. Generally speaking, the High Court does not deal with sentence itself, taking the view that it is not the appropriate forum. However, it may deal with sentence if it is obvious what the sentence should be.

The powers of the High Court include a power to order a re-hearing of the case before the same or a different bench of justices whenever such a course is appropriate (see *Griffith v Jenkins* [1992] AC 76; *R v Farrand and Galland* [1989] Crim LR 573).

8.2.6 Case stated from the Crown Court

One may appeal by way of case stated to the High Court from the Crown Court on matters *not related* to a trial on indictment,. Thus, if the defendant has appealed to the Crown Court against conviction or has been committed to the Crown Court for sentence, either party may then appeal against the outcome, to the High Court by way of case stated, under the SCA 1981, s 28, on the basis that the final decision of the Crown Court was wrong in law or in excess of jurisdiction.

The procedure is much the same as for an appeal by case stated from the magistrates' court, with two main differences. The first is that it is usually the appellant who initially drafts the statement. The respondent also has the right to submit a draft. The judge, who was the judge at the hearing of the appeal or the committal, will read the drafts submitted to him and state a case on that basis. The second difference is that, whereas the initial time limit for seeking a case stated from the magistrates is fixed by statute, the time limit for initiating a case stated in the Crown Court may be extended before or after it has in fact expired: Crim PR, r 64.5.

For an example of the High Court hearing cases by way of case stated from the Crown Court, see *R (on the application of Westminster City Council) v Middlesex Crown Court* [2002] EWHC 1104 (Admin). The Law Commission has recommended the abolition of appeals by case stated from the Crown Court to the High Court; see its 2010 Report, No 324.

8.3 Application for judicial review

Judicial review is the method by which the High Court controls the activities of inferior tribunals, that is, magistrates' courts (and the Crown Court where the matter complained of does not relate to trial on indictment). The existence of a right of appeal to the Crown Court (MCA 1980, s 108) does not of itself preclude a person convicted by magistrates from seeking relief by way of judicial review where the complaint is of procedural impropriety, unfairness or bias.

Application for judicial review is made to the Queen's Bench Division of the High Court, specifically the Administrative Court (older case reports refer to the Divisional Court of the QBD).

The Court's permission to proceed is required whenever a claim is made for judicial review. Permission, however, should only be granted where the applicant has an apparently plausible complaint, and immaterial and minor deviations from the rules will not have this effect (*R v Hereford Magistrates' Court, ex p Rowlands* [1998] QB 110). In reaching this decision, the Divisional Court considered *R v Peterborough Justices, ex p Dowler* [1996] 2 Cr App R 561, which held that it was unnecessary to grant the defendant judicial review because, on the facts of the case, the procedural irregularity of which he complained could be rectified on appeal to the Crown Court. The court in *Ex p Rowlands* did not doubt the correctness of the decision in *Ex p Dowler* on the facts, but held that it was not authority for the proposition that parties complaining of procedural irregularity or unfairness in the magistrates' court should be denied permission to apply for judicial review. To hold otherwise would be to deprive a defendant of the right to a proper trial before the magistrates with a right of appeal to the Crown Court, and would emasculate the supervisory jurisdiction of the High Court over the decisions of the magistrates. See also *R (on the application of Stone) v SW Surrey Magistrates' Court* [2012] EWHC 642 (Admin).

Note that the right to apply to the Administrative Court for judicial review of a decision of the Crown Court on matters *not relating* to a trial on indictment includes the right to apply for review of a decision of the Crown Court after it has decided an appeal against a decision of the magistrates. See, for example, *R v Aylesbury Crown Court, ex p Lait* [1998] Crim LR 264. In *R (P) v Liverpool City Magistrates* (2006) 170 JP 453 the High Court held that judicial review was a more appropriate remedy where it was alleged that there had been unfairness in the way that the trial had been conducted. An appeal by way of case stated is more appropriate where it is alleged that the magistrates have made an error of law.

As with appeals by way of case stated, proceedings in the magistrates' court should usually be complete before an application for judicial review is made. Criminal trials should not be punctuated by applications to test rulings: *Hoar-Stevens v Richmond Magistrates' Court* [2003] EWHC 2660 (Admin). Exceptional cases may arise, however, perhaps where a party seeks a prohibiting order (see **8.3.1.3**): *R v North East Essex Magistrates* [2006] EWHC 3145 (Admin).

8.3.1 Prerogative orders

The High Court exercises its control by the use of prerogative orders, namely quashing, mandatory and prohibiting orders (previously *certiorari, mandamus* and prohibition).

8.3.1.1 Quashing orders

A quashing order has the effect of quashing the original decision, usually this is a conviction and only exceptionally an acquittal. In addition, the High Court may:

- remit the case to the court concerned with a direction to reconsider it and reach a decision in accordance with the finding of the High Court (SCA 1981, s 31(5)).
- substitute for an unlawful sentence one which the court had the power to pass (SCA 1981, s 43(1)).

It is usually said that a quashing order will be issued in three situations:

(a) There is an error on the face of the record. However in a magistrates' court, the record is brief, and in any event magistrates rarely give full reasons for their decisions. If the magistrates in fact do give reasons, or include them in any affidavit they are swearing for consideration of the High Court, the High Court will treat those reasons as part of the record.

(b) The court has acted in excess of jurisdiction. See, for example, *R v Tunbridge Wells Justices, ex p Tunbridge Wells Borough Council* (1996) 160 JP 574, where the justices adjourned the case, part heard, after a submission of no case to answer was made. The High Court set aside the decision to accept the submission, which was subsequently pronounced in open court by a different bench of magistrates, as *ultra vires or outside of the powers of the court.* See also *R v Parker and the Barnet Magistrates' Court, ex p DPP* (1994) 158 JP 1061. The High Court may also set aside a sentence if it is one which the magistrates have no power to pass, but such an error is rare. However, in very limited circumstances, the High Court will treat a sentence which is so harsh and oppressive that no reasonable tribunal could have passed it as being in excess of jurisdiction, and quash it accordingly, even though it was in fact within the court's powers (see *R v St Albans Crown Court, ex p Cinnamond* [1981] QB 480). But such a course is exceptional, and should only be followed when an appeal against sentence to the Crown Court has failed (*R v Battle Justices, ex p Shepherd* (1983) 5 Cr App R (S) 124). But see also on this point, *R v Bradford Justices, ex p Wilkinson* [1990] 1 WLR 692 and *R v Truro Crown Court, ex p Adair* [1997] COD 296. The appropriate test for interfering with sentence was set out in *Ex p Adair* as follows:

> It would perhaps seem more helpful to ask the question whether the sentence or order in question falls clearly outside the broad area of the lower court's sentencing discretion.

(c) Where the court acts in breach of the rules of natural justice. Any court is under a duty to act fairly, there being two aspects of this duty:

(i) No person may be a judge in his or her own cause. See, for example, *Dimes v Grand Junction Canal* (1852) 3 HLC 759 and *R v Altrincham Justices, ex p Pennington* [1975] 1 QB 549.

(ii) The court must hear both sides of the case. The rule will be relied on where there has been some procedural irregularity which has prejudiced the appellant. The test laid down in *R v Gough* [1993] AC 646, 'Was there a real danger that the appellant did not receive a fair trial?' was considered in *Re Medicaments and Related Cases of Goods (No 2)* [2001] 1 WLR 700. The Court of Appeal reviewed *R v Gough* and all the authorities in the light of the Human Rights Act 1998, and concluded that, once European Convention case law had been taken into account, 'a modest adjustment' to *R v Gough* was required. The approach should be as follows. The court must ascertain all the circumstances that have a bearing on the suggestion of bias. It must then ask whether those circumstances would lead a fair-minded and informed observer to conclude that there was a real possibility or a real danger (which were the same thing) of bias. One circumstance will be any explanation offered by the judge. If this explanation is not accepted by one party, it becomes something for the court to take account of from the point of view of a fair-minded observer, thereby avoiding the necessity of the court ruling on whether the explanation should be accepted or rejected.

There are many and varied examples of the application of this principle to be found in the law reports, and the following are included merely by way of example:

— *R v Thames Magistrates' Court, ex p Polemis* [1974] 1 WLR 1371 (where the defendant was not given sufficient time to prepare his case);

- *R v Marylebone Justices, ex p Farrag* [1981] Crim LR 182 (where a verdict of guilty was announced before defence counsel's closing speech);
- *R v Romsey Justices, ex p Gale* [1992] Crim LR 451 (where one of the magistrates, during the prosecution case, prepared a note of what he proposed the bench should say if it were to convict);
- *R v Ely Justices, ex p Burgess* [1992] Crim LR 888 (where the justices travelled to view the crime scene with the prosecutor, and did not allow the defendant to be present—either or both of these factors would allow the conviction to be quashed);
- *R v Hendon Justices, ex p DPP* [1994] QB 167 (where the magistrates announced an acquittal without hearing prosecution evidence and without having a good reason to refuse to hear witnesses);
- *Vincent v The Queen* [1993] 1 WLR 862, PC (where the fact that the defendant, following normal practice, was not given detailed notice of the evidence against him was not sufficient to establish that he had been denied a fair hearing);
- *R v Newbury Justices, ex p Drake* [1993] COD 24 (where the allegedly partisan demeanour of the clerk was held not to have affected the magistrates' decision);
- *R v Nottingham Justices, ex p Fraser* (1995) 159 JP 612 (where the magistrates took into account the adequacy of the defendant's legal representation);
- *R v Worcester Justices, ex p Daniels* (1997) 161 JP 121 (where a member of the bench failed to give full attention to the defendant's evidence, and had been reading material unconnected with the trial).

The High Court has on occasion issued a quashing order even though the failure to provide the defence with the necessary information lay with the prosecuting authority and not with the court itself. Consider the following examples:

- *R v Leyland Justices, ex p Hawthorn* [1979] QB 283 (where the defence were not informed of witnesses who could assist their case);
- *R v Knightsbridge Crown Court, ex p Goonatilleke* [1986] QB 1 (where the store detective failed to tell the police that he had a conviction for wasting police time);
- *R v Liverpool Crown Court, ex p Roberts* [1986] Crim LR 622 (where the police did not inform the defence of an additional statement made by the victim which was inconsistent with another statement and with his testimony);
- *R v Bolton Justices, ex p Scally* [1991] 1 QB 537 (where a lack of care meant that medical kits used for testing the level of alcohol in the blood were themselves contaminated with alcohol).

Note: A quashing order to quash an acquittal on the ground that it had been procured by fraud or perjury should seldom if ever be made (*R v Portsmouth Crown Court, ex p DPP* [1994] COD 13, DC).

8.3.1.2 Mandatory orders

A mandatory order compels an inferior tribunal to carry out its duties. It will be ordered when the court refuses to act when it should; not when it *has* acted and made a mistake. The appropriate remedy in the latter case would be a quashing order. See, for example, *R v Hendon Justices, ex p DPP* [1994] QB 167.

8.3.1.3 Prohibiting orders

A prohibiting order will be made to stop the court acting in excess of its powers. Parties do not have to wait for the final outcome of the hearing, and if there is genuine doubt as to the court's powers, the court will adjourn, so that the opinion of the High Court can be sought.

8.3.2 Discretion

The power to award any of the prerogative orders is entirely discretionary, and even though the appellant has established a prima facie case, the order sought may still be refused by the Administrative Court. See, again, *R v Battle Justices, ex p Shepherd* (1983) 5 Cr App R (S) 124.

8.3.3 Procedure

This works as a civil matter, rather confusingly. Hence the appellant becomes a 'claimant'. Under the SCA 1981, s 31, the Civil Procedure Rules, Part 54 and PD 54A the procedure is as follows:

(a) Within three months of the decision, a claimant must submit a claim form for judicial review, identifying himself as well as any interested parties. Notwithstanding the time limit, a claimant must act 'promptly'. The claim form must also provide a detailed statement of the grounds on which judicial review is being sought and the remedy sought. The claimant must supply a statement of the facts, as well as any written evidence on which he relies, including a copy of the court's order (where relevant). A defendant who opposes the claim must file an acknowledgment of service and provide a summary of their grounds for contesting the claim.

(b) The claim for judicial review requires the court's permission to proceed. This is usually determined without a hearing. If there is no hearing, the judge will simply read the papers in chambers and make a decision. If the applicant specifically applies for a hearing, one may be held, and this may be in court.

(c) If permission is refused, the applicant has seven days in which to file a request for the matter to be reconsidered at a hearing before the Divisional Court.

(d) If permission is granted, the defendant has 35 days to serve detailed grounds for resisting the claim, together with any evidence. The claimant must file a skeleton argument not less than 21 working days prior to the hearing; the defendant must do likewise not less than 14 days before the hearing; PD 54A, para 15.1.

(e) The hearing itself consists of legal argument from counsel, witness statements and affidavit evidence. Oral evidence is not usually called, though it may be necessary to do so in order to establish the error of the court below.

(f) The court will reach a decision, and make any appropriate orders.

8.3.4 Bail

Magistrates have no power to grant bail where there is an application for judicial review. The application for bail must be made to the High Court judge in chambers under the Criminal Justice Act 1948, s 37(1)(d). However, if the application is from the Crown Court on a matter not relating to trial on indictment, the Crown Court may grant bail.

8.3.5 Judicial review from the Crown Court

Judicial review is rare, though possible, from the Crown Court; see, for example, *R v Harrow Crown Court, ex p Dave* [1994] 1 WLR 98. In *R v Carlisle Crown Court* [2009] EWHC 3540 (Admin) it was said that there was no room to appeal from the Crown Court when hearing an appeal from the magistrates' court 'and attempts to challenge such a decision by judicial review are normally inappropriate and should be firmly discouraged. However, there may be rare occasions when a claim for judicial review is not inappropriate . . .'. The present case was not to be considered as procedurally out of order but was to be regarded as exceptional. See also **3.11.2**—seeking judicial review of decisions by Crown Court judges to refuse bail to defendants.

8.4 Case stated and judicial review compared

In many situations, an appellant could apply for either a case to be stated or judicial review, and in some respects the two types of appeal are similar. However, by appealing by way of case stated, the appellant is challenging the actual decision of the court, alleging, for example, that a statute has been misapplied. In some circumstances this may be said of judicial review, but judicial review tends to be directed, not at the decision itself, but more at the decision-making process. It is the legality of the process which is under review, not whether the decision is right or wrong.

If both remedies do apply, the appellant should appeal by way of case stated, as all the facts can then be placed before the High Court (*R v Ipswich Crown Court, ex p Baldwin* [1981] 1 All ER 596 and *R v Oldbury Justices, ex p Smith* (1995) 159 JP 316). See also *R v Ipswich Justices, ex p D* (5 December 1994); *R v Gloucester Crown Court, ex p Chester* [1998] COD 365; and *Blackstone's Criminal Practice* at D29.42.

8.5 Appeal to the Supreme Court

A decision of the High Court in a criminal case or matter is appealed directly to the Supreme Court, and there is no right of appeal to the Court of Appeal (see Administration of Justice Act 1960, s 1). The appeal can be made if the following conditions are satisfied:

- the High Court certifies that the case involves a point of law of general public importance; and
- leave is granted by either the High Court or the Supreme Court.

8.6 Possible future developments

The Law Commission published a Report, No 324, in July 2010, looking at the jurisdiction of the High Court in relation to criminal cases. In summary, the Law Commission recommended:

- the abolition of appeal by way of case stated from the Crown Court (as serving no real purpose);
- the suspension of judicial review applications from the time that a case is sent to the Crown Court to the end of the trial (in particular, to remove issues around the concept of 'a matter relating to a trial on indictment') except where the accused challenges a refusal of bail; and
- the introduction of two new forms of statutory appeal.

These new appeals would be: (a) by a child or young person against a judge's refusal to impose reporting restrictions, and (b) in cases where a judge's decision 'has the potential to involve a real and immediate risk to a person's life'. The Commission gives as an example of the latter situation the following: a judge orders D1 to disclose his defence statement to D2. This would reveal to D2 that D1 has assisted the police and may lead D2 to threaten the life of D1. This situation would be 'irreversible' and therefore the decision ought to be capable of challenge before it takes effect.

The Law Commission's website notes that it 'awaits the Government's response' to these recommendations.

9 Disclosure

We have already seen that, where the defendant is to be tried in the Crown Court, the process whereby the case is sent to the Crown Court requires the prosecution to serve on the defence copies of the statements of the prosecution witnesses who will be called. Moreover, in the case of summary and either-way offences, Part 21 of the Criminal Procedure Rules provides that, by no later than the beginning of the day of the first hearing in the case, the prosecutor must, if so requested, provide 'initial details' to the defence. Those 'initial details' must include a summary of the prosecution case and/or any written statements (or other documents) setting out the facts or matters on which the prosecution case will be based (ie written statements of the prosecution witnesses). It should also be noted that good practice requires that the prosecution should provide the defence with the statements of the prosecution witnesses prior to any summary trial (whether the offence is summary or triable either way).

The Criminal Procedure and Investigations Act 1996 (CPIA) creates additional duties of disclosure. The Act is supplemented by a Code of Practice issued under the CPIA 1996, by the Attorney-General's Guidelines: *Disclosure of Information in Criminal Proceedings*, and by *Disclosure: A Protocol for the Control and Management of Unused Material in the Crown Court*, all of which may be found in Appendix 4 of *Blackstone's Criminal Practice,* and by Part 22 of the Criminal Procedure Rules (in the supplement to *Blackstone's Criminal Practice*). *R v K* [2006] EWCA Crim 724 (affirmed in *R v L* [2007] EWCA Crim 764), emphasised the importance of compliance with the Protocol.

9.1 The duty of the investigating officer

The investigating officer is under a duty to retain material obtained in a criminal investigation which may be relevant to that investigation. Paragraph 5.4 of the Code of Practice issued under s 23 of the CPIA 1996 provides a non-exhaustive list of the material that should be retained:

(a) Crime reports (including crime report forms, relevant parts of incident report books or police officers' notebooks).

(b) Custody records.

(c) Records derived from tapes of telephone messages (eg 999 calls) containing descriptions of the alleged offence or offender.

(d) Final versions of witness statements (and draft versions where their content differs from the final version).

(e) Interview records.

(f) Communications between police and experts (eg forensic scientists) and reports of work carried out by experts.

(g) Any material casting doubt on the reliability of a confession.

(h) Any material casting doubt on the reliability of a witness.

(i) Any other material that would fall within the test for primary prosecution disclosure (see later).

9.2 Prosecution disclosure

Section 3 of the CPIA 1996 (as amended by the CJA 2003) requires the prosecutor to:

> *. . . disclose to the accused any prosecution material which might reasonably be considered capable of undermining the case for the prosecution against the accused or of assisting the case for the accused.*

This is an objective test, covering a very wide range of material. Paragraph 6 of the Attorney-General's Guidelines on Disclosure state that, in deciding whether material satisfies the disclosure test, consideration should be given (amongst other things) to:

(a) the use that might be made of it in cross-examination;

(b) its capacity to support submissions that could lead to:

  (i) the exclusion of evidence;

  (ii) a stay of proceedings, where the material is required to allow a proper application to be made;

  (iii) a court or tribunal finding that any public authority had acted incompatibly with the accused's rights under the ECHR;

(c) its capacity to suggest an explanation or partial explanation of the accused's actions;

(d) the capacity of the material to have a bearing on scientific or medical evidence in the case.

Paragraph 7 notes that, whilst individual items of material viewed in isolation may not reasonably be considered to be capable of undermining the prosecution case or assisting the accused, several items taken together might have that effect.

The prosecution should inform the defence if any prosecution witnesses have relevant previous convictions. In *Her Majesty's Advocate v Murtagh* [2009] UKPC 36 (a Scottish case, but the rules on disclosure are very similar to those in England and Wales), Lord Hope of Craighead noted (at [28]) that 'information about a witness's previous convictions . . . falls within the scope of the witness's private life'. It follows that release of that information to the accused or his solicitor will engage the rights of the witness under Article 8(1) of the ECHR. Release of that information will be incompatible with those rights unless the interference can be justified under Article 8(2). His Lordship went on to say (at [30]) that, 'Materiality in this context must depend on whether the information could have any possible bearing on the witnesses's credibility or character . . . Previous convictions which would be relevant to a legitimate attack on their character or to their credibility would plainly be relevant to the accused's defence'. At [32], his Lordship said that, 'a conviction for an offence many years ago which was, on any view, of a trivial nature only and was not repeated would fall well outside the threshold of what was relevant. Other cases where care will need to be taken are where the conviction that might not be material was for an offence of a sensitive nature, disclosure of which could seriously affect the witness's relationship with others such as his neighbours, employer or members of his family.'

Under s 7A of the 1996 Act (inserted by the CJA 2003), there is a continuing duty on the prosecution to disclose unused material that falls within the ambit of s 3. Section 7A provides as follows:

Continuing duty of prosecutor to disclose

(1) This section applies at all times—

  (a) after the prosecutor has complied with section 3 or purported to comply with it, and

  (b) before the accused is acquitted or convicted or the prosecutor decides not to proceed with the case concerned.

(2) The prosecutor must keep under review the question whether at any given time (and, in particular, following the giving of a defence statement) there is prosecution material which—

  (a) might reasonably be considered capable of undermining the case for the prosecution against the accused or of assisting the case for the accused, and

  (b) has not been disclosed to the accused.

(3) If at any time there is any such material as is mentioned in subsection (2) the prosecutor must disclose it to the accused as soon as is reasonably practicable . . .

(4) In applying subsection (2) by reference to any given time the state of affairs at that time (including the case for the prosecution as it stands at that time) must be taken into account.

(5) Where the accused gives a defence statement [or an updated defence statement],

(a) if as a result of that statement the prosecutor is required by this section to make any disclosure, or further disclosure, he must do so . . .

(b) if the prosecutor considers that he is not so required, he must . . . give to the accused a written statement to that effect.

(6) For the purposes of this section prosecution material is material—

(a) which is in the prosecutor's possession and came into his possession in connection with the case for the prosecution against the accused, or

(b) which . . . he has inspected in connection with the case for the prosecution against the accused.

. . .

(8) Material must not be disclosed under this section to the extent that the court, on an application by the prosecutor, concludes it is not in the public interest to disclose it and orders accordingly.

. . .

9.3 Defence disclosure

Where the case is to be tried in the Crown Court, the defence *must* supply a 'defence statement' to the prosecution (see s 5 of the CPIA 1996); where the case is to be tried in the magistrates' court, the defence *may* supply such a statement (see s 6 of the CPIA 1996).

The content of the defence statement is governed by s 6A of the CPIA 1996. This requires the accused to set out the nature of his defence, including any particular defences on which he intends to rely, and indicate any points of law he wishes to take; special provision is made for cases where the defence is one of alibi. Section 6A provides:

6A Contents of defence statement

(1) For the purposes of this Part a defence statement is a written statement—

(a) setting out the nature of the accused's defence, including any particular defences on which he intends to rely,

(b) indicating the matters of fact on which he takes issue with the prosecution,

(c) setting out, in the case of each such matter, why he takes issue with the prosecution,

(ca) setting out particulars of the matters of fact on which he intends to rely for the purposes of his defence, and

(d) indicating any point of law (including any point as to the admissibility of evidence or an abuse of process) which he wishes to take, and any authority on which he intends to rely for that purpose.

(2) A defence statement that discloses an alibi must give particulars of it, including—

(a) the name, address and date of birth of any witness the accused believes is able to give evidence in support of the alibi, or as many of those details as are known to the accused when the statement is given;

(b) any information in the accused's possession which might be of material assistance in identifying or finding any such witness in whose case any of the details mentioned in paragraph (a) are not known to the accused when the statement is given.

(3) For the purposes of this section evidence in support of an alibi is evidence tending to show that by reason of the presence of the accused at a particular place or in a particular area at a particular time he was not, or was unlikely to have been, at the place where the offence is alleged to have been committed at the time of its alleged commission.

. . .

Under s 6B of the CPIA 1996 (not in force at April 2015), the accused, prior to the trial, must provide an updated defence statement, or a written statement that there are no changes to be made to the defence statement previously served.

Section 6C of the CPIA 1996 requires the defence to identify any witnesses they propose to call. This is a mandatory duty, whether the case is to be heard in a magistrates' court or in the Crown Court. Section 6C provides:

6C Notification of intention to call defence witnesses

(1) The accused must give to the court and the prosecutor a notice indicating whether he intends to call any persons (other than himself) as witnesses at his trial and, if so—

(a) giving the name, address and date of birth of each such proposed witness, or as many of those details as are known to the accused when the notice is given;

(b) providing any information in the accused's possession which might be of material assistance in identifying or finding any such proposed witness in whose case any of the details mentioned in paragraph (a) are not known to the accused when the notice is given.

. . .

(4) If, following the giving of a notice under this section, the accused—

(a) decides to call a person (other than himself) who is not included in the notice as a proposed witness, or decides not to call a person who is so included, or

(b) discovers any information which, under subsection (1), he would have had to include in the notice if he had been aware of it when giving the notice, he must give an appropriately amended notice to the court and the prosecutor.

In an attempt to allay fears that people might be put off testifying as defence witnesses, or encouraged to change their evidence, s 21A of the CPIA 1996 requires the Secretary of State to publish a Code of Practice giving guidance to police officers (and others charged with the duty of investigating offences) in relation to the arranging and conducting of interviews of people whose particulars are given to the prosecution because they are alibi witnesses or because they fall within s 6C. Section 21A(2) requires that:

The code must include (in particular) guidance in relation to—

(a) information that should be provided to the interviewee and the accused in relation to such an interview;

(b) the notification of the accused's solicitor of such an interview;

(c) the attendance of the interviewee's solicitor at such an interview;

(d) the attendance of the accused's solicitor at such an interview;

(e) the attendance of any other appropriate person at such an interview taking into account the interviewee's age or any disability of the interviewee.

Because of the potentially damaging effects of failure to comply with the obligations imposed by these defence disclosure provisions, s 6E(2) of the CPIA states that:

If it appears to the judge at a pre-trial hearing that an accused has failed to comply fully with section 5, 6B or 6C, so that there is a possibility of comment being made or inferences drawn under section 11(5), he shall warn the accused accordingly.

Section 6D of the 1996 Act (not in force at April 2015) requires the defence to reveal the identity of any experts who have been instructed on behalf of the defence, whether or not they are to be called as defence witnesses. It provides:

6D Notification of names of experts instructed by accused

(1) If the accused instructs a person with a view to his providing any expert opinion for possible use as evidence at the trial of the accused, he must give to the court and the prosecutor a notice specifying the person's name and address.

. . .

Section 5 of the CPIA 1996 makes provision for the service of defence statements on co-defendants, if the court so orders. It provides:

> (5A) *Where there are other accused in the proceedings and the court so orders, the accused must also give a defence statement to each other accused specified by the court.*
>
> (5B) *The court may make an order under subsection (5A) either of its own motion or on the application of any party.*
>
> . . .

This essentially gives statutory effect of the decision of the Court of Appeal in *R v Cairns* [2003] 1 WLR 796, that the prosecution would sometimes have to disclose the statement of one co-defendant to the other where it might assist the defence of that other defendant.

Ensuring the accuracy and completeness of the defence statement is important because of the adverse inferences that can be drawn under s 11 of the CPIA 1996 (see later). Moreover, s 6E makes it important to take great care in the drafting of defence statements for another reason: it makes provision for the jury to be shown the defence statement (or updated defence statement if there is one). Section 6E provides as follows:

> (4) *The judge in a trial before a judge and jury—*
>
> (a) *may direct that the jury be given a copy of any defence statement, and*
>
> (b) *if he does so, may direct that it be edited so as not to include references to matters evidence of which would be inadmissible.*
>
> (5) *A direction under subsection (4)—*
>
> (a) *may be made either of the judge's own motion or on the application of any party;*
>
> (b) *may be made only if the judge is of the opinion that seeing a copy of the defence statement would help the jury to understand the case or to resolve any issue in the case.*
>
> . . .

To remove any doubt as to whether a defence statement served by the defendant's solicitor is to be regarded as being given on behalf of the defendant, s 6E(1) of the CPIA 1996 provides that where the accused's solicitor 'purports to give on behalf of the accused' a defence statement or an updated defence statement, that statement 'shall, unless the contrary is proved, be deemed to be given with the authority of the accused'.

Defence statements are normally drafted by the defendant's solicitor, but counsel may be instructed to draft the defence statement. Counsel so instructed must ensure that the accused:

- understands the importance of the accuracy and adequacy of the defence statement; and
- has had the opportunity of carefully considering the statement drafted by counsel and has approved it.

In *R v Wheeler* (2000) 164 JP 565 the defendant was charged with and convicted of an offence contrary to s 170(2) of the Customs and Excise Management Act 1979 following his arrest at Gatwick airport when he was found to be concealing drugs internally. At trial, an inconsistency had become apparent between the defence statement which had been served by his solicitors (in which it was said that the accused knew he was carrying the drugs when he arrived in the UK) and his evidence during cross-examination (in which he maintained that he believed he had regurgitated all of the packets before travelling to the UK). The defence statement had not been signed and the defendant alleged that his solicitor had made a mistake in serving an incorrect statement of his case. Although the trial judge referred to the alleged mistake in his summing-up, he did not provide the jury with specific guidance. The Court of Appeal held that the judge had erred in failing to give specific directions as to the inconsistency, given that the jury would be affected by it. The court said that it was advisable that defence statements were signed by a defendant rather than served by solicitors on a defendant's behalf without procedures being followed to verify accuracy. It should be noted, however, that the court has no power to order the defence statement to be signed by the accused (*R (Sullivan) v Maidstone Crown Court* [2002] 1 WLR 2747). The template for a defence statement which is available on the Ministry of Justice website offers the option of a signature from either the defendant or his solicitor; see <https://www.justice.gov.uk/courts/procedure-rules/criminal/docs/2011/crim-pr-form-part22-defence-statement-aug-2011.pdf>.

9.3.1 Time limits

The Criminal Procedure and Investigations Act 1996 (Defence Disclosure Time Limits) Regulations 2011 (SI 2011/209) set out the relevant time limits. Under reg 2(1), the 'relevant period' for s 5 (compulsory disclosure in Crown Court cases), s 6 (voluntary disclosure in magistrates' court cases) and s 6C (notification of intention to call defence witnesses) begins with the day on which the prosecutor complies (or purports to comply) with s 3 (the initial duty of the prosecutor to disclose relevant material to the defence). In the case of proceedings in a magistrates' court, the defence statement (if any) and the notification under s 6C must be served before the expiry of the end of a period of 14 days beginning with the first day of the 'relevant period' (reg 2(2)). In Crown Court cases, the period for compliance is 28 days beginning with the first day of the relevant period (reg 2(3)). Where the relevant period would otherwise expire on a Saturday, Sunday, Christmas Day, Good Friday or any bank holiday, the relevant period is treated as expiring on the next working day (reg 2(4)).

Under reg 3, the court may extend (or further extend) the relevant period by as many days as it specifies in the order. The court may only make such an order on an application by the accused and must be satisfied that it would be 'unreasonable' to require the accused to give a defence statement under s 5 or s 6 (as the case may be), or to give notice under s 6C, within the relevant period. The application for an extension must be made within the relevant period (ie before the relevant period has expired), and must specify the grounds on which it is made and the number of days by which the accused wishes the relevant period to be extended. There is no limit on the number of applications that may be made for extensions of time.

9.4 Sanctions for non-compliance by the defence

The penalties for non-compliance by the defence with their disclosure obligations under the CPIA 1996 are set out in s 11. Section 11 applies in three cases:

(a) Where the accused is to be tried in the Crown Court (and so is required by s 5 of the Act to provide a defence statement) and the accused:
  (i) fails to give an initial defence statement under s 5; or
  (ii) provides an initial defence statement but does so late; or
  (iii) fails to provide an updated defence statement, or a statement that there are no changes (when this obligation comes into force); or
  (iv) provides an updated statement (or a statement that there are no changes) but does so late (again, when this obligation is implemented); or
  (v) sets out inconsistent defences in the defence statement; or
  (vi) at the trial, puts forward a defence which was not mentioned in his defence statement or which is different from any defence set out in that statement; or
  (vii) at the trial, relies on a matter which was not mentioned in his defence statement but which should have been so mentioned; or
  (viii) at the trial adduces evidence in support of an alibi without having given particulars of the alibi in the defence statement; or
  (ix) at the trial, calls an alibi witness without having given appropriate notice of the alibi, or details of that particular witness, in the defence statement.

(b) Where the accused is to be tried in a magistrates' court and gives an initial defence statement voluntarily but does so late or does any of the things set out in paras (iii) to (ix) in the preceding paragraph.

(c) Where the accused gives a witness notice (under s 6C) but does so late or, at the trial, calls a witness who was not included, or not adequately identified, in a witness notice.

Under s 11(5), where s 11 applies:

(a) *the court or any other party may make such comment as appears appropriate;*

(b) *the court or jury may draw such inferences as appear proper in deciding whether the accused is guilty of the offence concerned.*

Section 11(6) provides that where adverse inferences could be drawn for failure to mention a point of law (including any point as to the admissibility of evidence or an abuse of process) or an authority used to support legal argument, comment by another party may be made only with the leave of the court.

Similarly, s 11(7) provides that where the failure in question is a failure to comply with the witness notice requirements, comment by another party may only be made with the leave of the court. Section 11(9) stipulates that where the accused calls a witness whom he has failed to include, or to identify adequately, in a witness notice, the court must have regard to whether there is any justification for the failure.

Under s 11(8), where the accused puts forward a defence which is different from any defence set out in his defence statement, the court must have regard (a) to the extent of the differences in the defences, and (b) to whether there is any justification for it.

Section 11(10), importantly, confirms that 'a person shall not be convicted of an offence solely on an inference drawn under subsection (5)'.

The sanctions for non-compliance are limited to those set out in s 11. For example, in *Murphy v DPP* [2006] EWHC 1753 (Admin), the Divisional Court said that a defendant does not lose his entitlement to disclosure under the CPIA merely because he serves his defence statement out of time. Similarly, in *R (Tinnion) v Reading Crown Court* [2009] EWHC 2930 (Admin); (2010) 174 JP 36, the defendant was being tried in the Crown Court (by way of an appeal from the youth court). The judge refused to allow the defendant to call two alibi witnesses because no notice had been given to the Crown of the intention to call those two witnesses as alibi witnesses (and they had not been named by the defendant when he was interviewed by the police). Given that the trial was an appeal from a summary trial, the provision of a defence statement would have been voluntary (under s 6 of the 1996 Act). However, David Clarke J (at [8]) said that:

> Even if the Recorder had been right to hold that the claimant was under a requirement to provide a defence statement, either in the Youth Court or in the Crown Court on appeal, with details of his alibi witnesses, it does not follow that the failure to comply with this requirement rendered the evidence inadmissible. The sanction against a defendant who fails to give such notice is not that a witness cannot be called, but that adverse comment can be made and cross-examination can be conducted, and that the court or jury may draw such inference as is proper from the failure to give such notice . . .

It followed that the Crown Court had no power to prevent the witnesses being called, and so the Divisional Court directed that the appeal be reheard before a different judge and justices.

In *R v Rochford* [2010] EWCA Crim 1928; [2011] 1 WLR 534, the Court of Appeal ruled that, where there is a breach of s 6A, either because there is no defence statement or because it does not contain what it should, the court has no power to punish the defendant for contempt of court. Hughes LJ also made the point (at [22]) that a lawyer cannot properly advise a defendant not to file a defence statement: 'It is not open to a lawyer to advise his client to disobey the client's statutory obligation.' His Lordship added (at [25]) that: 'The lawyer's duty is to explain the statutory obligation that [the defendant] has and to explain the consequences which follow from disobedience of it'.

9.5 Public interest immunity

Public interest immunity (PII) enables the prosecution to withhold material that would otherwise have to be disclosed under the CPIA. Material can only be withheld on the basis of PII with the permission of the court. Common examples of cases where PII is raised are where the prosecution wish to protect the identity of an informant whom the prosecutor does not intend to call as a witness at the trial (as in *R v Turner* [1995] 1 WLR 264) or where the police wish to keep secret the location of an observation post from which they were watching the movements of the accused (as in *R v Johnson* [1988] 1 WLR 1377).

Paragraph 65 of the Attorney-General's Guidelines on Disclosure, dealing with applications for non-disclosure in the public interest, states that before making an application to the court to withhold material that would otherwise fall to be disclosed, on the basis that disclosure would give rise to a real risk of serious prejudice to an important public interest:

> *. . . prosecutors should aim to disclose as much of the material as they properly can (for example, by giving the defence redacted or edited copies or summaries). Neutral material or material damaging to the defendant need not be disclosed and there is no need to bring it to the attention of the court. Only in truly borderline cases should the prosecution seek a judicial ruling on whether material in its possession should be disclosed.*

In *Rowe and Davis v United Kingdom* (2000) 30 EHRR 1, the European Court held that:

> . . . Article 6(1) requires, as indeed does English law, that the prosecution authorities should disclose to the defence all material evidence in their possession for or against the accused (para 61).

However, the Court went on to hold that:

> the entitlement to disclosure of relevant evidence is not an absolute right. In any criminal proceedings there may be competing interests, such as national security or the need to protect witnesses at risk of reprisals or keep secret police methods of investigation of crime, which must be weighed against the rights of the accused. In some cases it may be necessary to withhold certain evidence from the defence so as to preserve the fundamental rights of another individual or to safeguard an important public interest. However, only such measures restricting the rights of the defence which are strictly necessary are permissible under Article 6(1). Moreover, in order to ensure that the accused receives a fair trial, any difficulties caused to the defence by a limitation on its rights must be sufficiently counterbalanced by the procedures followed by the judicial authorities (para 61).

In *R v H; R v C* [2004] UKHL 3; [2004] 2 AC 134, the House of Lords considered the question of PII and the potential role for 'special independent counsel' in PII hearings. The Court of Appeal had certified two points of law of general public importance were involved in its decision:

> (1) Are the procedures for dealing with claims for public interest immunity made on behalf of the prosecution in criminal proceedings compliant with article 6 of the European Convention for the Protection of Human Rights and Fundamental Freedoms?
>
> (2) If not, in what way are the procedures deficient and how might the deficiency be remedied?

The procedure for determining claims of PII had been set out in *R v Ward* [1993] 1 WLR 619 and *R v Davis* [1993] 1 WLR 613 at 617–618. The Court of Appeal had identified three classes of case, which Lord Bingham (in *R v H*) summarised in the following terms (at [20]):

> In the first, comprising most of the cases in which a PII issue arises, the prosecution must give notice to the defence that they are applying for a ruling of the court, and must indicate to the defence at least the category of the material they hold (that is, the broad ground upon which PII is claimed), and the defence must have the opportunity to make representations to the court. There is thus an *inter partes* hearing conducted in open court with reference to at least the category of the material in question. The second class comprises cases in which the prosecution contend that the public interest would be injured if disclosure were made even of the category of the material. In such cases the prosecution must still notify the defence that an application to the court is to be made, but the category of the material need not be specified: the defence will still have an opportunity to address the court on the procedure to be adopted but the application will be made to the court in the absence of the defendant or anyone representing him. If the court considers that the application falls within the first class, it will order that procedure to be followed. Otherwise it will rule. The third class, described as 'highly exceptional', comprises cases where the public interest would be injured even by disclosure that an *ex parte* application is to be made. In such cases application to the court would be made without notice to the defence. But if the court considers that the case should be treated as falling within the second or the first class, it will so order.

The procedural regime established by *R v Ward* and *R v Davis* is largely replicated in r 22.3 of the Criminal Procedure Rules, which deals with prosecutors' applications for public interest rulings. Under r 22.3(2), the prosecutor must serve notice of the application on the court, on any person who the prosecutor thinks would be directly affected by disclosure of the material and on the defendant, but only to the extent that serving it on the defendant would not disclose what the prosecutor thinks ought not be disclosed. The application must explain why it would not be in the public interest to disclose that material, and why no measure (eg disclosure of a summary or an edited copy) would adequately protect both the public interest and the defendant's right to a fair trial (r 22.3(3)). Where the prosecutor serves only part of the application on the defendant, the prosecutor must, in the part that is only for the court, explain why the prosecutor has withheld it from the defendant (r 22.3(4)). Under r 22.3(5), the court may order that the application be served on the defendant (if this has not already taken place). Rule 22.3(6) requires the court to determine the application at a hearing, which will be in private, unless the court otherwise directs; if the court so directs, the hearing may take place, wholly or in part, in the defendant's absence. Under r 22.3(7), at a hearing at which the defendant is present, the court will generally hear representations by the prosecutor and any other person served with the application, and then by the defendant, in the presence of them all, and then further representations by the prosecutor and any such other person in the defendant's absence. Importantly, under r 22.3(8), the court may only determine the application if satisfied that it has been able to take adequate account of such rights of confidentiality as apply to the material, and the defendant's right to a fair trial.

Lord Bingham, in *R v H*, gave guidance (at [36]) on how the courts should approach PII hearings:

> When any issue of derogation from the golden rule of full disclosure comes before it, the court must address a series of questions:
>
> (1) What is the material which the prosecution seek to withhold? This must be considered by the court in detail.
>
> (2) Is the material such as may weaken the prosecution case or strengthen that of the defence? If No, disclosure should not be ordered. If Yes, full disclosure should (subject to (3), (4) and (5) below) be ordered.
>
> (3) Is there a real risk of serious prejudice to an important public interest (and, if so, what) if full disclosure of the material is ordered? If No, full disclosure should be ordered.
>
> (4) If the answer to (2) and (3) is Yes, can the defendant's interest be protected without disclosure or disclosure be ordered to an extent or in a way which will give adequate protection to the public interest in question and also afford adequate protection to the interests of the defence?
>
> This question requires the court to consider, with specific reference to the material which the prosecution seek to withhold and the facts of the case and the defence as disclosed, whether the prosecution should formally admit what the defence seek to establish or whether disclosure short of full disclosure may be ordered. This may be done in appropriate cases by the preparation of summaries or extracts of evidence, or the provision of documents in an edited or anonymised form, provided the documents supplied are in each instance approved by the judge. In appropriate cases the appointment of special counsel may be a necessary step to ensure that the contentions of the prosecution are tested and the interests of the defendant protected (see paragraph 22 above). . . . In cases of exceptional difficulty the court may require the appointment of special counsel to ensure a correct answer to questions (2) and (3) as well as (4).
>
> (5) Do the measures proposed in answer to (4) represent the minimum derogation necessary to protect the public interest in question? If No, the court should order such greater disclosure as will represent the minimum derogation from the golden rule of full disclosure.
>
> (6) If limited disclosure is ordered pursuant to (4) or (5), may the effect be to render the trial process, viewed as a whole, unfair to the defendant? If Yes, then fuller disclosure should be ordered even if this leads or may lead the prosecution to discontinue the proceedings so as to avoid having to make disclosure.
>
> (7) If the answer to (6) when first given is No, does that remain the correct answer as the trial unfolds, evidence is adduced and the defence advanced?
>
> It is important that the answer to (6) should not be treated as a final, once-and-for-all, answer but as a provisional answer which the court must keep under review.

His Lordship continued (at [37]):

> Throughout his or her consideration of any disclosure issue the trial judge must bear constantly in mind the overriding principles referred to in this opinion. In applying them, the judge should involve the defence to the maximum extent possible without disclosing that which the general interest requires to be protected but taking full account of the specific defence which is relied on. There will be very few cases indeed in which some measure of disclosure to the defence will not be possible, even if this is confined to the fact that an *ex parte* application is to be made. If even that information is withheld and if the material to be withheld is of significant help to the defendant, there must be a very serious question whether the prosecution should proceed, since special counsel, even if appointed, cannot then receive any instructions from the defence at all.

Lord Bingham concluded (at [39]) that:

> Provided the existing procedures for dealing with claims for public interest immunity made on behalf of the prosecution in criminal proceedings are operated with scrupulous attention to the governing principles referred to and continuing regard to the proper interests of the defendant, there should be no violation of Article 6 of the Convention.

The main focus of *R v H* was the appointment of special independent counsel to represent the interests of the defendant but who is not permitted to disclose to the defendant the secret material that is disclosed to counsel in order to make representations on behalf of the defendant. Such counsel is not, in the ordinary sense, professionally responsible to the defendant. Special counsel may be appointed when it is in the interests of justice to do so. However, the House of Lords said that the need must be shown; such an appointment will 'always be exceptional, never automatic; a course of last and never first resort. It should not be ordered unless and until the trial judge is satisfied that no other course will adequately meet the overriding requirement of fairness to the defendant' (at [22]).

The House of Lords in *R v H* also gave general guidance on PII hearings in magistrates' courts. Lord Bingham affirmed the approach taken in *R (DPP) v Acton Youth Court* [2001] EWHC Admin 402; [2001] 1 WLR 1828 at [44].

> If PII applications are confined, as they should be, to material which undermines the prosecution case or strengthens that of the defence, the bench will not be alerted to material damaging to the defendant. If it is, the principles which should govern the court's decision whether to recuse itself are the same as in the case of any other tribunal of fact, but the court's duty of continuing review ordinarily militates in favour of continuing the proceedings before the court which determines the PII application. If a case raises complex and contentious PII issues, and the court has discretion to send the case to the Crown Court for trial, the magistrates' court should carefully consider whether those issues are best resolved in the Crown Court. The occasions on which it will be appropriate to appoint special counsel in the magistrates' court will be even rarer than in the Crown Court.

9.6 Defence applications for disclosure

Once the defendant has supplied a defence statement, the prosecutor has to reconsider whether there is any unused material which might undermine the prosecution case or support the defence case. The prosecutor must then (under s 7A(5) of the 1996 Act) either make such further disclosure as is necessary or give to the defendant a written statement that there is no such material. Under s 8(1) and (2) of the 1996 Act, where a defendant has given a defence statement (and the prosecutor has taken the steps required by s 7A(5), or has failed to comply with s 7A(5)) and has reasonable cause to believe that there is prosecution material which should be disclosed under s 7A but has not been, the defence may apply to the court for an order requiring the prosecutor to disclose that material. The application may be resisted by the prosecution if, for example, public interest immunity applies to the material (s 8(5)).

The procedure for the defendant's application for prosecution disclosure is set out in r 22.5 of the Criminal Procedure Rules. Under r 22.5(3), the application (served on the prosecution and the court) must describe the material that the defendant wants the prosecutor to disclose, explain why the defendant thinks there is reasonable cause to believe that the prosecutor has that material, and why it should be disclosed under the 1996 Act. If the defendant wants a hearing, the application must explain why a hearing is needed. Under r 22.5(4), the court may determine the application at a hearing (in public or in private) or without a hearing; however, the court cannot require the prosecutor to disclose material unless the prosecutor is present or has had at least 14 days in which to make representations (r 22.5(5)).

9.7 Third party disclosure

Sometimes material that may weaken the prosecution case or support the defence case is in the hands of a third party. For example, the accused might be charged with a sexual offence involving a child, and the child's school, or the relevant social services department, might have records of false allegations made by the child who is the alleged victim of the offence (as in *R v Brushett* [2001] Crim LR 471). If the material comes into the hands of the police, it should be retained and would fall within the ordinary disclosure regime under the CPIA 1996. Otherwise, if the third party is not prepared to hand over the material needed by the defence, the accused can seek a witness summons (using the procedure laid down by s 2 of the Criminal Procedure (Attendance of Witnesses) Act 1965 in Crown Court cases, or s 97 of the Magistrates' Courts Act 1980 in magistrates' court cases). The accused has to be able to show that the third party is likely to be able to give or produce material evidence in the case, and that it is in the interests of justice to issue a summons. Rule 28.5(3) of the Criminal Procedure Rules requires the applicant to serve the application on the proposed witness (unless the court otherwise directs) and, if the court so directs, on any a person to whom the proposed evidence relates. Under r 28.6(1), a person served with an application for a witness summons requiring production of a document or other evidence may object to its production on the ground that either it is not likely to be material evidence, or that the duties or rights (including rights of confidentiality) of the proposed witness or of any person to whom the document relates outweigh the reasons for issuing a summons. Under r 28.6(2), the court may require the proposed witness to make the document or thing available for the objection to be assessed by the court. In the context of disclosure, a third party would be to able to argue, for example, that the evidence should not be disclosed on grounds of public interest immunity (as previously mentioned) or because disclosure would infringe the right to privacy under Article 8 of the ECHR. In *Brushett*, Otton LJ summarised the law as follows:

> (i) to be material evidence documents must be not only relevant to the issues arising in the criminal proceedings, but also documents admissible as such in evidence;
>
> (ii) documents which are desired merely for the purpose of possible cross-examination are not admissible in evidence and, thus, are not material . . . ;
>
> (iii) whoever seeks production of documents must satisfy the Justices with some material that the documents are 'likely to be material' in the sense indicated, likelihood for this purpose involving a real possibility, although not necessarily a probability;
>
> (iv) it is not sufficient that the applicant merely wants to find out whether or not the third party has such material documents . . .

The Court cited with approval *Re M (a minor)* [1990] 2 FLR 36 (at 43B):

> In a disputed case, there is another public interest taken into account, namely the public interest in the due administration of justice . . . On the application of a party to the proceedings for disclosure of relevant documents the judge has a duty to weigh up competing public interest in the balancing operation referred to by Lord Edmund-Davies in *D v NSPCC* [1978] AC 171 . . . It is for the court on the application to decide whether the public interest in protecting the social work records overrides the public interest that the party to the proceedings should obtain the information he or she is seeking in order to obtain legal redress . . . None of this invalidates the general principle of public interest immunity, but it will undoubtedly have an effect on the balancing operation to be conducted by the judge.

10

Indictments

10.1 What is an indictment?

The indictment is the formal document which sets out the charge(s) to be tried in the Crown Court. The key legislative provisions governing the form and content of indictments are to be found in ss 3 and 5 of the Indictments Act 1915, s 2 of the Administration of Justice (Miscellaneous Provisions) Act 1933 and in Part 14 of the Criminal Procedure Rules.

10.1.1 What does an indictment contain?

The indictment begins with a heading, which contains a unique reference number for the case, identifies the location of the Crown Court and the name of the defendant(s).

Each charge faced by the defendant is contained in a separate 'count'.

10.1.2 What does a count contain?

Section 3(1) of the Indictments Act 1915 provides that the indictment must contain 'a statement of the specific offence or offences with which the accused person is charged, together with such particulars as may be necessary for giving reasonable information as to the nature of the charge'. The form and content of the indictment is governed by r 14.2 of the Crim PR. Under r 14.2(1) each count must contain:

(a) a statement of the offence charged that:
  (i) describes the offence in ordinary language, and
  (ii) identifies any legislation that creates it; and
(b) such particulars of the conduct constituting the commission of the offence as to make clear what the prosecutor alleges against the defendant.

Each count is therefore divided into two parts:

- 'Statement of Offence', which sets out the name of the offence (eg 'theft') and, where the offence is a statutory one, the statutory provision which creates the offence (eg s 1 of the Theft Act 1968).
- 'Particulars of Offence', giving factual information about the charge; this must disclose the essential elements of the offence.

Further guidance on drafting indictments can be found in Chapter 24 of the *Drafting* manual. Guidance on how to draft counts in respect of particular offences is given in the commentary relating to individual offences in Part B of *Blackstone's Criminal Practice*.

A single count must only allege one offence. If a count alleges more than one offence, it is said to be 'duplicitous', and the defence can ask the court to quash the count. For example, a count which alleges that the defendant 'on 16 August 2015 assaulted John Smith and on 17 August 2015 assaulted Peter Jones' is alleging two separate offences and so would be quashed.

It is possible, however, for several acts to constitute a single offence. Rule 14.2(2) of the Crim PR provides that 'more than one incident of the commission of the offence may be included in a count if those incidents taken together amount to a course of conduct having regard to the time, place or purpose of commission'. In *DPP v Merriman* [1973] AC 584, it was said that a number of acts may properly be said to amount to a single offence if they form part of the 'same transaction'. For example, in *R v Wilson* (1979) 69 Cr App R 83, the defendant was charged in one count with stealing a number of different items from Debenhams (three jumpers, a pair of shorts, two pairs of trousers, four dimmer switches and a cassette tape) and in another count with stealing a number of different items from Boots (eight records and a bottle of aftershave). The defence sought to argue that each count was duplicitous, on the basis that the goods had been stolen from different departments of the stores in question and so there should have been separate counts relating to each department. The Court of Appeal held that where counts in an indictment each charge theft of a number of separate items from different departments of the same store, those counts are not bad for duplicity, since it is legitimate to charge in a single count one activity, even though that activity may involve more than one act. The various acts of theft in each store had amounted to a single course of conduct, and so those acts could legitimately be regarded as amounting to a single offence of theft against each store.

Similarly, in *DPP v McCabe* [1992] Crim LR 885, it was held that an allegation that the defendant stole 76 library books between two specified dates was a single offence and so a count alleging this theft was not bad for duplicity. However, a count which alleged that the defendant stole £200 from A one day and £200 from B the next would be duplicitous because there are two separate acts of theft. See also *Barton v DPP* [2001] EWHC Admin 223.

Part II 14A.10 of the *Criminal Practice Directions* says that circumstances in which such a count may be appropriate include, but are not limited to:

(a) the victim on each occasion was the same (or there was no identifiable individual victim, eg in a case of the unlawful importation of controlled drugs or of money laundering);
(b) the alleged incidents involved a 'marked degree of repetition in the method employed or in their location, or both';
(c) the alleged incidents 'took place over a clearly defined period, typically (but not necessarily) no more than about a year';

In any event, the defence must be 'such as to apply to every alleged incident without differentiation'. Where what is in issue differs between different incidents, a single 'multiple incidents' count will not be appropriate.

If a section of a statute creates one offence which may be committed in a number of ways, the alternatives may properly be charged in a single count. If, however, the section creates more than one offence, each offence the prosecution wish the jury to consider must be put in a separate count. A good example of this principle (in practice, if not in strict legal theory) may be seen in the offence of handling stolen goods (s 22 of the Theft Act 1968). Handling effectively comprises two offences. The first is that of dishonestly receiving stolen goods; the second comprises all the other ways of handling (these ways are all different ways of committing a single offence). The various ways of committing the second form of handling can, and usually will, be charged in a single count. However, a single count which charged both receiving and the other forms of handling together would be regarded as defective.

Thus, there are two basic handling counts; either:

- AB on [date] dishonestly received stolen goods, namely [description of goods], knowing or believing the same to be stolen goods; or
- AB on [date] dishonestly undertook or assisted in the retention, removal, disposal or realisation of stolen goods, namely [description of goods], by or for the benefit of another, or dishonestly arranged to do so, knowing or believing the same to be stolen goods.

If a count is duplicitous (in that it charges more than one offence), the defence may make an application to quash the indictment. However, the prosecution may counter this application by asking for leave to amend the indictment under s 5(1) of the Indictments Act 1915, thus splitting the duplicitous count into two separate counts.

Duplicity as a ground of appeal against conviction was considered in *R v Levantiz* [1999] 1 Cr App R 465, where several discrete acts of supplying a controlled drug had been alleged in a single count in the indictment. The Court of Appeal held that, where a count is duplicitous, that count is not void and the conviction is not necessarily unsafe. It follows that an appeal against conviction on that count can be dismissed if the Court of Appeal decides that the conviction is safe despite the irregularity in the indictment. In deciding whether a conviction based on a duplicitous count is safe, it is submitted that the court should ask itself whether the accused was prejudiced by the duplicitous nature of the count. If it is the case that the defendant must have been guilty of everything alleged in the count—or nothing alleged in the count—it is unlikely that he would have been prejudiced by the duplicity.

Each count in an indictment is a separate entity (see **Figure 10.1**). In *R v O'Neill* [2003] EWCA Crim 411, the defendant was charged in an indictment which included a count that was defective, in that it was based on a statutory provision which had not been in force at the relevant time. The Court of Appeal confirmed that even if one count charges an offence not known to the law, any other counts in the same indictment can stand and need not be quashed.

10.1.3 Who draws up the indictment?

The indictment is normally drafted by the Crown Prosecution Service. In complex cases, however, counsel may be instructed to advise on evidence and to draft the indictment. The document is then sent to the Crown Court, where it is signed by an officer of the court.

No. 2015/12345

INDICTMENT

THE CROWN COURT AT CROYDON

THE QUEEN v ANDREW JAMES CLARKE

ANDREW JAMES CLARKE is charged as follows:

COUNT 1

Statement of Offence

Burglary, contrary to s 9(1)(b) of the Theft Act 1968

Particulars of Offence

ANDREW JAMES CLARKE, on 3 November 2015, having entered a dwelling, namely 27 Acacia Avenue Croydon, as a trespasser, stole therein a television set and video recorder belonging to John Mark Richardson.

COUNT 2

Statement of Offence

Unlawful wounding, contrary to s 20 of the Offences Against the Person Act 1861

Particulars of Offence

ANDREW JAMES CLARKE, on 3 November 2015, unlawfully and maliciously wounded John Mark Richardson.

Figure 10.1 This is an example of an indictment containing two counts

Under r 14.1 of the Crim PR, the prosecutor must serve the indictment on the Crown Court officer not more than 28 days after service on the defendant and on the Crown Court (as part of the transfer procedure under s 51 or 51A of the Crime and Disorder Act 1998) copies of the documents containing the evidence on which the charge(s) are based. The Crown Court may extend this 28-day limit, even after it has expired (see r 14.1(2)). Rule 14.1(3) requires the court officer at the Crown Court to endorse any paper copy of the indictment made for the court with a note to identify it as the indictment served by the prosecution and the date on which the draft indictment was served on the court officer, and to serve a copy of the indictment on all parties. It is apparent from these provisions that the 'draft indictment' becomes an 'indictment' once it is served on the Crown Court.

By virtue of s 2(6ZA)–(6ZC) of the Administration of Justice (Miscellaneous Provisions) Act 1933, objections to an indictment based on an alleged failure to observe procedural rules may not be taken after the start of the trial (ie when the jury have been sworn); for this purpose a preparatory hearing does not mark the start of trial.

Where there is more than one defendant, the order in which the names of defendants are placed on an indictment is the responsibility of the prosecutor, who has a discretion as to that order. The mere fact that a co-defendant named later on the indictment might give evidence adverse to a defendant after that defendant has testified provides no basis for regarding the prosecution's exercise of its discretion in drafting the indictment as improper. Nor does it provide grounds for severing the indictment and ordering a separate trial since, in principle, defendants jointly charged should be tried in a single trial: *R v Cairns* [2002] EWCA Crim 2838; [2003] 1 WLR 796.

10.2 Joinder of counts

Rule 14.2(3) of the Crim PR provides that an indictment may contain more than one count if all the offences charged:

(a) are founded on the same facts; or

(b) form or are a part of a series of offences of the same or a similar character.

10.2.1 Founded on the same facts

Two offences are founded on the same facts if they arise from a single incident or are part of the same 'transaction' (eg assaulting the householder in the course of a burglary).

One offence can also arise from the same facts as another if one would not have been committed but for the other. For example, in *R v Barrell and Wilson* (1979) 69 Cr App R 250, the indictment charged assault and affray (arising out of a single incident) and attempting to pervert the course of justice (based on attempts to prevent prosecution witnesses from testifying). The defence objected to the joinder of the latter charge. However, it was held by the Court of Appeal that the phrase 'founded on the same facts' does not mean that, for charges to be properly joined in the same indictment, the facts in relation to the respective charges must be identical in substance or virtually contemporaneous; rather, the test is whether the charges have 'a common factual origin'. That test was satisfied in *Barrell and Wilson*: the allegation of attempting to pervert the course of justice would not have arisen but for the allegations of assault and affray, and so it could legitimately be said that the charges had a common factual origin.

In *R v Roberts* [2008] EWCA Crim 1304; [2009] 1 Cr App R 20, police officers searched the defendant's home. A bag containing drugs was found in the kitchen. Two firearms were found in the bedroom. The defendant was charged with unlawful possession of drugs and with firearms offences. He argued that the drugs counts and firearms counts should not appear on the same indictment. The Court of Appeal repeated that the phrase 'founded on the same facts' in r 14.2 does not mean that the facts in relation to the respective charges must be identical in substance or virtually contemporaneous. Rather, the test is whether the charges have a common factual origin. In the present case, joinder was proper. At [12] and [13], Latham LJ said:

> . . . the facts upon which each of the counts was based was [sic] the finding in the one premises at the same time of the drugs and the firearms. In our judgment, that . . . falls into the category of case where the factual connection is established by the coincidence of time and place . . .

10.2.2 Series of similar offences

For two offences to belong to a series of similar offences, there must be a 'nexus' between them. In deciding whether such a nexus exists, regard must be had to the degree of similarity between the offences both in law and on the facts. This approach was confirmed in *Ludlow v Metropolitan Police Commissioner* [1971] AC 29, where the House of Lords upheld the joinder of a count alleging attempted theft at a public house in Acton on 20 August 1968 and a count alleging robbery at a public house in Acton on 5 September 1968.

In *R v Ferrell* [2010] UKPC 20; [2011] 1 All ER 95, the defendant had been convicted of two counts of possession of a controlled drug (counts 1 and 3), two counts of possession of a controlled drug with intent to supply (counts 2 and 4) and nine counts of concealing or transferring the proceeds of drug trafficking (counts 7 to 15). One of the issues raised on appeal was whether counts 7 to 15 were properly joined with counts 1 to 4. At [9], Lord Clarke noted that the question was 'whether, in the circumstances of this case there is a sufficient nexus between the offences charged in the money laundering counts and in the drugs counts'. His Lordship went on to say that the Privy Council accepted that there was both a legal and factual nexus between the two sets of counts. Counts 1 to 4 all dealt with the supply of drugs; the drugs would have been sold for money, which would then need to be banked and, in all likelihood, laundered. On the facts, it was open to the jury to infer that the money was indeed the proceeds of drug dealing. This was so even though all the money laundering counts related to transactions that predated the possession of the drugs in the drugs counts; in the absence of a credible explanation to the contrary, it was open to the jury to infer that the defendant had had a system of selling drugs and laundering the money over an extended period (at [10] and [11]). It was open to the jury to reject the defendant's explanation (that the money derived from smuggling tobacco, not drugs) and to conclude that there was no reasonable doubt that the money came from earlier dealing in drugs (at [12]). The Privy Council was therefore satisfied that the two sets of counts charged a series of offences of a similar character which could and should be tried together, and so were properly joined (at [14]).

The decision on joinder necessarily has to be taken by the judge before the start of the trial, and before the jury will have had a chance to consider any explanation put forward by the accused. It is therefore submitted that prosecutors should err on the side of caution and draft separate indictments where there is any uncertainty as to whether the counts could be properly joined in the same indictment.

The decision in *Ferrell* may be regarded as somewhat surprising on its facts, but in *R v Marsh* (1985) 83 Cr App R 165, Mustill LJ said, at 171, that:

> It is noteworthy that Lord Pearson [in *Ludlow*] did not suggest that two separate hurdles had to be surmounted, but simply that both the law and the facts should be taken into account in considering whether the offences are similar or dissimilar. Obviously, if the offences do not have any similar legal characteristics, then strong similarities of fact will have to exist to permit joinder under the rule. But we do not understand Lord Pearson to be suggesting that the absence of legal similarity as opposed to factual similarity necessarily means that the offences cannot be described as similar in character.
>
> In this connection it is noteworthy that Lord Pearson quoted with approval from the judgment of this Court in *Kray* (1969) 53 Cr App R 569, to the effect that 'All that is necessary to satisfy the rule is that the offences should exhibit such similar features as to establish a prima facie case that they can properly and conveniently be tried together'.
>
> It follows that the test for joinder requires consideration of how similar (or dissimilar) the charges are, both in law and on their facts.

10.3 Joinder of defendants

A count in an indictment can name more than one defendant if it is alleged that there was more than one participant in the offence (*DPP v Merriman* [1973] AC 584). Where one person is alleged to have aided and abetted the other, that person can either be charged specifically with aiding and abetting, or as a principal offender. In practice, however, secondary participants are usually charged as principal offenders. So, if it is alleged that D1 carried out a burglary and D2 acted as look-out, the usual practice would be to charge them jointly (in the same count) with burglary (the prosecutor will explain in the opening speech to the jury what roles each of the accused are alleged to have played in the offence).

It is permissible to join defendants in an indictment even if the defendants are not charged with the same offence (ie they are charged in separate counts), provided that the offences are sufficiently linked so that they can properly be joined under r 14.2(3). In *R v Assim* [1966] 2 QB 249, for example, there were two defendants. The charges arose out of a fracas at a nightclub. A receptionist at a nightclub (D1) had tried to prevent a customer from leaving without paying and was alleged to have wounded the customer; another customer had intervened and was allegedly assaulted by a doorman (D2). Given the fact that this was effectively a single incident with a number of participants, it was held that there was sufficient nexus for the two separate counts (one against D1 and the other against D2) to be joined in the same indictment.

10.4 Discretion to order separate trials

Section 5(3) of the Indictments Act 1915 provides that where (either before the trial or at any stage of a trial) the court is of the opinion that the defendant may be:

> prejudiced or embarrassed in his defence by reason of being charged with more than one offence in the same indictment, or that for any other reason it is desirable to direct that the person should be tried separately for any one or more offences charged in an indictment, the court may order a separate trial of any count or counts of such indictment.

This power to order separate trials of offences on an indictment is technically known as 'severing the indictment'. It applies both to a defendant who seeks separate trials for a number of different offences and to co-defendants seeking separate trials from each other.

This power can only be exercised where joinder of the offences is proper under r 14.2(3) of the Crim PR, and so cannot be used to cure the defect where counts are joined improperly (see *R v Newland* [1988] QB 402).

The power to order separate trials applies where a single trial would 'prejudice' or 'embarrass' the defendant(s) or if there is some other 'good reason' (s 5(3)). In *Ludlow*, the House of Lords said that where counts are properly joined, they should normally be tried together unless the defendant can show a 'special feature' justifying separate trials. In other words, the burden rests on the defendant to show that exceptional circumstances merit separate trials.

Relevant considerations include the following:

(a) How easy or difficult will it be for the jury to disentangle the evidence relating to the different counts?

(b) Is one of the counts likely to arouse hostility in the minds of the jurors, creating a risk that they will not approach the other counts with open minds?

(c) Is the strength of the evidence relating to the counts disproportionate, with the risk that the jury will think that if the defendant is guilty of the charge supported by the stronger evidence, he must also be guilty of the charge in respect of which the evidence is weaker?

(d) Is the evidence on all the counts weak, creating a risk that the jury may convict on the basis of an overview of the case rather than considering the evidence in respect of each count separately?

It has to be borne in mind that the effect of these risks can often be minimised, if not removed altogether, by appropriately worded directions from the judge on how to approach the task of analysing the evidence.

Where there are two defendants and they seek separate trials, it has to be shown that a fair trial cannot be achieved without severance. Judges are generally reluctant to order separate trials of defendants charged with the same offence: if there are separate trials, the cost of the proceedings will be doubled, the witnesses will have to testify twice and there is a risk of inconsistent verdicts.

In *R v Lake* (1976) 64 Cr App R 172, for example, the prosecution evidence included material which was admissible against D1 but inadmissible against D2. D2 argued that he should be tried separately, since the jury would otherwise hear the inadmissible evidence. The Court of Appeal upheld the judge's refusal to order separate trials, on the basis that the judge's direction to the jury was sufficient to ensure that the jury would disregard evidence that was inadmissible against D2 when considering the case against that defendant, even if the same evidence was admissible against D1. Similarly, separate trials were not thought necessary in *R v Grondkowsik and Malinowski* [1946] KB 369, even though the defendants were blaming each other (running so-called 'cut-throat' defences). In *R v Miah* [2011] EWCA Crim 945, the Court of Appeal proceeded on the basis that it is only in 'very exceptional' cases that a judge should exercise his judgment in favour of ordering a separate trial for one or more defendants pursuant to s 5(3) of the Indictment Act 1915. At [59], Aikens LJ said that:

> the fact that a co-defendant is running a 'cut throat' defence is common and is very seldom a successful ground, standing alone, for severance. Nor is the fact that one co-defendant has implicated another in the offences charged in the course of a police interview, which is denied by that second co-defendant and which is not admissible as evidence against him. Further, there is always the possibility that a co-defendant who has made an exculpatory statement in interview but at the same time has implicated co-defendants will decide not to give evidence at the trial and rely on just his police interview. Those factors are commonplace.

10.5 Misjoinder

If an indictment contains counts which should not be joined together, because the rules for joinder are not satisfied, there is no power to 'sever' the indictment (ie to order separate trials). In *R v Newland* [1988] QB 402, the defendant was charged with a drugs offence and three counts alleging assaults which were wholly unconnected with the drugs charge. The trial judge simply ordered separate trials (purporting to 'sever' the indictment under the Indictments Act 1915, s 5(3)), so that the drugs offence and the assault charges were tried separately. The Court of Appeal held that the judge had no power to 'sever' the indictment under s 5(3), since this power applies only to a valid indictment, and the indictment in the present case was defective because it failed to comply with what is now r 14.2(3) of the Crim PR. The court went on to say that the trial judge should have deleted from the indictment either the drugs charge or the assault charges, and proceeded with the trial on that indictment. The allegations deleted from the indictment could only be proceeded with if the prosecution brought fresh proceedings in the magistrates' court in respect of them or else sought a voluntary bill of indictment.

In *R v Follett* [1989] QB 338, however, a differently constituted Court of Appeal accepted a rather simpler solution. In this case, the indictment was again invalid because it contained counts which were not sufficiently linked. The Court of Appeal upheld the decision of the trial judge to stay proceedings on the indictment as drafted and to give the prosecution leave to serve fresh indictments (each one complying with r 14.2(3)). The effect of this is that the defective indictment remains in existence but becomes irrelevant. Two or more separate trials then follow, based on the new indictments.

It follows that, where there has been misjoinder, the situation can be remedied either by:

- deleting one or more counts from the indictment, leaving only counts which can properly be joined under r 14.2(3) (the course of action taken in *Newland*); or

- staying the existing indictment and allowing the prosecution to serve fresh indictments, each indictment containing only counts which can properly be joined under r 14.2(3) (the course of action taken in *Follett*).

There was authority to the effect that an indictment containing improperly joined counts was invalid (and so if a defendant was to be convicted on such an indictment, all the convictions would have to be quashed). However, that line of authority was based on a misreading of *Newland*. In *R v Smith* [1997] QB 836, three summary offences were added to an indictment under CJA 1988, s 40; joinder of two of those summary offences was improper because there was no sufficient link with the indictable offence which was also on the indictment. The Court of Appeal held that convictions for offences which are correctly joined are valid convictions. Accordingly, the convictions for the indictable offence and the correctly joined summary offence stood; only the convictions for the two improperly joined summary offences were quashed. Similarly, in *R v Lockley and Sainsbury* [1997] Crim LR 455, the appellants were charged with conspiracy to commit burglary and dangerous driving (the car they used in connection with the burglary was dangerously defective). Both offences are indictable offences and so only r 14.2(3) of the Crim PR had to be considered. The Court of Appeal held that the dangerous driving charge was improperly joined and confirmed that CJA 1988, s 40 and r 14.2(3) are in all material respects in the same terms (and so the same principles regarding misjoinder and the consequences thereof must apply to both). The court went on to hold that misjoinder does not nullify the whole indictment. It followed that only the conviction(s) on the wrongly joined count(s) should be quashed. It is thus clear that misjoinder of counts does not render the entire indictment invalid. In *R v McGrath* [2013] EWCA Crim 1261, the Court of Appeal confirmed that misjoinder of counts does not render the entire indictment invalid.

10.6 Deciding the contents of the indictment

In most cases, the counts on the indictment are the same as the charges which were sent for trial to the Crown Court from the magistrates' court. However, it is possible for the indictment to contain different charges from the original ones. Under s 2(2) of the Administration of Justice (Miscellaneous Provisions) Act 1933, the indictment may contain, as well as or instead of the original charges, any counts which are disclosed in the prosecution witness statements and which can properly be joined in the same indictment.

Rule 14.2(5) of the Crim PR states that an indictment may contain any count 'charging substantially the same offence' as one for which the defendant was sent for trial, or 'any other count based on the prosecution evidence already served which the Crown Court may try'.

In *R v Lombardi* [1989] 1 WLR 73, the Court of Appeal emphasised that counts for which there is evidence in the prosecution papers, but in respect of which the accused was not sent for trial, can only be added to the indictment if they are in substitution for offences which were sent for trial, or could lawfully be joined in the indictment which results from the sending of the original offence(s) to the Crown Court (on the basis that they arise from the same facts as, or form a series of offences of the same or similar character to, the original charge).

Some examples may help to illustrate the effect of s 2(2) of the 1933 Act.

EXAMPLE 1

The defendant is sent for trial on a charge of burglary. The prosecutor, when drafting the indictment, takes the view that, although there is ample evidence of theft, the evidence relating to the element of trespass is very weak. The prosecutor could draft a count for theft in place of the burglary charge on which the defendant was sent for trial (and so the defendant would be tried for theft, not burglary).

EXAMPLE 2

The magistrates send the defendant for trial on a charge of theft but the prosecutor subsequently decides that there is sufficient evidence to prove that the theft was committed in the course of a burglary. The prosecutor could indict the defendant for burglary instead of theft (and so the defendant would be tried for burglary, not theft).

EXAMPLE 3

The defendant is sent for trial on a single charge of robbery. The prosecution witness statements include evidence that the defendant was brandishing a gun at the time of the robbery. The allegation of possession of a firearm arises from the same facts as the robbery, so the prosecutor could add a charge alleging a firearms offence even though the defendant was not sent for trial in respect of that offence.

EXAMPLE 4

The defendant is charged with handling stolen goods. In the course of investigating the handling charge, the police search the defendant's home and find a quantity of drugs. There is no link at all between the stolen goods and the drugs. The defendant is sent for trial only on the handling offence. The prosecutor cannot add a drugs charge to the handling charge, because the defendant was not sent for trial in respect of it and joinder of the two charges would not be permissible under r 14.2(3), as there is no sufficient link between the two charges. The prosecutor cannot put the drugs charge in a separate indictment, because the defendant was not sent for trial in respect of the drugs charge.

In *Lombardi*, Lord Lane CJ also confirmed that, where the magistrates have sent a defendant to the Crown Court on more than one charge, the prosecution may prefer a number of separate indictments if they feel that it is appropriate to do so.

Similarly, if the magistrates send two or more defendants for trial at the same time, it is open to the prosecution to draft separate indictments against them if the prosecution feel that it would be appropriate to do so. If defendants are not sent for trial at the same time, it is nevertheless open to the prosecution to join those defendants in the same indictment (assuming r 14.2(3) is satisfied); this is so even if an indictment in respect of a defendant who has been sent for trial has already been signed (see *Criminal Practice Directions*, Part II 14A.2).

Paragraph 6.1 of the Code for Crown Prosecutors (Selection of charges) is relevant when the indictment is drafted (as well as at the earlier stage when the original charges are selected). It states that prosecutors should select charges which:

(a) reflect the seriousness and extent of the offending supported by the evidence;

(b) give the court adequate powers to sentence and impose appropriate post-conviction orders; and

(c) enable the case to be presented in a clear and simple way.

10.7 Alternative counts

It is possible for counts to appear on an indictment in the alternative. For example, the indictment might contain one count alleging wounding with intent (s 18 of the Offences Against the Person Act 1861) and a separate count alleging unlawful wounding (s 20 of the 1861 Act). This is appropriate where the prosecutor is unsure whether there is sufficient evidence to prove the more serious offence. Nothing on the face of the indictment indicates that the counts are alternatives, so this fact has to be explained to the jury.

10.8 Specimen counts

A 'specimen' (or 'sample') count is where the defendant is charged with one or more offences occurring on specific occasions, but the prosecution allege that such conduct was representative of other criminal conduct of the same kind on other occasions which are not the subject of specific charges. However, the use of specimen counts can be problematic, given that a defendant can only be sentenced for offences to which he has pleaded guilty (or been found guilty). In *R v Smith; R v Tovey* [2005] EWCA Crim 530; [2005] 2 Cr App R (S) 100, the Court of Appeal said that, in preparing the indictment, the prosecution should always have in mind, in a situation of multiple offending, the need to provide the sentencing judge with sufficient examples (and no more) of the offending to enable the judge to impose a sentence which properly reflects the offender's criminal behaviour. It is also important to draft the counts that are included in the indictment so as to establish the period during which the offending occurred (eg whether the offences occurred regularly over a significant period).

10.9 Amending the indictment

Under s 5(1) of the Indictments Act 1915, where, either before the trial or at any stage during the trial, it appears to the court that the indictment is defective, the court is empowered to make such order for the amendment of the indictment as it thinks necessary to meet the circumstances of the case unless, having regard to the merits of the case, the required amendments cannot be made without injustice.

In *R v Pople* [1951] 1 KB 53, it was held that it is not necessary that an indictment, in order to be 'defective' within the meaning of s 5(1), must be bad on its face. On the contrary, said the court, any alteration in matters of description may be made in order to meet the evidence in the case so long as the amendment causes no injustice to the accused. In that case, the Court of Appeal upheld the decision of the trial judge to allow the indictment to be amended at the close of the prosecution case to allege the obtaining by deception of a cheque rather than alleging the obtaining of a sum of money for which the cheque was drawn. The court held that the defendant was not prejudiced, since the substance of the allegation was unaltered.

In *R v Collison* (1980) 71 Cr App R 249, the defendant was charged with one count of wounding with intent (s 18 of the Offences Against the Person Act 1861). The jury were unable to reach either a unanimous or a majority verdict on this count. The judge allowed the prosecution to add a further count of unlawful wounding (contrary to s 20 of the 1861 Act). The Court of Appeal held that no injustice to the defendant had resulted from the amendment since the lesser s 20 offence was effectively already before the jury, since the jury could have acquitted the defendant of the s 18 offence and convicted him of the s 20 offence under s 6(3) of the Criminal Law Act 1967.

The important question in deciding whether or not to allow an amendment once the trial has started is whether the defence case would have been conducted differently had the amendment taken place at the outset. For example, in *R v Harris, The Times*, 22 March 1993, the defendant was charged with rape but, at the close of the defence case, the prosecution applied to add an alternative count alleging attempted rape to the indictment. The judge allowed this amendment, but the Court of Appeal held that this decision was wrong, since the defence case would have been put differently (different cross-examination of prosecution witnesses and different defence evidence). Similarly, in *R v Thomas* [1983] Crim LR 619, the Court of Appeal quashed a conviction where a count of receiving stolen property was added to an indictment which hitherto alleged only theft. This amendment took place after the close of the prosecution case and the defence would have cross-examined the prosecution witnesses differently if both allegations had been made at the outset. In *R v Foster* [2007] EWCA Crim 2869; [2008] 1 WLR 1615, Sir Igor Judge P said (at [65]):

> . . . it is now common practice to permit amendments to the indictment at any stage of the trial, whether by amending or adding or substituting new counts, provided that these steps may be taken without unfairness to the accused. Whether unfairness results will usually depend on the purpose of the amendment, the stage of the trial at which the amendment is sought, the degree, if any, to which the defendant is required by the amendment to meet a new prosecution case and whether he would be disadvantaged in the presentation of his defence.

The amendment may take the form of inserting a new count in the indictment, whether in addition to, or instead of, the original count (*R v Johal* [1973] QB 475). Where there is no injustice to the defendant, an indictment can even be amended under s 5(1) so as to add a new defendant (*R v Palmer* [2002] EWCA Crim 892).

In *R v Thompson* [2011] EWCA Crim 102, the court had to decide whether an indictment can be amended to add counts in respect of matters which have arisen after the date when the case was sent for trial. It was held, following *R v Osieh* [1996] 1 WLR 1260, that this is possible. However, Thomas LJ said (at [29]) that 'Although, in our judgment, there is the power to amend the indictment to add matters subsequent to the [sending], . . . circumstances in which it might be done are likely to be rare'. His Lordship added (at [32]) that the real issue 'is whether there is any prejudice or injustice to a defendant or to the fair and proper conduct of an orderly trial if this is done'.

11 Crown Court trial

11.1 Pre-trial hearings

There are several different pre-trial hearings which may take place.

11.1.1 Early guilty plea hearings

In order to maximise the credit for pleading guilty at the earliest reasonable opportunity, a defendant who was not able to formally indicate a guilty plea in the magistrates' court (as will be the case where the offence is triable only on indictment, and so there is no 'plea before venue' hearing in the magistrates' court), and who wishes to enter a guilty plea, should request an 'early guilty plea hearing' (see **Chapter 13**).

11.1.2 Preliminary hearings

Part I 3A.9 of the *Criminal Practice Directions* states that the magistrates' court or the Crown Court should order a 'preliminary hearing' where there are case management issues which call for such a hearing, or the trial is likely to last for more than four weeks, or it would be desirable to set an early trial date, or the defendant is a child or young person. If there is to be a preliminary hearing, it should be held between 14 and 21 days after the case is sent for trial.

11.1.3 Plea and case management hearings

Where the magistrates' court does not order an early guilty plea hearing or a preliminary hearing, it must order a Plea and Case Management Hearing (PCMH) to be held within approximately 13 weeks after the case has been sent for trial where the defendant is in custody (within approximately 16 weeks where the defendant is on bail) (Part I 3A.10 of the *Criminal Practice Directions*). In a case where the defendant intends to plead not guilty, the effectiveness of the PCMH is dependent on the presence of the trial advocate or of an advocate who is able to make decisions about the conduct of the case and give the court the assistance which the trial advocate could be expected to give (para 3A.13). Additional pre-trial hearings should be held only for some compelling reason; where necessary, the power to give, vary or revoke a direction without a hearing should be used (para 3A.15).

An essential part of the PCMH is the completion of the advocates' questionnaire, a standard form which requires the parties to provide detailed information required to assist with active case management by the court.

Under s 40 of the CPIA 1996, the court may make rulings, which have binding effect, as to: (a) any question as to the admissibility of evidence; (b) any other question of law relating to the case. The extent to which courts exercise the power to make these rulings at this hearing is a matter for the court, after considering representations. Such rulings can be varied or discharged, but only if there has been a material change of circumstance since the order was made and if the judge is satisfied that it is in the interests of justice to do so. There is no appeal from rulings made at PCMHs (though a defendant who is subsequently convicted may base an appeal against conviction on such rulings).

11.1.4 Preparatory hearings

Under the CPIA 1996, s 29, a Crown Court judge may, 'on an application by one of the parties or of his own motion', order a preparatory hearing to take place if it appears to the judge that the indictment 'reveals a case of such complexity, a case of such seriousness or a case whose trial is likely to be of such length, that substantial benefits are likely to accrue from a hearing . . .'.

Thus a preparatory hearing can be held on the basis that the case appears to be:

- complex; or
- serious; or
- lengthy.

Section 29(2) sets out the purposes of the preparatory hearing. These include:

- *identifying issues which are likely to be material to the determinations and findings which are likely to be required during the trial;*
- *assisting the comprehension by the jury of any such issues;*
- *expediting the proceedings before the jury;*
- *assisting the judge's management of the trial;*
- *considering questions as to the severance or joinder of charges.*

Section 31(3) empowers the judge to make rulings as to:

(a) any question as to the admissibility of evidence;

(b) any other question of law relating to the case;

(c) any question as to the severance or joinder of charges.

Section 35 makes provision for appeals from rulings made by the judge at a preparatory hearing to the Court of Appeal. Where leave to appeal has been granted, the preparatory hearing may continue, but the trial cannot begin until the appeal has been determined or abandoned.

In *R v I* [2009] EWCA Crim 1793; [2010] 1 Cr App R 10, the Court of Appeal sought to reduce the number of preparatory hearings. At para 21, Hughes LJ said:

> It is emphatically not the case that most heavy fraud or similar cases will nowadays call for a preparatory hearing. Virtually the only reason for directing such a hearing nowadays is if the judge is going to have to give a ruling which ought to be the subject of an interlocutory appeal. Such rulings are few and far between and do not extend to most rulings of law. An interlocutory appeal can be a most beneficial process in a few, very limited, circumstances . . .

At para 22, Hughes LJ went on to say that:

> Given the co-extensive powers of case management outside the preparatory hearing regime, courts ought to be very cautious about directing a preparatory hearing under s 29 of the CPIA . . . ; in particular, the desire of one party to test a ruling by interlocutory appeal is not a good enough reason for doing so, unless the point is one of the few which is genuinely suitable for that procedure . . . and there is a real prospect of such appeal being both capable of resolution in the absence of evidence and avoiding significant wastage of time at the trial.

In *R v Quillan* [2015] EWCA Crim 538, the Court of Appeal (at [10]–[11]) said that there may be 'special circumstances where a trial will be very long and very costly and where a ruling on a point of law in relation to the legal basis on which a count in the indictment is founded may determine whether or not a trial is required at all', in which case it may be appropriate for there to be a preparatory hearing.

11.1.5 Abuse of process

One application that may be made at an early stage of the proceedings is for those proceedings to be 'stayed' because they amount to an 'abuse of process'. The effect of such a stay is that the proceedings are effectively terminated. In R *v Beckford* [1996] 1 Cr App R 94, Neill LJ said (at 100) that the 'constitutional principle which underlies the jurisdiction to stay proceedings is that the courts have the power and the duty to protect the law by protecting its own purposes and functions'. His Lordship quoted the words of Lord Devlin in *Connelly v DPP* [1964] AC 1254 (at p 1354), that the courts have 'an inescapable duty to secure fair treatment for those who come or are brought before them'. Neill LJ went on (at 101) to note that the jurisdiction to stay proceedings can be exercised in many different circumstances but that two main strands could be detected in the authorities:

(a) cases where the court concludes that the accused cannot receive a fair trial;

(b) cases where the court concludes that it would be unfair for the accused to be tried.

The former focuses on the trial process itself; the latter is relevant where the accused should not be standing trial at all (irrespective of the fairness of the actual trial).

Two key questions are apparent from the case law on abuse of process:

(1) To what extent is the accused prejudiced?

(2) To what degree are the rule of law and the administration of justice undermined by the behaviour of the investigators or the prosecution?

There is no definitive list of complaints which are capable of amounting to abuse of process, but it is possible to derive some categories of abuse from the case law. Examples include: lengthy delay which causes prejudice to the accused; failure to honour an undertaking given to the accused; failure to secure evidence or destruction of evidence; tactical manipulation or misuse of procedures in order to deprive the accused of some protection provided by the law, or taking unfair advantage of a technicality; entrapment; abuse of executive power.

The procedure to be followed when making an abuse of process application to stay proceedings in the Crown Court is contained in Part I 3C of the *Criminal Practice Directions*. In summary, this requires written notice of the application to be given to the prosecutor (and to any co-accused) and to the court at least 14 days before the date fixed for trial. The notice has to specify the nature of the application, and set out the grounds upon which it is made. The advocate appearing for the applicant must serve a skeleton argument on the court and on the other parties at least five working days before the application is due to be heard. The prosecution advocate must serve a responsive skeleton argument at least two working days before the hearing. The skeleton arguments must set out any propositions of law to be advanced, together with any authorities (identifying specific passages) that are relied on.

It should be noted that the abuse of process jurisdiction of magistrates' courts is narrower than that of the Crown Court: where it is contended that a summary trial should not take place because it would be unfair to try the defendant (as opposed to the question being whether he can have a fair trial), the issue of abuse of process has to be dealt with by the High Court, not in the magistrates' court (*Nembhard v DPP* [2009] EWHC 194 (Admin); *R (Smith) v CPS* [2010] EWHC 3593 (Admin)).

11.1.6 Bail

In *R v Central Criminal Court, ex p Guney* [1996] AC 616, the House of Lords held that a defendant who has not previously surrendered to the custody of the court, surrenders to the custody of the court at the moment of arraignment. The result is that the Crown Court judge then has to decide whether or not to grant bail; unless the judge grants bail, the defendant will remain in custody pending and during the trial.

In *R v Evans* [2011] EWCA Crim 2842; (2012) 176 JP 139, the defendant's advocate went into the courtroom where the case was likely to be heard and told the usher that the defendant was in the building. The defendant later walked out of the building and did not return. When his case was called on, he was not there and a bench warrant for his arrest was issued. He was subsequently dealt with for the offence of failing to surrender to bail, contrary to s 6(1) of the Bail Act 1976. Hughes LJ (at para 20) summarised the practical effect of *Guney* thus:

> once arraignment has taken place, however informal its particular circumstances may be, the court must review the question of bail and if a surety is involved direct a fresh taking of a reconnaissance . . . whenever else it may happen surrender is deemed to have taken place on arraignment.

His Lordship went on to say (at para 27) that surrender is normally accomplished by way of entry into the dock. However, in the Crown Court, 'surrender may also be accomplished by the commencement of any hearing before the judge where the defendant is formally identified and whether he enters the dock or not'. Consequently, the court rejected (at para 28) the suggestion that reporting to the usher amounts to surrender. The court reasoned (at para 29) that:

> in the absence of either stepping into the dock in a Crown Court or in such a court being formally identified for the purposes of hearing, the defendant has not put himself into anything which can properly be called 'custody'. Nor . . . has he overtly subjected himself to the directions of the court.

His Lordship added (at para 32) that:

> once a defendant arrives at the Crown Court building he is in one sense not entirely at liberty to come and go as he wishes. That, however, does not seem to us to mean that he has thereby surrendered. Indeed it is common ground that mere arrival at the Crown Court building does not constitute surrender and could not do so. The correct analysis seems to us to be not that he has surrendered but that he knows that he may be required at any moment to do so and in consequence he would be very unwise to wander away.

It follows that:

> in the absence of special arrangements either particular to the court or particular to the individual case, surrender to the Crown Court is accomplished when the defendant presents himself to the custody officers by entering the dock or where a hearing before the judge commences at which he is formally identified as present.

Moreover, 'if there has been no previous surrender, as ordinarily there will have been, it is also accomplished by arraignment' (per Hughes LJ at para 36).

In *R v Maidstone Crown Court, ex p Jodka* (1997) 161 JP 638, the Divisional Court held that bail granted by magistrates ceases when the defendant surrenders to the custody of the Crown Court, whether or not the defendant is arraigned at the hearing at which he or she surrenders. Where the magistrates grant bail subject to a surety, the responsibility of that surety under the magistrates' court order ceases once the defendant surrenders to the custody of the Crown Court. If the Crown Court wishes to grant bail subject to the same surety, the court must consider the position of that surety before imposing such a condition. The Court of Appeal in *Evans* confirmed that this is so. Hughes LJ (at para 33) said:

> It is important to remember that if a Magistrates' Court commits on bail with or without a condition that a surety provide a recognisance, that bail and recognisance lapse on the first appearance in the Crown Court. It cannot in law carry through subsequent adjournments in that Crown Court. On the other hand, the Crown Court, if it renews bail, does have the power to make the recognisance continuous for all future appearances. All that underlines the importance of attention being paid to the terms of a defendant's bail, particularly at the conclusion of the first hearing in the Crown Court. At that point conditions of bail should always be considered. Of course it is sufficient to do so briefly by simply re-imposing conditions previously placed there by the magistrates, if that is appropriate and especially if there is no objection. But in both surety cases and non-surety cases an assessment of bail is required at the end of the first hearing in each Crown Court.

It follows from this that the question of bail will have to be considered at the PCMH. In any event, if the defendant is on bail before the trial, this bail effectively expires at the start of the trial. Therefore, a defendant who was on bail before the trial, and so surrendered to the custody of the court at the start of the trial, will only be released from custody if the judge grants bail. So a very brief bail application has to be made at the lunchtime adjournment and the end of each day. Such applications should be made in the absence of the jury (as refusal might prejudice them against the accused). Part III 19G.2 of the *Criminal Practice Directions* states that, once a trial has begun the further grant of bail, whether during short adjournments (eg at lunchtime) or overnight, is in the discretion of the judge, adding that it 'may be a proper exercise of this discretion to refuse bail during the short adjournment if the accused cannot otherwise be segregated from witnesses and jurors'. Paragraph 19G.3 goes on to say that an accused who was on bail while on remand (ie before the trial) should not be refused bail during the trial unless the judge is of the opinion that there are 'positive reasons to justify this refusal'. The *Practice Directions* suggest that such reasons might include:

(a) that a point has been reached where there is a real danger that the accused will abscond, either because the case is going badly for the defence, or for any other reason;
(b) that there is a real danger that the accused may interfere with witnesses, jurors or co-defendants.

Paragraph 19G.4 adds that, once the defendant has been found guilty, 'a further renewal of bail should be decided in the light of the gravity of the offence, any friction between co-defendants and the likely sentence to be passed in all the circumstances of the case'.

11.1.7 Adjournments

The existence of the various forms of pre-trial hearing should mean that the trial can go ahead on the date that is fixed. However, there may still be occasions when an adjournment is sought. In *R v Chaaban* [2003] EWCA Crim 1012, Judge LJ (at para 36) said that adjournments must be justified and, if at all possible, should be avoided. However, his Lordship noted that the decision whether or not to adjourn is pre-eminently a matter for the trial judge, and so the Court of Appeal will not interfere with that decision unless it can be demonstrated that the decision to refuse an adjournment was wholly unreasonable and caused real (as opposed to fanciful) prejudice to the defendant, thereby undermining the safety of the conviction.

11.2 The arraignment

At the arraignment (which usually takes place at the PCMH, unless the defendants has indicated that he intends to plead guilty, in which case the plea will be entered at an early guilty plea hearing), the indictment is 'put' to the defendant, in that he or she is asked to plead guilty or not guilty. The proceedings will go something like this:

Clerk of the Court: 'Are you Michael Smith?'
Smith: 'Yes.'
Clerk: 'Michael Smith, you are charged in an indictment containing one count of robbery contrary to s 8 of the Theft Act 1968. The particulars of the offence are that on 8 December 2014 you robbed Alice Jones of £450 in cash. Michael Smith, to this indictment do you plead guilty or not guilty?'

If the indictment contains more than one count, each count will be put to the defendant separately, so that a separate plea is entered on each. The defendant must enter their plea personally (not through counsel or solicitor).

11.2.1 Presence of defendant

The defendant must be present at the arraignment in order to enter a plea. If the defendant fails to attend court on the date fixed for the trial, a bench warrant for the defendant's arrest will usually be issued. The court also has a discretion to proceed with the trial in the absence of the defendant. However, Crim PR, r 38.2(1)(b) provides that the court must not proceed if the defendant is absent, unless the court is satisfied both that the defendant has waived the right to attend and that the trial will be fair despite the defendant's absence. Moreover, Part III 19E.2 of the *Criminal Practice Directions* says that the court must exercise its discretion 'with due regard for the interests of justice', adding that the 'overriding concern must be to ensure that such a trial is as fair as circumstances permit and leads to a just outcome. If the defendant's absence is due to involuntary illness or incapacity it would very rarely, if ever, be right to exercise the discretion in favour of commencing or continuing the trial.' Paragraph

19E.3 goes on to say that, in the Crown Court, proceeding in the absence of a defendant is a step which ought normally to be taken 'only if it is unavoidable', and the court must exercise its discretion to allow the trial to take place or continue in the defendant's absence 'with the utmost care and caution'. The Practice Directions refer to *R v Jones* [2002] UKHL 5; [2003] 1 AC 1, where it was held that circumstances to be taken into account before proceedings in the defendant's absence include:

(a) the conduct of the defendant;
(b) the disadvantage to the defendant;
(c) the public interest, taking account of the inconvenience and hardship to witnesses, and especially to any complainant, of a delay (if the witnesses have attended court and are ready to give evidence, that will weigh in favour of continuing with the trial);
(d) the effect of any delay;
(e) whether the attendance of the defendant could be secured at a later hearing; and
(f) the likely outcome if the defendant is found guilty.

In *R v O'Hare* [2006] EWCA Crim 471, it was said that it should be made clear to each defendant that if he fails to attend a trial, the trial may well proceed in his absence and without legal representation.

Part III 19E.3 of the *Criminal Practice Directions* says that, even if the defendant is voluntarily absent, it is still generally desirable that he or she is represented. In *R v Kepple* [2007] EWCA Crim 1339, the Court of Appeal said that where the defendant is being tried *in absentia* but counsel continues to act, counsel should conduct the case, on the basis of any instructions already received from the client, as though the client were still present in court but had decided not to give evidence. Counsel is free to use any material contained in the brief, and may cross-examine prosecution witnesses (to put the absent defendant's case to them or to cast doubt upon the coherence or accuracy of their accounts) and may call defence witnesses.

11.2.2 Procedure on a plea of guilty

If the defendant pleads guilty to all the counts on the indictment, the prosecution will summarise the facts of the offence(s) and tell the court about the defendant's antecedents, that is basic details about them (education, employment, income, etc), based on what the defendant has told the police, together with details of any relevant previous convictions. The court will in fact have a complete list of the defendant's previous convictions, but will invite the prosecution to read out only those that are relevant.

If the defendant pleads guilty to some charges but not guilty to others, the sentencing on the offences to which there was a guilty plea will usually be postponed until the trial of the charges on which there was a not guilty plea has been concluded.

11.2.3 The *Newton* hearing

In some cases, the defendant may plead guilty to an offence but on a factual basis that is less serious than the version of events put forward by the prosecution. The procedure to be adopted by the court in such a case was laid down in *R v Newton* (1982) 77 Cr App R 13. This is dealt with in **Chapter 13**.

11.2.4 Prosecution offering no evidence; leaving counts on the file

If the defendant pleads not guilty to some or all of the counts on the indictment, the next stage (which will take place some time after the PCMH) is to empanel a jury. However, it may be that new evidence has come to light showing that the wrong person has been charged or considerably weakening the case against this defendant, or it may be that a vital witness has refused to testify (and, although a person can be compelled to give evidence, a reluctant witness may well do more harm than good). In that case the prosecution will offer no evidence against the defendant, in which case a finding of not guilty is entered under the Criminal

Justice Act 1967, s 17. An alternative to offering no evidence is for the prosecution to ask the judge to direct that one or more counts be left on the file marked 'not to be proceeded with without the leave of the Crown Court or the Court of Appeal'.

If the defendant pleads guilty to some counts but not guilty to others, and the prosecution are content for the defendant to be dealt with solely on the basis of the counts to which he has pleaded guilty, prosecuting counsel may agree not to proceed with the counts to which the defendant pleads not guilty (either by offering no evidence in respect of them or asking for them to be left on the file). Leaving a count on the file is not an acquittal, whereas offering no evidence does result in an acquittal. Nonetheless, counts which have been left on the file would not be reactivated save in very unusual circumstances (eg where the Court of Appeal sets aside the guilty pleas because the pleas were entered under duress).

11.2.5 Plea of guilty to an alternative offence

The Criminal Law Act 1967 (CLA), s 6(1)(b), provides that the defendant may plead not guilty to the offence on the indictment but guilty to a lesser offence of which the jury would be able to convict him under the CLA 1967, s 6(3). For example, the offence of robbery is committed by a person who commits theft together with actual or threatened violence. If the accused admits the theft but denies the use or threat of violence, a plea of 'not guilty to robbery but guilty to theft' could be offered. In *R v Yeardley* [2000] QB 374, it was held (following *R v Hazeltine* [1967] 2 QB 857) that where the defendant pleads not guilty to the offence on the indictment but guilty to a lesser offence, the guilty plea becomes a nullity if the prosecution choose to proceed with the offence on the indictment. The obvious solution is to add the lesser offence to the indictment (the defendant then pleads guilty to one count and not guilty to the other).

11.2.6 Different pleas from different defendants

If there is more than one defendant and one pleads guilty and the others not guilty, it is a matter for the judge whether to sentence the one who has pleaded guilty immediately or at the end of the trial of the other defendant(s). The argument in favour of postponing sentence is that, at the end of the trial, the judge will have a much better idea of who did what. However, it is a little more difficult if the defendant who pleads guilty also indicates a willingness to 'turn Queen's evidence', giving evidence against the other accused. This will attract a substantial discount in sentence, well beyond the one-third normally credited to those who simply plead guilty. Such a person becomes a competent witness for the Crown after pleading guilty. However, if sentence is postponed, it may seem that the sentence imposed after the defendant has given evidence depends more on the quality of the evidence given than on the extent of the defendant's guilt; on the other hand, if the defendant is sentenced before giving evidence but then has a change of mind, the lenient sentence given on the basis of the promised testimony cannot be altered (see *R v Stone* [1970] 1 WLR 1112). The Court of Appeal, in *R v Weekes* (1980) 74 Cr App R 161, said that sentence should normally be postponed until after the trial of the other defendant(s). However, in *R v Clement*, *The Times*, 12 December 1991, the court observed that it is a matter for the judge whether the defendant is sentenced sooner or later.

If one defendant pleads guilty but another pleads not guilty, the jury should not be told about the guilty plea of the other defendant (unless, of course, that defendant gives evidence for the prosecution). For example, in *R v Manzur and Mahmood* [1997] 1 Cr App R 414, three people had been charged with rape. One defendant pleaded guilty, the other two pleaded not guilty, saying that the victim had consented to sexual intercourse. The judge allowed the jury to be told of the third defendant's plea of guilty. The Court of Appeal accepted the argument that the jury might have taken the view, on the basis of the third defendant's guilty plea, that the two appellants must have known that the victim was not consenting and so might not have given proper consideration to the evidence of the two appellants that they believed the woman to be consenting to intercourse. The admission of the evidence of the plea of the third defendant was therefore unduly prejudicial to the appellants and so a retrial was ordered.

11.2.7 Change of plea

The defendant may change plea from not guilty to guilty at any stage of the trial before the jury has returned a verdict. The defence simply asks for the indictment to be put again and the defendant then pleads guilty. The jury usually returns a formal verdict of guilty; however, in *R v Poole* [2002] 1 WLR 1528, the Court of Appeal held that where a defendant pleads not guilty but then changes the plea to guilty during the course of the trial, there is no requirement that the judge should ask the jury for a formal verdict of guilty. It is permissible for the judge simply to discharge the jury and proceed to sentencing.

The defendant can change plea from guilty to not guilty at any stage of the trial prior to the passing of sentence, but only with the permission of the judge (*S v Recorder of Manchester* [1971] AC 481). The judge will want some explanation for the change of heart and may take into account matters such as the legal advice the accused has received, their age and level of intellect, and experience of criminal proceedings. Permission to withdraw the guilty plea is unlikely to be given unless the defendant did not realise that he had a defence when he pleaded guilty (*R v McNally* [1954] 1 WLR 933). In *R v Drew* [1985] 1 WLR 914, Lord Lane CJ (at 923) said that it would be appropriate only in rare cases to allow a defendant to change an unequivocal plea of guilty to one of not guilty. This is particularly so in cases where the accused has been advised by experienced counsel.

In *R v Sheikh* [2004] EWCA Crim 492; [2004] 2 Cr App R 13, the defendants applied to withdraw their pleas of guilty. The basis of their application was that they had not been informed that they could be made the subject of confiscation proceedings in the event of conviction. The trial judge refused to allow a change of plea, and the Court of Appeal upheld the refusal. The court said that it is well accepted that, quite apart from cases where the plea of guilty is equivocal or ambiguous, the court retains a residual discretion to allow the withdrawal of a guilty plea where not to do so might work an injustice. Examples might be where a defendant has been misinformed about the nature of the charge or the availability of a defence, or where he has been put under pressure to plead guilty in circumstances where he is not truly admitting guilt. Commonly, however, it is reserved for cases where there is doubt that the plea represents a genuine acknowledgement of guilt.

A court has no jurisdiction to allow a defendant to change his plea from guilty to not guilty after sentence has been passed (*R v Evans* [2011] EWCA Crim 2842 (per Hughes LJ, at para 7)).

11.2.8 Securing attendance of witnesses

Where the prosecution or defence wish to secure the attendance of a witness, but have reason to believe that the witness will not attend voluntarily, they can apply for a witness summons under the Criminal Procedure (Attendance of Witnesses) Act 1965, ss 2–4. The court may issue a witness summons if it is satisfied that the witness is likely to be able to give material evidence and that it is in the interests of justice to do so (s 2(1)). The procedure is set out in r 28.3 of the Crim PR.

If the judge is satisfied (by evidence on oath) that a witness in respect of whom a witness summons is in force is unlikely to comply with it, the judge may issue a warrant for the arrest of the witness (s 4(1)).

11.3 The jury

11.3.1 Who can serve?

Under the Juries Act 1974, s 1 (as amended by the Criminal Justice Act (CJA) 2003), 'every person shall be qualified to serve as a juror in the Crown Court . . . and be liable accordingly to attend for jury service when summoned under this Act' if on the electoral roll, ordinarily resident in the United Kingdom for any period of at least five years since attaining the age of 13 and not disqualified from jury service. The Criminal Justice and Courts Act 2015 amended the Juries Act 1974 to increase the upper age limit for jury service to 75.

Under Sch 1, the following are disqualified from jury service:

- those liable to be detained under the Mental Health Act 1983 or lacking capacity (within the meaning of the Mental Capacity Act 2005) to serve as a juror;
- those currently on bail in criminal proceedings; and
- those with certain previous convictions (depending on the sentence imposed: those sentenced to imprisonment for five years or more are disqualified for life; those sentenced to less than five years, or who have received a community order, are disqualified for ten years).

Everyone else is required to serve when summoned to do so.

R v Abdroikov [2007] UKHL 37; [2007] 1 WLR 2679 concerned three unrelated trials. In two cases, the trial jury had included among its members a serving police officer, and in the third case it included a solicitor employed by the CPS. The House of Lords held (by a 3:2 majority) that the question to be asked was whether, on the particular facts of each of the cases, a fair-minded and informed observer would conclude that there was a real possibility that the jurors in question were biased, having regard to the fact that Parliament had declared that such persons were eligible to sit on juries, envisaging that any objection to their sitting would be the subject of judicial decision. They went on to hold that the convictions should be quashed in the case where one of the jurors was an employee of the CPS (that fact was enough to create a suspicion of bias in a case where the prosecution was brought by the CPS) and in the case where one of the jurors was a serving police officer who worked in the same area as police witnesses in the case; however, the conviction should not be quashed in the other case, where the police officer who was on the jury did not work in the same area as the police witnesses. It follows that, if an issue arises as to whether a member of the jury may be unsuitable to sit on that jury, the test in *Porter v Magill* [2002] 2 AC 357, 494 has to be applied in order to determine whether or not the requirements of fairness have been met.

The effect of this ruling was considered in *R v Alan I* [2007] EWCA Crim 2999. Nelson J (at para 29) said that in all cases the test is one of apparent bias. This will depend on the facts. If, for example, a potential juror knows a witness personally, it is common for such a juror to stand down. Where, however, the witness he knows is not contentious and not to be called, but is taken simply as read as an agreed statement, there may well be no possibility of bias. It is therefore necessary for the judge to make all appropriate factual enquiries. Usually, this is by posing questions, either in court or in writing to the potential juror. The manner in which the questions are asked will depend on the circumstances. Sometimes a few questions in open court will suffice. In other cases, where the information might be sensitive, or more detail is required, the matter may have to be dealt with in writing. His Lordship went on to hold (at paras 35 and 36) that any potential juror who knows witnesses who are to be called to give oral evidence should be stood down at the outset, 'unless it can be said with certainty that the evidence of the witnesses who are known will play no contested part in the determination of the matter'.

The Court of Appeal gave further guidance in *R v Khan* [2008] EWCA Crim 531; [2008] 3 All ER 502. Lord Phillips CJ said that 'the fact that a police juror may seem likely to favour the evidence of a fellow police officer will not, automatically, lead to the appearance that he favours the prosecution'. It would not do so, for example, if the police evidence is not challenged or does not form an important part of the prosecution case (para 29). Similarly, the 'mere suspicion that a juror might, by reason of having been employed as a prison officer in a prison where the defendant was held, have acquired knowledge of that defendant's bad character could not, of itself, lead an objective observer to conclude that the juror had an appearance of bias' (para 120). Moreover, there can be no objection to a member of the CPS sitting in a case prosecuted by some other prosecuting authority (para 97). *Khan* was followed in *R v J* [2009] EWCA Crim 1638, where a serving police officer had been a member of the jury (indeed she acted as forewoman). Richards LJ (at para 26) summarised the effect of *Khan* as follows:

> [T]he court drew a distinction between partiality towards the case of one of the parties and partiality towards a witness, stating that a conviction will not necessarily be quashed because a juror is shown to have had reason to favour a particular witness; this will happen only if it has rendered the trial unfair

or given an appearance of unfairness. To decide that, it is necessary to consider two questions: (i) would the fair minded observer consider that partiality of the juror to the witness may have caused the jury to accept the evidence of that witness? and (ii) would the fair minded observer consider that this may have affected the outcome of the trial?

The effect of having a police officer as a member of the jury was considered by the European Court of Human Rights in *Hanif and Khan v UK* [2011] ECHR 2247. The Court noted that there was nothing to suggest that there had been actual partiality on the part of the police officer, and so the question was whether there were 'sufficient guarantees to exclude any objectively justified doubts as to his impartiality' (at para 142). The Court regarded it as important that the defence case 'depended to a significant extent upon his challenge to the evidence of the police officers' (para 146), and went on (at para 148) to say that:

. . . where there is an important conflict regarding police evidence in the case and a police officer who is personally acquainted with the police officer witness giving the relevant evidence is a member of the jury, jury directions and judicial warnings are insufficient to guard against the risk that the juror may, albeit subconsciously, favour the evidence of the police.

In the present case, the juror in question had known one of the officers in the case for ten years and, although not from the same station, had worked with him on three occasions. The other witnesses who supported that officer's account of events were also police officers. On this basis, the Court found (at para 149) that there had been a violation of Article 6(1) of the Convention since the trial had not taken place before an impartial tribunal.

In *Armstrong v UK* [2014] ECHR 1368, there were two police officers (one retired, one still serving) on the jury. The European Court of Human Rights rejected the claim that the trial had therefore been unfair. This was partly on the basis that this was 'not a case where a police officer who was personally acquainted with a police officer witness giving relevant evidence was a member of the jury' (see para 43) and the defence case 'did not depend to any significant extent—if at all—upon a challenge to the evidence of the police officer witnesses' (see para 44).

No one is entitled to refuse to do jury service. However, s 9(2) of the Juries Act 1974 provides that a person who has been summoned for jury service may seek excusal if they can show a 'good reason' for this, and s 9A(1) enables a person summoned for jury service to seek deferral of the summons (and so, if the dates specified in the summons clash with the person's holiday arrangements or business commitments, attendance can be deferred to a later date). The discretion to excuse or defer is exercised by the Jury Central Summoning Bureau (JCSB) which administers the jury summoning system on behalf of the Crown Court. The JCSB works on the basis that deferral is always preferable to excusal.

Section 9B of the Juries Act 1974 enables a person to be excused from jury service because he or she is not capable of acting effectively as a juror because of a physical disability. Rule 39.2 of the Crim PR makes provision for an appeal against a summoning officer's decision in relation to excusal or deferral of jury service.

11.3.2 Empanelling the jury

Rule 38.6(4) of the Criminal Procedure Rules states that:

The court must select the jury by drawing at random each juror's name from among those so summoned and—

(a) announcing each name so drawn; or

(b) announcing an identifying number assigned by the court officer to that person, where the court is satisfied that that is necessary.

The ability to identify a juror by using a number rather than their name will be relevant in cases where there is a fear of jury intimidation.

Rule 38.6(6) goes on to provide that the jury selected must comprise no fewer than 12 jurors and that it may, where the court expects the trial to last for more than four weeks, comprise as many as 14 jurors to begin with.

Under r 38.6(7), where a jury comprising more than 12 jurors is selected, the court must explain to them that:

(a) the purpose of selecting more than 12 jurors to begin with is to fill any vacancy or vacancies caused by the discharge of any of the first 12 before the prosecution evidence begins;
(b) any such vacancy or vacancies will be filled by the extra jurors in order of their selection from the panel;
(c) the court will discharge any extra juror or jurors remaining by no later than the beginning of the prosecution evidence; and
(d) any juror who is discharged for that reason then will be available to be selected for service on another jury, during the period for which that juror has been summoned.

Rule 38.7(2) stipulates that, no later than the beginning of the prosecution evidence, if the jury then comprises more than 12 jurors, the court must discharge any in excess of 12 in reverse order of their selection from the panel.

The provision for having more than 12 jurors at the start of the trial is intended to prevent a trial from collapsing at its early stages because one or more jurors have to be discharged (eg where it becomes apparent during the prosecution opening that one of the jurors is acquainted with a party to the case).

Under r 38.6(9), the oath or affirmation taken by each juror is as follows:

'I swear by Almighty God [or I do solemnly, sincerely and truly declare and affirm] that I will faithfully try the defendant and give a true verdict according to the evidence.'

11.3.3 Challenging potential jurors

There are two main types of challenge.

11.3.3.1 Standby

The first type of challenge is the right of the prosecution to stand a juror by. Under Crim PR, r 38.8(3), a prosecutor who exercises the prosecution right without giving reasons to prevent the court selecting an individual juror must announce the exercise of that right before the juror completes the oath or affirmation. The judge will then explain to that juror that he or she cannot sit on this jury but may be required to sit on another one. Prosecuting counsel does not have to give any reasons for the challenge. The fact that the prosecution would seem to have an advantage over the defence (who no longer have any right of peremptory challenge) led the Attorney-General to issue guidelines on the related issues of use of the standby and jury vetting (see Appendix 2 to *Blackstone's Criminal Practice* for the full text). In many cases there will be no check at all on potential jurors. However, in ordinary cases the names of the potential jurors may be put through the Police National Computer to see if any have previous convictions which mean that they are disqualified from jury service. In cases involving national security and terrorism, however, a more thorough check is carried out. Unsuitable jurors can then simply be stood by. Another case where use of the standby is appropriate, according to the Guidelines, is where the person is manifestly unsuitable to sit on this jury. An example might be the person who is clearly unable to read the words on the card which contains the jury oath and so is unsuitable for a case which involves perusal of documentary evidence.

It should be noted that the judge also has power to stand a juror by, but this power is exercised only very rarely. Some judges had used it (at the request of the defence) to try to secure a racially balanced jury so that some members shared the defendant's ethnic origin. However, in *R v Ford* [1989] QB 868, the Court of Appeal ruled that this practice was unlawful. *Ford* was followed in *R v Smith* [2003] EWCA Crim 283; [2003] 1 WLR 2229, where a black defendant was tried, by an all-white jury, on an indictment which alleged that he had caused serious injury to a white victim. It was held that the jury-summoning procedure in the Juries Act 1974 is not inconsistent with Article 6 of the European Convention on Human Rights. The court said that it is not unfair that a black defendant is tried by a randomly selected all-white jury, nor would a fair-minded and informed observer consider it unfair. Pill LJ added (at para 40) that consideration of the evidence in the present case did not require knowledge of the traditions or social circumstances of a particular racial group (even though there was a racial element to the offence); rather it was a common situation of violence outside a club. Similarly, in *R v Tarrant* [1998] Crim LR 342, it was held that the judge cannot use his discretion to discharge individual jurors so as to interfere with the composition of the jury panel by selecting jurors from outside the court's catchment area, in order to minimise the risk of intimidation.

11.3.3.2 Challenge for cause

The other important form of challenge (and the only one open to the defence) is the challenge for cause. Rule 38.8(2) of the Criminal Procedure Rules provides that a party who objects to the selection of an individual juror must tell the court of the objection after the juror's name or number is announced but before the juror completes the oath or affirmation, and must explain the objection. It will usually be the defence who challenge for cause (given that the prosecution can simply stand a juror by without giving reasons).

This form of challenge is used in cases where it is suspected that a potential juror might be biased. It should be remembered that, although the names of potential jurors are available for inspection by the prosecution and defence, it is unlikely that any checks will have been carried out apart from the check for previous convictions. The defence is unlikely to have information to show that a particular juror is biased (unless the defendant happens to recognise the person in question). Further (and this is different from the position in the United States) no questions may be asked of a potential juror unless the challenging party has already established a prima facie case that the person is likely to be biased (see *R v Chandler* [1964] 2 QB 322). An example of how this operates may be seen in the trial of the Kray brothers, presided over by Lawton J (see *R v Kray* (1969) 53 Cr App R 412). A national newspaper had published a colourful account of the allegations against the Krays. The judge was persuaded that anyone who had read this material might well be biased against the defendants. He therefore allowed the defence to ask each of the jurors whether they had read the material in question. If a juror said yes, that person was then successfully challenged. However, a more restrictive view was taken by the Court of Appeal in *R v Andrews* [1999] Crim LR 156. The appellant claimed that her conviction for murder was unsafe because of adverse pre-trial publicity. It was argued on her behalf that potential jurors should have been asked whether they had read or heard the reports in question. It was held that such questioning of jurors (whether done orally or by means of a questionnaire) is of doubtful efficacy and may even be counter-productive (by reminding the jurors of the publicity); it should therefore only be done in the most exceptional circumstances. In *Montgomery v HM Advocate; Coulter v HM Advocate* [2001] 2 WLR 779, the Privy Council (hearing a Scottish appeal) held that where there has been prejudicial pre-trial publicity, the court is entitled to expect the jury to follow the directions which they receive from the trial judge and to return a verdict based only on the evidence they have heard in court. On that basis, a defendant may be regarded as having received a fair trial even if there has been adverse pre-trial publicity. Likewise, in *R v Abu Hamza* [2006] EWCA Crim 2918; [2007] QB 659, the Court of Appeal observed that the fact that there has been adverse publicity is no reason for not proceeding with the trial if the judge concludes that it will be possible to have a fair trial (per Lord Phillips CJ, at para 92).

To challenge for cause, counsel merely says 'challenge' before the juror takes the oath. If it is a straightforward case (eg the juror knows the defendant), counsel will simply state that this is the case and the judge will ask that person to leave the jury box. If it is more complicated, the jurors who have already been sworn and the rest of the jury in waiting will be asked to leave court and counsel will have to explain the basis of the challenge and (if the judge so directs) question the challenged juror.

The test for bias which is to be applied is the test set out in *Porter v Magill* [2002] 2 AC 357, where the House of Lords said that the test for bias is whether a fair-minded and informed observer, having considered the facts, would conclude that there was a real possibility of bias on the part of the tribunal (per Lord Hope, at para 103).

11.3.3.3 Replacement of juror after successful challenge

When a juror has been stood by or successfully challenged, he or she is replaced by another member of the jury in waiting.

11.3.4 Discharge of jurors

11.3.4.1 Discharge of individual jurors during the trial

Under the Juries Act 1974, s 16, up to three jurors may be discharged during the course of the trial in case of illness or other necessity (eg bereavement). What constitutes necessity is a matter for the trial judge. In *R v Hanberry* [1977] QB 924, for example, a juror was discharged because the trial went on longer than expected and she would otherwise have had to cancel a holiday.

If more than three jurors can no longer serve, the trial has to be abandoned; a fresh trial will take place later.

11.3.4.2 Discharge of entire jury

The entire jury may be discharged if, for example:

(a) The jury hears evidence that is inadmissible and prejudicial to the defendant: where evidence that is prejudicial to the defendant has inadvertently been adduced, it is not automatically the case that the jury should be discharged, since in some instances a direction to the jury to ignore the inadmissible evidence might be sufficient (*R v Weaver* [1968] 1 QB 353). Whether or not the jury should be discharged is a matter for the discretion of the trial judge. The test to be applied is the usual test for bias, namely whether there is a real possibility of injustice occurring because the jury, having heard the prejudicial matter, may be biased (*R v Docherty* [1999] 1 Cr App R 274). In *R v Lawson* [2005] EWCA Crim 84; [2007] 1 Cr App R 20, Auld LJ, at para 65 (cited with approval in *R v Mills* [2008] EWCA Crim 3001, per Beatson J, at para 24) said:

> Whether or not to discharge the jury is a matter for evaluation by the trial judge on the particular facts and circumstances of the case . . . It follows that every case depends on its own facts and circumstances, including: 1) the important issue or issues in the case; 2) the nature and impact of improperly admitted material on that issue or issues, having regard, inter alia to the respective strengths of the prosecution and defence cases; 3) the manner and circumstances of its admission and whether and to what extent it is potentially unfairly prejudicial to a defendant; 4) the extent to and manner in which it is remediable by judicial direction or otherwise, so as to permit the trial to proceed . . . The test is always the same, whether to continue with the trial would or could, by reason of the admission of the unfairly prejudicial material, result in an unsafe conviction.

(b) The jury cannot agree on a verdict (see **11.10.5**).

(c) An individual juror has to be discharged and there is a risk that he or she may have contaminated the rest of the jury (eg because that juror knows that the defendant has previous convictions which have not been ruled admissible or that the defendant is facing further trials for other offences). Where a juror has specialised knowledge of something relevant to the case against the defendant, and has communicated that knowledge to the rest of the jury, the judge is obliged to discharge the jury since the defendant has had no opportunity to challenge what amounts to new evidence or to put forward their own explanation (*R v Fricker, The Times*, 13 July 1999; *R v Pouladian-Kari* [2013] EWCA Crim 158).

If members of the jury misbehave during the course of the trial, the jury should be discharged if there is a 'real danger of prejudice' to the accused (*R v Spencer* [1987] AC 128). In *R v Sawyer* (1980) 71 Cr App R 283, for example, some jurors were seen in conversation with prosecution witnesses during an adjournment. The trial judge questioned them and it transpired that the conversation had been on subjects unconnected with the trial. The decision of the judge not to discharge the jury was upheld by the Court of Appeal. In *R v Azam* [2006] EWCA Crim 161, the Court of Appeal said that the judge must make a judgment whether the interests of justice require the discharge of the jury; if the judge concludes that there are 'real grounds for doubting the ability of the jury to bring an objective judgment to bear' on the issues, the jury should be discharged. That decision requires a balanced judgment of the things said to create the risk of bias in the jury, while also taking account of the directions that may be given to the jury to address and extinguish the risk (per Sir Igor Judge P, at para 50).

In *Sookram v R* [2011] UKPC 5, one of the defendants changed his plea to guilty during the course of the trial. The issue arose whether the trial of the remaining defendant should start again with a fresh jury. Lord Brown, at paras 19 and 20, said that where a co-accused (B) changes plea, justice requires the jury to be discharged and the accused (A) to be tried afresh by a new jury only where it is 'possible to point to a particular unfairness which could be seen to result from A continuing to be tried by the same jury'. This would be the case, for example, where 'B's subsequent acceptance of his guilt necessarily carries with it the inference that A too is guilty' or where evidence had been led against B which was not admissible against A but was nevertheless highly prejudicial to A. In such cases, the jury should be discharged unless B's plea of guilty is admissible in evidence against A, or appropriate directions to the jury will substantially nullify its prejudicial effect on A's case, or there is 'other good reason' not to discharge the jury. Where the jury is discharged from giving a verdict, the defendant is not regarded as having been acquitted and so can be re-tried.

11.3.5 Outline of the trial

Rule 38.9(2) of the Criminal Procedure Rules sets out the sequence of events where the defendant has entered a plea of not guilty:

(a) where there is a jury, the court must (i) inform the jurors of each offence charged in the indictment to which the defendant pleads not guilty, and (ii) explain to the jurors that it is their duty, after hearing the evidence, to decide whether the defendant is guilty or not guilty of each offence;

(b) the prosecutor may summarise the prosecution case (ie make an opening speech);

(c) the prosecutor must introduce the evidence on which the prosecution case relies (ie calling 'live' witnesses and reading witness statements);

(d) at the end of the prosecution evidence, the court, either on the defendant's application (ie a submission of no case to answer) or on its own initiative, may direct the jury to acquit on the ground that the prosecution evidence is insufficient for any reasonable court properly to convict, but must not do so unless the prosecutor has had an opportunity to make representations;

(e) (assuming the case is to proceed) at the end of the prosecution evidence, the court must ask whether the defendant intends to give evidence in person and, if the answer is 'no', then the court must satisfy itself that there has been explained to the defendant (i) the right to give evidence in person, and (ii) that if the defendant does not give evidence in person, or refuses to answer a question while giving evidence, the court may draw such inferences as seem proper (under CJPOA 1994, s 35);

(f) the defendant may summarise the defence case (ie make an opening speech), but only if the defence intend to call at least one witness other than the defendant to give evidence in person about the facts of the case;

(g) the defendant may then (i) give evidence in person, (ii) call another witness, or witnesses, to give evidence in person, and (iii) introduce any other evidence;

(h) a party may introduce further evidence if it is then admissible (eg because it is in rebuttal of evidence already introduced);

(i) the prosecutor may make final representations (ie make a closing speech), but only if (i) the defendant has a legal representative, or (ii) the defendant has called at least one witness, other than the defendant, to give evidence in person about the facts of the case, or (iii) the court so permits;

(j) the defendant may make final representations (ie make a closing speech).

Under r 38.9(5), where there is more than one defendant, this procedure applies to each of them in the order in which their names appear in the indictment, or in an order directed by the court.

We will now examine some of these stages in greater detail.

11.3.6 Preliminary instructions to the jury

Part VI 39G.3 of the *Criminal Practice Directions* says that the judge should, at the start of the trial, give the jury clear guidance on a number of matters:

(a) the need to 'try the case only on the evidence and to remain faithful to their oath or affirmation';

(b) the 'prohibition on internet searches for matters related to the trial, issues arising or the parties';

(c) the importance of 'not discussing any aspect of the case with anyone outside their own number or allowing anyone to talk to them about it, whether directly, by telephone, through internet facilities such as Facebook or Twitter or in any other way';

(d) the importance of 'taking no account of any media reports about the case';

(e) the 'collective responsibility' of the jury for ensuring that the conduct of each member is consistent with the jury oath and that the directions of the trial judge about the discharge of their responsibilities are followed;

(f) the need to 'bring any concerns, including concerns about the conduct of other jurors, to the attention of the judge at the time, and not to wait until the case is concluded' (making the point that, unless that is done while the case is continuing, it may not be possible to deal with the problem at all).

11.3.7 Witnesses

Rule 38.11(2) of the Criminal Procedure Rules requires that, unless the court otherwise directs, a witness waiting to give evidence must not wait inside the courtroom, unless that witness is either a party or an expert witness.

Rule 38.11(4) sets out the process for eliciting evidence from the witness. It provides that it must happen in the following sequence:

(a) the party who calls a witness may ask questions in examination-in-chief;

(b) if the witness gives evidence for the prosecution—

    (i) the defendant, if there is only one, may ask questions in cross-examination, or

    (ii) subject to the court's directions, each defendant, if there is more than one, may ask such questions, in the order their names appear in the indictment or as directed by the court;

(c) if the witness gives evidence for a defendant—

    (i) subject to the court's directions, each other defendant, if there is more than one, may ask questions in cross-examination, in the order their names appear in the indictment or as directed by the court, and

    (ii) the prosecutor may ask such questions;

(d) the party who called the witness may ask questions in re-examination arising out of any cross-examination.

11.4 The prosecution case

After the indictment has been read to the jury, counsel for the prosecution opens the Crown's case:

May it please your Honour [or your Lordship, if a High Court judge or sitting at the Old Bailey], members of the jury, I appear to prosecute and my learned friend Miss Singh appears for the accused.

11.4.1 The opening speech

The purpose of the prosecution opening speech is to give the jury an overview of the prosecution case. The jury will be reminded of the charge(s) which the defendant faces, which should be explained in everyday language. Counsel will probably tell the jury what witnesses will be called by the prosecution and what it is hoped they will establish. Counsel will also mention the burden of proof and the standard of proof, and make it clear that anything said about the law is subject to what the judge will say in the summing-up.

If counsel for the defence takes the view that an objection should be taken to the admissibility of some of the evidence which the prosecution will be calling, but no ruling on admissibility was sought at the PCMH, then he or she should inform counsel for the prosecution. The prosecutor will then omit any reference to the disputed material from the opening speech, and the judge will then be asked to rule on the admissibility of the evidence at the appropriate moment.

In *R v Lashley* [2005] EWCA Crim 2016, the Court of Appeal said that an opening address by counsel for the prosecution should not address the law, save in cases of real complication and difficulty where counsel believes (and the trial judge agrees) that the jury may be assisted by a brief and well-focused submission (per Judge LJ, at para 13).

11.4.2 The prosecution evidence

At the conclusion of the opening speech, prosecuting counsel calls the evidence. It is the rule that the prosecution must call all the witnesses whose evidence was included in the bundle of statements on the basis of which the defendant was sent for trial. If one witness is expected to duplicate the evidence of another (eg the second police officer present at an interview with the accused), the prosecution may 'tender' that second witness for cross-examination. This means that the witness is called into the witness box by counsel for the prosecution and, having been identified and their relevance to the case established, will then be told to stay there in case the defence has any questions. The only exceptions to the rule that the prosecution must call (or tender for cross-examination) all the witnesses whose evidence was served as part of the sending process are those set out in *R v Russell-Jones* [1995] 1 Cr App R 538 at 544:

- the defence has consented to the written statement of that witness being read to the court;
- counsel for the prosecution takes the view that the evidence of that witness is no longer credible; or
- counsel for the prosecution takes the view that the witness would so fundamentally contradict the prosecution case that it would make more sense for that person to be called as a witness by the defence.

The other side of the coin is that the prosecution can *only* call as witnesses people whose evidence was served as part of the sending process or whose statements have been subsequently disclosed to the defence by way of a notice of additional evidence (a copy of the witness statement is served on the defence along with a notice saying that the prosecution will be adducing the evidence of this witness at trial). There is no time limit within which a notice of additional evidence must be served, but if it is served just before the trial, so that the defence has had insufficient time to adjust its preparation in the light of the new evidence, then the judge should grant an adjournment.

11.4.2.1 Taking evidence from the witnesses

Each witness called by the prosecution, having taken the oath (or affirmed) to 'tell the truth, the whole truth and nothing but the truth', is examined in chief by counsel for the prosecution (unless that witness is only being tendered for cross-examination) and may produce (ie identify) items of real evidence which then become exhibits in the case.

Each witness is then subject to cross-examination by the defence. Cross-examination is not limited to matters arising from the examination-in-chief, but must be relevant to the issues arising in the case. The cross-examination is followed by re-examination by the prosecution.

Under the CJA 2003, s 139(1), witnesses may, whilst giving evidence, refresh their memory from documents made or verified by them at an earlier time if they testify that the document records their recollection of the matter at that earlier time, and that their recollection of the matter is likely to have been significantly better at that time than it is at the time of the oral evidence.

11.4.2.2 Formal admissions

If the defendant pleads not guilty, that puts the prosecution to proof of each and every element of the offence(s) on the indictment to which a plea of not guilty has been entered. The only exception to this is where the defence has made a formal admission under the CJA 1967, s 10. This provides that either party in a criminal case (though, in practice, it is usually the defence) may admit any fact which would otherwise be in issue and this admission is conclusive evidence of the fact admitted. Under r 38.13(2), unless the court otherwise directs, a written record must be made of the admission.

11.4.2.3 Reading witness statements

Formal admissions are not very common. Usually, where evidence is not disputed by the defence (eg the loser of stolen property where the defence case is not that the property was not stolen but rather that the defendant was not the thief), they will consent to the prosecution reading out the written statement of the witness who provides the uncontroversial evidence (under s 9 of the Criminal Justice Act 1967; see also Part 27 of the Crim PR). If a witness says some things which are not disputed by the defence but others which are, that witness will have to give oral evidence (since it would not be appropriate for the written statement to be read to the court) and it will become apparent from the cross-examination by the defence which parts of that witness's evidence are disputed.

Under Crim PR, r 38.12, where the court permits a party to introduce in evidence the written statement of a witness, each relevant part of the statement must be read or summarised aloud, or the court and the jury must read the statement and its gist must be summarised aloud.

When the written statement of a witness is read to the court with the consent of the defence, the judge should explain to the jury that the contents of the witness statement are not in dispute and so the defence has consented to the statement being read to the jury without the maker having to attend court. The jury should be told that the evidence is just as good as evidence given 'live'. Counsel, in reading the statement, must read out the declaration signed by the maker of the statement, that it is true to the best of that person's knowledge and belief and is made knowing that a prosecution may be brought if the statement contains anything which the maker knows or believes to be false.

There are also instances where a statement may be read to the jury *without* the consent of the defence. These are set out in the CJA 2003, particularly s 114 and s 116, and include cases where a witness does not testify because of fear. In order to satisfy the requirements of s 116(2)(e), the court must hear oral evidence (eg from a police officer) as to the fear of the witness (*R v Belmarsh Magistrates' Court, ex p Gilligan* [1998] 1 Cr App R 14, following *Neill v North Antrim Magistrates' Court* [1992] 4 All ER 846.

Where a statement has been read to the jury without the consent of the defence, the jury must be warned to use particular care when considering that witness statement, since the maker of the statement was not in court to be cross-examined as to its contents.

11.4.2.4 Defence objections to prosecution evidence

If counsel for the prosecution agrees with the defence suggestion made before the start of the trial that certain evidence is inadmissible, the prosecutor should (via the Crown Prosecution Service representative or the police officer in charge of the case) warn the relevant witness not to give that particular evidence. If this involves evidence which will come into the possession of the jury (eg interview notes, which count as real evidence and may be exhibited and so handed to the jury), this evidence may well have to be edited.

If, however, the prosecution do not accept that the evidence in question is inadmissible, the question of admissibility may be dealt with at the PCMH, at which the judge is empowered to give binding rulings on the admissibility of evidence. Otherwise, the objection is made (in the absence of the jury) during the course of the trial. If the objection is made during the course of the trial, the prosecution evidence is called in the usual way until the part of the evidence to which there is objection is reached. At that point the jury are invited to retire to the jury room.

Although s 82 of PACE 1984 expressly preserves the common law rules on the admissibility of evidence, objections to prosecution evidence are usually made under PACE 1984, s 76 (which applies only to confessions) or s 78 (which applies to all prosecution evidence).

Where the defence invoke s 76 and allege that a confession has been obtained by oppression or in circumstances likely to render any confession unreliable, the prosecution must prove beyond reasonable doubt that the confession was not so obtained. The requirement for the prosecution to *prove* that the confession was not obtained improperly means that they must call evidence on the point and so a *voir dire* (sometimes called a 'trial within a trial') takes place in the absence of the jury. Unless the witness is in the middle of giving (or has already given) evidence in the course of the trial, a witness giving evidence on a *voir dire* takes a special form of oath in which they swear (or affirm) to 'answer truthfully all such questions as the court may ask'. Each prosecution witness called in the *voir dire* may be cross-examined by the defence. When the relevant prosecution witnesses have given evidence, the defence may call evidence (including the evidence of the defendant); each defence witness may be cross-examined by the prosecution.

After the evidence has been called, both counsel may address the judge and the judge then rules on the admissibility of the confession. In *Mitchell v The Queen* [1998] AC 695, it was held by the Privy Council that where a judge conducts a *voir dire* and holds that a confession is admissible, the judge should not tell the jury of the ruling (the trial should simply continue with the prosecution adducing evidence of the confession). If the judge indicates that he has ruled against the accused, this might lead the jury to think that the judge does not believe the accused.

If the objection to the prosecution evidence is brought *solely* on the basis of s 78, that it would be unfair to the defence for the evidence to be admitted, the judge may hold a *voir dire* but is not obliged to do so. Such applications may be dealt with on the basis of submissions by counsel if the factual basis for the submissions is agreed between prosecution and defence (eg if the custody record discloses breaches of the Codes of Practice under PACE 1984 and the only question to be determined is whether the evidence thereby obtained should be excluded under s 78). These submissions will, of course, be heard in the absence of the jury. The judge gives a ruling and the trial then proceeds, either with or without the disputed evidence.

It should be noted that if inadmissible evidence is heard by the jury, the judge has to consider whether the prejudicial effect can be cured by an appropriate direction (repeated in the summing-up) or whether the jury should be discharged and a new trial take place.

11.4.3 Special measures

Sections 16–33 of the Youth Justice and Criminal Evidence Act 1999 (YJCEA) contain provision for various 'special measures' which the court can direct in respect of certain witnesses:

- screening the witness from the accused (s 23);
- giving evidence by live link (s 24) (note that s 51 of the CJA 2003 enables a court to allow witnesses, other than the defendant, to give evidence through a live link in criminal proceedings, and s 33A of the YJCEA 1999 allows defendants to testify via a live link in certain limited circumstances);
- ordering the removal of wigs and gowns while the witness gives evidence (s 25);
- giving evidence in private, in a sexual case or where there is a fear that the witness may be intimidated (s 26);

- video recording of evidence-in-chief (s 27) (note that s 137 of the CJA 2003 extends the circumstances in which evidence-in-chief can take the form of a video-recorded statement);
- video recording of cross-examination and re-examination where the evidence-in-chief of the witness has been video recorded (s 28);
- examination through an intermediary in the case of a young or incapacitated witness (s 29); (note that s 33BA of the YJCEA, when brought into force, will make similar provision for defendants);
- provision of aids to communication for a young or incapacitated witness (s 30).

All witnesses under the age of 18 are eligible for special measures.

The procedure for making an application for special measures is contained in Part 29 of the Crim PR. Under r 29.3, a party who wants the court to make a special measure direction must apply in writing not more than 14 days after the defendant pleads not guilty. Under r 29.10, the applicant must explain how the witness is eligible for assistance and why the special measures sought would be likely to improve the quality of the witness's evidence. Rule 29.11 makes provision for applications to vary or discharge a special measures direction; such applications must be based on a material change of circumstances since the direction was made (see s 20 of the 1999 Act).

Rule 3.13(1)(c)(iii) of the Crim PR provides that the Crown Court may hold a pre-trial hearing where 'such a hearing is required to set ground rules for the conduct of the questioning of a witness or defendant'. Rule 3.9(7) makes more detailed provision for 'ground rules' hearings, at which the court can give directions for the appropriate treatment and questioning of vulnerable witnesses and defendants:

Where directions for appropriate treatment and questioning are required, the court must—

(a) invite representations by the parties and by any intermediary; and

(b) set ground rules for the conduct of the questioning, which rules may include—

(i) a direction relieving a party of any duty to put that party's case to a witness or a defendant in its entirety,

(ii) directions about the manner of questioning,

(iii) directions about the duration of questioning,

(iv) if necessary, directions about the questions that may or may not be asked,

(v) where there is more than one defendant, the allocation among them of the topics about which a witness may be asked, and

(vi) directions about the use of models, plans, body maps or similar aids to help communicate a question or an answer.

11.5 Submission of no case to answer

After the prosecution witnesses have all testified, the defence may make a submission that there is no case to answer (colloquially called 'a half-time submission').

This submission is made in the absence of the jury. Counsel for the defence makes the submission and counsel for the prosecution then has the right to reply.

The submission is governed by the principles laid down in *R v Galbraith* [1981] 1 WLR 1039 at 1042 (per Lord Lane CJ):

(a) The submission should succeed if the judge comes to the conclusion that the prosecution evidence, taken at its highest, is such that a jury, properly directed, could not properly convict on it. In this case the judge should direct the jury to acquit on the count(s) in respect of which the submission has succeeded. If there are other counts on the indictment and either no submission was made in respect of them or a submission was made but failed, the trial proceeds on those counts.

(b) The submission should fail if the strength or weakness of the prosecution case depends on the view to be taken of the reliability of a witness and, on one possible view, there is evidence on which a reasonable jury, properly directed, could convict. In this case, the matter should be left to the jury and the trial should be allowed to take its course with the jury being left in ignorance about what has happened.

The basis for this distinction is that questions relating to the credibility of witnesses are matters of fact which are within the exclusive province of the jury. However, regard should be had to the ruling of Turner J in *R v Shippey* [1988] Crim LR 767. His Lordship found no case to answer because of 'really significant inherent inconsistencies' in the complainant's evidence, which he found to be 'frankly incredible'. In other words, the judge can have regard to the sheer improbability of what the witness says and to internal inconsistencies in the evidence. If no reasonable jury could believe the witness whose evidence is central to the prosecution case, then the submission of no case to answer should succeed.

Where the only evidence against the accused is identification evidence, the special considerations highlighted in *R v Turnbull* [1977] QB 224 should be borne in mind, and the case withdrawn from the jury if the evidence is weak. Lord Widgery CJ, at pp 229–230 said that:

> When, in the judgment of the trial judge, the quality of the identifying evidence is poor, as for example when it depends solely on a fleeting glance or on a longer observation made in difficult conditions . . . [t]he judge should then withdraw the case from the jury and direct an acquittal unless there is other evidence which goes to support the correctness of the identification.

The test to be applied on a submission of no case to answer was considered in *R v Goring* [2011] EWCA Crim 2. The Court of Appeal (at para 35) referred with approval to a decision of the Supreme Court of South Australia, *Questions of Law Reserved on Acquittal (No 2 of 1993)* (1993) 61 SASR 1, in which King CJ had said:

> [I]t is not the function of the judge in considering a submission of no case to choose between inferences which are reasonably open to the jury. He must decide upon the basis that the jury will draw such of the inferences which are reasonably open, as are most favourable to the prosecution . . . Neither is it any part of his function to decide whether any possible hypotheses consistent with innocence are reasonably open on the evidence . . . He is concerned only with whether a reasonable jury could reach a conclusion of guilty beyond reasonable doubt and therefore exclude any competing hypothesis as not reasonably open on the evidence.
>
> . . . If there is direct evidence which is capable of proving the charge, there is a case to answer no matter how weak or tenuous might [sic] consider such evidence to be. If the case depends upon circumstantial evidence, and that evidence, if accepted, is capable of producing in a reasonable mind a conclusion of guilt beyond reasonable doubt and thus is capable of causing a reasonable mind to exclude any competing hypotheses as unreasonable, there is a case to answer. There is no case to answer only if the evidence is not capable in law of supporting a conviction. In a circumstantial case, that implies that even if all the evidence for the prosecution was accepted and all inferences most favourable to the prosecution which are reasonably open were drawn, a reasonable mind could not reach a conclusion of guilty beyond reasonable doubt, or to put it another way, could not exclude all hypotheses consistent with innocence, as not reasonably open on the evidence.

Leveson LJ, in *Goring*, continued (at para 37):

> It has long been a principle that, absent good reason (such as the witness being unworthy of belief), the prosecution is obliged to call all witnesses who give direct evidence of the primary facts and which the prosecution, when serving statements, consider to be material, even if there are inconsistencies between one witness and another: see *R v Russell-Jones* [1995] 1 Cr App R 538. Further, although taking the prosecution at its highest does not mean 'picking out all the plums and leaving the duff behind' (see per Turner J in *R v Shippey* [1988] Crim LR 767), it is necessary to make an assessment of the evidence as a whole and not simply consider the credibility of individual witnesses or evidential inconsistencies between witnesses. It is for the jury to decide what evidence to accept and what evidence to reject and the fact that a witness called by the Crown gives evidence in some respects inconsistent with the inferential case being advanced by the Crown cannot, by itself, be determinative of a submission of no case to answer: it is obviously, however, a factor to be taken into account.

In *R v Vaid* [2015] EWCA Crim 298, Gross LJ (at [20]) noted that when considering (pursuant to *R v Galbraith*) whether the prosecution evidence, taken at its highest, is such that a jury properly directed could properly convict on it, 'the question is whether a reasonable jury could, on one possible view of the evidence, reject all realistic possibilities consistent with innocence, not whether all reasonable juries would do so'.

If defence counsel notices an error on the part of the prosecution, he or she should take the point at the outset, and not wait until the close of the prosecution case. For example, in *R v Gleeson* [2003] EWCA Crim 3357; [2004] 1 Cr App R 29, the defendant was charged with common law conspiracy. The charge was inappropriate and the trial judge accepted a submission of no case to answer. However, the judge also gave the prosecution leave to amend the indictment to allege statutory conspiracy. The Court of Appeal held that, just as a defendant should not be penalised for errors on the part of his legal representatives in the conduct of his defence if he is unfairly prejudiced by them, so also the prosecution should not be frustrated by errors on the part of the prosecutor, unless such errors have irremediably rendered a fair trial for the defendant impossible. It is contrary to defence counsel's professional duty, and not in the legitimate interests of the defendant, to take advantage of procedural errors by the prosecution by delaying in identifying those errors as issues in the case until the last possible moment (per Auld LJ at para 35). The point was made that a criminal trial is not a game; its object is to ensure that the guilty are convicted and the innocent acquitted (para 36).

The importance of the defence raising issues at an early stage, and not leaving it until the close of the prosecution case, was reiterated in *R v Penner* [2010] EWCA Crim 1155. Thomas LJ (at paras 16–19) said:

> . . . [T] he issues in this case should have been identified at the PCMH . . . [I]t is essential that counsel at the PCMH stage carefully examine and identify the issues. As counsel in this case failed to do so, when the point, as he tells us, occurred to him in the course of cross-examination, it was then his duty to have identified it to the judge, before going any further with his cross-examination. He should not have left the matter for half time. He should have told the judge that there was a new issue and asked the judge how this matter should be dealt with . . . It is no longer possible to have cases conducted in the way in which this case was conducted by counsel for the appellant, where points occur to someone and then an attempt is made to ambush the prosecution by a submission of no case to answer. . . [I]f counsel had identified the issue, even if it occurred to him late (in a proper manner and not by means of submission at half time) then the Crown would have had an opportunity, if there had been any evidence in this case, to correct and bring before the trial court proper evidence. It is no longer permissible for the ambush of the type that it might be suggested happened in this case, to be performed in the future.

In *R v Powell* [2006] EWCA Crim 685, the court said that where a submission of no case to answer is made but rejected, the judge should give brief reasons for deciding that there is sufficient evidence to go before a jury (to enable the defence to understand clearly the grounds upon which the application has failed and to demonstrate that the judgment has been made on a rational basis rather than a personal whim).

If the judge wrongly refuses to uphold a submission of no case to answer, this constitutes an error of law. Any evidence called afterwards (ie by the defence) is irrelevant on appeal as no evidence would have been called by the defence if the submission had been upheld. So if, in the course of giving evidence, the accused makes damaging admissions, those admissions will have to be ignored by the Court of Appeal: see, for example, *R v Smith* [2000] 1 All ER 263.

It should be borne in mind that the Criminal Justice and Public Order Act 1994 (CJPOA), s 34(2)(c), provides that adverse inferences can be drawn from failure to answer police questions when the court is considering a submission of no case to answer. However, s 34(2)(c) can only be relied upon to take the case past half-time if a fact has been relied on by the defence which brings s 34 into play. This would be the case where, for example, the defence cross-examine prosecution witnesses on the basis of facts that were not mentioned by the defendant when questioned by the police (see *R v Webber* [2004] UKHL 1; [2004] 1 WLR 404).

11.6 The defence case

The defence is under no obligation to call any evidence, and so it would be possible for counsel for the defence simply to address the jury on the basis that the prosecution evidence has failed to show beyond reasonable doubt that the defendant is guilty. This may be appropriate where there is only just a case to answer. However, the CJPOA 1994, s 35, enables adverse inferences to be drawn by the jury if the accused either fails to give evidence or fails without good cause to answer questions put by the prosecution. It follows that the accused should, in the vast majority of cases, be advised to give evidence. If a defendant decides not to testify, despite advice to the contrary by counsel, that defendant should be asked to endorse a note on counsel's brief confirming their decision not to give evidence (see *R v Bevan* (1993) 98 Cr App R 354).

The defence case may start with an opening speech outlining the evidence the defence will be calling and showing how it will rebut the evidence called by the prosecution (though opening speeches are rarely made by the defence, unless the case is a complex one). In any event, the defence is not allowed to make an opening speech unless it will be calling at least one witness to the facts of the case, in addition to the evidence of the defendant (see Crim PR, r 38.9(2)(f)). So, if the only defence evidence is from the accused and/or character witnesses, there can be no opening speech.

11.6.1 The defence evidence

If the defendant does give evidence, then he or she must be called as the first defence witness, unless the judge gives leave to the contrary (PACE 1984, s 79).

Each defence witness takes the oath (or affirms) and is then examined in chief on behalf of the defendant, cross-examined by the prosecution and (if necessary) re-examined on behalf of the defence.

11.7 Closing speeches

At the close of the defence case the prosecution may make a closing speech. However, the prosecution have no right to make a closing speech if the defendant is unrepresented and has called no witnesses as to the facts of the case apart from his or her own testimony (see Crim PR, r 38.9(2)(j) and *R v Cojan* [2014] EWCA Crim 2512). In a fairly straightforward case the prosecution may, in any event, forgo their closing speech.

The defence always has the right to make a closing speech and this right should never be waived. It is a vital speech, giving counsel the chance to show how reasonable doubt has been cast on the prosecution case.

11.8 Two or more defendants

Where two or more defendants are charged in the same indictment, and those defendants are separately represented (which will be the case where they are putting forward inconsistent defences), their cases will be presented in the order in which their names appear on the indictment. So if the indictment is against D1, D2, and D3, the order is:

D1 opening speech

D1's witnesses (starting with D1)

- Examination-in-chief by D1's counsel
- Cross-examination on behalf of D2
- Cross-examination on behalf of D3

Cross-examination by prosecution

Re-examination by D1's counsel (if necessary)

D2 opening speech

D2's witnesses (starting with D2)

Examination-in-chief by D2's counsel

Cross-examination on behalf of D1

Cross-examination on behalf of D3

Cross-examination by prosecution

Re-examination by D2's counsel (if necessary) and so on

D3 opening speech, evidence and witnesses

Closing speeches are in the order: prosecution, D1, D2, D3.

If the defendants are jointly represented, they are regarded as putting forward a joint defence. Their counsel may make an opening speech. Then D1 may give evidence, followed by D2, then D3, and then any other witnesses the defence wish to call.

11.9 The summing-up

After the prosecution and defence counsel have made their closing speeches, the judge sums the case up to the jury. The judge must do this in all cases, however simple the case may seem. Although traditionally the judge produces the summing-up without reference to counsel, in *R v Taylor* [2003] EWCA Crim 2447, the Court of Appeal said that, where complex directions are to be given to the jury, counsel in the case should be permitted to consider and comment upon the draft directions before the judge addresses the jury.

Rule 38.14(2) of the Crim PR requires the judge, before the jury retire to consider their verdict, to:

(a) give the jury directions about the relevant law;

(b) summarise for the jury the evidence relevant to the issues they must decide;

(c) give the jury such questions, if any, as the court invites jurors to answer in coming to a verdict;

(d) direct the jury to retire to consider its verdict.

A summing-up should contain the following elements:

(a) *The respective functions of judge and jury*. Questions of law are for the judge and questions of fact are for the jury. The judge is entitled to express a view on the facts but should always make it very clear that if he or she seems to be expressing a view on the facts, then the jury must feel free to disregard that view. See *R v Jackson* [1992] Crim LR 214.

(b) *Burden and standard of proof*. It is for the prosecution to prove the case against the accused, not for the accused to prove his or her innocence. Before convicting, the jury must be 'satisfied so that they are sure' (a preferred formulation to the time-honoured 'beyond reasonable doubt'). The judge should not expand on what is meant by 'sure', as this is likely to generate confusion. See *Ferguson v The Queen* [1979] 1 WLR 94 and *R v McVey* [1988] Crim LR 127. In *R v Stephens* [2002] EWCA Crim 1529 (a case in which the jury sought additional guidance on how sure they had to be before convicting), the Court of Appeal stated that it is not helpful for a judge to direct a jury to distinguish between being sure and being certain and a judge should avoid doing so. If necessary, a judge should direct a jury that telling them to be sure is the limit of the help that can be given. If the case (exceptionally) involves a legal burden on the defendant (eg to show lawful authority or reasonable excuse for possession of an offensive weapon: Prevention of Crime Act 1957, s 1) then the jury must be told that the standard is to the balance of probabilities, ie more likely than not.

(c) *The law and the evidence*. There should be an explanation of the law involved and how it relates to the facts of the case. The judge should remind the jury of the main features of the prosecution and defence evidence, even if the case is a straightforward one (see *R v McVey* [1988] Crim LR 127 and *R v Gregory* [1993] Crim LR 623). In *R v Bowerman* [2002] 2 Cr App R 189, the Court of Appeal emphasised the importance of the summing-up as a means of focusing the jury's attention on the issues to be decided. This involves fitting the evidence that has been heard into the legal framework of the charge(s), so that the jury knows what the prosecution must prove and what (if anything) the defence has said in response. In going through the evidence which has been heard, the judge must be careful to present both the prosecution and defence stories even-handedly (*R v Marr* (1989) 90 Cr App R 154). For example, it is important that the defence case is put fully and fairly before the jury (*R v Gaughan* [1990] Crim LR 880). The judge must avoid sarcastic and extravagant language which disparages the defence case (*R v Berrada* (1989) 91 Cr App R 131). If there is an appeal, the Court of Appeal will look at the overall effect of the summing-up (*R v Berrada* (1989) 91 Cr App R 131). In *R v Spencer* [1995] Crim LR 235, for example, the defendant's conviction was held to be unsafe as a result of excessive and largely one-sided comments made by the judge when directing the jury. It was said by Henry LJ that some comment is permissible, but not to the extent that the rehearsal of the evidence is interrupted and the jury's task made more difficult. See also *R v Farr* (1999) 163 JP 193, where a conviction was quashed, and a retrial ordered, because the summing-up failed to refer to a number of the key features of the defence case and, instead of being fair and balanced, resembled a speech for the prosecution. Indeed, where the case against the defendant is strong, and the defence correspondingly weak, the judge has to be scrupulous to ensure that the defendant's defence is presented to the jury in an even-handed and impartial manner (*R v Reid, The Times*, 17 August 1999).

(d) *Identification evidence*. If the case against the accused depends on identification evidence, there should be a warning about the special need for care when examining identification evidence, as a witness may appear convincing yet also be mistaken. The factors which should be taken into account in assessing the quality of the evidence should be set out: see *R v Turnbull* [1977] QB 224. Lord Widgery CJ (at p 228) said:

> First, whenever the case against an accused depends wholly or substantially on the correctness of one or more identifications of the accused which the defence alleges to be mistaken, the judge should warn the jury of the special need for caution before convicting the accused in reliance on the correctness of the identification or identifications. In addition he should instruct them as to the reason for the need for such a warning and should make some reference to the possibility that a mistaken witness can be a convincing one and that a number of such witnesses can all be mistaken. Provided this is done in clear terms the judge need not use any particular form of words.
>
> Secondly, the judge should direct the jury to examine closely the circumstances in which the identification by each witness came to be made. How long did the witness have the accused under observation? At what distance? In what light? Was the observation impeded in any way, as for example by passing traffic or a press of people? Had the witness ever seen the accused before? How often? If only occasionally, had he any special reason for remembering the accused? How long elapsed between the original observation and the subsequent identification to the police? Was there any material discrepancy between the description of the accused given to the police by the witness when first seen by them and his actual appearance? If in any case, whether it is being dealt with summarily or on indictment, the prosecution have reason to believe that there is such a material discrepancy they should supply the accused or his legal advisers with particulars of the description the police were first given. In all cases if the accused asks to be given particulars of such descriptions, the prosecution should supply them. Finally, he should remind the jury of any specific weaknesses which had appeared in the identification evidence.

> Recognition may be more reliable than identification of a stranger; but even when the witness is purporting to recognise someone whom he knows, the jury should be reminded that mistakes in recognition of close relatives and friends are sometimes made.

(e) *More than one count or defendant.* If there is more than one count or more than one defendant, a warning must be given that each count and each defendant must be considered separately. Where evidence is admissible against one defendant but not the other (eg a police interview in which a defendant implicates both himself and a co-accused), the judge must instruct the jury to disregard the evidence in so far as it relates to the other defendant. In a case where there are co-defendants and each defendant denies responsibility for the alleged crime, the jury should be directed that: (i) the case for and against each defendant should be considered separately; (ii) the case should be decided on all of the evidence, including the evidence of the co-defendant(s) and the defendant whose case they are considering; (iii) when considering a co-defendant's evidence against the particular defendant whose case they are considering, they should bear in mind that he or she may have an interest to serve; (iv) they should assess the evidence of a co-defendant in the same way as any other witness in the case (see *R v Jones and Jenkins* [2003] EWCA Crim 1966; [2004] 1 Cr App R 5, per Auld LJ, at para 47).

(f) *Previous convictions.* The judge's summing-up must reflect the principles governing the admissibility of previous convictions under ss 98–112 of the Criminal Justice Act 2003. The jury should be told that they may take the defendant's record into account when deciding whether or not he or she committed the offence(s) charged. However, the jury must also be warned that bad character cannot by itself prove the defendant's guilt (and so it would be wrong to jump to the conclusion that a defendant is guilty just because of previous bad character). In *R v Hanson* [2005] EWCA Crim 824; [2005] 1 WLR 3169, Rose LJ (at para 18) said that the judge:

> should warn the jury clearly against placing undue reliance on previous convictions. Evidence of bad character cannot be used simply to bolster a weak case, or to prejudice the minds of a jury against a defendant. In particular, the jury should be directed: that they should not conclude that the defendant is guilty or untruthful merely because he has these convictions; that, although the convictions may show a propensity, this does not mean that he has committed this offence or been untruthful in this case; that whether they in fact show a propensity is for them to decide; that they must take into account what the defendant has said about his previous convictions; and that, although they are entitled, if they find propensity as shown, to take this into account when determining guilt, propensity is only one relevant factor and they must assess its significance in the light of all the other evidence in the case.

So far as the relevance of previous convictions to the defendant's credibility is concerned, in *R v Campbell* [2007] EWCA Crim 1472; [2007] 1 WLR 2798, Lord Phillips CJ (at para 30) said that:

> The question of whether a defendant has a propensity for being untruthful will not normally be capable of being described as an important matter in issue between the defendant and the prosecution. A propensity for untruthfulness will not, of itself, go very far to establishing the commission of a criminal offence. To suggest that a propensity for untruthfulness makes it more likely that a defendant has lied to the jury is not likely to help them. If they apply common sense they will conclude that a defendant who has committed a criminal offence may well be prepared to lie about it, even if he has not shown a propensity for lying whereas a defendant who has not committed the offence charged will be likely to tell the truth, even if he has shown a propensity for telling lies. In short, whether or not a defendant is telling the truth to the jury is likely to depend simply on whether or not he committed the offence charged. The jury should focus on the latter question rather than on whether or not he has a propensity for telling lies.

Where the defendant has no previous convictions, the jury should be directed that this is relevant both to the credibility of the defendant as a witness (a person of good character is more likely to be truthful) and to the likelihood that he or she committed the offence (a person with good character is less likely to commit a crime) (see *R v Vye* [1993] 1 WLR 471; *R v Aziz* [1996] AC 41; *R v Gray* [2004] EWCA Crim 1074; [2004] 2 Cr App R 30).

(g) *Failure by accused to testify*. In *R v Cowan* [1996] QB 373, Lord Taylor CJ (at p 381) gave guidance on what should be said in the summing-up if the defendant decides not to testify. The jury should be directed that:

(i) the burden of proof remains on the prosecution;

(ii) an inference from failure to give evidence cannot on its own prove guilt (CJPOA, s 38(3));

(iii) they must be satisfied (on the basis of the evidence called by the prosecution) that the prosecution have established a case to answer before inferences can be drawn from the accused's silence; and

(iv) they can draw an adverse inference from the accused's silence only if they conclude that the silence can only sensibly be attributed to the accused having no answer to the charge or none that stands up to cross-examination.

In *R v Birchall* [1999] Crim LR 311, the Court of Appeal emphasised that where the defendant fails to testify, the trial judge must tell the jury that they should not start to consider whether to draw adverse inferences from the failure to testify until it has concluded that the Crown's case against the defendant is sufficiently compelling to call for an answer.

Thus, there are two key steps before adverse inferences can be drawn under s 35:

(i) Are the jury satisfied that the prosecution have established a case to answer against the defendant?

(ii) Have the jury rejected any explanation put forward by the defendant for his refusal to give evidence?

If the answer to these questions is 'yes', the jury may draw adverse inferences from the defendant's silence.

(h) *Failure to answer police questions*. In *R v Condron* [1997] 1 WLR 827, the Court of Appeal said that the guidelines set out in *R v Cowan* [1996] QB 373 regarding the drawing of adverse inferences where the accused fails to testify are equally applicable where the accused fails to answer questions when being interviewed by the police. Detailed guidance was given in *R v Argent* [1997] 2 Cr App R 27, where the Court of Appeal set out the conditions which have to be satisfied before adverse inferences can be drawn from a person's failure to answer police questions (CJPOA, s 34). Lord Bingham CJ (at pp 32–33) said that the conditions include:

(i) the alleged failure must take place before the person has been charged;

(ii) the alleged failure must occur during questioning under caution;

(iii) the questioning must be directed at trying to discover whether and by whom the alleged offence has been committed;

(iv) the alleged failure must be a failure to mention a fact relied on by the defendant in his or her defence;

(v) the fact must be one which this particular defendant (not some hypothetical reasonable accused) could reasonably be expected to have mentioned when being questioned, taking account of all the circumstances existing at that time (eg the time of day, the defendant's age, experience, mental capacity, state of health, sobriety, personality and access to legal advice).

It should be borne in mind that a defendant may rely on a fact even if that defendant does not give evidence of that fact. In *R v Webber* [2004] UKHL 1; [2004] 1 WLR 404, the House of Lords confirmed that s 34 might apply if a defendant fails to mention when questioned by the police a significant matter on which he seeks to rely at trial (a) by giving evidence of it, (b) by adducing evidence of it from another witness, or (c) by putting it to a prosecution witness (per Lord Bingham, at para 34). Thus, adverse inferences can be drawn under s 34 even if the accused does not testify at the trial. Where the judge decides that it is not appropriate for the jury to draw adverse inferences from the defendant's silence, the jury should be specifically directed not to draw adverse inferences (*R v McGarry* [1999] 1 Cr App R 377). In *R v Betts and Hall* [2001] 2 Cr App R 257, the defendants had elected to remain silent in interviews with the police following legal advice. Kay LJ (at para 54) said that, 'If it is a plausible explanation that the reason for not mentioning facts is that the particular [defendant] acted on the advice of his solicitor and not because he had no, or no satisfactory, answer to give then no inference can be drawn'. His Lordship said (at para 57) that the jury should be directed that, 'If . . . you are satisfied that the true explanation for [the] defendant's failure is that he did not at that time have any answer to the allegations that were being put to him, or that he realised that such explanation as he had would not at that stage stand up to questioning or investigation by the police and that the advice of the solicitor did no more than to provide him with a convenient shield behind which to hide, then and only then can you draw such inferences as you consider proper from his failure.' The approach taken by the Court of Appeal in this case was approved by the European Court of Human Rights in *Beckles v UK* (2003) 36 EHRR 13.

(i) *Adverse inferences under the CPIA*. Where the defendant fails to provide a defence statement setting out the defence case, or does so late, or sets out inconsistent defences in the defence statement, or presents to the court a defence which is inconsistent with the defence statement, or presents alibi evidence without having given details of the alibi to the prosecution, adverse inferences may be drawn by the jury (see s 11). The judge must therefore give an appropriate direction to the jury.

(j) *Lies by defendant*. Where there is evidence before the jury that the defendant has lied about something, and there is a risk of the jury thinking that, because the defendant has lied, he or she must therefore be guilty of the offence charged, they should be directed that proof of lying is not proof of guilt, and that an innocent defendant might lie. In *R v Lucas* [1981] QB 720, Lord Lane CJ, at p 724, said that the lie must be deliberate; it must relate to a material issue; the motive for the lie must be a realisation of guilt and a fear of the truth (and so 'the jury should in appropriate cases be reminded that people sometimes lie, for example, in an attempt to bolster up a just cause, or out of shame or out of a wish to conceal disgraceful behaviour from their family'); and the statement must be clearly shown to be a lie.

(k) *Alibi*. Where the defendant has relied on an alibi and the prosecution have sought to prove that the alibi was false, the judge should direct the jury to the effect that 'even if you conclude that the alibi was false, that does not entitle you to convict the defendant. The Crown must still make you sure of his guilt. An alibi is sometimes invented to bolster a genuine defence.' A failure to give such a direction does not, however, automatically render a conviction unsafe. The Court of Appeal will consider whether the jury might have come to a different conclusion had the direction been given (*R v Harron* [1996] 2 Cr App R 457 and *R v Lesley* [1996] 1 Cr App R 39).

(l) *Corroboration*. Where an accomplice testifies as a prosecution witness against a defendant, there is no duty to warn the jury about the dangers of convicting on the basis of that evidence (CJPOA 1994, s 32). However, the trial judge nevertheless has a discretion to give such a warning (*R v Makanjuola; R v Easton* [1995] 1 WLR 1348). The Court of Appeal will only rarely interfere with the exercise of this discretion.

(m) *Expert witness*. Where there has been evidence from an expert witness, the jury should be directed that they are not bound by the opinion of the expert witness (*R v Stockwell* (1993) 97 Cr App R 260; *R v Fitzpatrick* [1999] Crim LR 832).

(n) *Failure to call defence witness*. It should be noted that it is generally inappropriate for the judge to comment on the failure of the defence to call a particular witness, as such comment can easily detract from what is said about the burden of proof (see *R v Wheeler* [1967] 1 WLR 1531, 1535; *R v Wright* [2000] Crim LR 510).

(o) *Reaching a verdict*. Part VI 39K.1 of the *Criminal Practice Directions* says that, at the conclusion of the summing-up, a number of directions are required. In particular it is important to direct the jury:

   (i) That their verdict must be unanimous in respect of each count and each defendant.

(ii) Not to think about majority verdicts unless and until given further directions.

(iii) That they will need to select one of their number to chair their discussions and speak on their behalf.

In *R v Wang* [2005] UKHL 9; [2005] 1 All ER 782, the House of Lords held that there are no circumstances in which a judge is entitled to direct a jury to return a verdict of guilty.

Until March 2010, use was made of 'specimen directions' which had been issued by the Judicial Studies Board (now the Judicial College). However, these specimen directions have now been replaced by the *Criminal Bench Book*. This contains a summary of relevant law, bullet-pointed ingredients for directions and illustrative examples to guide the judge in the crafting of appropriate directions. This publication is freely available at <http://www.judiciary.gov.uk>.

11.9.1 Written directions

Rule 38.14(3) says that the court 'may give the jury directions and questions in writing'.

In *R v Thompson* [2010] EWCA Crim 1623; [2011] 1 WLR 200, Lord Judge CJ considered the desirability of providing written material for jurors. His Lordship said (at para 13):

> The trial judge must decide whether to reduce his directions of law, or some of them, into writing, or whether written steps to verdict which may be particularly useful if there are several possible bases for conviction, or several possible offences, or defences to consider, may be of assistance to the jury. It has become much more common for a written extract of the central or critical part of the directions of law, or written steps to verdict, to be provided. Whether either practice will be helpful to a jury in a particular case must remain for the judgment of the judge. In a single issue case he may conclude that no document is needed. In others, he may be concerned that reducing directions to writing would either burden the jury with over-long material or would isolate, potentially unfairly, and give prominence to, some parts of the directions rather than others. In others, it will be apparent that either the central parts of the legal direction will be helpful if reduced to writing, or, more often perhaps, that a one-page 'steps to verdict' written analysis will enable the jury to remember the more discursive legal directions and apply them systematically. If the former practice is adopted, the judge will make it clear to the jury that the written document does not cover every area of law and that the directions given orally are equally binding on them. All such written documents will of course be discussed with counsel before they are finalised . . .

11.10 The verdict

11.10.1 The jury's retirement

The jury are put in the charge of a jury bailiff, who takes an oath to take the jurors to a private place and not to allow anyone to speak to them. The jurors then go off to the retiring room to consider their verdict.

Section 13 of the Juries Act 1974 enables the court to allow the jury to separate after (as well as before) they have been sent out to consider their verdict (formerly, separation was only permitted before the jury had been sent out to consider their verdict). In *R v Oliver* [1996] 2 Cr App R 514, at p 520, the Court of Appeal gave guidance on the directions which should be given to a jury which are allowed to separate before delivering their verdict. The direction should cover the following matters:

1. That the jury must decide the case on the evidence and the arguments that they have seen and heard in court, and not on anything they may have seen or heard or may see or hear outside the court.
2. That the evidence has been completed and that it would be wrong for any juror to seek for or to receive further evidence or information of any sort about the case.
3. That the jury must not talk to anyone about the case, save to the other members of the jury and then only when they are deliberating in the jury room. They must not allow anyone to talk to

them about the case unless that person is a juror and he or she is in the jury room deliberating about the case.

4. When they leave court they should try to set the case they are trying on one side until they return to court and retire to their jury room to continue the process of deliberating about their verdict or verdicts.

Where a jury are sent to a hotel overnight, they must be told not to continue their deliberations in the hotel but only to discuss the case when they have returned to court the following day (otherwise, discussions might take place without all jurors being present) (*R v Tharakan* [1995] 2 Cr App R 368).

When deliberating, the jury are allowed to have with them any exhibit in the case. In *R v Tonge* (1993) 157 JP 1137 the Court of Appeal considered what should be done if the jury (after they have retired) ask to hear the tape recording of the defendant's interview at the police station. It was said that if the tape recording has not been played in open court during the trial and the jury ask to hear the tape, it should usually be played in open court. However, if the tape has already been played in court, the jury may be allowed to hear it again in the jury room.

Once the jury have retired, any communication between the judge and jury has to take place in open court in the presence of the entire jury, both counsel and the defendant (*Ramstead v The Queen* [1999] 2 AC 92). Where the judge receives a note from the jury, the procedure laid down in *R v Gorman* [1987] 1 WLR 545 should be followed: unless the note has nothing to do with the trial, the judge should, in open court (but in the absence of the jury), state the contents of the note and seek submissions from both counsel. The judge should then send for the jury and deal with the query in open court (per Lord Lane CJ, at pp 550–551).

Once the jury have retired to consider their verdict, no further evidence can be adduced before them (*R v Owen* [1952] 2 QB 362). In *Owen*, the jury came out of retirement to ask whether the premises where a sexual assault was alleged to have taken place would have been occupied or not at the relevant time. The Court of Appeal held that no further evidence can be called after the jury have retired to consider their verdict. However, in *R v Hallam* [2007] EWCA Crim 1495, Toulson LJ said (at para 22) that there is no longer an absolute rule to the effect that evidence cannot be admitted after the retirement of the jury; rather, 'the question is what justice requires'. The same view was expressed by Gage LJ in *R v Khan* [2008] EWCA Crim 1112 (at para 39), where his Lordship said that, although historically there was an absolute principle that no further evidence should be given after the judge's summing-up has been concluded and the jury have retired, in recent years this principle has been 'subject to some relaxation'.

11.10.2 Taking the verdict

Each time the jury come into court, they are asked by the clerk, 'Have you reached a verdict upon which you are all agreed?' If they have come back with a query, the answer will of course be 'no'. If they have come back with a verdict, the answer will be 'yes'. A verdict must be taken on each count of the indictment separately. However, if two counts were in the alternative and the jury convict on the first (and most serious) count, they will be discharged from giving a verdict on the second.

11.10.3 Alternative verdicts

It is possible for the jury to acquit the defendant of the count on the indictment but to convict of another offence, sometimes known as a 'lesser included offence'. The Criminal Justice Act 1967, s 6, provides that where allegations in an indictment amount to or include, whether expressly or by implication, an allegation of another offence which may be tried on indictment, then the jury may acquit of the offence charged and convict of that other offence.

'Express inclusion' means that if certain words are deleted, the allegation of another offence remains. For example, if the indictment alleges that 'AB on 1st December 2015 entered 4 Gray's Inn Place as a trespasser and stole therein a laptop computer, the property of City University London', and the words 'entered 4 Gray's Inn Place as a trespasser and' are deleted, that leaves a valid count alleging theft. So if the jury feel that the prosecution have failed to prove trespass, an essential ingredient of burglary, but nonetheless find that the defendant stole the goods in question, they can convict of theft. See, for example, *R v Lillis* [1972] 2 QB 236.

'Implied inclusion' means that the lesser offence is either a necessary step towards committing the offence charged on the indictment or else is an offence which, in the vast majority of cases, is a step on the road to committing the offence charged. See *Metropolitan Police Commission v Wilson* [1984] AC 242. So, for example, theft is a valid alternative verdict to a charge of robbery (where the jury decides there was no assault); sexual assault is a valid alternative to rape. Section 47 of the Offences Against the Person Act 1861 is a valid alternative to s 20 of that Act (*R v Savage* [1992] 1 AC 714); s 20 is a valid alternative to s 18 of the Act (*R v Mandair* [1995] 1 AC 208).

Under s 6(3A) of the Criminal Law Act 1967, an offence falls within the jurisdiction of the Crown Court for these purposes if it is an offence to which s 40 of the CJA 1988 applies, even if a count charging the offence is not included in the indictment. Thus, the jury may acquit the accused of the offence on the indictment but convict of an offence under s 40 of the 1988 Act, even though that offence is a summary offence (provided, of course, that it is expressly or impliedly included in the offence that does appear on the indictment). For example, if the accused is charged with assault occasioning actual bodily harm (s 47 of the Offences Against the Person Act 1861) but the jury find that no actual bodily harm was caused, they may acquit of that charge but convict of common assault (to which s 40 of the 1988 Act applies) even though that charge does not appear on the indictment.

There are also some specific statutory provisions which enable the jury to convict the defendant of a summary offence if they acquit the defendant of an indictable offence. For example, the Theft Act 1968, s 12(4), provides that taking a conveyance without the owner's consent is a valid alternative verdict to a charge of theft, and the Road Traffic Offenders Act 1988, s 24, provides (inter alia) that careless driving is a valid alternative verdict to a charge of dangerous driving, causing death by dangerous driving, causing death by careless driving, or causing death by careless driving when under influence of drink or drugs.

Of course a jury will only be aware of its power to convict of a lesser included offence if it is told that it can do so; and even if the possibility is raised by counsel, the judge can decide to direct the jury not to consider that possibility.

In *R v Coutts* [2006] UKHL 39; [2006] 1 WLR 2154, it was said that an alternative verdict should be left to the jury only if it is 'obviously raised by the evidence'. In *R v Foster* [2007] EWCA Crim 2869; [2008] 1 WLR 1615, Sir Igor Judge P said (at para 61):

> . . . not every alternative verdict must be left to the jury. In addition to any specific issues of fairness, there is . . . a proportionality consideration. The judge is not in error if he decides that a lesser alternative verdict should not be left to the jury if that verdict can properly be described in its legal and factual context as trivial, or insubstantial, or where any possible compromise verdict would not reflect the real issues in the case. He must, of course, reconsider any decision he may have reached about alternative verdicts in the light of any question which the jury may see fit to ask . . . However when the defence to a specific charge amounts to the admission or assertion of a lesser offence, the primary obligation of the judge is to ensure that the defence is left to the jury . . . the judge must examine whether the absence of a direction about a lesser alternative verdict or verdicts would oblige the jury to make an unrealistic choice between the serious charge and complete acquittal which would unfairly disadvantage the defendant . . .

In *R v Caven* [2011] EWCA Crim 3239, Aikens LJ summarised the law thus (at [12]):

> The general principles to be derived from *R v Coutts* and *R v Foster* are . . . as follows: (1) before any requirement to leave an alternative verdict to the jury arises, that alternative verdict must be 'obviously' raised on the evidence. The alternative verdict must suggest itself to the mind of 'any ordinary knowledgeable and alert criminal judge' . . . (2) That test will generally only be passed if the alternative verdict is one to which a jury could reasonably come; which must mean that the alternative is one which really arises on the issues as presented at the trial. (3) There is no duty to put an alternative verdict if such a verdict would be remote from the real point of the case. (4) However, each case must depend on its particular facts.

(5) The evidence, disputed and undisputed, and the issues of law and fact to which it gives rise, must be examined . . . A judge will not be in error if he decides that a lesser alternative verdict should not be left to the jury if that verdict can properly be described in its legal and factual context as trivial, or insubstantial, or where any possible compromise verdict would not reflect the real issue in the case . . . (6) Where the defence to a specific charge amounts to the admission or assertion of a lesser offence, the primary obligation of the judge is to ensure that that defence is left to the jury. If it is not, then the summing-up will be seriously defective and the conviction unsafe. (7) A judge may have to reconsider a decision not to leave an alternative verdict to the jury in the light of any question which the jury may see fit to ask . . . (8) At all stages the judge has to ask the question: will the absence of a lesser alternative verdict oblige the jury to make an unrealistic choice between the serious charge and a complete acquittal in a way which would unfairly disadvantage the defendant . . . We emphasise that these are principles, not tramlines, and that each case depends upon its particular facts.

In *R v Lahaye* [2005] EWCA Crim 2847; [2006] 1 Cr App R 11, the Court of Appeal said that it is better if the availability of the alternative charge appears on the face of the indictment. This removes the need for the judge to exercise discretion as to whether or not the jury can consider a lesser offence.

Under s 6(3) of the 1967 Act, a verdict on a lesser offence is only possible if the jury acquits of the offence actually on the indictment. In *R v Collison* (1980) 71 Cr App R 249, for example, the jury were unable to agree on an acquittal. To enable it to convict of a lesser offence, that offence had to be added to the indictment as a new count (and the decision to do this, even though the jury had been considering its verdict for some time, was upheld on appeal as the defence would not have been conducted any differently).

11.10.4 Majority verdicts

The Juries Act 1974, s 17, provides that a majority verdict may be accepted after the jury have been considering their verdict for two hours, or such longer time as the judge thinks appropriate given the nature and complexity of the case. As a matter of practice, the jury are given a further ten minutes in which to settle into the retiring room and elect a foreman. The procedure to be adopted is set out in Part VI 39Q of the *Criminal Practice Directions*.

Should the jury return before a period of two hours and ten minutes (or such longer time as the judge thinks reasonable) has elapsed since the jury retired to consider its verdict, the foreman should be asked, 'Have you reached a verdict upon which you are all agreed? Please answer "Yes" or "No"'. If the jury have reached a unanimous verdict, the foreman should be asked, 'What is your verdict?' If the jury have not reached a unanimous verdict, they should be sent out again for further deliberation with a direction to arrive, if possible, at a unanimous verdict (para 39Q.2).

When the judge decides that (subject to the two hour, ten minute minimum) the jury have had long enough to reach a verdict, they will be called back into court. Again, the foreman will be asked if they have reached a unanimous verdict. If they have not, the judge will tell them to retire once more and will direct them that they should continue to endeavour to reach a unanimous verdict but that, if they cannot, a majority verdict will be accepted (para 39Q.3).

The only permissible majorities (bearing in mind that up to three jurors may be discharged during the course of the trial due to illness or other necessity) are:

12 jurors: 11–1 or 10–2
11 jurors: 10–1
10 jurors: 9–1

If the jury has been reduced to nine jurors, only a unanimous verdict is acceptable.

When the jury returns into court after the majority verdict direction has been given, the foreman will be asked, 'Have at least ten [or nine as the case may be] of you agreed on your verdict?' If the answer is 'Yes', the foreman will be asked 'What is your verdict? Please only answer "guilty" or "not guilty"'. If the verdict is 'not guilty', that is the end of the matter. If the verdict is 'guilty', the foreman will be asked, 'Is that the verdict of you all or by a majority?' If the answer is that it was a majority verdict, the foreman will be asked, 'How many of you agreed to the verdict and how many dissented?' (para 39Q.4)

The reason for this slightly complicated procedure is to prevent it being known that a verdict of 'not guilty' was a majority verdict, and to ensure that a verdict of 'guilty' was that of a permissible majority.

Under s 17(3) of the Juries Act 1974, the foreman *must* state in open court the number of jurors who respectively agreed to and dissented from the verdict before the judge can accept a majority verdict of guilty. In *R v Austin* [2002] EWCA Crim 1796, the court confirmed that a majority verdict of guilty will be a nullity if the words used by the clerk of the court and the foreman are not such that it would be clear to an ordinary person how the jury was divided.

11.10.5 Reaching a verdict

No pressure should be put on the jury to reach a verdict (*R v Duggan* [1992] Crim LR 513). However, the judge can enquire whether there is a reasonable prospect of a verdict being reached; the judge may tell the jury that if there is no reasonable prospect of them reaching a verdict they will be discharged and if there is, then they can have as much time as they need (*R v Modeste* [1983] Crim LR 746).

In *R v Watson* [1988] QB 690, the Court of Appeal provided a model direction to be given to a jury which is having trouble reaching a verdict:

> Each of you has taken an oath to return a true verdict according to the evidence. No one must be false to that oath, but you have a duty not only as individuals but collectively. That is the strength of the jury system. Each of you takes into the jury box with you your individual experience and wisdom. Your task is to pool that experience and wisdom. You do that by giving your views and listening to the views of the others. There must necessarily be discussion, argument and give and take within the scope of your oath. That is the way in which agreement is reached. If, unhappily, [ten of] you cannot reach agreement you must say so.

In *R v Arthur* [2013] EWCA Crim 1852, Pitchford LJ (at para 43) said that it is undesirable to give a *Watson* direction before or at the time of the majority verdict direction (because its effect may be to undo the benefit of the majority verdict direction), adding that the *Watson* direction is 'rarely given by trial judges' and, when it is given, it is 'only as a last resort following a prolonged retirement after the majority verdict direction has been given'. In *R v M* [2014] EWCA Crim 2590, Bean LJ (at [20]) said that:

> there are cumulative tests which must be satisfied before a *Watson* direction can be given: (i) it requires exceptional circumstances, which is why it is rarely given; and even then (ii) it can only be given as a last resort where prolonged retirement following the giving of a majority direction.

Where the defendant is charged with a number of offences and the jury indicates that they have agreed on verdicts on some, but not all, of the offences, it is good practice to take the verdicts on those counts upon which the jury are agreed before they carry on to consider the other counts (*R v F* [1994] Crim LR 377).

11.10.6 Discharge of the jury

If the jury cannot reach a verdict within what the judge holds to be a reasonable time, the jury will be discharged. This does not count as an acquittal and there is every chance that there will be a retrial. There is a convention that if a jury disagrees on the first trial and then a second jury also disagrees, the prosecution will then formally offer no evidence. However, this is no more than a convention; there is no rule of law that forbids a prosecutor from seeking a second retrial after a jury has disagreed (*R v Byrne* [2002] EWCA Crim 632; [2002] 2 Cr App R 21). Nonetheless, the jurisdiction which permits a second retrial after two jury disagreements must be exercised with 'extreme caution' (*R v Bell* [2010] EWCA Crim 3; [2010] 1 Cr App R 27).

11.11 Sentence

If the defendant is convicted of some or all of the counts on the indictment, the judge will proceed to the sentencing stage (if necessary, after an adjournment for a pre-sentence report to be prepared). Rule 38.16(3) requires the prosecutor to summarise the prosecution case, if the sentencing court has not heard evidence (and so this is not necessary where the judge has just presided over the trial), and also to identify in writing any offence that the prosecutor proposes should be taken into consideration in sentencing, to provide information relevant to sentence (including details of any previous convictions recorded against the defendant, and any statement of the effect of the offence on the victim, the victim's family or others) and to identify any other matters relevant to sentence, including any sentencing guidelines (or guideline cases) and the aggravating and mitigating features affecting the defendant's culpability and the harm associated with the offence.

After the prosecutor has addressed the court, counsel for the defence makes a plea in mitigation.

11.12 Less common pleas

Most of this chapter has been devoted to cases which involve straightforward pleas of guilty or not guilty. Other situations are sometimes encountered, for example where the defendant is unfit to enter a plea, or seeks to rely on the 'double jeopardy' rule.

11.12.1 Fitness to plead

A person is unfit to plead if incapable of understanding the proceedings and so unable to put forward any defence, challenge any juror for cause, give proper instructions to defence counsel or follow the evidence (see *R v Podola* [1960] 1 QB 325). In *R v Erskine* [2009] EWCA Crim 1425; [2009] 2 Cr App R 29, Lord Judge CJ said (at para 88) that 'provided the defendant can understand the proceedings, he will be deemed fit to plead'. His Lordship added that 'a defendant is not to be deemed unfit to plead merely because he will not accept what appears to be eminently sensible advice from his legal advisers'. The issue of fitness to plead can be raised either by the prosecution or the defence.

The procedure to be followed is contained in s 4 of the Criminal Procedure (Insanity) Act 1964. The court may postpone consideration of the question of fitness to plead until any time up to the opening of the defence case, if this is in the defendant's interests (s 4(2) of the 1964 Act). This enables a submission of no case to answer to be made before the question of fitness has to be determined. Under s 4(5) the question of fitness is to be determined 'by the court without a jury'.

If the defendant is found fit to plead, the trial takes its normal course. If, however, the defendant is found unfit to plead, a jury has to decide whether the defendant committed the *actus reus* of the offence. The procedure for this is governed by s 4A of the 1964 Act. If the question of fitness was determined at the start of the trial, a jury must be empanelled to determine whether the defendant committed the *actus reus*. If determination of the question was postponed and the defendant is found unfit to plead, the jury trying the substantive offence must determine whether the defendant committed the *actus reus* (s 4A(5)). If it is found that the defendant did not commit the *actus reus*, he or she is acquitted. If it is found that the defendant is not fit to plead, a hospital order (with or without a restriction order) or a supervision order may be made, or the court may grant an absolute discharge (s 5). The procedure to be followed is helpfully summarised by Thomas LJ in *R v Norman* [2008] EWCA Crim 1810; [2009] 1 Cr App R 13 (at para 34).

In *R v H* [2003] UKHL 1; [2003] 1 All ER 497, the House of Lords held that the procedure laid down by the 1964 Act for determining whether the accused has done the act or omission charged against him does not involve the determination of a criminal charge but is, in any event, compatible with the rights of the accused under Article 6 of the ECHR.

See also r 38.10 of the Crim PR.

11.12.2 Double jeopardy: *autrefois acquit* and *autrefois convict*

The principle of *autrefois acquit* and *convict*, sometimes known as the rule against 'double jeopardy', comprises the following elements (derived from *Connelly v DPP* [1964] AC 1254):

(a) A person should not be tried for a crime in respect of which he has previously been acquitted or convicted.

(b) A person should not be tried for a crime of which he could on some previous occasion have been convicted by way of an alternative verdict under s 6(3) of the Criminal Law Act 1967. For example, where the defendant was tried for rape, the jury could, if it acquitted him of rape, convict him instead of the lesser offence of sexual assault; it follows that the defendant should not be tried, on a later occasion, for sexual assault arising out of that incident.

(c) A person should not be tried for a crime, proof of which would necessarily entail proof of a crime of which he has previously been acquitted. In *R v Forest of Dean Justices, ex p Farley* [1990] RTR 228, it was said that there is an almost invariable rule that a person who has been tried for a lesser offence should not be tried again on the same facts for a more serious offence (eg a person acquitted of theft should not be tried for robbery, of which theft is an essential ingredient, arising out of the same incident).

(d) The defendant cannot be tried for a crime which is in effect the same, or substantially the same, as one of which he has previously been acquitted or convicted (or of which he could have been convicted by way of alternative verdict).

In *R v Beedie* [1998] QB 356, the Court of Appeal held that, in all cases except the first, the court has a discretion whether or not to strike out the later prosecution.

In *R v Dabhade* [1993] QB 329, it was held that where a charge is dismissed (without a hearing on the merits) on the ground that it is defective as a matter of law or because the evidence available to the prosecution is insufficient to sustain a conviction on the charge as laid, it cannot properly be said that the defendant was ever in jeopardy of conviction, and so the *autrefois* principle does not apply. This is particularly the case where the prosecution substitutes a new charge which is regarded as more appropriate to the facts. The consensual dismissal of the original charge does not give rise to the application of the doctrine of *autrefois acquit*.

In *R v J* [2013] EWCA Crim 569; [2014] 2 WLR 701, Sir John Thomas P said that the 'scope of *autrefois* is narrow and the offence, as well as the facts, must be the same for the plea of *autrefois* to apply' (para 23), adding that, in 'any case where the narrow application of the principle would result in unfairness or injustice to a defendant amounting to oppression, the remedy lies in the power of the court to stay the proceedings' (para 29).

The *autrefois* principle does not apply: where the defendant is re-prosecuted following the quashing of an indictment; where the prosecution serves a notice of discontinuance but reserves the right to institute proceedings at a later date under the Prosecution of Offences Act 1985, s 23(9); where the first jury was discharged from giving a verdict; or where the High Court quashes an acquittal (under the Criminal Procedure and Investigations Act 1996, ss 54–57), where someone has been convicted of interfering with, or intimidating, a juror or witness in the original trial.

Moreover, Part 10 of the CJA 2003 provides, by way of exception to the normal rule against 'double jeopardy', for retrials in certain cases. CJA 2003, s 75, restricts the possibility of retrial following acquittal to 'qualifying offences' (listed in Part 1 of Sch 5). Under s 76, the prosecution may apply to the Court of Appeal for an order quashing the defendant's acquittal and ordering him to be re-tried. Such an application may only be made with the written consent of the DPP. Only one application for an acquittal to be quashed may be made in respect of any acquittal, giving the prosecution only one further 'bite at the cherry'. The Court of Appeal can only order a retrial where the requirements of ss 78 and 79 are satisfied. Section 78 requires there to be 'new and compelling evidence against the acquitted person in relation to the qualifying offence'. In *R v Dobson* [2011] EWCA Crim 1256; [2011] 2 Cr App

R 8, Lord Judge CJ said (at para 7) that 'compelling evidence' for these purposes 'does not mean that the evidence must be irresistible, or that absolute proof of guilt is required'. Under s 78(2), evidence is 'new' if it was not adduced in the proceedings in which the person was acquitted; and evidence is 'compelling' if it is 'reliable', 'substantial' and 'appears highly probative of the case against the acquitted person'. Under s 79, an order for retrial can only be made if, in all the circumstances, it is in the interests of justice for the court to make such an order. Section 79(2) provides that this question is to be determined having regard to whether existing circumstances make a fair trial unlikely (having regard to the length of time since the qualifying offence was allegedly committed); whether it is likely that the new evidence would have been adduced in the earlier proceedings against the acquitted person but for a failure by an officer or by a prosecutor to act with due diligence or expedition; and whether, since those proceedings, any officer or prosecutor has failed to act with due diligence or expedition.

11.13 Trial by judge alone

Section 44 of the CJA 2003 makes provision for trial by judge alone in cases where there is a danger of jury tampering.

The judge may only make such an order if satisfied that 'there is evidence of a real and present danger that jury tampering would take place' (s 44(4)) and 'notwithstanding any steps (including the provision of police protection) which might reasonably be taken to prevent jury tampering, the likelihood that it would take place would be so substantial as to make it necessary in the interests of justice for the trial to be conducted without a jury' (s 44(5)). Section 44(6) gives some examples of cases where there may be evidence of a real and present danger that jury tampering would take place:

- a case where the trial is a retrial and the jury in the previous trial was discharged because jury tampering had taken place;
- a case where jury tampering has taken place in previous criminal proceedings involving the defendant or any of the defendants;
- a case where there has been intimidation, or attempted intimidation, of any person who is likely to be a witness in the trial.

The word 'examples' indicates that this is not intended to be an exhaustive list of the cases where s 44 may apply.

Under the CJA 2003, s 45, an application for an order under s 44 must be made at a preparatory hearing; all parties must be given an opportunity to make representations about the application.

Section 46 of the CJA 2003 makes provision for the discharge of a jury because of jury tampering. Before discharging the jury in such a case, the judge must allow the parties an opportunity to make representations. The judge may then make an order that the trial is to continue without a jury if satisfied that jury tampering has taken place, and that to continue the trial without a jury would be fair to the defendant(s) (s 46(3)). Under s 46(4), if the judge considers that it is necessary in the interests of justice for the trial to be terminated, the trial must be terminated; in such a case the judge may (under subs (5)) order that any new trial must be conducted without a jury.

In *R v T* [2009] EWCA Crim 1035; [2010] 1 WLR 630, Lord Judge CJ said (at para 16) that the judge has to be satisfied that the conditions in s 44 of the CJA 2003 are fulfilled to the criminal standard (ie beyond reasonable doubt).

In *R v J* [2010] EWCA Crim 1755, Lord Judge (at para 8) said that trial without a jury must remain 'the decision of last resort, only to be ordered when the court is sure (not that it entertains doubts, suspicions or reservations) that the statutory conditions are fulfilled'.

Section 17 of the Domestic Violence, Crime and Victims Act 2004 makes further provision for Crown Court trial without a jury. It permits a judge, on application by the prosecution, to order such trial of some, but not all, of the counts on the indictment if three conditions are satisfied, namely:

- the number of counts included in the indictment is likely to mean that a trial by jury involving all of those counts would be impracticable;
- each count or group of counts which would be tried with a jury can be regarded as a sample of counts which could be tried without a jury;
- it is in the interests of justice for an order to be made.

In deciding whether or not to make an order, the judge must have regard to any steps which might reasonably be taken to facilitate a trial by jury, but a step is not to be regarded as reasonable if it could lead to the possibility of a defendant receiving a lesser sentence than would be the case if that step were not taken.

Section 19 sets out the effect of an order under s 17: where, in the course of the proceedings to which the order relates, a defendant is found guilty by a jury on a count which can be regarded as a sample of other counts to be tried in those proceedings, those other counts may be tried without a jury in those proceedings. Where the defendant is subsequently found guilty, the judge must give a judgment which states the reasons for the conviction.

Section 18 requires that applications under s 17 must be determined at a preparatory hearing (under s 29 of the Criminal Procedure and Investigations Act 1996).

11.14 Unrepresented defendants

Where the defendant is unrepresented:

- the trial judge may ask questions to test the reliability of the prosecution witnesses and may ask whether the defendant wishes particular matters to be put to the witnesses;
- the jury should be instructed (at the start of the trial and in the summing-up) that the defendant is entitled to be unrepresented and should also be warned of the difficulty of doing so properly; and
- the judge should prevent repetitious questioning of prosecution witnesses by the defendant.

It should be borne in mind that the YJCEA, s 34, provides that no person charged with a sexual offence may cross-examine the complainant, either in connection with that offence, or in connection with any other offence (of whatever nature) with which that person is charged in the proceedings. Under s 35, unrepresented defendants are not allowed to cross-examine in person a child who is either the complainant of, or a witness to the commission of, a sexual offence, kidnapping, false imprisonment or abduction. Section 36 gives courts the power to prohibit unrepresented defendants from cross-examining witnesses in cases where a mandatory ban does not apply under ss 34 and 35, but where the court is satisfied that the quality of evidence given by the witness on cross-examination is likely to be diminished if the cross-examination is conducted by the accused in person, and would be likely to be improved if that were to be prohibited, and that it would not be contrary to the interests of justice to do so.

Where a prosecutor is faced by an unrepresented defendant, he may have greater obligations to ensure a fair trial. See *BSB Handbook*, Part Two—the Code of Conduct guidance at gC5.

12

Appeals to the Court of Appeal

12.1 The Criminal Division of the Court of Appeal

Traditionally, the Criminal Division of the Court of Appeal has entertained appeals from the Crown Court on all matters relating to a trial on indictment, and appeals against any sentence imposed by the Crown Court following a committal for sentence. Appeals on matters *not* relating to a trial on indictment, such as when the Crown Court hears an appeal from a decision of the magistrates, have been heard in the High Court, either on appeal by way of case stated, or on an application for judicial review (see **Chapter 8**).

The phrase 'not relating to trial on indictment' was considered in *Re Smalley* [1985] AC 622, approved in *R v Ashton* [1994] 1 AC 9. The court did not define these words but held that the test to be applied was whether the decision of the Crown Court was one affecting the conduct of a trial, given in the course of a trial or by way of pre-trial directions. The following are examples of matters within the definition:

- an order to estreat the recognisance of a surety (*Re Smalley*);
- a ruling given at a pre-trial hearing (*R v Southwark Crown Court, ex p Johnson* [1992] COD 364, DC);
- an order staying the whole or part of an indictment (*R v Manchester Crown Court, ex p DPP* [1994] 1 AC 9);
- a decision, after argument, as to the date of the trial (*R v Southwark Crown Court, ex p Ward* [1995] COD 140).

Since these cases, s 58 of the CJA 2003 has come into force, which allows the prosecution to appeal against the trial judge's rulings, in certain circumstances discussed in **12.2**.

12.1.1 Composition of the court

If the Court of Appeal is hearing an appeal against conviction, the court must comprise at least three judges. Occasionally, if the court is dealing with a case of exceptional complexity or significance, the court will consist of five or seven judges. If the court is dealing with an appeal against sentence, it is usual for two judges only to sit. However, it is rare to have more than one judgment delivered, in order to make for certainty of the law.

The Court of Appeal itself consists of up to 38 Lords Justices of Appeal, and a number of ex-officio judges including the Lord Chief Justice. In addition, the Lord Chief Justice may ask either of the following to sit in the Criminal Division:

- any High Court judge, who may deal with any case that comes before the Court of Appeal, except a case in which he was either the trial judge or passed sentence; but see *R v Sampson* (unreported, 24 October 2006, CA) where the defendant was sentenced to life imprisonment with a minimum recommendation of 12 years. The defendant appealed against the recommendation, as it happened, to the same High Court judge, now elevated, who had imposed the original tariff. Dismissing the appeal, it was held that the crucial point was that the judiciary, and not the executive, should set the tariff; or

- in certain circumstances, circuit judges, who may sit in appeals specified as suitable by the Lord Chancellor, except that they may not sit on any appeal from the decision of a High Court judge (s 9(1) of the Senior Courts Act 1981, as amended by s 52 of the Criminal Justice and Public Order Act 1994).

12.1.2 The court's Registrar

The administrative work of the Criminal Division is carried out by the Registrar of Criminal Appeals, who receives all notices and applications, and in turn serves all relevant notices on the parties to the appeal. In addition, the Registrar will obtain necessary transcripts, exhibits or other material.

Under the Criminal Procedure Rules, Part 65.2(2), the court and the parties have the same powers and duties concerning case management as they would under Part 3. Thus, the Registrar:

(a) must fulfil the duty of active case management under r 3.2;

(b) in fulfilling that duty may exercise any of the powers of case management under—

  (i) r 3.5 (the court's general powers of case management);

  (ii) r 3.10(3) (requiring a certificate of readiness); and

  (iii) r 3.11 (requiring a party to identify intentions and anticipated requirements), subject to the directions of the court.

Under the Crim PR, Part 65.2(3), the Registrar must nominate a case progression officer under r 3.4.

Certain additional powers have been conferred on the Registrar by virtue of the Criminal Appeal Act 1995 and the Criminal Procedure Rules. See **12.7.1**.

12.1.3 The right of appeal

The statute governing the right to appeal is the Criminal Appeal Act 1968, as amended by the Criminal Appeal Act 1995, referred to in this chapter as the CAA 1968 and the CAA 1995 respectively. The changes effected by the CAA 1995 came into effect on 1 January 1996, unless otherwise indicated. Students should also refer to the Crim PR, Parts 65–73, as appropriate, and *The Guide to Commencing Proceedings in the Court of Appeal Criminal Division*, issued in October 2008, which provide practical advice. You can access the Guide online at <http://www.justice.gov.uk/downloads/courts/court-of-appeal/criminal-division/proc_guide.pdf>.

12.2 Appeal against a terminating or evidentiary ruling

Sections 57–74 of the CJA 2003 permit the prosecution to appeal against certain of the trial judge's rulings, namely a 'terminating ruling' or an 'evidentiary ruling'. A terminating ruling is one that has the effect of stopping the case, such as a ruling that there is no case to answer or that the proceedings should be stayed. An evidentiary ruling is one which relates to matters such as the inclusion or exclusion of evidence. Such rulings may have a serious and detrimental effect on the way the prosecution develops its case. It seems inevitable that some evidentiary rulings will form part of an appeal against a terminating ruling.

An appeal against a ruling only lies with leave of the trial judge or the Court of Appeal (s 57(4)). See further Crim PR, Part 67.

12.2.1 The general right of appeal in respect of rulings

The procedure for appeal is fairly complex, but in essence is as follows, under the CJA 2003, ss 58–61 and the Crim PR, Part 67:

(a) Following the ruling, the prosecution informs the court that it intends to appeal or requests an adjournment to consider whether to appeal. It must also inform the court that it agrees that, if leave to appeal is not granted or the appeal is abandoned, the defendant should be acquitted.

(b) The trial judge may agree to or refuse the request for an adjournment. If an adjournment is granted and the prosecution decide to appeal, it must inform the court at the adjourned hearing. If an adjournment is refused, the prosecution must decide either to continue with the appeal, or lose the right to do so.

(c) Where there are two or more offences, the prosecution must indicate which offence is the subject of the appeal.

(d) Where the trial judge has ruled that there is no case to answer, and the prosecution has informed the court that it intends to appeal, it may also nominate other rulings made in the course of the trial.

(e) The trial judge must decide whether to:

  (i) adjourn the case and expedite the appeal. The Court of Appeal may reverse the order to expedite;

  (ii) adjourn the case and not order that the appeal is expedited;

  (iii) discharge the jury and not order that the appeal is expedited.

(f) Once the prosecution has informed the court that it intends to appeal the ruling, the ruling has no effect whilst the appeal is pursued. Any consequences of the ruling equally have no effect, and no steps should be taken in consequence of the ruling. Such a consequence seems to include that a defendant who has been detained in custody prior to and during the trial will continue to be detained, even though the trial judge has decided that there is no case to answer. One can envisage conflict between the application of the defence for bail, which the trial judge is minded to give, and the clear wording of the section.

12.2.2 Power of the Court of Appeal on an appeal under s 58

On hearing an appeal under s 58 of the CJA 2003, the Court of Appeal may confirm, reverse or vary any ruling to which the appeal relates:

(a) Where the challenged ruling is that there is no case to answer and the Court of Appeal confirms that ruling, order that the defendant be acquitted of that offence.

(b) Where the challenged ruling is no case to answer and the Court of Appeal reverses or varies the ruling, it must consider making one of the following orders:

  (i) an order that proceedings are resumed in the Crown Court, if necessary in the interests of justice; or

  (ii) an order that a fresh trial should commence in the Crown Court, if necessary in the interests of justice; or

  (iii) order that the defendant be acquitted of that offence (s 61(3)–(4) of the CJA 2003).

The Criminal Justice and Immigration Act 2008, s 44 introduced a requirement that the Court ought not to choose the 'acquittal' option, in (b)(iii) above, unless it had concluded that the defendant could not receive a fair trial (s 69(5) of the CJA 2003). For examples of an appeal against a terminating ruling see *R v NW and Others* [2008] EWCA Crim 2, where the prosecution appealed against the judge's acceptance of a submission of no case to answer, and *R v C and Others* [2009] EWCA Crim 2614.

In *R v M and T* [2009] EWCA Crim 2848, the Court of Appeal said: 'the position of a trial judge . . . must be acknowledged and respected. That acknowledgement finds its expression in the principle that this court will not interfere with such a terminating ruling unless the conclusion of the judge, refusing to let the case go before the jury, is outwith the range of reasonable conclusion. That high hurdle, which a prosecution must overcome is because this court is so much worse placed to make the sort of assessments and judgments this judge had to make . . .'.

12.2.3 The right of appeal in respect of evidentiary rulings

A separate set of provisions, the CJA 2003, ss 62 and 63, not in force at the time of writing (April 2015), applies to evidentiary rulings. Nothing in these sections affects the right of the prosecution to appeal under s 58 (s 62(11)). The ruling must be one which significantly weakens the prosecution case (s 63(2)).

In order to come within these sections, the ruling must:

- be made before the close of the prosecution case (s 62(2)); and
- relate to one of the qualifying offences in Sch 4 (s 62(9)). These are the most serious offences and include murder, manslaughter, rape, arson, endangering life and war crimes.

In order to appeal against the trial judge's evidentiary ruling, the procedure is as follows:

(a) The prosecution informs the court, before the opening of the defence case, that it intends to appeal against the ruling, and specifies to which ruling or rulings the appeal relates.

(b) For the avoidance of doubt, s 62(8) defines the opening of the defence case as the earliest of the following events:

   (i) evidence begins to be adduced on behalf of the defendant;

   (ii) it is indicated to the court that no evidence will be adduced on behalf of the defendant; or

   (iii) the defence make an opening speech.

(c) Leave of the trial judge or the Court of Appeal must be obtained. This will only be given if the court is satisfied that the ruling significantly weakens the prosecution case (s 63(l) and (2)).

Note that a ruling which was an 'evidentiary ruling' within the meaning of s 62(9) could also be a ruling within s 58(1): *R v Y* [2008] EWCA Crim 10, where it was held that since the appealed ruling was a ruling about what evidence the Crown would be permitted to adduce in its attempt to prove the offences for which the defendant had been indicted, the judge's ruling fell within s 58(1) notwithstanding that it was also an evidentiary ruling.

12.2.4 Power of the Court of Appeal in an appeal under s 62

On hearing an appeal under s 62, the Court of Appeal may, by virtue of s 66:

(a) confirm, reverse or vary any ruling to which the appeal relates;

(b) in addition, the Court of Appeal must, in respect of each offence, make one of the following orders:

   (i) an order that the proceedings be resumed in the Crown Court;

   (ii) an order that a fresh trial take place in the Crown Court;

   (iii) an order that the defendant be acquitted of that offence, if the prosecution indicates that it does not intend to continue with the prosecution of the offence.

12.3 The appeal against conviction

By virtue of the CAA 1968, s 2, as substituted by the CAA 1995, s 2, a person convicted on indictment may appeal on the single ground that the conviction is 'unsafe' (see **12.3.2**). Leave to appeal is always required (see **12.3.5**).

12.3.1 Grounds of appeal: the 1968 Act

Prior to 1996, the Court of Appeal would allow an appeal if one of the three grounds of appeal, set out here, were made out. The proviso to this was that the Court of Appeal could dismiss the appeal if no miscarriage of justice had actually occurred. This was known as 'exercising' or 'applying' the proviso. In this situation the Court of Appeal in effect agreed that a ground of appeal had been made out but that the ground was so trivial that the jury would inevitably come to the same conclusion. The grounds were as follows:

(a) *The conviction was unsafe or unsatisfactory.* In deciding whether the conviction was unsafe or unsatisfactory, the Court of Appeal considered the case as a whole and asked itself the subjective question 'whether we are content to let the matter stand as it is, or whether there is not some lurking doubt in our minds which makes us wonder whether an injustice has been done'. See *R v Cooper* [1969] 1 QB 267 per Widgery LJ, applied in *R v O'Leary* (1988) 87 Cr App R 387.

(b) *The trial judge made a wrong decision on a question of law.* If an appeal was on the basis of a wrong decision by the trial judge on a question of law, even if this could be demonstrated, the Court of Appeal still had to consider whether the judgment of the trial court should be set aside on that account. In effect, it considered the proviso. See *R v Moghal* (1977) 65 Cr App R 56.

(c) *There was a material irregularity in the course of the trial.* An appeal on the basis that there was a material irregularity succeeded if there had been a procedural error during the trial. But the irregularity had to be major and material; that is, serious enough to have affected the course of the trial.

12.3.2 Grounds of appeal: the 1995 Act

12.3.2.1 The test in the 1995 Act

The CAA 1995 abolished the three grounds of appeal and the proviso, replacing them with the single test of the safety of the conviction.

The CAA 1995, s 2 provides as follows:

In section 2 of the 1968 Act (disposal of appeal against conviction), for subsection (1) (grounds on which Court of Appeal are to allow or dismiss appeal including the proviso) substitute—

(1) Subject to the provisions of this Act, the Court of Appeal—

(a) shall allow an appeal against conviction if they think that the conviction is unsafe; and

(b) shall dismiss such an appeal in any other case.

The Act does not contain any definition of the word 'unsafe'. The meaning of the word has, however, been considered by the Court of Appeal in the following cases.

In *R v Chalkley* [1998] QB 848, it was described as 'in essence much the same as the intertwined and overlapping provisions of the old test, as was intended by the Royal Commission in recommending it, the Government in promoting it, the senior judiciary in supporting its parliamentary passage and Parliament in enacting it'.

At one time, it was thought that the 'lurking doubt' test had been swept away by the amendments to s 2, see, for example, *R v Farrow*, *The Times*, 20 October 1998 (reported as *R v F* [1999] Crim LR 306), where the Court of Appeal described the 'new' test as simple and clear and one upon which it was undesirable to impose any gloss, in particular, that of 'lurking doubt'. However, the court in many subsequent cases has continued to ask itself whether it was left with a lurking doubt. See, for example, *R v Conley* [2005] EWCA Crim 63, where Auld LJ said that the 'lurking doubt' test continued to be a tool available to the Courts Martial Appeal Court as an application of the test of unsafety of a conviction in s 2, as amended. If the court 'has a lurking doubt, or feels unease, about the safety of a conviction, then, in the words of section 2(1)(a) of [the] Act, it "thinks that the conviction is unsafe", and is bound to quash it'.

More recently in the case of *Pope* [2013] 1 Cr App R 214, Lord Judge CJ when giving judgment observed:

> Where it arises for consideration at all, the application of the 'lurking doubt' concept requires reasoned analysis of the evidence or the trial process, or both, which leads to the inexorable conclusion that the conviction is unsafe. It can therefore only be in the most exceptional circumstances that a conviction will be quashed on this ground alone, and even more exceptional if the attention of the court is confined to a re-examination of the material before the jury.

Thus, *Pope* does not dispense with the concept of 'lurking doubt', but confirms that the court will be concerned with the safety of the conviction.

12.3.2.2 The modern approach

The traditional approach of the Court of Appeal when dealing with misdirections of law, inadmissible material placed before the jury or a failure to direct a jury on a material point due to oversight or error, was frequently to quash the conviction. A new approach was set out in *R v Lambert* [2006] EWCA Crim 827. The correct approach was to decide whether the defendant's trial had been so prejudiced as a result that it would have called for the discharge of the jury or the conviction being quashed. The starting point was not to assume that the trial process had been vitiated as a result of the error(s).

A similar new approach can be seen in relation to procedural failures. In *R v Knights* [2002] EWCA Crim 2954 the Court of Appeal held that 'the purpose of rules of procedure is not usually to give or take away a court's jurisdiction'; rather, procedural requirements 'provide a convenient and just machinery enabling the court to exercise its jurisdiction'.

In *R v Soneji* [2005] UKHL 49, the House of Lords rejected a distinction between rules of procedure which were mandatory or directory. 'Instead . . . the emphasis ought to be on the consequences of non-compliance, and posing the question whether Parliament can fairly be taken to have intended total invalidity'. At [23] in dealing with the interests of justice in that case, Lord Steyn concluded '. . . that the rigid mandatory and directory distinction, and its many artificial refinements, have outlived their usefulness'.

In *R v Ashton* [2006] EWCA Crim 794, Fulford J stated:

> 4. . . . in our judgment it is now wholly clear that whenever a court is confronted by failure to take a required step, properly or at all, before a power is exercised ('a procedural failure'), the court should first ask itself whether the intention of the legislature was that any act done following that procedural failure should be invalid. If the answer to that question is no, then the court should go on to consider the interests of justice generally, and most particularly whether there is a real possibility that either the prosecution or the defence may suffer prejudice on account of the procedural failure. If there is such a risk, the court must decide whether it is just to allow the proceedings to continue.
>
> 5. On the other hand, if a court acts without jurisdiction if, for instance, a magistrates' court purports to try a defendant on a charge of homicide, then the proceedings will usually be invalid.

12.3.3 The Criminal Appeal Act 1968 and the Human Rights Act 1998

The power of the Court of Appeal to uphold a conviction of an appellant if it is 'safe' must now be read in the light of Article 6 of the ECHR, which confers on the defendant the right to a fair trial. The relationship between the safety of the conviction and the fairness of the trial has been the subject of some discussion in the Court of Appeal. On one hand, the Court of Appeal may find that the conviction is safe even though there has been some irregularity or misdirection in the trial that would render it 'unfair'; that is, the defendant is guilty. On the other hand, a conviction may be quashed because the trial was unfair even though the defendant is clearly guilty; that is, the conviction would be 'safe'.

A review of all the cases in which the Court of Appeal has dealt with these different approaches is beyond the scope of this manual, but the following cases are worthy of note: *Condron v United Kingdom* [2000] Crim LR 679; *R v Francom* [2001] 1 Cr App R 17; *R v Davis* [2001] 1 Cr App R 8; and *R v Togher* [2001] 3 All ER 463.

In *Condron* the European Court of Human Rights stressed the need for the Court of Appeal to examine the fairness of the trial, rather than the safety of conviction, stating: 'The question whether or not the rights of the defence guaranteed to an accused under Article 6 of the Convention were secured in any given case cannot be assimilated to a finding that his conviction was safe in the absence of any enquiry into the issue of fairness'.

In *Francom*, where the trial judge had failed to direct the jury at all, the Court of Appeal accepted that the term 'unfair' in the context of Article 6 had to be given a broad meaning favourable to the accused. It was not limited to the safety of the conviction itself, but encompassed the entire prosecution process. Lord Woolf went on to say:

> A misdirection of the jury could result in a breach of Article 6. But it may not do so. In the same way it may not make a conviction unsafe. It all depends on the circumstances of the case. In a case such as the present, we would expect this court to approach the issue of lack of safety in exactly the same way as the [European Court of Human Rights] approaches the lack of fairness. The directions, which a judge gives at trial are designed to achieve the very fairness required by Article 6(1). As we understand the jurisprudence of the ECHR, that court does not adopt a technical approach to the question of fairness. The European Court is interested . . . in requiring fairness of the trial in all circumstances.

Later he continued:

> The test which we have to apply before upholding the conviction is whether, notwithstanding the non-direction, we are satisfied that no reasonable jury could have come to a different conclusion from that which was reached by the jury, if they were properly directed. That approach not only means there must not be a lack of safety, it also means there must be no unfairness because the non-direction or misdirection must not affect the accused's right to a fair trial.

In *Davis*, the European Court of Human Rights decided that there had been a violation of the appellant's right, which was not cured by the appeal process. Mantell LJ stated that:

> The court is concerned with the safety of the conviction. A conviction can never be safe if there is doubt about guilt. However the converse is not true. A conviction may be unsafe even where there is no doubt about guilt, but the trial process has been vitiated by serious unfairness or significant legal misdirection. That being so, there is no tension between s 2(1)(a) of the Criminal Appeal Act 1968 and s 3(1) of the Human Rights Act 1998.

Later he said:

> [W]e are satisfied that the two questions (i.e. safety and fairness) must be kept separate and apart. The European Court of Human Rights is charged with enquiring into whether there has been a breach of a Convention right. This court is concerned with the safety of the conviction. That the first question may intrude upon the second is obvious. To what extent it does so will depend upon the circumstances of the particular case.

In *Togher*, an appeal following a plea of guilty, Lord Woolf CJ said, after discussing *Condron*:

> Now that the Convention is part of our domestic law, it would be most unfortunate if the approach identified by the European Court and the approach of this court continued to differ unless this is inevitable because of provisions contained in this country's legislation or the state of our case law.

Moreover, in *Togher* Lord Woolf said, 'We would expect . . . that the approach of this court applying the test of lack of safety would produce the same result as the approach of the European Court applying the test of lack of fairness'.

For a more recent view on this issue, consider *R (Dowsett) v Criminal Cases Review Commission* [2007] EWHC 1923 (Admin), where it was said that the Court of Appeal does not quash convictions simply because the European Court of Human Rights has found a breach of the ECHR.

12.3.4 Errors commonly before the Court of Appeal

Some errors occur commonly and the following cases are intended to illustrate the way the Court of Appeal approaches such errors. This list includes cases decided both before and after the CAA 1995, and it may be that some of the pre-1995 cases would now be decided differently, particularly in view of the Human Rights Act 1998 (HRA) and the Criminal Procedure Rules. This list is not intended to be exhaustive.

(a) *The wrongful admission or exclusion of evidence.* If the wrongful admission or exclusion of evidence renders the conviction unsafe, the Court of Appeal will quash the conviction, unless it is satisfied that had the error not been made, the proper verdict would nevertheless have been guilty: *R v Stirland* [1944] AC 315.

(b) *Defects in the indictment.* For example, the indictment is bad for duplicity or falls foul of Crim PR, r 14.2(3).

(c) *Failure or misdirection by the trial judge on the burden or standard of proof.* Such a non-direction or misdirection will often lead to the quashing of the conviction, but see *R v Edwards* (1983) 77 Cr App R 5, where the trial judge did not direct the jury as to the standard of proof. The conviction was upheld because the evidence against the defendant was overwhelming and the jury had been reminded of the standard by both counsel in any event.

(d) *A wrong rejection of no case to answer.* Prior to 1995, if the trial judge wrongly rejected a submission of no case to answer, the appeal succeeded and the proviso was not applied. Had the trial judge not erred in law, the defendant would have been acquitted and no matter what evidence was adduced in the trial subsequently, the acquittal would not have been affected (*R v Cockley* (1984) 79 Cr App R 181). In *R v Smith* [1999] 2 Cr App R 238, the Court of Appeal reached the same conclusion applying the new test, even though, in this case, the defendant admitted guilt during cross-examination. See also *R v Broadhead* [2006] EWCA Crim 1705, where it was held that the new test in s 2 did not alter this situation.

(e) *Interventions by the trial judge.* If there are a large number of interventions by the trial judge, which effectively prevent the proper development of the defence case, then the conviction is likely to be quashed (see *R v Matthews and Matthews* (1984) 78 Cr App R 23, *R v Whybrow*, *The Times*, 14 February 1994 and *R v Ahmed*, *The Times*, 9 March 1995). In *R v Cameron* [2001] Crim LR 587, the Court of Appeal upheld the actions of the trial judge who conducted the cross-examination of the 14-year-old complainant in a rape case after she refused to respond to questions put by defence counsel.

    See also *R v Garrett* [2005] EWCA Crim 1169, where the conviction was quashed due, inter alia, to the cumulative effect of the trial judge's questions to the jury in a short and straightforward case.

    In *R v Tatton* [2009] EWCA Crim 1896, it was held that the trial judge had wrongly questioned the appellant on the details of the information she had provided on her legal aid form, for the purpose of establishing that it was not consistent with her evidence that she was financially sound and had no need to resort to the theft which was alleged.

(f) *Failure or misdirection by the trial judge on law.* This will lead to the quashing of the conviction if the misdirection causes the conviction to be unsafe. See, for example, *R v James* [1997] Crim LR 598, where, on a charge of robbery, the trial judge did not direct the jury that the use of force had to be with the intention of stealing. The Court of Appeal quashed the conviction, holding that it was crucial to direct the jury on this element as well as the theft element. In *R v Clarke* [2006] EWCA Crim 3427, the convictions for murder and manslaughter were quashed due to errors in the summing-up in relation to these offences and inadequate directions in relation to evidence of bad character. The court observed:

    > It is commonplace and much to be recommended that the judge, however experienced, should pass their written directions to the jury on issues such as the distinction between murder and manslaughter, so long as they are couched in clear terms, shown to counsel in advance and are not too lengthy.

(g) *Failure to deal with the essential thrust of the defence case.* For an example, see *R v Osborn* [2002] EWCA Crim 2935, where the Court of Appeal quashed the conviction of a defendant charged with wounding with intent to do grievous bodily harm where the possibility of accident, raised at the trial, was not mentioned in the summing-up.

In *R v Stephenson* [2005] EWCA Crim 3111, the conviction for possession with intent to supply was quashed because the trial judge introduced a new factual basis for the commission of the offence in his summing-up to the jury.

Note, however, that it is not part of the trial judge's duty to construct the defence of someone who has not given evidence, although he is right to remind the jury of what the appellant said prior to the trial: *R v Hillier and Farrar* (1993) 97 Cr App R 349.

(h) *Errors by defence counsel.* The Court of Appeal will not allow an appeal on the basis that defence counsel's actions were mistaken or unwise, though in the case of 'flagrantly incompetent advocacy' it will quash the conviction (*R v Ensor* [1989] 1 WLR 497). In *R v Clinton* [1993] 1 WLR 1181, the appeal was on the basis that the appellant was not advised to give evidence but should have been. The Court of Appeal said that the crucial issue was not counsel's incompetence, but the effect on the trial and the verdict, and quashed the conviction. The approach taken in *Clinton* was approved in *R v Scollan* [1999] Crim LR 566. In *R v Nangle* [2001] Crim LR 506, the Court of Appeal said that if the failures of defence counsel mean that the defendant has been deprived of his right to a fair trial, it may be compelled to intervene. However, if no unfairness has been caused the court will be slow to intervene. In *R v JT* [2001] EWCA Crim 1096, the Court of Appeal said that despite the incompetent handling of the case by the solicitors, the conviction for robbery was safe because the shortcomings caused no prejudice. In *R v Doherty* [1997] 2 Cr App R 218, the Court of Appeal set out the guidance and procedure to be followed where the appeal involves criticism of trial counsel. Guidance issued in December 1995 by the Bar Council was quoted with approval by the Lord Chief Justice. In particular, an appeal on this basis should not be pursued unless 'it can be demonstrated that in the light of the information available to him at the time, no reasonably competent counsel would sensibly have adopted the course taken by him at the time when he took it'. In *R v Pluck* [2002] EWCA Crim 3166, the Court of Appeal held that decisions made by defence counsel in good faith after proper consideration of the arguments, and after discussion with the defendant if appropriate, did not render the conviction unsafe. See also *R v Hobson* [1998] 1 Cr App R 31, *R v Nasser, The Times*, 19 February 1998 and *Boodram v Trinidad and Tobago* [2002] 1 Cr App R 12.

The point arose again in slightly unusual contexts in *R v Shatwell and Lea* [2002] EWCA Crim 215 and *R v Hall* [2002] EWCA Crim 1881. In the first case, the defendants' appeal was rejected, as the fact that prosecution were represented by Queen's Counsel did not mean that the defendants had been deprived of their right to a fair trial on the basis of an inequality of arms. What was required was that the chosen advocate had competently presented the defence, and, in this case, no valid criticism could be made. In the second case, leading counsel had been diagnosed with a terminal illness just before the trial, and the defendant argued that he had not received a fair trial, as the illness may have affected counsel's ability to make decisions regarding his defence. The Court of Appeal dismissed the appeal, holding that the question was whether the conduct of the case fell below the proper standard so that the defendant did not receive a fair trial. In this case, the decisions made by counsel were within the range of decisions which competent counsel could have made. In *Sealey* [2002] UKPC 52, it was held that, where credibility is an issue of central importance, the failure of defence counsel to raise the issue of the defendant's good character rendered the trial defective.

The test when assessing if the conduct of a legal adviser had been such as to render a defendant's trial unfair was whether the conduct of the legal adviser had been unreasonable in the *Wednesbury* sense and whether as such it had had an actual effect on the fairness of the trial: *R v Bolivar, R v Lee* [2003] EWCA Crim 1167.

(i) *A refusal by the trial judge to exercise discretion in favour of the defence.* The Court of Appeal is generally reluctant to interfere with the exercise of the trial judge's discretion, and will usually do so only if the discretion was exercised on the wrong basis (eg *R v Morris* [1991] Crim LR 385) or if the discretion was not exercised at all (eg *R v Dubarry* (1977)

64 Cr App R 7) or if the decision was perverse (eg *Dures* [1997] 2 Cr App R 247, applying the general principle stated in *Quinn* [1995] 1 Cr App R 480). See *Blackstone's Criminal Practice* 2015, D26.22.

(j) *A failure by the trial judge to direct the jury to ignore his views*. In *R v Dow* [2003] EWCA Crim 3621, the trial judge's failure to direct the jury, inter alia, that they should ignore his views unless they coincided with the jury's own was not enough to lead to the quashing of the conviction.

In *R v Herbert* [2009] EWCA Crim 2518, the trial judge's direction to the jury to be prepared to 'give and take' did not render the conviction unsafe.

(k) *The residual discretion of the CA*. Even where the trial process cannot be faulted, there remains in the Court of Appeal a residual discretion to set aside a conviction where it is felt it would be unsafe or unfair to allow it to stand: *R v B* [2003] All ER (D) 67, where the defendant was put in an impossible position to defend himself, having regard to the 30-year delay, even though the judge had warned the jury fairly and carefully with ample warning of the difficulties faced by the defendant, and the very limited evidence which was available. This was one of the residual cases where, in the interests of justice, the conviction had to be set aside. In *R v D and Others* [2007] EWCA Crim 2485, the trial lasted approximately 11 months but was really disrupted with an inadequate summing-up. The strong prosecution evidence was hardly challenged but nevertheless there were issues which the jury had to decide and the Court of Appeal came to the conclusion that the jury were 'deprived of the fair opportunity to reach rational conclusions . . . [T]he trial process was so defective and the failure of the summing up to cure those defects so great that the verdicts were unsafe'.

(l) *Inconsistencies in the verdicts*. Where the verdict of guilty on one count is inconsistent with the verdict of not guilty on another, the conviction may be quashed if they are so inconsistent as to call for the interference of the court. See, for example, *R v Loi* [2003] EWCA Crim 801.

Cases of this type require scrutiny of the facts and circumstances by the Court of Appeal (*Burke* [2006] EWCA Crim 3122). In *Ahmadzai* [2009] EWCA Crim 2031, the Court of Appeal reiterated that it was for the appellant to show a logical inconsistency between verdicts, not for the Court of Appeal to seek an explanation. The fact that verdicts were surprising was insufficient to render a conviction unsafe.

See also *Gilmartin* [2013] EWCA Crim 2631 and *Formhals* [2014] 1 WLR 2219 where the court stated that: 'It will be a rare case indeed where a failure to reach a verdict can be said to be logically inexplicable when contrasted with or set against a verdict or verdicts which have been reached'. The court went on to say that such an argument would require 'the closest scrutiny'.

(m) *Improper comment*. It is clear that the law is for the judge and the facts are for the jury. This does not prevent the judge from expressing an opinion, in strong terms if appropriate, as long as he leaves the issues to the jury. Nevertheless, he should not suggest that he does not believe a witness, and certainly not the defendant: *R v Iroegbu, The Times*, 2 August 1988.

A number of cases have attempted to define the test to apply when looking at whether the court has gone beyond the limit of proper judicial comment. In *Re Medicaments and Related Classes of Goods (No 2)* [2001] 1 WLR 700, Lord Phillips of Worth Matravers MR summarised the court's conclusions, at 726–7:

> 85. . . . The court must first ascertain all the circumstances, which have a bearing on the suggestion that the judge was biased. It must then ask whether those circumstances would lead a fair-minded and informed observer to conclude that there was a real possibility, or a real danger, the two being the same, that the tribunal was biased.

This was approved by Lord Hope of Craighead in *Porter v Magill* [2002] 2 AC 357, who added that:

> I would however delete from it the reference to 'a real danger'. Those words no longer serve a useful purpose here, and they are not used in the jurisprudence of the Strasbourg court. The question is whether the fair-minded and informed observer, having considered the facts, would conclude that there was a real possibility that the tribunal was biased.

For examples of alleged bias see *R v C* [2005] EWCA Crim 2170, where the trial judge said to defence counsel: 'I am not having the jury misled by you', 'Are you content with half-truths', 'You cannot have your cake and eat it' and 'Do you take any notice of anything that anybody says to you?'. These remarks were unwarranted and so prejudicial that the conviction was quashed. See also *R v Cordingley* [2007] EWCA Crim 2174.

A further example is found in *Cole* [2008] EWCA Crim 3234, where the court quashed a conviction for dangerous driving following inappropriate and hostile interventions by the trial judge, which culminated in a note sent to defence counsel setting out in bold the '6Ps': 'Prior Planning Prevents Piss Poor Performance'.

(o) *Composition of the jury*. Traditionally, people involved in the administration of justice, such as police officers, crown prosecutors, barristers and judges, have been excluded from sitting on a jury. This exclusion was removed by the CJA 2003, s 321 and Sch 33. There have, as a result, been a number of cases in which the defendant has appealed on the basis that, by virtue of the presence of a member of the previously excluded category on his jury, the jury has been biased. In *R v Abdroikov, Green and Wilkinson* [2007] UKHL 37, the House of Lords repeated that justice should not only be done, but should manifestly and undoubtedly be seen to be done, which now equates with the right to a fair trial under Article 6 of the European Convention. The appellants argued that, though there was no actual bias, justice is not seen to be done where one of those charged to decide whether the appellant was guilty or not, is employed full-time by a body dedicated to promoting the success of one side in the adversarial trial process. Lord Bingham said:

> It must in my view be accepted that most adult human beings, as a result of their background, education and experience, harbour certain prejudices and predilections of which they may be conscious or unconscious. I would also, for my part, accept that the safeguards established to protect the impartiality of the jury, when properly operated, do all that can reasonably be done to neutralise the ordinary prejudices and predilections to which we are all prone. But this does not meet the central thrust of the case made . . . for the appellants: that these cases do not involve the ordinary prejudices and predilections to which we are all prone but the possibility of bias (possibly unconscious) which, as he submits, inevitably flows from the presence on a jury of persons professionally committed to one side only of an adversarial trial process, not merely (as the Court of Appeal put it) 'involved in some capacity or other in the administration of justice'. [The] expectation that each doubtful case would be resolved by the judge on a case by case basis is not, he pointed out, met if neither the judge nor counsel know of the identity of a police officer or the juror, as appears to be the present practice.

This case led to a number of other appeals, for example *R v Khan* [2008] EWCA Crim 531, where Lord Phillips CJ said:

> Where an impartial juror is shown to have had reason to favour a particular witness, this will not necessarily result in the quashing of a conviction. It will only do so if this has rendered the trial unfair, or given it an appearance of unfairness. To decide this it is necessary to consider two questions:
>
> (i) would the fair minded observer consider that partiality of the juror to the witness may have caused the jury to accept the evidence of that witness? If so,
>
> (ii) would the fair minded observer consider that this may have affected the outcome of the trial?

If the answer to both questions is in the affirmative, then the trial will not have the appearance of fairness. If the answer to the first or the second question is in the negative, then the partiality of the juror to the witness will not have affected the safety of the verdict and there will be no reason to consider the trial unfair. The mere fact that a member of the jury is a member of the police or a CPS employee will not of itself justify quashing the conviction. Witnesses who fall into this category should be identified at the outset so that if necessary that juror could be stood down. See also *R v C* [2008] EWCA Crim 1033 and *R v J* [2009] EWCA Crim 1638.

The same issue arose in different circumstances in *R v Cornwall* [2009] EWCA Crim 2458, where one of the jurors was a *Sun* newspaper journalist. He was described by the QC for the appellant as an outspoken polemicist who held strong and well-publicised views on issues such as law and order, soft judges, knife crime, drugs and immigration which could be characterised as populist and tendentious. It was therefore argued that his presence on the jury gave rise to the real possibility or real danger of bias. The argument was rejected by the Court of Appeal.

The court would be entitled, rarely and exceptionally, to hear evidence from jurors to resolve issues of alleged jury bias: *R v Adams* [2007] 1 Cr App R 34. Leave of the Court of Appeal should first be obtained before any juror is interviewed.

(p) *Unduly long trials*. In *R v A and Others* [2007] EWCA Crim 2485, the trial was estimated to last four months but lasted for 11 months and was really disrupted, with an inadequate summing-up. The Court of Appeal held that the verdicts were unsafe and quashed the convictions.

(q) *Comment on the failure of the accused to testify*. An error when directing the jury about the consequences of a failure to testify may give rise to a ground of appeal. The trial judge must be careful to make the jury aware of the inferences, which may properly be drawn from such a failure. At the same time, the direction must comply with the requirement that the accused receive a fair trial under the provisions of the ECHR (*Birchall* [1999] Crim LR 311).

Under s 6C of the Criminal Procedure and Investigation Act 1996, a defendant must give notice to the court and the prosecution of any person other than him or herself that he or she intends to call to give evidence (in force since 2010). The notice must contain the name, address and date of birth of the proposed witness, or as much information as possible in order to assist in identifying or finding any such witness.

If the defendant calls a witness about whom the prosecution and court were not given notice, adverse comment can be made to the jury about the failure to serve a notice or an amended notice, or on the late service of a notice. The witness can be cross-examined about why the information was withheld and as such their credibility can be called into question.

As a result of s 6C, the decision in *R (Kelly) v Warley JJ* [2007] EWHC 1836 (Admin); [2008] 1 WLR 2001, in which the Divisional Court had ruled that the courts' general powers of case management do not extend to require the defence to notify their witnesses, has been set aside.

Where a trial judge removes a defence from a jury's consideration, the prosecution must still prove an affirmative case and it remains for the jury to return its own voluntary verdict. It is never right for the trial judge to direct the jury to convict: see *R v Kelleher* [2003] EWCA Crim 3525, where the defence was self-defence, and, on the evidence, the only proper verdict was guilty and the conviction was safe.

The deliberations of the jury are immune from examination, and the Court of Appeal will not intervene where, after an unambiguous verdict, a juror subsequently alleges that the verdict was not unanimous. As a matter of policy, the verdict is final. Further, jurors should be protected from pressure or inducement to alter their views. This position is not altered by the HRA 1998: see *R v Millward* [1999] 1 Cr App R 61, and *R v Lewis* [2001] EWCA Crim 935. In *R v Mirza* [2004] UKHL 2, the House of Lords said there was a distinction between investigating conduct of a trial, which was permissible, and allowing evidence of a jury's deliberations on appeal, which was not. Note also *R v Young* [1995] QB 324, where the use, by some members of the jury, of a ouija board during the overnight adjournment to determine the defendant's guilt was held to be outside the course of the jury deliberations and therefore reviewable by the Court of Appeal.

12.3.5 Leave to appeal

By virtue of the CAA 1968, as amended, leave to appeal against conviction is always required. Leave may be given either by the trial judge, or by the Court of Appeal itself.

The CAA 1968, s 1 provides as follows:

> *(2) An appeal under this section lies only—*
>
> *(a) with the leave of the Court of Appeal; or*
>
> *(b) if, within 28 days of the date of conviction, the judge of the court of trial grants a certificate that the case is fit for appeal.*

As to (a), the power to grant leave of the Court of Appeal is usually exercised by the single judge: see **12.6.3.** Where leave to appeal is limited to one or only some of the grounds of appeal, the Court of Appeal will not allow other grounds to be argued without leave: *R v Jackson* [1999] 1 All ER 572.

As to (b), the certificate may be granted either:

- on the judge's own initiative, in which case the judge drafts the question which he or she considers ought to be raised (it is then read to counsel for their comment); or
- on counsel's application (in which case counsel normally drafts the question and the application itself is made in chambers with a shorthand writer present).

See generally the Crim PR, Part 68.4.

It will be rare for the defendant to ask the trial judge for a certificate that the case is fit for appeal. Such a certificate should only be sought in exceptional circumstances, and the normal rule is that it should be left to the Court of Appeal, whether as the single judge or the full court, to consider when a case is suitable for the granting of leave to appeal: *R v Inskip* [2005] EWCA Crim 3372. The mere fact that a judge has a difficult exercise of evaluation before reaching a conclusion that a case should go to the jury is plainly an insufficient reason for the grant of a trial judge's certificate.

There must be a particular and cogent ground of appeal on which the appellant will have a substantial chance of succeeding (*R v Bansal* [1999] Crim LR 484). If the trial judge has certified the case as fit for appeal, he or she may also grant the defendant bail: *R v Grant* (1990) 12 Cr App R (S) 441.

See also the *Criminal Practice Directions*, Part 19H.3:

> The first question for the judge is then whether there exists a particular and cogent ground of appeal. If there is no such ground there can be no certificate, and if there is no certificate there can be no bail. A judge should not grant a certificate with regard to sentence merely in the light of mitigation to which he has, in his opinion, given due weight, nor in regard to conviction on a ground where he considers the chance of a successful appeal is not substantial. The judge should bear in mind that, where a certificate is refused, application may be made to the Court of Appeal for leave to appeal and for bail; it is expected that certificates will only be granted in exceptional circumstances.

Under the Proceeds of Crime Act 2002, the person (designated by the statute) who has applied for a restraint order under ss 40–41 (prohibiting the person specified in the order from dealing with any 'realisable property') or the person affected by the order may appeal against the decision of the Crown Court with leave of the Court of Appeal. A further appeal may be made to the Supreme Court, but a certificate from the Court of Appeal that the case involves a point of law of general public importance is not required, nor is leave to appeal from either the Court of Appeal or the Supreme Court.

12.3.6 Appeals after a plea of guilty

The defendant may appeal against conviction after a plea of guilty, but only if he can bring his case within CAA 1968, s 2, that is to say demonstrate that the conviction was unsafe, and only in limited circumstances. In coming to a determination of whether the conviction was unsafe, the court should consider whether the appellant had been fit to plead, had known what he was doing, had intended to plead guilty and had done so unequivocally having received advice from counsel (*R v Lee* (1984) 79 Cr App R 108).

Some examples of the circumstances that may give rise to an appeal are:

(a) Following erroneous advice from counsel or a failure to advise of a possible defence (*R v Boal* (1992) 95 Cr App R 272). See also *Sadighpour* [2013] 1 WLR 2725.

(b) Where the plea was founded on an incorrect ruling of law on admitted facts, which left an accused with no legal escape from a verdict of guilty (*R v Chalkley* [1998] QB 848). If, on the other hand, the defendant pleaded guilty because he realised that as a result of the ruling the evidence against him was so strong that his case was hopeless, no appeal against conviction would apply. In such cases, the accused should plead not guilty and appeal in the normal way. *Chalkley* was followed in *R v Llewellyn* [2001] EWCA Crim 1555.

The second, wider, approach was preferred in *R v Togher* [2001] 3 All ER 463, to the effect that a plea of guilty following a material irregularity could also found an appeal. In particular, the word 'unsafe' should be applied in a way compatible with the ECHR. Fairness of the trial and the safety of conviction went together. Denial of a fair trial almost inevitably rendered the conviction unsafe. However, see *Dowsett* [2007]; see **12.3.2**.

Note that where the appellant appeals after a plea of guilty, a verdict of guilty of an alternative offence may be substituted by the Court of Appeal under CAA 1968, s 3A, as substituted by CJA 2003, s 316.

12.3.7 Single right of appeal

Under the CAA 1968, the appellant has the right to bring an appeal before the Court of Appeal. If that appeal is dismissed, he or she has no right to bring a second appeal on the same matter (see *R v Pinfold* [1988] QB 462). Two apparent exceptions were recognised in *Pinfold*:

- where an appellant seeks to revive an abandoned appeal;
- where, owing to some defect in the procedure, the appellant has, on the first appeal being dismissed, suffered an injustice, such as where he or she was not notified of a hearing date.

In *R v Thomas* [2002] EWCA Crim 941, the Court of Appeal held that it was not bound by the rule in *Pinfold* when dealing with a case which had been referred to it by the Criminal Cases Review Commission (see **12.13**). The power to make such a re-determination, however, should be limited to 'exceptional circumstances'. The court found it difficult to envisage such exceptional circumstances, but concluded that they would have to be such as to convince the court that if the case had been argued in that way on the previous occasion, it would, not might, have quashed the conviction. In any event, the court should be very slow to differ from the earlier judgment.

Difficulties may arise, however, where the Court of Appeal allows the appeal on one ground, but does not bother to hear the other grounds, considering that it would be a waste of time, the appeal already having succeeded on one ground. The problem is that if the Crown were to appeal to the Supreme Court, which reinstated the conviction, the appellant would be precluded from pursuing any further appeals. There are two possible solutions. The first is for the Court of Appeal to consider all remaining grounds of appeal whenever the Crown indicates that it intends to appeal to the Supreme Court: *R v Berry* [1994] Crim LR 276. The second solution is for the Supreme Court to consider all the other grounds of appeal as if it were the Court of Appeal: *R v Mandair* [1995] 1 AC 208.

It appears that the appellant has a separate right of appeal on the basis that the proceedings were a nullity, as the powers of the Court of Appeal to issue a *venire de novo* (an order returning the proceedings to the point immediately before the error, so that it can be corrected) exist independently of CAA 1968. See also *R v Laming* (1990) 90 Cr App R 450.

12.3.8 Appeals in the case of death

Prior to the CAA 1995, there was no procedure whereby the conviction of a deceased person could be challenged on appeal. The CAA 1995, s 7 inserts an entirely new provision into the CAA 1968. Section 44A now gives a person approved by the Court of Appeal the right to begin or continue an appeal after the death of the deceased.

The persons approved by the Court of Appeal under s 44A(3) (as amended by the Civil Partnership Act 2004, s 261(1)) must be one of the following:

- the widow, widower or surviving civil partner of the deceased;
- his or her personal representatives;
- any other person who, by family or other similar relationship with the deceased, has a substantial financial or other interest in the determining of the appeal.

The application for approval must be made within one year of death (s 44A(4)).

R v Whelan [1997] Crim LR 659, is believed to be the first application under this section. A widow was held to be entitled to continue her deceased husband's appeal against conviction for assault on his daughter, where only death had prevented him from pursuing the appeal himself.

12.4 Receiving evidence on an appeal

Under the CAA 1968, as amended by the CAA 1995, s 4, the Court of Appeal may receive any evidence if it considers that it is necessary or expedient in the interests of justice. The decision to receive fresh evidence is case- and fact-specific and the discretion is a wide one, which focuses on the interests of justice: *R v Erskine and Williams* [2009] EWCA Crim 1425.

The CAA 1968, s 23, as amended, provides as follows:

> *(1) For purposes of an appeal or an application for leave to appeal under this part of this Act [appeals against conviction and/or sentence and references to the Court of Appeal by the Home Secretary] the Court of Appeal may, if they think it necessary or expedient in the interests of justice—*
>
> *(a) order the production of any document, exhibit or other thing connected with the proceedings, the production of which appears to them necessary for the determination of the case;*
>
> *(b) order any witness to attend for examination and be examined before the court, (whether or not he was called in the proceedings from which the appeal lies); and*
>
> *(c) receive any evidence which was not adduced in the proceedings from which the appeal lies.*
>
> *(1A) . . .*
>
> *(2) The Court of Appeal shall, in considering whether to receive any evidence, have regard in particular to—*
>
> *(a) whether the evidence appears to the Court to be capable of belief;*
>
> *(b) whether it appears to the Court that the evidence may afford any ground for allowing the appeal;*
>
> *(c) whether the evidence would have been admissible in the proceedings from which the appeal lies on an issue which is the subject of the appeal; and*
>
> *(d) whether there is a reasonable explanation for the failure to adduce the evidence in those proceedings.*
>
> *(3) Subsection (1)(c) above applies to any evidence of a witness (including the appellant) who is competent but not compellable . . .*
>
> *(4) For purposes of an appeal or an application for leave to appeal under this Part of this Act, the Court of Appeal may, if they think it necessary or expedient in the interests of justice, order the examination of any witness whose attendance might be required under subsection (1)(b) above to be conducted, in a manner provided by rules of court, before any judge or officer of the Court or other person appointed by the Court for the purpose, and allow the admission of any depositions so taken as evidence before the Court.*

In *R v Pendleton* [2001] UKHL 66, the House of Lords considered that the correct test to be applied, where fresh evidence was to be admitted, was whether the conviction was safe, and not whether the accused was guilty. This was a matter for the judgment of the Court of Appeal, which should apply the test from the viewpoint of the effect of the fresh evidence on the minds of members of the court, and not the presumed effect on the minds of the trial jury. However, it would usually be appropriate for the court to ask itself the question, to test its provisional view, whether the evidence, if given at the trial, might reasonably have affected the decision of the trial jury to convict. If so, the conviction should be regarded as unsafe.

In *R v Hanratty* [2002] EWCA Crim 1141, the Court of Appeal held that the overriding consideration in deciding whether fresh evidence should be admitted was whether the evidence would assist the court to achieve justice, which may either be by upholding a conviction which was safe or setting it aside if it was unsafe. Fresh evidence may be admitted where, though not relevant to a specific ground of appeal, it was relevant to the overall question of the guilt or innocence of the appellant. Where the issue before the court was the safety of the conviction, that is, the guilt of the appellant, fresh evidence would usually be admitted. Where the issue before the court was the fairness of the proceedings, fresh evidence would not usually be admissible because it did not deal with the defect at the trial, unless it placed the defect in its context. This approach was particularly important where the court was dealing with old cases where standards have changed over the years. The court would be expected to enforce standards, but this did not apply where the rule was not in force at the time of the trial.

For other examples see *R v Winzar* [2002] EWCA Crim 2950, *R v Jacques* [2003] EWCA Crim 175, *R v Mynott* [2003] EWCA Crim 282 and *Bain v The Queen* [2007] UKPC 33.

In *Smith* [2014] 2 Cr App R 1(1) the court made clear its displeasure at the growing tendency of those convicted to dismiss trial counsel and instruct fresh counsel in order to criticise trial counsel and attempt to circumvent the strict application of s 23.

The following points may be noted about s 23 of the CAA 1968:

(a) The test for receiving evidence is that of the interests of justice. See *R v Jones*, [1997] 1 Cr App R 86, where the court received fresh medical evidence, even though there was no strong argument to do so, holding that it was expedient in the interests of justice.

(b) The section permits any evidence to be called before the Court of Appeal, whether or not it was called at the trial (*R v Mercer* [2001] EWCA Crim 638).

(c) If evidence is to be received, the matters contained in s 23(2) are important. These points, however, are merely matters to which the court should have regard and not conditions for the admissibility of the evidence namely:

    (i) whether the evidence appears to be capable of belief;
    (ii) whether the evidence affords any ground for allowing the appeal;
    (iii) whether the evidence would have been admissible;
    (iv) where there is a reasonable explanation for not calling the evidence at trial.

    In *Erskine* [2009] EWCA Crim 1425, Lord Judge CJ observed that the decision whether to admit fresh evidence is case- and fact-specific, it confers a wide discretion, which should focus on the interests of justice.

(d) Section 23(2)(a) provides that the evidence must be 'capable of belief', replacing the old test of 'likely to be credible'. In *R v Parks* [1961] 1 WLR 1484, it was held that 'likely to be credible' meant whether the witness's proof of evidence was intrinsically credible, and whether it fitted in with at least some of the other evidence in the case.

(e) As to whether there is a 'reasonable explanation' for the failure to adduce evidence at the trial, the case of *R v Beresford* (1972) 56 Cr App R 143, on precisely similar words, decided that the test was whether the evidence could have been obtained with 'reasonable diligence'. The court should be provided with all relevant information so that it can make a decision on this point.

(f) Rules on the receipt of fresh evidence have more relevance to factual evidence than to expert evidence, as experts are interchangeable to a certain extent, and if there is only one expert, and that expert is unavailable, the case may be postponed; see *R v Jones* [1997] 1 Cr App R 86. Fresh expert evidence will be received in appropriate circumstances, however. In *R v Latte* (1996) CLY 1388, fresh expert evidence was called and the Court of Appeal accepted that there was a reasonable explanation for not adducing the evidence at trial because the field of expertise (lighting and facial recognition) was highly specialised and not well known. In *Henderson, Butler and Oyediran* [2010] EWCA Crim 1269, the court said that where a defendant had made a 'tactical' decision at trial not to call expert evidence, that should not advantage them in terms of calling 'fresh' evidence at an appeal. The court emphasised that trial by jury should mean precisely that a defendant should not usually get 'two bites of the cherry' by being able to call expert evidence before the Court of Appeal.

(g) The role of the Court of Appeal is not to make a finding of fact but to assess new evidence that has become available since the trial and to make a decision on the safety of the earlier conviction (*R v Twitchell* [2000] 1 Cr App R 373).

(h) *R v Guppy* (1995) 16 Cr App R (S) 25, a decision on the old law, held that on a true construction of ss 11(3) and 23(1)(c), the Court of Appeal is empowered to receive fresh evidence of any witness, including the appellant, on an appeal against sentence. It would seem that this decision will be followed under the new formulation of s 23(1)(c).

(i) In *R v Ahluwalia* [1992] 4 All ER 889, the fresh evidence which the appellant wished to adduce raised a defence which was not raised at the trial (psychiatric reports as to the appellant's diminished responsibility). The Court of Appeal admitted the reports as fresh evidence, concluding that there may have been an arguable defence which, for some unexplained reason, was not raised at the trial.

See also *R v Moringiello* [1997] Crim LR 902, where the Court of Appeal did not allow fresh evidence to be called by the appellant's solicitor that the trial judge had fallen asleep during part of the evidence. Such an allegation had to be made at the time so that it could be known which parts of the evidence the judge was supposed to have missed.

12.5 Appeal against sentence

The right of appeal against sentence after conviction on indictment is found in CAA 1968, s 9. However, the Court of Appeal has always recognised that judges approach the question of sentencing in different ways, and must be allowed a measure of discretion in their approach. Thus, the court will not interfere merely because it would have passed a somewhat different sentence in a particular case.

For the purposes of s 9, the word 'sentence' includes 'any order made by a court when dealing with an offender': CAA 1968, s 50. Absolute and conditional discharges, hospital orders, compensation orders and costs all come within this definition.

Leave to appeal against sentence must always be obtained, either from the Court of Appeal, or by way of a certificate of the trial judge: CAA 1968, s 11(1) and (1A).

The following are the most widely accepted grounds of appeal:

(a) *The sentence is wrong in law.* Where the judge passes a sentence, which he has no jurisdiction to pass, such as one which exceeds the maximum that could legally be passed for the offence. However, appeals on such grounds are rare.

(b) *The sentence is manifestly excessive or wrong in principle.* This contention covers two situations:

   (i) *The sentence is manifestly excessive.* This is the most commonly used ground of appeal against sentence. Here the appellant is arguing that the right type of sentence has been imposed, but that it was outside the appropriate range for the offence and the offender. It is not enough that the sentence was severe.

   A sentence, which is manifestly excessive is also likely to be wrong in principle.

Courts are under a duty to follow Sentencing Guidelines, and should explain why one has not been followed. As to guideline cases, they represent guidelines only, and are not to be used as rules to be applied in every case.

(ii) *The sentence is wrong in principle.* An example is where the appellant argues that entirely the wrong type of sentence was imposed, such as a sentence of custody when non-custodial measures were appropriate; alternatively, where the judge combines two sentences, which are inconsistent with each other, such as a sentence of imprisonment and a community order.

(c) *The judge took the wrong approach to sentencing.* If the trial judge, in passing sentence, has taken into account an irrelevant consideration, such as the fact that the appellant has alleged that the police officers had fabricated their evidence, the sentence is likely to be reduced.

(d) *The judge followed the wrong procedure prior to sentence.* If, following a plea of guilty, there has been a dispute as to the facts of the case, and the judge accepts the prosecution version without any enquiry or investigation, then the Court of Appeal may feel obliged to reduce the sentence. See *R v Newton* (1983) 77 Cr App R 13 and, generally, **11.2.3** and **13.3.3**.

(e) *Disparity.* Any disparity between the sentence imposed on co-defendants is probably best seen as merely a factor that the Court of Appeal will take into account when considering an appeal against sentence. It is unlikely, on its own, to support a successful appeal against sentence, but the view of the court has been inconsistent. On the one hand, the court says that if the disparity is so marked that one of the former co-defendants is left with a burning sense of grievance, then it would be right to interfere (see *R v Dickinson* [1977] Crim LR 303). On the other hand, the court has also expressed the view that the mere fact that one sentence is wrong (the lighter sentence) is no reason for altering the right sentence and making two wrong sentences (see *R v Stroud* (1977) 65 Cr App R 150).

(f) *Sense of grievance.* If the sentencing procedure and the actual sentence, taken together, leave the offender with a justifiable sense of grievance, then the Court of Appeal may interfere, notwithstanding that the sentence is not in itself too severe, for example where the offender is sentenced to custody after reports have been ordered, leading him actually and legitimately to expect a non-custodial sentence if the reports are good, and the reports are good (see *R v Gillam* (1980) 2 Cr App R (S) 267, *R v Ward* (1982) 4 Cr App R (S) 103, *R v Jackson* [1996] Crim LR 355 and *R v Horton* (1985) 7 Cr App R (S) 299).

12.6 Procedure for appeal

Preliminary notes: The procedure is the same whether the appeal is against conviction or sentence. The procedure is governed by the CAA 1968, the Criminal Appeal Rules 1968 (SI 1968/1262), the Criminal Procedure Rules and 'the Guide', namely 'A Guide to Commencing Proceedings in the Court of Appeal Criminal Division', produced by the Registrar of Criminal Appeals. The latest version of the Guide was produced in 2008; see <http://www.justice.gov.uk/downloads/courts/court-of-appeal/criminal-division/proc_guide.pdf>. Students should also be familiar with the relevant passages in the *Criminal Practice Directions*.

The Registrar's 'Guide' encourages prompt action from counsel following conviction. Counsel should see the convicted person immediately following the hearing and give oral advice on the prospects of appeal.

If an appeal is to be pursued, within 28 days of conviction (or sentence if the appeal is against sentence) notice of application for leave to appeal should be lodged at the Crown Court at which the proceedings took place. If appealing against conviction, counsel should observe the 28-day limit, even if there are practical difficulties, such as a delay between conviction and sentence.

The notice of application for leave to appeal is in a standard form (Form NG), which includes:

- the name and address of the applicant;
- the name of the court where he or she was tried, the name of the judge and the dates of his or her appearances;
- the offences of which he or she was convicted and the sentence imposed; and
- the application being made.

This will include not only the application for leave but also, where appropriate, any of the following:

- leave to appeal out of time;
- an application for a representation order;
- an application for bail pending determination of the appeal;
- leave to be present at the hearing; or
- leave to call witnesses.

The grounds of appeal (see **12.6.2**) must be attached to the notice of appeal. The form and grounds are lodged at the Crown Court where the proceedings took place, and are then forwarded to the Criminal Appeal Office by the Crown Court.

Note that where the trial judge has certified that the case is fit for appeal, the appellant simply gives notice of appeal and the Registrar lists the case for a full hearing by a court.

For the format and content of the grounds, please see the *Drafting* manual.

12.6.1 Transcripts

Once the Registrar at the Criminal Appeal Office has the notice and grounds, he or she may then order a transcript of any necessary part of the trial or summing-up as specified by counsel in the grounds of appeal. It is rare to request a transcript of the entire case and counsel should not do so unless it is essential. In conviction cases, a transcript of the summing-up, and proceedings up to and including verdict is invariably obtained. In sentencing cases the Registrar will obtain a transcript of the sentencing judge's remarks as a matter of course.

12.6.2 Grounds of appeal

12.6.2.1 Settling the grounds

Once counsel has received a copy of the transcript, the grounds of appeal can be set out in full, or 'perfected', as counsel will now have, for example, the exact words with which the judge directed the jury. Counsel has 14 days to perfect the grounds of appeal.

Grounds must be settled sufficiently clearly to enable the Registrar and subsequently the court to identify the material relied on. No particular form of words is required, but each point on which appeal is being made should be clearly identified, and set out in sufficient detail for the court to identify clearly the matters relied on. It is often convenient to make these points in chronological order. The grounds should refer to the transcript by page and paragraph number, and should cite any authorities upon which counsel proposes to rely. If counsel wishes to call a witness at the appeal, the reason why such a course is necessary should be explained fully. Further, any document referred to should be clearly identified.

The *Criminal Practice Directions*, Part X 68C.2 provide as follows:

> 68C.2 Advocates should not settle grounds unless they consider that they are properly arguable. Grounds should be carefully drafted: the Court is not assisted by grounds of appeal which are not properly set out and particularised. Should leave to amend the grounds be granted, it is most unlikely that further grounds will be entertained.
>
> In line with the Registrar's 'Guide' (para A2–4), the grounds and advice should be contained in a single combined document, bearing the title 'Grounds of Appeal' and should contain positive grounds only.

12.6.2.2 Skeleton arguments

Prior to the new *Criminal Practice Directions*, which originally took effect from 7 October 2013, a skeleton argument was required in all conviction appeals. The position has now changed and the Court of Appeal has moved to a position of encouraging skeleton arguments in complex cases. The *Criminal Practice Directions 2014*, Part X 68F.1–3 provide as follows:

> 68F.1 Advocates should always ensure that the Court, and any other party as appropriate, has a single document containing all of the points that are to be argued. The appeal notice must comply with the requirements of Part 68. In cases of an appeal against conviction, advocates must serve a skeleton argument when the appeal notice does not sufficiently outline the grounds of appeal, particularly in cases where a complex or novel point of law has been raised. In an appeal against sentence it may be helpful for an advocate to serve a skeleton argument when a complex issue is raised.
>
> 68F.2 The appellant's skeleton argument, if any, must be served no later than 21 days before the hearing date, and the respondent's skeleton argument, if any, no later than 14 days before the hearing date, unless otherwise directed by the Court.
>
> 68F.3 A skeleton argument, if provided, should contain a numbered list of the points the advocate intends to argue, grouped under each ground of appeal, and stated in no more than one or two sentences. It should be as succinct as possible. Advocates should ensure that the correct Criminal Appeal Office number appears at the beginning of the respondent's notice and any skeleton argument and that their names are at the end.

In order to assist the court, the Criminal Appeal Office prepares a summary of the cases coming before it, once the single judge grants leave to appeal. The summary is entirely objective and does not contain any advice about how the court should deal with the case or any view about its merits. See *Criminal Practice Directions*, Part X 68G.1.

The summary consists of two parts. Part I is provided to all advocates in the case (para 68G.2), and to unrepresented appellants, unless a judge of the High Court or the Registrar directs to the contrary in a case involving material of an explicitly salacious or sadistic nature (para 68G.5). Part I generally contains, according to para 68G.2:

- particulars of the proceedings before the Crown Court;
- particulars of the proceedings before the Court of Appeal;
- the facts of the case as drawn from the transcripts, advice of the advocates, witness statements and/or exhibits;
- the submissions and rulings, summing-up and sentencing remarks.

The contents of the summary are a matter for the writer, but if an advocate wishes to suggest any significant alteration, he or she should write to the Registrar. If the writer does not agree, the summary and the letter are put before the court.

Part II is for the court alone, and contains:

- a summary of the grounds of appeal;
- in appeals against sentence (and applications for such leave) summaries of the antecedent histories of the parties and any relevant pre-sentence, medical or other reports (para 68G.6).

12.6.3 The single judge

The application for leave to appeal, and any other applications (see **12.6**), are placed before the single judge. No oral submission or arguments are heard by the single judge, who decides the matter on the basis of the papers before him or her.

If it would assist the single judge when determining the question of leave, the views of the prosecution can be sought in relation to the grounds of appeal. Examples of cases where the prosecution response is thought appropriate include grounds relating to issues of jury irregularity, public interest immunity and cases with high media interest (Crim PR, r 68.6).

The single judge or Registrar also has the power to refer an application for leave directly to the full court, for example where a case involves a novel point of law.

If the single judge refuses to grant leave, the applicant has 14 days to renew the application before the full court, whose decision is final. When applying for leave to the single judge, or to the full court, the applicant should bear in mind the court's power to order 'loss of time' (see **12.8.1**).

The court has power to extend the 14-day time limit, but very rarely does so (see *R v Dixon* [2000] 1 WLR 782).

Where the single judge grants leave in respect of certain grounds of appeal, but expressly refuses leave in respect of others, the latter grounds may only be argued on appeal with leave of the full court (*R v Jackson* [1999] 1 All ER 572). Further guidance on this issue was given in *R v Cox and Thomas* [1999] 2 Cr App R 6.

12.7 Powers of the single judge

Most of the powers of the Court of Appeal, short of deciding the appeal itself, are exercised by the single judge of the court under the CAA 1968, s 31. The single judge has power to:

(a) Grant leave to appeal.

(b) Allow the appellant to be present at the hearing of the appeal. Under the CAA 1968, s 22(1), the appellant is entitled to be present at the hearing of an appeal even if he or she is in custody. However, if the appellant is in custody, he or she is not entitled to be present if the appeal is on the ground of law alone, nor on any preliminary application, without leave.

(c) Order a witness to attend for examination. The court may order a witness to appear before it, in pursuance of an appeal under the CAA 1968, s 23 (fresh evidence). This has the advantage of allowing both parties to the appeal to cross-examine.

(d) Allow bail pending the appeal hearing. Under the CAA 1968, s 19, the court has the power to grant bail to an appellant pending the hearing of the appeal. However, bail is granted only rarely, and only where it appears that the appeal is likely to be successful or where the sentence is so short that it is likely to have been served before the appeal can be heard. In deciding whether to grant bail, the true test is, 'are there exceptional circumstances which would drive the court to the conclusion that justice can only be done by the granting of bail?' (per Geoffrey Lane LJ in *R v Watton* (1979) 68 Cr App R 293). The length of time until the hearing of the appeal may be a relevant factor in the decision to grant bail, but in those circumstances the Court of Appeal will usually expedite the hearing of the appeal. The Crown Court may only grant bail in circumstances where a certificate that the case is fit for appeal has also been granted.

(e) Make, vary or discharge orders, for example as to whether the appellant is in custody or on bail pending retrial.

(f) Make orders as to the costs of the appeal, including the granting of a representation order.

(g) Give directions for loss of time (see **12.8.1**).

12.7.1 Powers of the Registrar

By virtue of the CAA 1968, s 31A, inserted by the CAA 1995, s 6, certain of these powers may be exercised by the Registrar. These are:

- to extend the time within which notice of application for leave to appeal may be given;
- to give a live link direction;
- to order a witness to attend for examination;
- to vary the conditions of bail granted by either the Court of Appeal or the Crown Court. However, he or she may not do so unless satisfied that the prosecution does not object to the variation (s 31A(3)).

If the Registrar refuses any of these applications, the appellant may apply to the single judge.

In addition to these powers, the Registrar may, like the single judge on examining the grounds of appeal, decide that the appeal has a good chance of success and refer the application for leave to the court. The court may then both grant leave to appeal and dispose of the appeal at one hearing. Alternatively, if the Registrar considers that the notice of appeal or notice of application for leave to appeal does not show any substantial ground of appeal, he may refer it to a court for summary determination, and where the court considers the appeal or application frivolous or vexatious and it can be disposed of without adjourning for a full hearing, it can dismiss the appeal or application summarily: CAA 1968, s 20 as substituted by CAA 1988.

12.8 Powers of the Court of Appeal

12.8.1 Following appeal against conviction

Having heard the appeal against conviction the Court of Appeal may do any of the following:

(a) Dismiss the appeal.

(b) Allow the appeal and quash the conviction.

(c) Allow part of the appeal and dismiss the other part. If it does this, the court may pass a new sentence on the remaining conviction, but this must not be greater than the sentence as a whole passed by the convicting court (CAA 1968, s 4(3)). For example, the defendant is convicted of two offences and sentenced to one year's imprisonment on each to run consecutively. On appeal, one conviction is quashed. The Court of Appeal may increase the sentence on the remaining conviction to up to two years, this being the total imposed by the convicting court.

(d) Find the appellant guilty of an alternative offence. Under the CAA 1968, s 3, if the appellant has been convicted of one offence, but the jury, under the Criminal Law Act 1967, s 6, could have found him or her guilty of another offence, then the court may substitute a conviction for that other offence. Thus, if the jury have convicted of murder, the court may substitute a verdict of guilty of manslaughter. Further, if the defendant is charged with two counts in the alternative, and is convicted on one but the jury are discharged from giving a verdict on the other, the court may reverse the verdicts. The court must consider that the jury were satisfied of facts which proved him or her guilty of the other offence. See *R v Spratt* [1980] 1 WLR 554 and *R v Peterson* [1997] Crim LR 339. Section 4(3) of the CAA 1968 applies. The power under s 3 to find the appellant guilty of an alternative offence only applies where the appellant pleaded not guilty at the trial (*R v Horsman* [1998] QB 531).

    The CJA 2003, s 316, however, created a new s 3A, under which a defendant who has pleaded guilty may be found guilty of an alternative offence. This applies where the defendant has been convicted of an offence to which he has pleaded guilty; if he has not so pleaded, he could have pleaded guilty to or been found guilty of another offence, and it appears to the Court of Appeal that the original plea of guilty indicates an admission by the appellant of facts which prove him guilty of the other offence. In these circumstances, the Court of Appeal may, instead of allowing or dismissing the appeal, substitute for the appellant's plea of guilty a plea of guilty to the other offence. It may also pass sentence on the substitute offence, but not of greater severity than the sentence imposed by the original court.

(e) Determine the appeal summarily under the CAA 1968, s 20 as amended. If the Registrar considers that an appeal or application for leave to appeal has no real merit, he or she may put it before the court for 'summary determination'. The court may, if it is of the opinion that the appeal or application is frivolous or vexatious and can be disposed of without a full hearing, simply dismiss it without a full hearing and without hearing argument from either side. This process is to discourage groundless appeals or applications, and applies to all appeals, whether on points of pure law, fact or mixed fact and law.

(f) Order a retrial. Under the CAA 1968, s 7, the court may order a retrial if it considers that a retrial is required in the interests of justice. The power to order a retrial is generally available, whether the appeal is on the basis of fresh evidence, or because of some irregularity or misdirection in the trial. In deciding whether to order a retrial, the court will take into account the length of time since the original trial, whether the defendant has been in custody, the apparent strength of the evidence and the degree of publicity surrounding the case, if any. Where a retrial is ordered a new indictment must be preferred by the Court of Appeal and arraignment must usually be within two months of the quashing of the conviction (s 8 of the CAA 1968).

(g) Make an order for loss of time. Under the CAA 1968, s 29(1), the Court of Appeal can direct that all or part of the time spent in custody pending the determination of the appeal does not count towards the term of any custodial sentence which has been imposed. Such directions may be given where either the single judge or the full court refuse leave to appeal. In *Fortean* [2009] EWCA Crim 437, it was made clear that counsel's support of an application does not mean an order for loss of time will automatically be avoided. Where a single judge has indicated that an application is without merit, an applicant should expect the full court to order loss of time (*Brind* [2008] EWCA Crim 934).

The *Criminal Practice Directions*, Part X 68E.1–2 provide:

> 68E.1 Both the Court and the single judge have power, in their discretion, under the Criminal Appeal Act 1968 sections 29 and 31, to direct that part of the time during which an applicant is in custody after lodging his notice of application for leave to appeal should not count towards sentence. Those contemplating an appeal should seek advice and should remember that a notice of appeal without grounds is ineffective and that grounds should be substantial and particularised and not a mere formula. When leave to appeal has been refused by the single judge, it is often of assistance to consider the reasons given by the single judge before making a decision whether to renew the application. Where an application devoid of merit has been refused by the single judge he may indicate that the Full Court should consider making a direction for loss of time on renewal of the application. However the Full Court may make such a direction whether or not such an indication has been given by the single judge.
>
> 68E.2 Applicants and counsel are reminded of the warning given by the Court of Appeal in *R v Hart and Others* [2006] EWCA Crim 3239, [2007] 1 Cr App R 31, [2007] 2 Cr App R (S) 34 and should 'heed the fact that this court is prepared to exercise its power ... The mere fact that counsel has advised that there are grounds of appeal will not always be a sufficient answer to the question as to whether or not an application has indeed been brought which was totally without merit.'

In addition to its statutory powers, the Court of Appeal has inherent powers, independent of the CAA 1968, to issue a writ of *venire de novo*. If there has been such an irregularity at the trial that the trial can be said to have been a nullity, and the appellant was never in danger of a valid conviction, then the court may order the writ of *venire de novo* to be issued and the appellant may be retried. The irregularity has to be so fundamental that there could not be said to have been a trial (*R v Rose* [1982] AC 822, followed in *R v Booth, Holland and Wood* [1999] 1 Cr App R 457).

In any event, there should always be a proper hearing of an appeal which is before the court. In *R v Owens and Another* [2006] EWCA Crim 2206, the Crown and the defence purported to have reached an agreement as to the disposal of the appeals. This was unacceptable:

> such a compromise was in [the court's] experience unprecedented, and [they] were unable to proceed on that basis. Of course, there are occasions, for instance where new evidence comes forward on appeal, where the Crown indicates that it is not minded to resist an appeal. Even in such circumstances, however, the matter is fully opened to the court, so that the court can form its own view of the situation and resolve the matter for itself. In the present case, however, the suggested compromise had no logical or intellectual basis in the appeal, and simply represented a 'deal'. It was described by counsel as a

'compromise'. It was unacceptable. It showed a fundamental misunderstanding of the function of the court in determining appeals in accordance with section 2 of the Criminal Appeal Act 1968, namely to allow an appeal against conviction if the court considers the conviction unsafe, and to dismiss the appeal in any other case.

See also Patrick O'Connor, 'The Court of Appeal Retrials and Tribulations' [1990] Crim LR 615.

12.8.2 Following appeal against sentence

Having heard the appeal against sentence the court may:

- quash any sentence or order which is the subject of the appeal;
- substitute any sentence that was available to the Crown Court, except that it may not deal with the appellant, taking the sentence as a whole, more severely than he or she was originally dealt with: CAA 1968, s 11(3). Note that this rule is subject to two qualifications:
  (i) by making an order for loss of time, the Court of Appeal may effectively increase the sentence. See **12.8.1**;
  (ii) the Attorney-General's Sentencing References (see **12.10**) are not appeals by the offender and therefore s 11(3) does not apply.

12.8.3 Following an appeal against sentence after summary conviction

Under the CAA 1968, s 10, the Court of Appeal also has the power to deal with an appeal against a sentence imposed by the Crown Court after the defendant has been convicted summarily. Section 10 covers two separate situations:

(a) After committal for sentence.

(b) Where summary conviction puts the appellant in breach of certain orders passed by the Crown Court.

12.8.4 The Human Rights Act 1998

The Human Rights Act 1998, s 4, provides the Court of Appeal (together with the other superior courts) with the power to make a declaration of incompatibility, i.e. that a provision of primary legislation is incompatible with Convention rights. Section 5 further provides that if the court is considering making such a declaration, the Crown is entitled to notice in accordance with rules of court. See now the Crim PR, r 65.12.

Section 5(2) of the 1998 Act entitles a Minister of the Crown (or person nominated by him or her), a member of the Scottish Executive, a Northern Ireland Minister or a Northern Ireland department, on giving notice, to be joined as a party to the proceedings.

12.9 The appeal against acquittal and order for retrial

12.9.1 The right to appeal

Since 2004, the prosecution may appeal against the acquittal of the defendant by the Crown Court, if certain conditions are satisfied, by virtue of CJA 2003, ss 75–97. It also applies to acquittals following a successful appeal against conviction.

The right to appeal under this section is not available for every offence, but only for the offences listed in Sch 5 to the Act. These are the most serious offences and include murder, manslaughter, rape, arson endangering life and war crimes. There is no appeal under these sections where the defendant was found guilty or found not guilty either by reason of insanity or in respect of which he has been found to be under a disability (CJA 2003, s 75(2)(a), (b) and (c)).

Note that s 75(4) makes provision for the retrial of offences where the offender was acquitted outside the UK.

In order to take advantage of this right to appeal, under the CJA 2003, s 76, a prosecutor applies to the Court of Appeal for an order:

- quashing a person's acquittal; and
- ordering his retrial for the offence..

12.9.2 Procedure

There is a two-stage procedure in applying for the above order.

(a) The order may only be applied for with the consent of the Director of Public Prosecutions (s 76). Such consent will only be given if:
   (i) there is new and compelling evidence (see later);
   (ii) it is in the public interest for the application to proceed; and
   (iii) it does not conflict with the Treaty obligations under Article 31 or 34 of the Treaty on European Union (the Articles essentially prevent the bringing of new proceedings as opposed to opening up old proceedings).

(b) The prosecutor must seek the leave of the Court of Appeal. The basic steps are as follows, as set out by the CJA 2003, s 80:
   (i) the prosecution must give notice of application to the Court of Appeal;
   (ii) within two days of such notice, the prosecutor must give notice to the person affected. This time limit may be extended if the person affected is outside the UK;
   (iii) the Court of Appeal must consider the application at a hearing;
   (iv) the person is entitled to be present at the hearing, and whether or not he is present, he is entitled to be represented;
   (v) the Court of Appeal may, if it thinks it necessary in the interests of justice, order the production of any document or exhibit or the appearance of any compellable witness;
   (vi) the Court of Appeal may hear more than one application at one hearing but only if the matters could be tried together on the same indictment.

12.9.3 New and compelling evidence

Section 78 of the CJA 2003 provides that there must be new and compelling evidence against the acquitted person. Under s 78(2), evidence is new if it was not adduced in the proceedings in which the person was acquitted, or from which he appealed. An example of such evidence is new testing techniques.

Under s 78(3), evidence is compelling if:

- it is reliable;
- it is substantial; and
- in the context of the outstanding issues, it appears highly probative of the case against the acquitted person. The outstanding issues are the issues in dispute in the proceedings in which the person was acquitted and, if those were appeal proceedings, any other issues remaining in dispute from earlier proceedings to which the appeal related.

See *R v A* [2009] 1 WLR 1947 as to what is meant by 'new and compelling' evidence. The Act did not require new evidence to be direct evidence, and strong supporting evidence could come with in the definition. In this case, the acquittal was quashed and a retrial ordered.

12.9.4 Determination by the Court of Appeal

If the Court of Appeal is dealing with an appeal against acquittal, it must make the order applied for and if not, must dismiss the application, if the requirements under the CJA 2003, ss 78 and 79 are not met (see earlier).

In addition, the Court of Appeal must be satisfied, under s 79 that it is in the interests of justice for the court to make the order. In determining whether it is in the interests of justice, the Court of Appeal will have regard, under s 79, to:

(a) whether existing circumstances make a fair trial unlikely;

(b) for the purposes of that question and otherwise, the length of time since the offence was committed;

(c) whether it is likely that the new evidence would have been adduced in the earlier proceedings against the acquitted person but for the failure by an officer or by a prosecutor to act with due diligence;

(d) whether since those proceedings (or since the commencement of this part of the Act, if later) any officer or prosecutor has failed to act with due diligence.

See by way of example, *R v Dunlop* [2006] EWCA Crim 1354, the first instance of this power being used. The defendant had been acquitted of murder but subsequently informally admitted the offences, and was recharged. At the retrial, he pleaded guilty to murder. See also *R v Miell* [2007] EWCA Crim 3130, where the Court of Appeal had to form its own view as to whether the acquitted person's subsequent plea of guilty to perjury at his trial constituted compelling evidence that he had committed the offence charged (murder). In *B and G* [2009] Crim LR 738, the issue about whether evidence was compelling was a different test to the jury's assessment of whether it was persuasive. In *Dobson* [2011] 1 WLR 3230 the court made it clear that compelling evidence did not have to be irresistible.

12.10 Other methods of appeal

12.10.1 The Attorney-General's Reference

Under the Criminal Justice Act 1972, s 36(1), where a defendant has been acquitted following a trial on indictment, the Attorney-General may refer any point of law that arose in the case to the Court of Appeal for its opinion. The purpose is to prevent potentially false decisions becoming too widely accepted. Whatever conclusion the Court of Appeal reaches on the point of law, the acquittal is not affected.

In order to bring proceedings under s 36, the Attorney-General serves a notice on the defendant within 28 days, containing the point of law to be argued, a summary of the argument and the authorities the Attorney-General relies on. The Court of Appeal must hear the argument from the Attorney-General or his representative, and may hear submissions from the defence. See Crim PR, Part 70.

Under s 36(3), the Court of Appeal may refer the point to the Supreme Court, either on its own initiative or following an application from either party. The Supreme Court then considers the matter and gives its opinion.

12.10.2 Reference by the Attorney-General on a matter of sentence

Under the CJA 1988, ss 35 and 36, the Attorney-General may refer a sentence, which includes any order made by a court when dealing with an offender, to the Court of Appeal for review if:

(a) he or she considers that the sentence was 'unduly lenient' (this may, but need not, be because the Attorney-General considers that the judge erred in law as to his powers of sentence);

(b) leave of the Court of Appeal is granted; and

(c) the offence was triable only on indictment, or was triable either way but specified as reviewable in an order made by the Home Secretary.

Reviewable offences are set out in the Criminal Justice Act 1988 (Reviews of Sentencing) Order 2006 (SI 2006/1116) (see *Blackstone's Criminal Practice* at D28.11) and include:

- indecent assault, threats to kill, cruelty to a person under 16, and attempts or incitement to commit any of these offences, certain serious fraud, smuggling, drug offences, racially or religiously aggravated assault, criminal damage, public order or harassment within these provisions.

If an offender is sentenced for two separate matters, only one of which is triable only on indictment or specified as reviewable, they are to be treated as having been passed in the same proceedings if they are passed on the same day, or passed on different days but ordered to be treated as one sentence by the sentencing court. Thus, sentences may be reviewed by the Court of Appeal even though they do not fall within (c) above.

The procedure for bringing a sentencing reference is the same as for bringing an appeal against sentence (see **12.6**). The Court of Appeal may quash any sentence, and impose such a sentence as it thinks appropriate, provided it is a sentence which the Crown Court had power to pass. See Crim PR, Part 70.

The correct approach to sentencing references was set out by the Court of Appeal in *Attorney-General's Reference (No 4 of 1989)* [1990] 1 WLR 41:

- the sentence must be *unduly* lenient, that is it must fall out of the range of sentences, which the judge could reasonably consider appropriate;
- assuming that it is unduly lenient, the court still has a discretion as to whether to exercise its powers;
- the court's powers are not confined to increasing the sentence.

According to *R v Krivec* [2007] EWCA Crim 922, mitigation might well justify a subsequent departure from established sentencing guidelines and trial judges should not hesitate to impose the right sentence merely because they fear a reference by the Attorney-General. Nor should the Attorney-General ignore the fact that a substantial departure from the guidelines will not automatically justify intervening. See also *R v Johnson* [2002] EWCA Crim 1418, where the court said that the distinction between 'lenient' and 'unduly lenient' should be kept in mind, and that the purpose of the provision was to avoid gross error, allay public concern and preserve public confidence in cases where a judge appears to have departed from the norms of sentencing generally applied.

For examples, see *R v Shaw, Attorney-General's Reference (No 28 of 1996)* [1997] 2 Cr App R (S) 206; *R v Harnett, Attorney-General's Reference (No 60 of 1996)* [1997] 2 Cr App R (S) 198; *Attorney-General's Reference (No 110 of 2002)* [2003] 2 Cr App R (S) 78; and *Attorney-General's References (Nos 14 and 15 of 2006)* [2007] 1 All ER 718.

Note that CJA 2003, s 271 provides that an offender may appeal against a minimum or whole life term in a murder case. The Attorney-General therefore may also refer such terms as being too lenient.

Further reading: Ralph Henham, '*Attorney-General's Reference* Revisited' (1998) 62(5) JCL 468.

12.11 Appeal to the Supreme Court (formerly the House of Lords)

Under the CAA 1968, s 33, either the prosecution or defendant may appeal from any decision of the Court of Appeal to the Supreme Court if:

- leave is granted by either the Court of Appeal or the Supreme Court; and
- the Court of Appeal certifies that the case raises a point of law of general public importance which ought to be considered by the Supreme Court. There is no appeal against the court's refusal to grant a certificate. See *R v Tang* [1995] Crim LR 813.

One of the effects of s 33 is that the prosecutor may appeal to the Supreme Court against the order of the Court of Appeal quashing the appellant's conviction. If the prosecutor is successful in the Supreme Court, the conviction will be restored.

Students are also referred to Crim PR, Part 74.

12.12 Reference to the European Court of Justice

Under the Crim PR, Part 75, the Court of Appeal has power to refer a case to the Court of Justice of the European Union at any time before the determination of an appeal for a preliminary ruling. This should not be confused with a case being taken to the European Court of Human Rights in Strasbourg; see *Blackstone's Criminal Practice* 2014, at D30.9, for a brief summary.

12.13 The Criminal Cases Review Commission

Prior to 1997, the Home Secretary had the power to refer a case, or any point arising in it, to the Court of Appeal (CAA 1968, s 17). The reference was made in the exercise of the Home Secretary's discretion and could be made whether or not the defendant had made an application to the Home Secretary for the reference to be made. In any event the defendant could not be prejudiced by the reference as the Court of Appeal had no power to order loss of time in these circumstances.

If the whole case was referred, it was treated as if it were an appeal to the Court of Appeal by the defendant, who was then able to raise any questions of law, fact or mixed law and fact.

However, it became clear that the power was not satisfactory. In practice, the Home Secretary only referred cases to the Court of Appeal where there was fresh evidence, or some other significant matter arose which had not been investigated at the trial. In 1991, the then Home Secretary announced the creation of a Royal Commission on Criminal Justice to examine the ways in which alleged miscarriages of justice were dealt with. As a result of the recommendations of the Royal Commission, the Criminal Cases Review Commission (the Commission) was established by the CAA 1995, replacing the Home Secretary's power to refer matters to the Court of Appeal. The Commission started work in 1997. Originally, the Commission had its own website, but it appears now on the Ministry of Justice website; see <http://www.justice.gov.uk/about/criminal-cases-review-commission>.

What follows is a general outline of the work of the Commission. A full discussion is beyond the scope of this manual.

12.13.1 Membership of the Commission

The Commission is a public body, independent of government and the courts. It must consist of at least 11 members, appointed by Her Majesty on the recommendation of the Prime Minister. At least one-third must be legally qualified. At least two-thirds must be persons who have knowledge or experience of any aspect of the criminal justice system.

12.13.2 Making the reference

The Commission may refer to the Court of Appeal any conviction or sentence following a trial on indictment, such a reference being treated as an appeal by the person concerned, under the CAA 1968, s 1 (CAA 1995, s 9). Section 11 makes similar provisions in relation to a person convicted in a magistrates' court, referring the matter to the Crown Court.

Under the CAA 1995, s 13, three conditions must be fulfilled before any matter will be referred to the Court of Appeal:

13 Conditions for making of references

(1) A reference of a conviction, verdict, finding or sentence shall not be made under any of sections 9 to 12 unless:

(a) the Commission consider that there is a real possibility that the conviction, verdict, finding or sentence would not be upheld were the reference to be made,

(b) the Commission so consider—

(i) in the case of a conviction, verdict or finding, because of an argument, or evidence, not raised in the proceedings which led to it or on any appeal or application for leave to appeal against it, or

(ii) in the case of a sentence, because of an argument on a point of law, or information, not so raised, and

(c) an appeal against the conviction, verdict, finding or sentence has been determined or leave to appeal against it has been refused.

(2) Nothing in subsection (1)(b)(i) or (c) shall prevent the making of a reference if it appears to the Commission that there are exceptional circumstances which justify making it.

The result of these conditions is that in general a reference will be made if there is an argument or information which previously was not available and which would lead to a real possibility that the conviction will be quashed.

In deciding whether to make a reference, the Commission should also have regard, under s 14(2) and (3), to the following:

(a) Any application or representations made to the Commission by or on behalf of the person to whom it relates. Note that the reference may be made without any application being made to it by the person to whom it relates (s 14(1)).
(b) Any other representations made to the Commission in relation to it.
(c) Any point on which it desires the assistance of the Court of Appeal.
(d) Any other matters which appear to the Commission to be relevant.

For an example of a reference by the Commission to the Court of Appeal, see *R v Bentley* [2001] 1 Cr App R 21.

12.13.3 Information for the parties

Where the Commission decides to refer the matter to the court, it shall inform the court, and any likely party to the proceedings, of its reasons for making the reference (s 14(4)). Further, where the Commission decides not to make a reference after an application has been made to it, the Commission must give the applicant the reasons for not so doing.

12.13.4 Investigations

The Commission has no power to carry out investigations into alleged miscarriages of justice. Instead, the police will be asked to carry out investigations for them, acting in a manner which is similar to the Independent Police Complaints Authority. The Commission may require an appropriate person from the body which carried out the original investigation to appoint someone to make enquiries and report back to the Commission (CAA 1995, s 19(1)). In the majority of cases this will be a police force, and the appropriate person will be the Chief Constable. The Chief Constable may be required to appoint someone from his own force or another force. See also *R (on the appeal of Boyle) v Criminal Cases Review Commission* [2007] EWHC 8 (Admin) for a discussion of the Commission.

12.13.5 Relationship with the Court of Appeal

For a discussion of the relationship between the Commission and the Court of Appeal, see *R v Criminal Cases Review Commission, ex p Pearson* [1999] 3 All ER 498, where the appellant was convicted of murder and wished the Commission to refer her case to the Court of Appeal. The Commission refused to do so, on the basis that there was no likelihood that the Court of Appeal would receive the fresh evidence that the appellant wished to adduce, and there was therefore no real possibility that the conviction would be quashed. The appellant sought judicial review, in which the following principles were set out:

(a) The role of the Commission was to try to predict the response of the Court of Appeal, and it could only do this by making its own assessment based on the same process of reasoning that the Court of Appeal might follow. To do so was not to usurp the function of the Court of Appeal.

(b) The Commission's reasoning did not include any defects, which would allow the court to interfere, and the conclusion of the Commission was not irrational and not legally misdirected. The issue was within the Commission's discretion and the only role for the court in such cases was to ensure that the Commission had acted lawfully.

Three final points may be made about the Commission:

(a) The Court of Appeal is not restricted to dealing with the matter on the point referred to, but may examine the case as a whole (s 14(5)).

(b) The Court of Appeal has the discretionary power, if practical considerations so demand, to adjourn an appeal referred to it by the Commission (see *R v Smith (No 2)* [1999] 2 Cr App R 444).

(c) Once a reference has been made to the Court of Appeal on whatever grounds, an appellant may put forward additional grounds of appeal that he or she has been advised could be pursued, arising from the original trial, despite the fact that the Commission has previously rejected them. The Commission does not act in the same way as the 'single judge'. See *R v Smith (No 3)* [2002] EWCA Crim 2907.

13

Procedure between conviction and sentence

13.1 Early guilty plea hearings

Part I 3A.6 of the *Criminal Practice Directions* says that, when a case has been sent for trial, the magistrates' court or the Crown Court may order an early guilty plea hearing, in accordance with directions given by the relevant presiding judge, where a guilty plea is anticipated. This is to allow the Crown Court to deal promptly with such a plea. This will generally be more relevant in the case of indictable-only offences, as the defendant can plead guilty at the 'plea before venue' hearing if the offence is triable either way. However, an early guilty plea hearing would be appropriate where a defendant entered a not guilty plea at the plea before venue hearing but then decides to plead guilty after the case has been sent to the Crown Court for trial. Paragraph 3A.7 says that sentence should normally be passed at an early guilty plea hearing (and so, if a pre-sentence report is required, it should be obtained before the hearing).

13.2 Adjournments

Except in cases where there is an early guilty plea hearing, the court does not necessarily pass sentence the same day that the offender pleads guilty or is found guilty. It has power to adjourn prior to passing sentence. In the magistrates' court, the maximum length of each adjournment after conviction is three weeks if the offender is in custody, or four weeks if the offender is on bail (MCA 1980, s 10(3)); the Crown Court's power to adjourn is one which it possesses at common law, with no specific restrictions on the length of each adjournment.

The presumption in favour of bail (under the Bail Act 1976, s 4) continues to apply during the period between conviction and sentence, unless the defendant has been committed to the Crown Court for sentence (in which case there is a discretion to grant bail, but no presumption in favour of bail). The grounds for refusing bail are the same as those which apply before conviction, but with the additional ground that the adjournment is for the purpose of preparing a report and it would be impracticable to do that if the offender were at liberty (see BA 1976, Sch 1, Part I, para 7). Where an offender has been remanded for reports and is granted bail the court may, at its discretion, include a condition that the offender must be available for interview, etc, so that the report can be compiled (BA 1976, s 3(6)(d)).

13.2.1 Adjournments for reports

Pre-sentence reports on offenders are often a vital factor in the sentencing decision, usually being produced by probation officers (for adult offenders) or social workers (for young offenders) but also in appropriate cases medical reports may be sought from doctors and psychiatrists. Sometimes it might be possible for a 'fast delivery' report (oral or written) to be prepared on the same day. In many cases, however, the court will have to adjourn for a pre-sentence report to be prepared.

13.2.2 Adjournments and 'legitimate expectation'

Where the court adjourns between conviction and sentence, it has to be made clear to the offender that all sentencing options remain open to the court when sentence is passed if that is the intention of the court. If the offender is led to believe that a particular type of disposal—for example, custody or, where the offender has been convicted of an either-way offence in the magistrates' court, committal for sentence—will not be used, the sentencer has to abide by this indication. In *Nottingham Magistrates' Court, ex p Davidson* [2001] 1 Cr App R (S) 167, Lord Bingham CJ (at p 169), said:

> If a court at a preliminary stage of the sentencing process gives to a defendant any indication as to the sentence which will or will not be thereafter passed upon him, in terms sufficiently unqualified to found a legitimate expectation in the mind of the defendant that any court which later passes sentence upon him will act in accordance with the indication given, and if on a later occasion a court, without reasons which justify departure from the earlier indication, and whether or not it is aware of that indication, passes a sentence inconsistent with, and more severe than, the sentence indicated, the court will ordinarily feel obliged, however reluctantly, to adjust the sentence passed so as to bring it into line with that indicated.

Similarly, in *Thornton v CPS* (2010) 174 JP 121, Aikens LJ (at para 49) said that:

> . . . it is imperative that magistrates do not put themselves in a position which binds the hands of another bench on the question of sentence unless they are absolutely certain that it is the right course to take. Forms can be used, and forms of words used, to ensure that no expectation about sentence, legitimate or otherwise, is engendered in the mind of defendants or their advisers.

13.3 The facts of the offence

If the accused pleads guilty, the first stage of the sentencing procedure is for the prosecution to present, briefly, the facts of the offence.

13.3.1 Presenting the facts

The prosecuting advocate summarises the prosecution case based on the statements made by the prosecution witnesses. The summary usually includes the circumstances and gravity of the offence, and the offender's response when questioned at the police station.

Prosecution advocates also have to be aware of the Attorney-General's guidelines: *Guidelines on Acceptance of Pleas and the Prosecutor's Role in the Sentencing Exercise*. These guidelines (which are in Appendix 2 of *Blackstone's Criminal Practice*), at para B4, make the point that the prosecution advocate:

> *. . . represents the public interest, and should be ready to assist the court to reach its decision as to the appropriate sentence. This will include drawing the court's attention to:*
>
> - *any victim personal statement or other information available to the prosecution advocate as to the impact of the offence on the victim;*
> - *where appropriate, to any evidence of the impact of the offending on a community;*
> - *any statutory provisions relevant to the offender and the offences under consideration;*
> - *any relevant sentencing guidelines and guideline cases; and*
> - *the aggravating and mitigating factors of the offence under consideration.*

The prosecution advocate may also offer assistance to the court by making submissions, in the light of all these factors, as to the appropriate sentencing range.

Rule 37.10(3) of the Criminal Procedure Rules states that, in the magistrates' court, the prosecutor must:

> *(a) summarise the prosecution case, if the sentencing court has not heard evidence;*
>
> *(b) identify any offence to be taken into consideration in sentencing;*

(c) *provide information relevant to sentence, including any statement of the effect of the offence on the victim, the victim's family or others; and*

(d) *where it is likely to assist the court, identify any other matter relevant to sentence, including—*

   (i) *aggravating and mitigating factors,*

   (ii) *the legislation applicable, and*

   (iii) *any sentencing guidelines, or guideline cases.*

Rule 38.16(3) makes almost identical provision for cases where the defendant pleads guilty or is found guilty in the Crown Court.

When presenting the facts, the prosecuting advocate should not try to make the offence seem as serious as possible so as to obtain a heavy sentence. The advocate must present the facts fairly in the light of the evidence contained in the prosecution witness statements, conceding to the defence any points in mitigation which are apparent from the statements, but equally giving full weight to any aggravating factors which make the offence a serious one of its type. In particular, if the offender (in any statements to the police) or defence advocate (in mitigation) puts forward a version of the facts of the offence which does not accord with the evidence the prosecution has available, the advocate should indicate that the prosecution cannot accept what the defence is saying about the offence (see **13.3.3**).

13.3.2 Victim Personal Statements

Victims of crime are invited to make a statement, known as a Victim Personal Statement (VPS), giving them a formal opportunity to say how a crime has affected them. Part VII F.3 of the *Criminal Practice Directions* says that if the court is presented with a VPS the guidance given in *R v Perkins* [2013] EWCA Crim 323 should be followed. In particular:

- The VPS must be the form of a witness statement made under s 9 of the CJA 1967, served in good time on the defence. The maker of a VPS may be cross-examined on its content.
- At the discretion of the court, the VPS may be read aloud in open court, in whole or in part, or it may be summarised.
- In all cases, 'it will be appropriate for a VPS to be referred to in the course of the sentencing hearing and/or in the sentencing remarks'.
- The court 'must pass what it judges to be the appropriate sentence having regard to the circumstances of the offence and of the offender, taking into account, so far as the court considers it appropriate, the impact on the victim. The opinions of the victim or the victim's close relatives as to what the sentence should be are therefore not relevant, unlike the consequences of the offence on them. Victims should be advised of this. If, despite the advice, opinions as to sentence are included in the statement, the court should pay no attention to them.'

13.3.3 Disputes about the facts after a guilty plea

The Attorney-General's *Guidelines on Acceptance of Pleas and the Prosecutor's Role in the Sentencing Exercise* (at Part C) require a written basis of plea to be prepared unless the defence has indicated that the guilty plea has been, or will be, tendered on the basis of the prosecution case (in other words, the defence accepts the prosecution case as it stands). Where there is any disagreement between the defence and the prosecution as to the facts, a written basis of plea should be produced.

It will quite often be the case that the defendant admits committing the offence and so pleads guilty to it, but on the basis that the facts of the offence are not as serious as the version being put forward by the prosecution. It may well be that the defence and the prosecution can agree on a version of facts that both are content with. However, the Attorney-General's guidelines make the point that the basis of a guilty plea 'must not be agreed on a misleading or untrue set of facts and must take proper account of the victim's interests'. The guidelines go on to say that, where the basis of plea 'cannot be agreed and the discrepancy between the two accounts is such as to have a potentially significant effect on the level of sentence, it is the duty of the defence advocate so to inform the court before the sentencing process begins. There remains an overriding duty on the prosecution advocate to ensure that the sentencing judge is made aware of the discrepancy and of the consideration which must be given to holding a *Newton* hearing to resolve the issue'.

In *R v Newton* (1982) 77 Cr App R 13, the Court of Appeal set out the procedure to be followed where the defendant pleads guilty but on a factual basis which is significantly different to the prosecution version. In such a case, the judge may:

- hear whatever evidence the parties wish to call on the disputed issue, and come down on one side or the other (this is usually referred to as a '*Newton* hearing'); or
- accept the defence version; or
- if the difference between the two versions amounts (in effect) to an allegation that the defendant committed an additional offence, empanel a jury to decide the issue (in such a case a count will be added to the indictment by way of amendment and a trial on that count will ensue, see *R v Eubank* [2002] 1 Cr App R (S) 4).

The defence have a duty to notify the Crown that a guilty plea will be put forward, but that the prosecution version of the facts will be contested, so that the prosecution can ensure the presence of any necessary witnesses to enable a *Newton* hearing to proceed (*R v Mohun* (1993) 14 Cr App R (S) 5).

When the judge conducts a *Newton* hearing, the rules of evidence should be strictly followed, and the prosecution have to prove their version of events to the criminal standard (*R v Kerrigan* (1993) 14 Cr App R (S) 179).

If the defendant declines to give evidence, the judge is entitled to proceed on the basis that, in the absence of any evidence from the defendant, the facts put forward by the prosecution are undisputed (*R v Mirza* (1992) 14 Cr App R (S) 64).

A *Newton* hearing need not be held where the defendant's story is so 'manifestly false' that the judge was entitled to reject the defence version without hearing evidence (*R v Hawkins* (1985) 7 Cr App R (S) 351; *R v Walton* (1987) 9 Cr App R (S) 107).

Where the alleged facts relied upon by the defence to reduce the gravity of the offence are exclusively within the offender's own knowledge, so that the prosecution cannot reasonably be expected to call evidence in rebuttal, the judge is entitled to reject the offender's evidence of what happened as unbelievable, notwithstanding that it is the only evidence there is (*R v Kerr* (1980) 2 Cr App R (S) 54). In *R v Tolera* [1999] 1 Cr App R (S) 25, Lord Bingham CJ (at p 32) said that where:

> the defendant, having pleaded guilty, advances an account of the offence which the prosecution does not, or feels it cannot, challenge, but which the court feels unable to accept, whether because it conflicts with the facts disclosed in the Crown case or because it is inherently incredible and defies common sense... it is desirable that the court should make it clear that it does not accept the defence account and why... The court should therefore make its views known and, failing any other resolution, a hearing can be held and evidence called to resolve the matter. That will ordinarily involve calling the defendant and the prosecutor should ask appropriate questions to test the defendant's evidence, adopting for this purpose the role of an *amicus* ['friend of the court'], exploring matters which the court wishes to be explored. It is not generally desirable that the prosecutor, on the ground that he has no evidence to contradict that of the defendant, should simply fold his hands and leave the questioning to the judge.

The Guidelines issued by the Sentencing Guidelines Council (now the Sentencing Council) in 2007, say that if, after the defendant pleads guilty, 'there is a *Newton* hearing and the offender's version of the circumstances of the offence is rejected, this should be taken into account in determining the level of reduction'. This means that the offender will receive less credit for pleading than would otherwise have been the case (but this applies only where the offender's version of events is rejected by the court).

Where the difference in version between the facts put forward by the defendant and those put forward by the prosecution amounts to an allegation by the prosecution that the defendant committed an additional offence (eg where the prosecution allege that the defendant committed a robbery and during the course of the robbery brandished a knife, but the defendant, whilst admitting robbery, denies possession of a knife), the proper course of action is to amend the indictment and add a count alleging the additional offence; a jury is then empanelled to try that additional offence. In such a case, a *Newton* hearing should not be held, since the defendant is entitled to have a verdict from a jury in respect of the additional offence (*R v Eubank* [2002] 1 Cr App R (S) 4).

If the judge wrongly fails to hold a *Newton* hearing, the Court of Appeal may vary the sentence to one which is appropriate on the basis that the defendant's version of events is correct (*R v Mohun* (1993) 14 Cr App R (S) 5).

In *R v Underwood* [2005] 1 Cr App R (S) 90, the Court of Appeal heard a number of appeals together to set out guidelines to re-emphasise the procedure to be adopted when dealing with a *Newton* hearing. Lord Judge (at paras 2–11) sets out a very useful summary of the principles to be derived from *Newton* and the subsequent case law:

2. The essential principle is that the sentencing judge must do justice. So far as possible the offender should be sentenced on the basis which accurately reflects the facts of the individual case . . .
3. The starting point has to be the defendant's instructions. His advocate will appreciate whether any significant facts about the prosecution evidence are disputed and the factual basis on which the defendant intends to plead guilty. If the resolution of the facts in dispute may matter to the sentencing decision, the responsibility for taking any initiative and alerting the prosecutor to the areas of dispute rests with the defence. The Crown should not be taken by surprise . . . In any event, whatever view may be formed by the Crown on any proposed basis of plea, it is deemed to be conditional on the judge's acceptance of it.
4. The Crown may accept and agree the defendant's account of the disputed facts. If so, the agreement should be reduced to writing and signed by both advocates. It should then be made available to the judge before the start of the Crown's opening, and, if possible, before he is invited to approve the acceptance of any plea or pleas . . . The Crown may reject the defendant's version. If so, the areas of dispute should be identified in writing and the document should focus the court's attention on the precise fact or facts which are in dispute.
5. The third, and most difficult, situation arises when the Crown may lack the evidence positively to dispute the defendant's account. In many cases an issue raised by the defence is outside the knowledge of the prosecution. The prosecution's position may well be that it had no evidence to contradict the defence assertions. That does not mean that the truth of matters outside its own knowledge should be agreed. In these circumstances, particularly if the facts relied on by the defendant arise from his personal knowledge and depend on his own account of the facts, the Crown should not normally agree the defendant's account unless it is supported by other material . . . Neither the prosecution nor the judge is bound to agree facts merely because . . . the prosecution cannot 'gainsay' the defendant's account . . .
6. . . . We emphasise that, whether or not the basis of plea is 'agreed', the judge is not bound by any such agreement and is entitled . . . to insist that any evidence relevant to the facts in dispute should be called . . .
7. The prosecuting advocate should assist the judge by calling any appropriate evidence and testing the evidence advanced by the defence. The defence advocate should similarly call any relevant evidence and, in particular, where the issue arises from facts which are within the exclusive knowledge of the defendant and the defendant is willing to give evidence in support of his case, be prepared to call him. If he is not, and subject to any explanation which may be proffered, the judge may draw such inferences as he thinks fit from that fact . . .
8. The judge must then make up his mind about the facts in dispute. He may, of course, reject evidence called by the prosecution . . . [H]e may equally reject assertions advanced by the defendant, or his witnesses, even if the Crown does not offer positive contradictory evidence.
9. The judge must, of course, direct himself in accordance with ordinary principles, such as, for example, the burden and standard of proof. In short, his self-directions should reflect the relevant directions he would have given to the jury. Having reached his conclusions, he should explain them in a judgment.

10. Again, by way of reminder, we must explain some of the limitations on the *Newton* hearing procedure.
   (a) There will be occasions when the *Newton* hearing will be inappropriate. Some issues require a verdict from the jury. To take an obvious example, a dispute whether the necessary intent under s.18 of the Offences against the Person Act 1861 has been proved should be decided by the jury. Where the factual issue is not encapsulated in a distinct count in the indictment when it should be, then, again, the indictment should be amended and the issue resolved by the jury. We have in mind, again for example, cases where there is a dispute whether the defendant was carrying a firearm to commit a robbery. In essence, if the defendant is denying that a specific criminal offence has been committed, the tribunal for deciding whether the offence has been proved is the jury.
   (b) At the end of the *Newton* hearing the judge cannot make findings of fact and sentence on a basis which is inconsistent with the pleas to counts which have already been accepted by the Crown and approved by the court. Particular care is needed in relation to a multi-count indictment involving one defendant, or an indictment involving a number of defendants, and to circumstances in which the Crown accepts, and the court approves, a guilty plea to a reduced charge . . .
   (e) Where the impact of the dispute on the eventual sentencing decision is minimal, the *Newton* hearing is unnecessary . . .
   (f) The judge is entitled to decline to hear evidence about disputed facts if the case advanced on the defendant's behalf is, for good reason, to be regarded as absurd or obviously untenable. If so, however, he should explain why he has reached this conclusion.
11. . . . If the issues at the *Newton* hearing are wholly resolved in the defendant's favour, the credit due to him should not be reduced. If for example, however, the defendant is disbelieved, or obliges the prosecution to call evidence from the victim, who is then subjected to a cross-examination, which, because it is entirely unfounded, causes unnecessary and in-appropriate distress, or if the defendant conveys to the judge that he has no insight into the consequences of his offence and no genuine remorse for it, these are all matters which may lead the judge to reduce the discount which the defendant would otherwise have received for his guilty plea, particularly if that plea is tendered at a very late stage. Accordingly, there may even be exceptional cases in which the normal entitlement to credit for a plea of guilty is wholly dissipated by the *Newton* hearing . . .

In *R v Cairns* [2013] EWCA Crim 467, Leveson LJ reiterated that the onus is on the defendant to identify the matters that are in dispute. His Lordship said (at para 4):

The admission comprised within the guilty plea is to the offence and not necessarily to all the facts or inferences for which the prosecution contend. Once again, however, the responsibility for determining the facts which inform the assessment of the sentence is that of the judge. In the normal course, when the contrary is not suggested, that assessment will be based on the prosecution facts as disclosed by the statements. If, however, the offender seeks to challenge that account, the onus is on him to do so and to identify the areas of dispute in writing, first with the prosecution and then with the court.

His Lordship added (at para 7) that, at the conclusion of a *Newton* hearing, 'in order to meet the requirements of the defendant and the wider public, the judge should provide a reasoned decision as to his findings of fact and thereafter, following mitigation, proceed to sentence'.

It should be noted that the principles established by *Newton* also apply in magistrates' courts. Rule 37.10(5) of the Crim PR says that:

Where the defendant pleads guilty but wants to be sentenced on a different basis to that disclosed by the prosecution case—

(a) the defendant must set out that basis in writing, identifying what is in dispute;

(b) the court may invite the parties to make representations about whether the dispute is material to sentence; and

(c) if the court decides that it is a material dispute, the court will—

   (i) invite such further representations or evidence as it may require, and

   (ii) decide the dispute.

Although this provision appears to suggest that, where the difference in versions put forward by the parties is significant (in that it would make a difference to the sentence passed), the court has a choice of hearing further representations or evidence, it is submitted that magistrates should follow the procedure laid down in *Newton*, and (if they are unwilling simply to accept the defence version of events) hear evidence (ie hold a *Newton* hearing) and then make findings of fact and sentence accordingly. Indeed, cases where it is possible to resolve such a factual dispute without hearing evidence are likely to be very rare, since the decision is likely to involve the court assessing the credibility of the evidence adduced by the parties.

13.3.4 Disputes about the facts after a not guilty plea

Post-conviction disputes about the circumstances of the offence are not limited to cases where the offender pleaded guilty, as a jury's verdict of guilty after a not guilty plea is not necessarily a total vindication of the prosecution's case. In such cases, it is for the judge to form a personal view of the evidence adduced before the jury, and decide what the facts of the offence were. The judge should not ask the jury the reasons for its verdict or what facts it found proved unless the verdict is inconsistent or ambiguous, in which case proper questions may be put by a judge inviting the jury to explain what they mean (per Humphreys J in *R v Larkin* [1943] KB 174, at 176). The judge is not obliged to adopt as a basis for sentencing the least serious version of events consistent with the jury's verdict (*R v Solomon* (1984) 6 Cr App R (S) 120), but should be 'extremely astute' to give the benefit of any doubt to a defendant about the basis on which a jury has convicted (per Watkins LJ in *R v Stosiek* (1982) 4 Cr App R (S) 205 at 208). In *R v Wood* (1991) 13 Cr App R (S) 207, the Court of Appeal said that it would only interfere with the finding of fact by a judge after hearing evidence in exceptional circumstances (eg where the court considers that no reasonable jury could have reached the judge's conclusion).

The view the judge takes of the facts must naturally be consistent with the jury's verdict. Thus, if the jury refuses to find the accused not guilty as charged but convicts of a lesser offence, the sentence must be appropriate to the lesser offence, notwithstanding that the judge is convinced there should have been a conviction for the more serious offence (*R v Hazelwood* (1984) 6 Cr App R (S) 52). The relevant principles were summarised by Leveson LJ in *R v Cairns* [2013] EWCA Crim 467. His Lordship said (at [8]):

> After conviction following a trial, the judge is bound to honour the verdicts of the jury but, provided he does so, is entitled to form his own view of the facts in the light of the evidence . . .

His Lordship referred to case of *R v McGlade* (1990) 12 Cr App R (S) 105, where Lord Taylor CJ had said (at p 109):

> [I]f the verdict of a jury leads inexorably to one version of the facts being found and only one version, the learned judge is bound to sentence upon that basis. But if the verdict of a jury leaves open some important issue which may affect sentence, then the learned judge, having heard all the evidence himself in the course of the trial, is free and, indeed, it is his duty to come to a conclusion, if he can, upon where the truth lies.

Leveson J went on (at para 9) to say that this did not mean that a *Newton* hearing is never appropriate after a trial: 'If an issue not relevant to guilt but relevant to sentence has not been canvassed in the trial, a further hearing may be necessary.'

13.4 Character and antecedents

After the prosecution summary of the facts or, in the case of a not guilty plea, immediately after the guilty verdict, the prosecution advocate provides the court with information about the 'character and antecedents' of the offender. Information about the 'character' of the offender will be wholly or principally concerned with any previous convictions.

Details of antecedents are usually provided by the prosecution advocate, provided that the defence have agreed that they are not in dispute. The information provided should include details of the offender's age, education, employment (past and present) domestic circumstances and income (if any).

13.5 Pre-sentence reports

A pre-sentence report is defined by CJA 2003, s 158 as a report, prepared by an 'appropriate officer', to assist the court in determining the most suitable method of dealing with the offender.

A pre-sentence report will usually be prepared by a probation officer (or, in the case of a young offender, by a social worker or member of a youth offending team). The report will include information about the offence, the various factors in the commission of the offence which are relevant to its seriousness, the offender's attitude towards the offence, background information about the offender and an assessment of the likelihood of the offender re-offending. Where appropriate, the report will also include consideration of what form of community order would best assist with the rehabilitation of the offender. The report will usually make proposals regarding an appropriate sentence.

A probation officer writing a report will draw upon a variety of sources. Of prime importance is the interview with the accused. The probation officer may also visit the offender's home and speak with family members. With permission, the probation officer might talk to the offender's employer. The probation officer will also have access to background sources of information, such as police antecedents and any records the probation service may have of previous contact with the offender. If the accused has recently been released from a custodial sentence, the probation officer may consult the authorities at the relevant establishment to see what effect the sentence apparently had. Where medical or psychiatric factors seem to have contributed to the offence, assistance might be sought from the offender's doctor, and the report might suggest the preparation of a full medical report.

Pre-sentence reports are usually produced in writing. However, under s 158(1A), the court may accept a pre-sentence report given orally in open court. This cannot be done, however, where the offender is under the age of 18 and the court is considering a custodial sentence; in such a case the report must be in writing (s 158(1B)).

By virtue of s 159, a copy of the report must be given to the offender or their legal representative (and, where the offender is under 18, their parent or guardian, unless that would be likely to create a risk of significant harm to the offender). The defence, in mitigation, may refer to passages in the report or perhaps read out particular sentences which are especially favourable. The defence can challenge assertions made in the report (in which case the probation officer may be required to attend for questioning in open court). The prosecution also receive a copy of the report (this enables the prosecution to draw the court's attention to any factual inaccuracies in the report).

13.5.1 The necessity for pre-sentence reports

Under the CJA 2003, s 156, when a court is deciding whether a custodial sentence should be imposed (and, if so, the length of that sentence), or whether a community order should be imposed (and, if so, what restrictions there should be on the offender's liberty), the court is under a duty to obtain and consider a pre-sentence report. This requirement does not apply, however, if the offender is aged 18 or over, and in the circumstances of the case, the court is of the opinion that it is 'unnecessary' to obtain a pre-sentence report (s 156(4)). This would apply, for example, where the appropriate sentence is clear, and the report would make no difference.

Failure to obtain a report does not invalidate a sentence but, on appeal, the appellate court must obtain one and consider it, unless it takes the view the court from which appeal is made was justified in thinking that a report was unnecessary, or is of the opinion that it is unnecessary (s 156(6) and (7)).

Where the offender is under the age of 18, s 156(5) and (8) require the court to obtain and consider a report unless there already exists a previous report and the court has considered the information in that report (if more than one report exists, the court should consider the most recent).

Even where there is no requirement for a report, the court may nonetheless consider it good sentencing practice to have one, especially if it is requested by the defence.

13.5.2 Medical reports

Under the CJA 2003, s 157, where the offender is (or appears to be) mentally disordered, the court must obtain and consider a medical report before passing a custodial sentence, unless the court is of the opinion that it is unnecessary to obtain such a report. The court is required to consider the likely effect of such a sentence on that condition and on any treatment which may be available for it. Moreover, by virtue of s 207, the court can only impose a community order or suspended sentence order which includes a mental health treatment requirement based on evidence from an appropriately qualified medical practitioner that the mental condition of the offender requires, and may be susceptible, to treatment. Likewise, under s 37 of the Mental Health Act 1983, the court can only make a hospital order or guardianship order in respect of a mentally disordered offender based on the evidence of two appropriately qualified medical practitioners that the offender's mental condition is such as to warrant such an order.

13.6 Defence mitigation

Defence counsel may call character witnesses, but this is comparatively unusual. The offender will not be called personally unless either there is a dispute about the facts of the offence, or it is a road traffic offence which carries mandatory disqualification unless the offender can show 'special reasons' for not disqualifying. In most cases, therefore, defence counsel will proceed immediately to make a plea in mitigation. (See the *Advocacy* manual, Chapter 41.)

There is no set pattern for a plea in mitigation, and what ought to be said will obviously vary from case to case. However, a plea in mitigation will usually include submissions about the facts of the offence, the circumstances which led up to it, and the offender's personal circumstances. Counsel has to form a judgment on the seriousness of the offence and the likely penalty, since the court's patience should not be tried by discussing non-custodial sentences at length in a case where the offence is clearly so serious that only a custodial sentence would be justified; conversely, counsel should not concede that the offender must go to prison if the case is one where a community sentence might be appropriate.

13.7 Sentencing indications: *R v Goodyear*

In *R v Goodyear* [2005] EWCA Crim 888; [2005] 1 WLR 2532, the Court of Appeal gave guidance on the procedure to be followed where a defendant in the Crown Court wishes to seek an indication from the judge of the maximum sentence that would be imposed if a guilty plea were to be tendered at that stage in the proceedings. The relevant principles are summarised in Part VII C of the *Criminal Practice Directions*:

- Any advance indication of sentence given by the judge should normally be confined to the maximum sentence if a plea of guilty were tendered at the stage at which the indication is sought (not the maximum possible sentence following conviction by the jury).
- The judge should not give an advance indication of sentence unless one has been sought by the defendant. However, the judge is entitled in an appropriate case to remind the defence advocate (in open court and in the presence of the defendant) that the defendant is entitled to seek such an indication.
- The judge retains an unfettered discretion to refuse to give an advance indication of sentence or to wait, for example until a pre-sentence report is available, before deciding whether to give one.

- Once an indication has been given, it is binding on the judge who has given it, and on any other judge who becomes responsible for the case.
- If, after a reasonable opportunity to consider the indication, the defendant does not plead guilty, the indication ceases to have effect.
- The defendant's advocate should not seek an indication without written authority, signed by the client, that the defendant wishes to seek an indication.
- The advocate is responsible for ensuring that the client fully appreciates that: (a) he or she should not plead guilty unless in fact guilty; (b) any sentence indication given by the judge remains subject to the entitlement of the Attorney-General (where it arises) to refer an unduly lenient sentence to the Court of Appeal; (c) any indication given by the judge reflects the situation at the time when it is given, and that if a guilty plea is not tendered in the light of that indication, the indication ceases to have effect.
- An indication should not be sought while there is any uncertainty between the prosecution and the defence about an acceptable plea (eg where there is a possibility of the defendant pleading guilty to a lesser offence), or about any factual basis relating to the plea. Any agreed basis should be reduced into writing before an indication is sought. The judge should not be asked to indicate levels of sentence which would vary depending on possible different pleas.
- If an indication is sought, the prosecution should normally enquire whether the judge is in possession of all the evidence relied on by the prosecution, including any victim personal statement, as well as any information of relevant previous convictions recorded against the defendant.
- Any sentence indication should normally be sought at the Plea and Case Management Hearing. The hearing should normally take place in open court, with a full recording of the entire proceedings, and both sides represented, in the defendant's presence.
- Any reference to a request for a sentence indication, or the circumstances in which it was sought, is inadmissible in any subsequent trial (should the defendant maintain a not guilty plea). Reporting restrictions should normally be imposed, to be lifted if and when the defendant pleads or is found guilty.

In *Attorney-General's Reference No 80 of 2005* [2005] EWCA Crim 3367, Rose LJ said (at para 29) that hearings involving an indication of sentence 'should normally take place in open court'. Moreover, if an indication is given, it is not appropriate for the judge 'to identify, by reference to a trial, the much longer sentence which he would impose compared with the sentence which he proposes if the defendant pleads guilty' (this comparison would be likely to apply undue pressure to the defendant).

13.8 Pronouncing sentence

A Crown Court judge or a district judge will normally pronounce sentence immediately after the defence mitigation; a bench of lay magistrates may wish to retire to consider sentence, and they may seek advice from the court legal adviser (clerk) on their sentencing powers. If the magistrates cannot agree, the decision on sentence may be taken by a majority.

Under the CJA 2003, s 174, the court is required to give reasons for the sentence that has been passed. In particular, the court must state its reasons for deciding on the particular sentence and must explain to the offender the effect of the sentence, the effects of non-compliance with any order that the offender is required to comply with as part of the sentence, any power the court has to vary or review any order forming part of the sentence and (if the sentence consists of or includes a fine) the effect of failure to pay a fine. The court also has to identify any Sentencing Council guidelines that are relevant to the offender's case and explain how the court has discharged its duty (under s 125 of the Coroners and Justice Act 2009) to comply with those guidelines; in particular, where the court was satisfied that it would be contrary to the interests of justice to follow the guidelines, the court must state why. Where, as a result of taking into account a guilty plea, the court imposes a punishment on the offender which is less severe than the punishment it would otherwise have imposed, the court must state that fact.

13.8.1 Variation of sentence

Under the PCC(S)A 2000, s 155, the Crown Court may vary or rescind a sentence within 56 days from the passing of the sentence. The variation must be made by the Crown Court judge who originally passed the sentence (if the judge was sitting with lay justices, as will be the case where the Crown Court was hearing an appeal from a magistrates' court, they do not have to be present for the variation). This power to vary may be used to correct technical errors in the original sentence.

Once the statutory period for variation has expired the Crown Court has no power to vary its sentence; any alteration would have to be made by the Court of Appeal.

The MCA 1980, s 142(1) empowers magistrates' courts to vary or rescind a sentence at any time if it is considered to be in the interests of justice to do so.

Rule 42.4(3) of the Crim PR provides that a party seeking a variation in sentence (whether in the magistrates' court or the Crown Court) must apply in writing as soon as reasonably practicable, explaining why the sentence should be varied and specifying the variation that the applicant proposes. Under r 42.4(4), the court cannot vary the sentence in the absence of the defendant unless either the court is making the variation which he has proposed, or else he has been given the opportunity to make representations at a hearing.

13.9 Taking other offences into consideration

The general rule is that the court can impose sentence only in respect of offences of which the offender has been convicted (whether by pleading guilty or being found guilty). There is one major exception to this rule, namely the practice of taking other offences into consideration.

Offences taken into consideration (or 'TICs' as they are often known) are offences of which the offender is not convicted, but which the offender admits and asks the court to bear in mind when passing sentence for the offences in respect of which there has been a conviction ('conviction offences'). A list is drawn up of the offences to be taken into consideration and the suspect signs the list. The offences with which the defendant is charged are prosecuted in the normal way and the defendant duly pleads guilty. Before sentence is passed, prosecuting counsel informs the court that the offender wants other matters to be considered. The court is handed the list of offences, signed by the offender, and the court asks for confirmation that the offender admits committing the offences in question and wants them taken into consideration. Prosecuting counsel will then give the court brief details of the nature of the offences.

The system of TICs is advantageous to the offender because (despite an increase in sentence to reflect the admission of guilt of other crimes) the agreement to 'wipe the slate clean' is good evidence of remorse (a mitigating factor which serves to reduce the sentence); also, as a matter of practice, where offences have been taken into consideration, they will not be the subject of separate prosecution (and the increase in sentence that results from such offences being taken into consideration is considerably less than the sentence that would be imposed if the offender were to be convicted—and sentenced separately—for those offences). In *R v Miles* [2006] EWCA Crim 256 Sir Igor Judge P, at paras 10 and 11, said:

> In relation to offences taken into consideration . . . : the sentence is intended to reflect a defendant's overall criminality. Offences cannot be taken into consideration without the express agreement of the offender. That is an essential prerequisite . . . If they are to be taken into account (and the court is not obliged to take them into account) they have relevance to the overall criminality. When assessing the

significance of TICs . . . the court is likely to attach weight to the demonstrable fact that the offender has assisted the police, particularly if they are enabled to clear up offences which might not otherwise be brought to justice. It is also true that cooperative behaviour of that kind will often provide its own very early indication of guilt, and usually means that no further proceedings at all need be started. They may also serve to demonstrate a genuine determination by the offender . . . to wipe the slate clean, so that when he emerges from whatever sentence is imposed on him, he can put his past completely behind him, without having worry or concern that offences may be revealed as that he is then returned to court.

. . . [T]he way in which the court deals with offences to be taken into consideration depends on context. In some cases the offences taken into consideration will end up by adding nothing or nothing very much to the sentence which the court would otherwise impose. On the other hand, offences taken into consideration may aggravate the sentence and lead to a substantial increase in it. For example, the offences may show a pattern of criminal activity which suggests careful planning or deliberate rather than casual involvement in a crime. They may show an offence or offences committed on bail, after an earlier arrest. They may show a return to crime immediately after the offender has been before the court and given a chance that, by committing the crime, he has immediately rejected. There are many situations where similar issues may arise. One advantage to the defendant, of course, is that if once an offence is taken into consideration, there is no likely risk of any further prosecution for it. If, on the other hand, it is not, that risk remains. In short, offences taken into consideration are indeed taken into consideration. They are not ignored or expunged or disregarded.

The Sentencing Council has issued a definitive Guideline on TICs. The Guideline states that:

When sentencing an offender who requests offences to be taken into consideration (TICs), courts should pass a total sentence which reflects all the offending behaviour. The sentence must be just and proportionate and must not exceed the statutory maximum for the conviction offence.

The court has discretion as to whether or not to take TICs into account. In exercising its discretion the court should take into account that TICs are capable of reflecting the offender's overall criminality. The court is likely to consider that the fact that the offender has assisted the police (particularly if the offences would not otherwise have been detected) and avoided the need for further proceedings demonstrates a genuine determination by the offender to 'wipe the slate clean'.

It is generally undesirable for TICs to be accepted in the following circumstances:

- where the TIC is likely to attract a greater sentence than the conviction offence;
- where it is in the public interest that the TIC should be the subject of a separate charge;
- where the offender would avoid a prohibition, ancillary order or similar consequence which it would have been desirable to impose on conviction. For example:
  - where the TIC attracts mandatory disqualification or endorsement and the offence(s) for which the defendant is to be sentenced do not;
- where the TIC constitutes a breach of an earlier sentence;
- where the TIC is a specified offence for the purposes of s 224 of the Criminal Justice Act 2003, but the conviction offence is non-specified; or
- where the TIC is not founded on the same facts or evidence or part of a series of offences of the same or similar character (unless the court is satisfied that it is in the interests of justice to do so).

The Guideline goes on to note that a magistrates' court cannot take into consideration an indictable-only offence, and that the Crown Court can take into account summary-only offences which are closely related to the indictable offence(s) before the court.

The Guideline makes it clear that the sentence imposed on an offender should, in most circumstances, be increased to reflect the fact that other offences have been taken into consideration.

13.10 Specimen or sample offences

A 'specimen' (or 'sample') count is where the defendant is charged with one or more offences occurring on specific occasions, but the prosecution allege that such conduct was representative of other criminal conduct of the same kind on other occasions which are not the subject of specific charges.

In *R v Clark* [1996] 2 Cr App R (S) 351, the defendant was convicted of a single count of indecent assault. This single count was said by the prosecution to reflect a series of offences committed over a two-year period. However, the defendant did not admit committing any offence. The judge passed sentence on the basis that the defendant had committed a series of offences. The Court of Appeal said that, having been convicted on a single count particularising a single act and not having admitted any offence beyond that, the defendant could only be sentenced on the basis of that single act. Similarly, in *R v Kidd; R v Canavan* [1998] 1 WLR 604, the Court of Appeal held that the defendant can only be sentenced for an offence which has been proved against him (ie where he pleads guilty to it or is found guilty of it) or which he has asked the court to take into consideration when passing sentence. Lord Bingham CJ (at p 608) thought it 'inconsistent with principle that a defendant should be sentenced for offences neither admitted nor proved by verdict'. Therefore, when passing sentence, the court must not take account of the fact that the charges are said by the prosecution to be 'specimen' or 'sample' charges. If the prosecution want other incidents to be taken account of, those other incidents must be the subject of individual charges (or offences 'taken into consideration'). In *R v T* [1999] 1 Cr App R (S) 419, the Court of Appeal said that if the prosecution wish to rely on a continuous course of conduct, they must give a sufficient number of instances of that course of conduct in distinct counts in the indictment.

However, in *R v Smith; R v Tovey* [2005] EWCA Crim 530; [2005] 2 Cr App R (S) 100, the Court of Appeal said that where an offender pleads guilty and admits that the plea embraces a wider course of conduct than that specifically charged, that is the equivalent of an informal invitation to the court to take into consideration the other offences, and so the judge can properly proceed to pass sentence on the wider basis admitted.

In *R v A* [2015] EWCA Crim 177, the Court of Appeal gave guidance on how to approach drafting the indictment where multiple offending is alleged (eg in a case involving sexual offences committed over a period of time). Fulford LJ (at [45]) noted that there are three possibilities open to the prosecution:

a) To include a count or counts in the indictment pursuant to rule 14.2(2) of the Criminal Procedure Rules 14.2(2), alleging a course of conduct [the rule provides that: 'More than one incident of the commission of the offence may be included in a count if those incidents taken together amount to a course of conduct having regard to the time, place or purpose of commission'.]

b) To request that the judge resorts to ss 17–19 of the Domestic Violence (Crime and Victims) Act 2004, which enables the judge in particular circumstance to try the outstanding allegations following conviction (after trial by jury) on sample counts; or

c) To include sufficient counts to enable the judge to impose a sentence which sufficiently represents what happened, but care is needed not to overload the indictment.

Fulford LJ went on (at [46]) to note that alleging a course of conduct, under r 14.2(2), may means that 'the extent, seriousness and timespan of the defendant's offending is unclear from the jury's verdict'. His Lordship went on to state (at [47]):

> In our judgment, the central answer to this problem is to be identified in the purpose underpinning multiple counts: it is to enable the prosecution to reflect the defendant's alleged criminality when the offences are so similar and numerous that it is inappropriate to indict each occasion, or a large number of different occasions, in separate charges. This provision allows the prosecution to reflect the offending in these circumstances in a single count rather than a number of specimen counts. However, when the prosecution fails to specify a sufficient minimum number of occasions within the multiple incident count or counts, they are not making proper use of this procedure. In cases of sustained abuse, it will often be unhelpful to draft the count as representing, potentially, no more than two incidents. Indeed, in this case, if there had been a multiple incident count alleging, for example, 'on not less than five occasions' with an alternative of one or more specimen counts relating to single incidents for the jury to consider if they were unsure the offending had occurred on multiple occasions, the judge would have had a solid basis for understanding the ambit of the jury's verdict and he would been able to pass an appropriate sentence. Therefore, the prosecution needs to ensure that there are one or more sufficiently broad course of conduct counts, or a mix of individual counts and course of conduct counts, such that the judge will be able to sentence the defendant appropriately on the basis of his criminality as revealed by the counts on which he is convicted. In most cases it will be unnecessary for the counts to be numerous, but they

should be sufficient in number to enable the judge to reflect the seriousness of the offending by reference to the central factors in the case: e.g. the number of victims, the nature of the offending and the length of time over which it extended. Therefore, in drafting the indictment, a balance needs to be struck between including sufficient counts to give the court adequate sentencing powers and unduly burdening the indictment ... [T]he indictment must be drafted in such a way as to leave no room for misinterpretation of a guilty verdict and regard must be had to the possible views reached by the jury and to the position of the judge, so as to enable realistic sentencing.

13.11 Deferring sentence

Section 1(1) of the PCC(S)A 2000 enables the court to defer passing sentence for the purpose of enabling the court, when it deals with him, to have regard to the offender's conduct after conviction (including, where appropriate, the making of reparation for the offence) or any change in the offender's circumstances. Under subs (2), the court may also have regard to the extent to which the offender has complied with requirements imposed under subs (3). By virtue of subs (3), the requirements can (with the consent of the offender) include undertaking to comply with requirements relating to the offender's conduct during the period of the deferment.

Section 1ZA makes specific provision for undertakings to participate in restorative justice activities (ie activities where the participants consist of, or include, the offender and one or more of the victims, which aim to maximise the offender's awareness of the impact of the offending concerned on the victims, and which give an opportunity to the victim(s) to talk about, or by other means express experience of, the offending and its impact).

Any deferment of sentence is limited to a period of six months (s 1(4)).

In *R v George* [1984] 1 WLR 1082, Lord Lane CJ said that the court should make it clear to the offender what particular purposes the court has in mind and what conduct is expected of the offender during the deferment. His Lordship went on to say (at p 1085) that:

the task of the court which comes to deal with the offender at the expiration of the period of deferment is as follows. First the purpose of the deferment and any requirement imposed by the deferring court must be ascertained. Secondly the court must determine if the defendant has substantially conformed or attempted to conform with the proper expectations of the deferring court, whether with regard to finding a job or as the case may be. If he has, then the defendant may legitimately expect that an immediate custodial sentence will not be imposed. If he has not, then the court should be careful to state with precision in what respects he has failed.

14 The principles of sentencing

14.1 Introduction

In this chapter we examine some of the principles which underpin the sentencing process. At its most basic, this involves considering:

- What sentence does the seriousness of the offence itself merit (in light of the harm caused by the offence and the culpability of the offender)?
- Can that sentence be reduced in light of mitigation relating to the offender?

14.2 Sentencing Council

Section 118 of the Coroners and Justice Act 2009 established the Sentencing Council (replacing both the Sentencing Guidelines Council (SGC) and the Sentencing Advisory Panel (SAP), which were established by the Criminal Justice Act 2003). The Council is chaired by a judicial member (currently Treacy LJ) appointed by the Lord Chief Justice with the agreement of the Lord Chancellor. Under s 120 of the Act, the Sentencing Council has to have regard to a number of matters including: the need to promote consistency in sentencing; the impact of sentencing decisions on victims of offences; the need to promote public confidence in the criminal justice system; and the cost of different sentences and their relative effectiveness in preventing re-offending.

Under s 121(4) of the 2009 Act, the guidelines should specify the range of sentences which the Council thinks appropriate for a court to impose on an offender convicted of the particular offence, and where the guidelines describe different categories of case (according to culpability and harm) the guidelines should specify the range of sentences appropriate for each category. Under subs (5), the guidelines should also specify appropriate starting points. They should also identify any specific aggravating or mitigating features likely to be relevant to the particular offence (subs (6)).

Under s 125(1), the court must, when sentencing an offender, follow any sentencing guidelines which are relevant to the offender's case unless 'satisfied that it would be contrary to the interests of justice to do so'. In particular, under subs (2), where sentencing guidelines have been issued in relation to the offence for which the court has to pass sentence, the court has to impose a sentence within the range specified in the guidelines for that offence (or for the category of that offence into which the present case falls, unless none of the categories sufficiently resembles the present case).

The duty imposed on the court by s 125 does not apply to offences committed before 6 April 2010. However, the existing guidelines issued by the Sentencing Guidelines Council are treated as if they were guidelines issued by the Sentencing Council.

In *R v Healey* [2012] EWCA Crim 1005, the Court of Appeal emphasised the importance of following the Sentencing Council's guidelines. Hughes LJ said (at [5]) that:

> There is deliberately built in to the guidelines issued by the Sentencing Council a good deal of flexibility . . . It does not, however, extend to deliberately disregarding the guidelines, not on the grounds that the

case has particular facts which warrant distinguishing it from the general level, but because the judge happens to take a different view about where the general level ought to be.

14.3 Statutory purposes of sentencing

The CJA 2003, s 142(1), sets out the objectives of sentencing, to which the courts are required to have regard when dealing with adult offenders. Those objectives are:

- punishment of offenders;
- reduction of crime (including reduction by deterrence);
- reform and rehabilitation of offenders;
- protection of the public;
- making of reparation by offenders to persons affected by their offences.

14.3.1 Young offenders

The CJA 2003, s 142A(2) (added by the Criminal Justice and Immigration Act 2008 but not yet in force) provides that, where the offender is under the age of 18, the court must have regard to the purposes of sentencing set out in subs (3), namely:

(a) the punishment of offenders,

(b) the reform and rehabilitation of offenders,

(c) the protection of the public, and

(d) the making of reparation by offenders to persons affected by their offences.

The notable omission in the case of offenders under the age of 18 is deterrence.

In addition to these purposes, a court dealing with a young offender must also have regard to:

(a) the principal aim of the youth justice system, which is to prevent offending (or re-offending) by persons aged under 18 (see s 37(1) of the Crime and Disorder Act 1998); and

(b) the welfare of the offender (in accordance with s 44 of the Children and Young Persons Act 1933).

14.4 The concept of seriousness

Seriousness determines whether a custodial, community or other sentence is the most appropriate, and is the key factor in deciding the length of a custodial sentence, the onerousness of requirements to be incorporated in a community sentence or the amount of any fine imposed.

14.4.1 'Thresholds'

The seriousness of the offence is an important factor in determining whether or not a particular type of sentence is, or might be, appropriate—in other words, whether the custody threshold or the community sentence threshold has been crossed. As regards custodial sentences, the CJA 2003, s 152(2) provides that:

The court must not pass a custodial sentence unless it is of the opinion that the offence, or the combination of the offence and one or more offences associated with it, was so serious that neither a fine alone nor a community sentence can be justified for the offence.

As regards community orders, s 148(1) provides that:

A court must not pass a community sentence on an offender unless it is of the opinion that the offence, or the combination of the offence and one or more offences associated with it, was serious enough to warrant such a sentence.

14.4.2 Culpability and harm

The CJA 2003, s 143(1) provides that:

In considering the seriousness of any offence, the court must consider the offender's culpability in committing the offence and any harm which the offence caused, was intended to cause or might foreseeably have caused.

Thus, 'culpability' is the initial factor in determining the seriousness of an offence. The SGC Guidance on Seriousness identifies four levels of culpability:

(a) *Intention* to cause harm: highest culpability when an offence is planned; the worse the harm intended, the greater the seriousness.

(b) *Recklessness* as to whether harm is caused (appreciates some harm would be caused but proceeds, giving no thought to consequences even though extent of risk would be obvious to most people).

(c) *Knowledge* of specific risks entailed by actions but does not intend to cause the harm that results.

(d) *Negligence*.

Culpability is greater if:

- the offender deliberately causes more harm than is necessary for the commission of the offence; or
- the offender targets a victim who is vulnerable (eg because of old age or youth, disability or by virtue of the job they do).

A number of general factors are relevant to assessing the seriousness of an offence. Factors indicating *higher culpability* include the following:

- Offence committed whilst on bail for other offences. This is a statutory aggravating factor: s 143(3) of the CJA 2003 provides that if the offence was committed while the offender was on bail, the court must treat that as an aggravating factor.
- Failure to respond to previous sentences.
- Offence was racially or religiously aggravated. Racial or religious aggravation is a statutory aggravating factor under s 145 of the CJA 2003, which provides that if the offence was racially or religiously aggravated, the court must treat this as an aggravating factor.
- Offence motivated by, or demonstrating, hostility to the victim based on his or her sexual orientation (or presumed sexual orientation) or disability (or presumed disability). Again, these are statutory aggravating features. Section 146(2) of the CJA 2003 provides that the court must treat circumstances as aggravating where the offence involved hostility based on the victim's actual or presumed sexual orientation, transgender identity or disability. Under s 146(4), it is immaterial whether or not the offender's hostility is based on other factors as well. For these purposes 'disability' means any physical or mental impairment: s 146(5).
- Previous conviction(s), particularly where a pattern of repeat offending is disclosed. The effect of previous convictions is dealt with by s 143(2) of the CJA 2003 (see later).
- Planning of an offence.
- An intention to commit more serious harm than actually resulted from the offence.
- Offenders operating in groups or gangs.
- 'Professional' offending.
- Commission of the offence for financial gain (where this is not inherent in the offence itself).
- High level of profit from the offence.
- An attempt to conceal or dispose of evidence.
- Failure to respond to warnings or concerns expressed by others about the offender's behaviour.

- Offence committed whilst on licence (ie following release from a custodial sentence).
- Offence motivated by hostility towards a minority group, or a member or members of it.
- Deliberate targeting of vulnerable victim(s).
- Commission of an offence while under the influence of alcohol or drugs.
- Use of a weapon to frighten or injure victim.
- Deliberate and gratuitous violence or damage to property, over and above what is needed to carry out the offence.
- Abuse of power.
- Abuse of a position of trust.

Factors indicating a *more than usually serious degree of harm* include:

- Multiple victims.
- An especially serious physical or psychological effect on the victim, even if unintended.
- A sustained assault or repeated assaults on the same victim.
- Victim is particularly vulnerable.
- Location of the offence (eg in an isolated place).
- Offence is committed against those working in the public sector or providing a service to the public.
- Presence of others, for example relatives, especially children or partner of the victim.
- Additional degradation of the victim (eg taking photographs of a victim as part of a sexual offence).
- In property offences, high value (including sentimental value) of property to the victim, or substantial consequential loss (eg where the theft of equipment causes serious disruption to a victim's life or business).

Paragraph 1.39 of the SGC guidance says that there may be exceptional local circumstances which may lead a court to decide that the prevalence of the offence should influence sentencing levels: this is only appropriate where there is appropriate evidence of prevalence and where there is a compelling need to treat the offence more seriously than elsewhere. In *R v Oosthuizen* [2005] EWCA Crim 1978; [2006] 1 Cr App R (S) 73, the Court of Appeal emphasised that if, in any particular city or town, statistics are available to the CPS or the local Criminal Justice Board which demonstrate a prevalence of a particular offence greater than that at a national level, those statistics should be made available to the sentencing court. In the absence of such statistics or other evidence identifying particular prevalence in a particular area, a judge, however experienced in a particular area, should not make the assumption that prevalence of that offence is more marked in that area than it is nationally.

Factors indicating *significantly lower culpability* include:

- a greater degree of provocation than normally expected;
- mental illness or disability;
- youth or age, where it affects the responsibility of the individual defendant;
- the fact that the offender played only a minor role in the offence.

14.5 Reduction in sentence for guilty plea

Pleading guilty is, in itself, good mitigation. Section 144(1) of the CJA 2003 requires the sentencer to have regard to the fact that the offender pleaded guilty and to take into account (a) the stage of the proceedings at which the offender indicated an intention to plead guilty, and (b) the circumstances in which that indication was given.

A reduction in sentence as a result of a guilty plea is appropriate because that plea avoids the need for a trial (enabling other cases to be disposed of more expeditiously); shortens the gap between charge and sentence; saves considerable cost; and saves victims and witnesses from having to give evidence.

A guilty plea was traditionally regarded as evidence of remorse on the part of the offender. However, para 2.4 of the SGC guidance says that the sentencer should address remorse separately, and so should decide the appropriate length of sentence (taking account of any evidence of remorse) before calculating the reduction for the guilty plea.

Discount for pleading guilty is based on a sliding scale, so that the offender gets more credit for pleading guilty at the earliest reasonable opportunity (and less credit for pleading guilty at a later stage). Under that sliding scale, the offender receives:

- the (normal) maximum of one-third where the guilty plea was entered at the first reasonable opportunity;
- a maximum of one-quarter where a trial date has been set;
- a maximum of one-tenth for a guilty plea entered at the 'door of the court' or after the trial has begun.

The importance of following the guidelines on the discount for pleading guilty was emphasised by the Court of Appeal in *R v Ladlow* [2011] EWCA Crim 3214. The judge had given full discount even though the pleas were entered on the date fixed for the trial. Davis LJ said (at para 34):

> It is most important that, so far as possible, consistency is maintained throughout the Crown Courts in England and Wales in this area. Indeed, those defendants who do plead guilty at the first reasonable opportunity and duly get the full discount may feel no real incentive to plead at an early stage if there is to become a perception that a plea even at the date of trial may attract a full discount, as happened here. Moreover, such an approach, if adopted, can give rise to real difficulties and perceptions of unfairness particularly where there are a number of co-accused, some of whom may plead at differing stages in the proceedings.

His Lordship added (at para 35) that, to give full discount for a late plea:

> goes against a principal rationale of the Sentencing Guidelines, which is to encourage pleas at the earliest possible moment . . . It can only tend to ratchet up costs and to undermine the overall rationale of the guidelines if defendants are encouraged to take their chances up until the door of the court. Shortly put, a late plea is better than a trial but it is not as good as an early plea.

His Lordship noted (at para 36) that there are cases (eg complex fraud or conspiracy cases) where the prosecution evidence as served is not complete by the time of the plea and case management hearing; in such cases, the possibility of full credit for a guilty plea may properly be kept open for a period of time. However, his Lordship found it difficult to envisage cases in which (in the absence of a change of circumstances, eg, the willingness of the prosecution at the door of the court to accept a plea to a lesser or alternative count) maximum credit for a plea can properly be given where a plea is only tendered for the first time on the day fixed for trial.

Guidance on what amounts to the 'first reasonable opportunity' was given in *R v Chaytors* [2012] EWCA Crim 1810. Royce J, giving the judgment of the Court of Appeal, said (at para 16):

> In our experience is often the case that judges make it clear that there should be no assumption that a plea at the plea and case management hearing will attract a one-third discount and they apply within the guideline a lesser discount on the basis that the first reasonable opportunity was earlier. That is an entirely proper approach and it should encourage early indications of willingness to plead, with all the consequential savings of cost and time . . .

His Lordship added (at para 19):

> In an increasing number of court centres now there is an early guilty plea scheme where early guilty plea hearings take place. In those centres there are practice guidance notes making it clear that there is a presumption that only a 25 per cent discount will be given if a guilty plea is entered at the plea and case management hearing rather than earlier . . . [A]s this scheme develops around the country it will be

increasingly difficult to maintain that a plea at the plea and case management hearing is the first reasonable opportunity.

In *R v Caley* [2012] EWCA Crim 2821, Hughes LJ, at [13], dealt with admissions by the accused when interviewed by the police:

> The right way for courts to deal with admissions in interview is not . . . by treating them as essential in every case to according the maximum one-third reduction for guilty plea. Rather, the variable circumstances of such admissions are best dealt with not by percentage adjustments prescribed in advance but by recognising them as a factor tending towards downwards adjustment to the sentence passed, to be assessed in the ordinary way by the judge along with other aggravating and mitigating factors, but before adjustment for plea of guilty.

His Lordship then went on to refer to *Chaytors*, and said (at para 18) that:

> absent particular considerations individual to the case, the first reasonable opportunity for the defendant to indicate (not necessarily enter) his plea of guilty, if that is his mind, is not the PCMH . . . The first reasonable opportunity is normally either at the Magistrates' Court or immediately on arrival in the Crown Court—whether at a preliminary hearing or by way of a locally-approved system for indicating plea through his solicitors.

Where the offender was caught 'red-handed', the discount for pleading guilty is reduced. The revised version of the SGC Guidelines, published in 2007, says that:

> 5.3 Where the prosecution case is overwhelming, it may not be appropriate to give the full reduction that would otherwise be given. Whilst there is a presumption in favour of the full reduction being given where a plea has been indicated at the first reasonable opportunity, the fact that the prosecution case is overwhelming without relying on admissions from the defendant may be a reason justifying departure from the guideline.
>
> 5.4 Where a court is satisfied that a lower reduction should be given for this reason, a recommended reduction of 20% is likely to be appropriate where the guilty plea was indicated at the first reasonable opportunity.

Giving credit for a guilty plea where the prosecution case is overwhelming was considered in *R v Wilson* [2012] EWCA Crim 386. Lord Judge CJ said (at para 27):

> On the face of it, even in the context of an overwhelming case, the starting point is the full reduction. Where a lesser reduction is considered appropriate, the recommendation is 20%, not as a mathematical calculation but as an indication of the likely level of reduction if the guilty plea has been indicated at the first available opportunity.

His Lordship added (at para 28) that, even in an overwhelming case, 'the guilty plea has a distinct public benefit. The earlier that it is indicated, the better for everyone'. His Lordship also emphasised (at para 32) 'the value to the victims of crime and the administration of justice of an early indication that the defendant does not require the issues to be tried'.

Where there is a *Newton* hearing (because the defendant puts forward a version of events that differs significantly from the prosecution version, and the court is not willing simply to accept the defendant's version), and the defendant's version of events is rejected, this is taken into account in determining the level of reduction in sentence. In other words, the defendant will lose some of the discount for pleading guilty in such a case. In *Caley*, Hughes LJ (at para 27) said that what (if any) reduction for plea should survive an adverse *Newton* finding will depend 'on all the circumstances of the case, including the extent of the issue determined, on whether lay witnesses have to give evidence and on the extra public time and effort that has been involved'.

It should also be noted that discount for pleading guilty can also be relevant to the type of sentence that is passed. Where the offence crosses the threshold for the imposition of a community or a custodial sentence, application of the reduction principle may properly form the basis for imposing a non-custodial sentence even though the custody threshold has been passed, or a fine or discharge rather than a community sentence. Where the reduction is applied in this way, the type of sentence imposed incorporates the reduction and so no further discount is appropriate (see para 2.3 of the SGC guidance).

14.6 Effect of previous convictions

The CJA 2003, s 143(2), provides that:

> *. . . the court must treat each previous conviction as an aggravating factor if (in the case of that conviction) the court considers that it can reasonably be so treated having regard, in particular, to—*
>
> *(a) the nature of the offence to which the conviction relates and its relevance to the current offence, and*
>
> *(b) the time that has elapsed since the conviction.*

In other words, an offence is to be regarded as more serious if committed by someone with relevant previous convictions (relevance depending on how recent the previous convictions are, and how similar in type they are to the present offence).

The approach prior to the implementation of the CJA 2003 was to regard the existence of relevant previous convictions as resulting in a 'progressive loss' of 'good character mitigation' (see, eg, *Carlton* (1994) 15 Cr App R (S) 335). This meant that an offender without relevant previous convictions would receive a discount in the sentence to reflect previous good character; the more relevant previous convictions recorded against the offender, the more discount was lost. Under the CJA 2003, however, the court should increase the sentence imposed on the offender in order to reflect previous convictions (on the basis that an offence is to be regarded as more serious if committed by someone with relevant previous convictions).

Moreover, a custodial sentence may be imposed because of previous failures to respond to non-custodial sentences. For example, where the offence crosses the custody threshold but the defence argue that mitigating circumstances justify the imposition of a community order instead, the court may reject the suggestion of a community order on the basis that such sentences have been tried previously but the offender has nonetheless committed further offences (see, eg, *Oliver & Little* [1993] 2 All ER 9). However, even if the offender has a very bad record, the defence may argue for a non-custodial sentence to give the offender 'one last chance' to break the cycle of offending (see, eg, *Bowles* [1996] 2 Cr App R (S) 248).

15

Non-custodial sentences in the magistrates' court

In this chapter we look at the various non-custodial sentences that may be imposed by a magistrates' court.

Most of the law relating to non-custodial sentences can be found in the Powers of Criminal Courts (Sentencing) Act 2000 (PCC(S)A).

15.1 Absolute discharge

An absolute discharge (PCC(S)A 2000, s 12(1)(a)) is ordered where the court decides that it is inappropriate to inflict any punishment. Such an order may be appropriate where the circumstances of the offence disclose little or no blame on the part of the offender (eg *R v O'Toole* (1971) 55 Cr App R 206, where an ambulance driver collided with another vehicle while responding to an emergency call).

15.2 Conditional discharge

Where a conditional discharge is imposed (PCC(S)A, s 12(1)(b)), the offender is discharged on condition that he or she does not commit a further offence during the period specified by the court (which can be up to three years). An offender who commits a further offence during the period of the conditional discharge can be re-sentenced for the offence in respect of which the conditional discharge was imposed, as well as being sentenced for the later offence.

One magistrates' court can deal with the breach of a conditional discharge imposed by another magistrates' court, but only with the consent of that court (s 13(8)). If the Crown Court is dealing with the breach of a conditional discharge imposed by a magistrates' court, the powers of the Crown Court when re-sentencing are limited to those of a magistrates' court (s 13(7)). If the conditional discharge was imposed by the Crown Court, only the Crown Court can re-sentence; so if a magistrates' court convicts someone of an offence committed in breach of a conditional discharge imposed by the Crown Court, the magistrates are empowered to commit the offender to the Crown Court to be dealt with for the breach of the conditional discharge (s 13(5)).

The court which re-sentences the offender for the original offence can impose any sentence which could have been passed when the conditional discharge was ordered (PCC(S)A 2000, s 13(6)).

15.3 Fines

More offenders are dealt with by means of a fine than by means of any other sentence.

15.3.1 The maximum fine

For summary offences, fines are expressed in terms of a standard scale containing five 'levels' (Criminal Justice Act 1982, s 37(2), as amended), shown in **Table 15.1**:

Table 15.1 **Standard scale of fines for summary offences**

Level	Maximum fine
1	£200
2	£500
3	£1,000
4	£2,500
5	Unlimited

For offences that are triable either way, the maximum fine is unlimited (Legal Aid, Sentencing and Punishment of Offenders Act 2012, s 85), save for those offences dealt with in the Legal Aid, Sentencing and Punishment of Offenders Act 2012 (Fines on Summary Conviction) Regulations 2015 (SI 2015/664).

15.3.2 Fixing the amount of the fine

The procedure for fixing the amount of a fine is set out in the CJA 2003, s 162. There are three stages:

(a) The court begins by deciding what fine is appropriate in light of the seriousness of the offence.

(b) Next, the court considers whether the fine should be reduced on the basis of any mitigating circumstances relating to the offender. The fine should also be reduced to reflect an early plea of guilty.

(c) Finally, the court takes account of the financial circumstances of the offender. The means of the offender can operate to increase or decrease the amount of the fine.

Under the CJA 2003, s 162, the court can make a 'financial circumstances order' against the offender, requiring the offender to provide a statement of means within the period specified in the order.

If the offender spent time remanded in custody but subsequently receives a fine rather than a custodial sentence for the offence, the fine should be reduced to reflect the time spent in custody (*R v Warden* [1996] 2 Cr App R 269).

The Magistrates' Courts Sentencing Guidelines produced by the Sentencing Council provide detailed guidance on fines.

15.3.3 Enforcement of fines

Where a fine is imposed, payment is due immediately. However, where the offender does not have the means to pay the fine forthwith, the magistrates are empowered to allow time for payment or to order payment by instalments (MCA 1980, s 75(1)). Where payment by instalments is ordered, the total fine should usually be one that the offender will be able to pay off within 12 months.

A magistrates' court, when it imposes a fine, may only fix a term of imprisonment in default if either the offence is punishable with imprisonment and it appears to the court that the offender has sufficient means to pay the fine immediately, or if it appears to the court that the offender is unlikely to remain long enough at an address where he can be found (so that enforcement of the fine by other methods is likely to be impossible) (MCA 1980, s 82(1)).

Enforcement of fines is carried out by the offender's local magistrates' court. If the offender fails to pay the fine or fails to pay the instalments as ordered, the magistrates' court can issue a summons requiring the offender to attend court or the court can issue a warrant for the offender's arrest (MCA 1980, s 83). At the hearing, the court will investigate the offender's means (and the offender can be required to produce evidence of income and outgoings).

Under s 85(1) of the Magistrates' Courts Act 1980, where a fine has been imposed by a magistrates' court, the court may at any time remit the whole or any part of the fine, but only 'if it thinks it just to do so having regard to a change of circumstances'. Under subs (2), where the court remits the whole or part of the fine after a term of imprisonment has been fixed (as will always be the case with Crown Court fines), it must also reduce the term by a proportionate amount (or remit the whole term if the whole fine is cancelled). It should be noted that the power to remit is restricted to fines; there is no equivalent power in respect of compensation orders (s 85(4)).

Assuming that the fine is not remitted, the court has at its disposal a wide array of enforcement mechanisms to ensure that fines are paid, including:

(a) A 'warrant of control' authorising seizure and sale of goods owned by the offender (s 62 of the Tribunals, Courts and Enforcement Act 2007).

(b) An 'attachment of earnings order', so that money is deducted from the offender's wages (Attachment of Earnings Act 1971).

(c) An order for deduction of money from the offender's income support, universal credit, state pension credit, job-seeker's allowance or employment and support allowance (Fines (Deductions from Income Support) Regulations 1992 (SI 1992/2182)).

(d) An attendance centre order, but only if the offender is under the age of 25 (MCA 1980, s 82(4A)).

(e) Under s 35 of the Crime Sentences Act 1997 (re-enacted in the CJA 2003, s 300(2)—not yet in force), where a court has the power to commit an offender to prison in default of payment of a fine (see later), the court may instead order the offender to comply with an unpaid work or curfew requirement.

(f) Under s 40 of the Crime (Sentences) Act 1997 (re-enacted in the CJA 2003, s 301—not yet in force), instead of committing an offender to custody in default of payment of a sum, the court may disqualify the offender from driving for a period of up to 12 months.

(g) Imprisonment, but only if either (i) the offence for which the fine was imposed is imprisonable, and the offender has sufficient means to pay forthwith, or (ii) the court is satisfied that the offender's failure to pay the fine is due to 'wilful refusal' or 'culpable neglect' and the court has considered or tried all other methods of enforcement but it appears to the court that they are inappropriate or have been unsuccessful (MCA 1980, s 82(4)).

Schedule 5 to the Courts Act 2003 puts in place an additional set of powers to aid the enforcement of fines to complement the other mechanisms for enforcement. For example, there is provision for fines to be increased in the event of non-payment (para 42A). The Act also enables the offender's vehicle to be clamped, and then sold, if a fine remains unpaid (para 38(1)(d)). Schedule 6 enables the court to allow an offender over the age of 18 to discharge a fine by means of unpaid work (under a 'work order').

15.4 Community sentences under the Criminal Justice Act 2003

The CJA 2003 effectively gives the court a 'pick-and-mix' menu to enable it to construct a community order that is appropriate to the particular offender.

The term 'community order' is defined by s 177(1) of the Act. This provides that where a person aged 18 or over is convicted of an offence, the court may make an order (a 'community order') imposing on him any one or more of the following requirements:

- an unpaid work requirement;
- a rehabilitation activity requirement;

- a programme requirement;
- a prohibited activity requirement;
- a curfew requirement;
- an exclusion requirement;
- a residence requirement;
- a foreign travel prohibition requirement;
- a mental health treatment requirement;
- a drug rehabilitation requirement;
- an alcohol treatment requirement;
- an alcohol abstinence and monitoring requirement;
- in a case where the offender is aged under 25, an attendance centre requirement;
- an electronic monitoring requirement (not yet in force).

Under s 177(3), where the court makes a community order imposing a curfew requirement or an exclusion requirement, it must normally impose an electronic monitoring requirement as well; under s 177(4), the court may impose an electronic monitoring requirement when it makes a community order containing any of the other requirements.

Under s 177(2A), where the court makes a community order, the order must include at least one requirement imposed for the purpose of punishment, or a fine for the offence in respect of which the community order is made, or both. This duty does not apply if there are exceptional circumstances which relate to the offence or to the offender, and which would make it unjust to do so (subs (2B)).

Under s 177(6), before making a community order imposing two or more different requirements, the court must consider whether, in the circumstances of the case, the requirements are compatible with each other. Moreover, s 217 requires the court to ensure, as far as practicable, that any requirement imposed by the order avoids any conflict with the offender's religious beliefs or with the requirements of any other relevant order to which he may be subject, and avoids any interference with the times, if any, at which he normally works or attends any educational establishment.

The maximum duration of a community order is three years (s 177(5)).

15.4.1 Restrictions on imposing community sentences

Under s 148(1) of the CJA 2003, the community sentence 'threshold' has to be crossed before a community sentence can be imposed. In other words, the offence must be sufficiently serious to justify a community order:

A court must not pass a community sentence on an offender unless it is of the opinion that the offence, or the combination of the offence and one or more offences associated with it, was serious enough to warrant such a sentence.

Moreover, under s 148(2), the court must ensure that the order is both suitable for the offender and commensurate with the seriousness of the offence:

Where a court passes a community sentence—

(a) the particular requirement or requirements forming part of the community order . . . must be such as, in the opinion of the court, is, or taken together are, the most suitable for the offender, and

(b) the restrictions on liberty imposed by the order must be such as in the opinion of the court are commensurate with the seriousness of the offence, or the combination of the offence and one or more offences associated with it.

Under s 150A, a community sentence can only be imposed if the offence is punishable with imprisonment, unless s 151(2) is applicable (this enables a community order to be made if the offender has previously been fined three or more times, even if the current offence does not justify a community sentence).

Section 166(2) makes it clear that a court is not prevented, after taking into account any mitigating matters that are relevant, from passing a community sentence even though it is of the opinion that the offence(s) is/are so serious that a community sentence could not normally be justified for the offence(s). In other words, the fact the case crosses the custody threshold does not mean that custody is inevitable. If there is sufficient mitigation, it is open to the court to impose a community sentence instead. Similarly, s 148(5) provides that the fact that a community sentence may be passed on the offender does not require a court to pass such a sentence.

15.4.2 Procedural requirements

Before deciding that the offence is sufficiently serious to merit a community sentence and before deciding what restrictions on the offender's liberty would be commensurate with the seriousness of the offence, and whether the offender is suitable for the imposition of particular requirements, the court must obtain and consider a pre-sentence report (unless, in the case of an offender who has attained the age of 18, the court takes the view that such a report is unnecessary): see s 156 of the CJA 2003.

15.4.3 Requirements that may be imposed under a community order

The requirements that may be imposed as part of a community order are listed in the CJA 2003, s 177(1).

15.4.3.1 Unpaid work requirement (ss 199, 200)

This is a requirement that the offender must perform unpaid work. The number of hours' work that may be required under an unpaid work requirement must be specified in the order and must be between 40 and 300. The court may only impose an unpaid work requirement if satisfied that the offender is a suitable person to perform such a requirement. Under s 200(2), the work should normally be performed during a period of 12 months. However, under subs (3), unless it is revoked, a community order imposing an unpaid work requirement remains in force until the offender has completed the number of hours specified.

15.4.3.2 Rehabilitation activity requirement (s 200A)

This is a requirement that the offender must, for the duration of the order, 'comply with any instructions given by the responsible officer to attend appointments or participate in activities or both' (s 200A(1)). An order imposing a rehabilitation activity requirement must specify the maximum number of days for which the offender may be instructed to participate in activities (s 200A(2)). Any instructions given by the responsible officer must be given with a view to promoting the offender's rehabilitation, but may have other purposes too (s 200A(3)). The activities that responsible officers may instruct offenders to participate in include activities forming an 'accredited programme', or activities whose purpose is reparative, such as restorative justice activities (s 200A(7)). For these purposes, an activity is a restorative justice activity if the participants include the offender and one or more of the victims (ie people affected by the offending in question), the aim of the activity is to maximise the offender's awareness of the impact of the offending concerned on the victims, and the activity gives the victim(s) an opportunity to talk about, or by other means express experience of, the offending and its impact (s 200A(8)).

15.4.3.3 Programme requirement (s 202)

This is a requirement that the offender must participate in an accredited programme (comprising a systematic set of activities) for the number of days specified in the order.

15.4.3.4 Prohibited activity requirement (s 203)

This is a requirement that the offender must refrain from participating in specified activities on specified days or for a specified period.

15.4.3.5 Curfew requirement (s 204)

This is a requirement that the offender must remain at a specified place for specified periods. The order may specify different places or different periods for different days, but may not specify periods which amount to less than two hours or more than 16 hours in any day. The order may only specify periods that fall within 12 months from the date when the order was made.

15.4.3.6 Exclusion requirement (s 205)

This has the effect of prohibiting the offender from entering a specified place for a specified period (which cannot be for more than two years). An exclusion requirement may provide for the prohibition to operate only during specified periods, and the order may specify different places for different periods or days.

15.4.3.7 Residence requirement (s 206)

This is a requirement that, during a period specified in the order, the offender must reside at a specified place. The court cannot specify a hostel or other institution as the place where the offender must reside, except on the recommendation of a probation officer.

15.4.3.8 Foreign travel prohibition requirement (s 206A)

This is a requirement prohibiting the offender from travelling, on specified days or for a specified period, to any country outside the UK (either generally or as specified in the order). The prohibition is limited to the period of 12 months from the date of the order.

15.4.3.9 Mental health treatment requirement (s 207)

This is a requirement that the offender must submit, during the period(s) specified in the order, to treatment by a registered medical practitioner or a chartered psychologist with a view to the improvement of the offender's mental condition. The treatment may be on an in-patient or out-patient basis. The court may only impose such a requirement if satisfied that the mental condition of the offender is such as requires (and may be susceptible to) treatment, but is not such as to warrant the making of a hospital order or guardianship order under the Mental Health Act 1983 and that the offender has expressed his willingness to comply with such a requirement.

15.4.3.10 Drug rehabilitation requirement (s 209)

This is a requirement that, during the period specified in the order ('the treatment and testing period'), the offender must submit to treatment by an appropriately qualified person with a view to the reduction or elimination of the offender's dependency on or propensity to misuse drugs; the order also requires that, for the purpose of ascertaining whether he has any drug in his body during that period, the offender must provide samples for testing. Such a requirement can only be imposed if the court is satisfied that the offender is dependent on, or has a propensity to misuse, drugs, and that his dependency or propensity is such as requires and may be susceptible to treatment. Also, the requirement must have been recommended to the court as being suitable for the offender by a probation officer, and the offender must have expressed willingness to comply with the requirement. The treatment required under the order can be on an in-patient or out-patient basis.

Sections 210 and 211 provide for review by the court where a drug rehabilitation requirement has been imposed.

15.4.3.11 Alcohol treatment requirement (s 212)

This is a requirement that the offender must submit, during a specified period, to treatment by a suitably qualified person with a view to the reduction or elimination of the offender's dependency on alcohol. Such a requirement may only be imposed if the court is satisfied that the offender is dependent on alcohol, and that this dependency is such as requires (and may be susceptible to) treatment. The court may not impose an alcohol treatment requirement unless the offender expresses willingness to comply with its requirements. The treatment can be on an in-patient or out-patient basis. Section 212A makes provision (not in force at the time of writing) for an alcohol abstinence and monitoring requirement, namely a requirement that the offender abstain from alcohol for a specified period (up to 120 days) and that the offender must submit to monitoring to ensure compliance with the requirement.

15.4.3.12 Alcohol abstinence and monitoring requirement (s 212A)

This is a requirement that the offender must abstain from consuming alcohol throughout a specified period (up to 120 days) and must submit to monitoring to ensure compliance. Such a requirement may be imposed only if (a) the consumption of alcohol by the offender is an element of the offence for which the order is to be imposed, or the court is satisfied that the consumption of alcohol by the offender was a factor that contributed to the commission of that offence; (b) the court is satisfied that the offender is not dependent on alcohol; and (c) the court does not include an alcohol treatment requirement in the order.

15.4.3.13 Attendance centre requirement (s 214)

Section 221(2) defines an 'attendance centre' as 'a place at which offenders aged under 25 may be required to attend and be given under supervision appropriate occupation or instruction'. Section 214 defines an attendance centre requirement as a requirement that the offender must attend an attendance centre for the specified number of hours, and must engage in occupation, or receive instruction, under the supervision of (and in accordance with instructions given by) the person in charge of the centre. The maximum total number of hours must be between 12 and 36. The offender cannot be required to attend an attendance centre on more than one occasion on any day, or for more than three hours on any occasion.

15.4.3.14 Electronic monitoring requirement (s 215)

Under s 215, an electronic monitoring requirement is a requirement for securing the electronic monitoring of the offender's compliance with other requirements under a community order (or, by virtue of an amendment which was not in force at the time of writing, to monitor the offender's whereabouts for a purpose other than ensuring compliance with such other requirements—thus allowing the court to impose electronic monitoring as a free-standing requirement).

15.4.3.15 Other duties of offenders subject to community orders

Section 220 imposes a duty on the offender to keep in touch with the assigned probation officer in accordance with such instructions as he may from time to time be given by that officer, and to notify any change of address. Section 220A requires the offender to seek the permission of the responsible officer or the court before changing their place of residence.

15.5 Credit for time spent on remand

Section 149(1) of the CJA 2003 provides that:

> *In determining the restrictions on liberty to be imposed by a community order . . . the court may have regard to any period for which the offender has been remanded in custody in connection with the offence . . .*

The SGC guidance on community sentences says that the court should seek to give credit for time spent on remand in all cases where the offender was remanded in custody prior to conviction/sentence. Thus, the offender may receive a more lenient community sentence to reflect the fact that he or she has already spent some time in custody in connection with the offence(s) for which sentence is now being passed.

The guidance adds that the court should make clear, when announcing sentence, whether or not credit for time on remand has been given and should explain its reasons for not giving credit when it considers that this is not justified, would not be practical or would not be in the best interests of the offender.

15.6 Breach of community orders under the Criminal Justice Act 2003

Schedule 8 to the CJA 2003 deals with breach, revocation and amendment of community orders.

Under para 5(1), if the probation officer who is supervising the offender is of the opinion that the offender has failed, without reasonable excuse, to comply with any of the requirements of a community order, the officer must give him a warning unless the offender has received such a warning during the last 12 months or the responsible officer decides to refer the matter back to the court (eg because the breach was a serious one). If a warning is given, it must inform the offender that if, within the next 12 months, he again fails to comply with any requirement of the order, he will be liable to be brought before the court (para 5(2)).

Paragraph 6(1), which deals with further non-compliance after a warning, is cast in mandatory terms. It provides that if the responsible officer has given the offender a warning under para 5 and, during the next 12 months, the offender again fails (without reasonable excuse) to comply with any of the requirements of the order, the officer *must* refer the case back to the court. Under para 7, the court can issue a summons, or an arrest warrant, to secure the offender's attendance. In *West Yorkshire Probation Board v Robinson & Tinker* [2009] EWHC 2517 (Admin); (2010) 174 JP 13, it was held that the probation officer has a discretion to give only one warning. After that first warning, the probation officer has no discretion as to what to do in the event of a further breach; if there is a failure to comply after the first warning, the matter must be referred back to the court.

Under para 9(1), if it is proved to the satisfaction of the court that the offender has failed without reasonable excuse to comply with any of the requirements of the community order, the court may deal with him in any one of the following ways:

> *(a) by amending the terms of the community order so as to impose more onerous requirements which the court could include if it were then making the order;*
>
> *(aa) by ordering the offender to pay a fine of an amount not exceeding £2,500;*
>
> *(b) where the community order was made by a magistrates' court, by dealing with him, for the offence in respect of which the order was made, in any way in which the court could deal with him if he had just been convicted by it of the offence;*
>
> *(c) where—*
>
> *(i) the community order was made by a magistrates' court,*
>
> *(ii) the offence in respect of which the order was made was not an offence punishable by imprisonment,*
>
> *(iii) the offender is aged 18 or over, and*
>
> *(iv) the offender has wilfully and persistently failed to comply with the requirements of the order, by dealing with him, in respect of that offence, by imposing a sentence of imprisonment for a term not exceeding 6 months.*

Option (a) would, for example, empower the court to add a new requirement or extend the duration of an existing requirement. The court may for this purpose extend the duration of the order by up to six months where the offender has breached a requirement in the order (para 9(3)).

Option (b) involves revocation of the order (if it is still in force at the date of the hearing) and then re-sentencing (subject to the limitations on the court's sentencing powers when it was first dealing with the offender). Paragraph 9(4) empowers the court to impose a custodial sentence even if the offence did not cross the custody threshold.

Option (c) enables the court to punish wilful and persistent non-compliance with a custodial sentence even though the offence for which the order was made was non-imprisonable. As with (b), the community order is revoked if this option is chosen.

When dealing with the non-compliance, the court must take into account the extent to which the offender has complied with the order (para 9(2)).

Where the order was made by the Crown Court, the magistrates' court dealing with the breach can commit him, in custody or on bail, to be dealt with by the Crown Court (para 9(6)). The options available to the Crown Court, set out in para 10, mirror those available to the magistrates' court.

The SGC guidance on community sentences gives the following guidance on sentencing for breach of a community order:

- The primary objective is to ensure that the requirements of the community sentence are completed.
- A court sentencing for breach must take account of the extent to which the offender has complied with the requirements of the community order, the reasons for breach and the point at which the breach has occurred.
- Custody should be the last resort, reserved for those cases of deliberate and repeated breach where all reasonable efforts to ensure that the offender complies have failed.
- Before increasing the onerousness of the requirements of a community sentence, the sentencer should take account of the offender's ability to comply and should avoid precipitating further breach by overloading the offender with too many or conflicting requirements.
- It may be necessary to consider re-sentencing to a differently constructed community sentence in order to secure compliance with the purposes of the original sentence.

From this it is clear that the emphasis is on achieving the objectives of the original sentence rather than punishing the offender for failure to comply with the terms of that original sentence.

In *West Yorkshire Probation Board v Boulter* [2005] EWHC 2342 (Admin); [2006] 1 WLR 232, it was held that a breach of a community order has to be proved to the criminal standard (namely, beyond reasonable doubt).

The fact that an appeal has been lodged does not prevent the probation service from instituting proceedings for breach of the order which was under appeal. In *West Midlands Probation Board v Sutton Coldfield Magistrates' Court* [2008] EWHC 15 (Admin) Dyson LJ said (at para 13) that:

> like any other sentence, a community order takes effect when it is imposed and it remains in full force and effect until and unless it is quashed on appeal or revoked or amended by order of the court. The lodging of an appeal does not of itself have any effect on the enforceability of the order.

His Lordship continued (at para 15):

> Although the concept of 'reasonable excuse' is broad, I do not consider that it can have been intended by Parliament to be stretched to include the mere fact that the defendant has lodged an appeal against the community order or the conviction on which it is based. To do that would be to undermine the general principle that community orders take effect from the date on which they are made and remain in force until and unless they are quashed on appeal or revoked or amended by order of the court. To accept non-compliance with a community order as a reasonable excuse merely because the defendant is appealing would amount to an acknowledgement that defendants may pick and choose whether and in what circumstances they will comply. That is wrong in principle.

15.6.1 Revocation of community orders other than for breach

Part 3 of Sch 8 deals with the revocation of community orders other than in the case of a breach of the requirement of the order. Paragraph 13 states that (provided the order is still in force) either the offender or the responsible officer may apply to the magistrates' court for the revocation of the order, or for the offender to be dealt with in some other way for the offence in respect of which the order was made, if—having regard to circumstances which have arisen since the order was made—it would be in the interests of justice to do so.

Under para 13(3), the circumstances in which a community order may be revoked include the fact that the offender is making good progress or is responding satisfactorily to supervision or treatment under the order. The revocation of the order may also be appropriate if, for example, the offender is taken ill or becomes disabled, and so becomes unable to complete the requirements of the order.

If the court re-sentences the offender, it must take into account the extent to which the offender complied with the original order (para 13(4)).

15.7 Commission of subsequent offences

Part 5 of Sch 8 deals with the powers of the court in relation to a community order where the offender is subsequently convicted for another offence.

Paragraph 21 provides that where an offender in respect of whom a community order made by a magistrates' court is in force is convicted of another offence by a magistrates' court, and it appears to the court that it would be in the interests of justice to do so, the magistrates' court may either (a) revoke the order, or (b) revoke the order and re-sentence the offender for the offence in respect of which the order was made, dealing with him in any way in which he could have been dealt with for that offence by the court which made the order. If it re-sentences him, the court must take into account the extent to which he complied with the order (para 21(3)), and the offender has a right of appeal to the Crown Court (para 21(4)).

If the magistrates' court is dealing with the later offence but the community order was made in the Crown Court, the magistrates may commit the offender, in custody or on bail, to appear at the Crown Court (para 22(1)). The options open to the Crown Court, set out in para 23, mirror the options available to the magistrates' court.

15.8 Surcharges

15.8.1 Victim surcharge

Section 161A of the Criminal Justice Act 2003 provides that, when a court is sentencing an offender for one or more offences, it must also order him to pay a 'surcharge' unless the court considers that it would be appropriate to make a compensation order, but the offender has insufficient means to pay both the surcharge and appropriate compensation, in which case the court must reduce the surcharge accordingly, if necessary to nil. This provision does not apply if the court grants an absolute discharge. The amount of the surcharge is set by the Criminal Justice Act 2003 (Surcharge) Order 2012 (SI 2012/1696), as amended, and varies according to whether or not the offender has attained the age of 18 and the sentence imposed for the offence. For offenders under the age of 18, the surcharge varies between £10 and £20; for offenders who have attained the age of 18, it varies between £15 and £120. Where a court imposes more than one sentence (eg when sentence is passed for more than one offence), a single surcharge is imposed, and the amount of that surcharge is based on the sentence which attracts the highest surcharge.

Money raised by the surcharge system is spent on a range of services for victims of crime and witnesses, such as witness care units and services to victims of domestic violence and sexual violence (through the Victims' Fund, which supports the development of community-based services for victims of sexual offending).

15.8.2 Criminal courts charge

Section 21A of the Prosecution of Offences Act 1985 (inserted by s 54 of the Criminal Justice and Courts Act 2015) requires magistrates' courts and the Crown Court, when sentencing an offender who had attained the age of 18 at the date of the commission of the offence, to order that offender to pay a charge in respect of the cost of providing the judiciary and the rest of the system of courts in connection with criminal proceedings. The Prosecution of Offences Act 1985 (Criminal Courts Charge) Regulations 2015 (SI 2015/796) specifies the amount of the charge, including the following:

- conviction by a magistrates' court for a summary offence on a guilty plea: £150;
- conviction by a magistrates' court for an either-way offence on a guilty plea: £180;

- conviction by a magistrates' court at a trial of a summary offence: £520;
- conviction by a magistrates' court at a trial of an either-way offence: £1,000;
- conviction by the Crown Court on a guilty plea: £900;
- conviction by the Crown Court at a trial on indictment: £1,200;
- Crown Court dismissing an appeal against conviction or sentence: £150;
- Court of Appeal dismissing an application for leave to appeal: £150.
- Court of Appeal dismissing an appeal against conviction or sentence: £200

Section 21E gives a magistrates' court a limited power to remit the charge if satisfied that the person has taken all reasonable steps to pay it, having regard to the person's personal circumstances, or that collection and enforcement of the charge is 'impracticable'. However, the charge may not be remitted while the offender is in prison, or (where the offender has made the application to a magistrates' court to remit the charge) before a period of two years has elapsed (12 months in any other case).

15.9 Ancillary orders

Following conviction, the court can make a number of ancillary orders in addition to passing sentence on the offender.

15.9.1 Compensation orders

Section 130 of the Powers of Criminal Courts (Sentencing) Act 2000 provides that the court, instead of or in addition to dealing with the offender in any other way, may make a compensation order. By virtue of subs (2A), the court *must* consider making a compensation order in any case where s 130 empowers it to do so. This requires the offender to pay compensation for any personal injury, loss or damage resulting from the offence of which the offender has been convicted (or which is taken into consideration). The amount of the order is whatever the court considers appropriate, having regard to any evidence and to any representations that are made by or on behalf of the accused or the prosecutor (s 130(4)). The court is required to give reasons if it does not make a compensation order in a case where it is empowered to do so (s 130(3)). If it would be appropriate both to impose a fine and to make a compensation order, but the offender has insufficient means to pay both, the court has to give preference to compensation, although it may impose a (suitably reduced) fine as well (s 130(12)).

Under s 131 of the 2000 Act, a compensation order made by a magistrates' court is unlimited where the offender has attained the age of 18. In *R v Stapylton* [2012] EWCA Crim 728, the court (at para 12) helpfully summarised some of the key principles:

> First, the court has no jurisdiction to make an order where there are real issues as to whether those to benefit have suffered any, and if so, what loss: *R v Horsham Justices ex p Richards* [1985] 1 WLR 986, 993. Thus in *R v Christopher Paul Watson* (1990–91) 12 Cr App R (S) 508, no award was made in favour of insurers because there was no evidence as to the loss. Coupled with that is that because compensation orders are for straightforward cases: *R v Donovan* (1981) 3 Cr App R (S) 192, a court should not embark on a detailed inquiry as to the extent of any injury, loss, or damage. If the matter demands such attention it is better left for civil proceedings. Further, compensation orders must not be made unless there is a realistic possibility of compliance (*R v Webb* (1979) 1 CR App R (S) 16). Orders should not be made if they will be protracted in effect, although much will turn on the nature of the offence and the offender: *R v Olliver* (1989) 1 Cr App R (S) 10.

15.9.2 Forfeiture and deprivation orders

Under s 143 of the Powers of Criminal Courts (Sentencing) Act 2000, where the defendant has been convicted of an offence, the court may make a deprivation order in respect of any property which has been lawfully seized from the offender, or which was in the offender's possession when apprehended for offence, and which has been used for the purpose of committing (or facilitating) the commission of any offence or was intended by the offender to be so used. The court must have regard to the value of the property, and likely financial and other effects on the offender of making the order.

Other legislation enables forfeiture orders to be made. For example, s 1 of the Prevention of Crime Act 1953 enables the court to order forfeiture (and disposal) of an offensive weapon following conviction; s 52 of the Firearms Act 1968 enables forfeiture (and disposal) of firearms following conviction; s 27 of the Misuse of Drugs Act 1971 enables forfeiture of property related to drugs or drug trafficking offences (it must be shown to be related to the offence of which the offender has been convicted; the property is then destroyed or dealt with in such other manner as the court may order).

15.9.3 Endorsement of driving licences and disqualification

Under s 34(1) of the Road Traffic Offenders Act 1988, where a person has been convicted of a road traffic offence involving obligatory disqualification, the court must order that he be disqualified from driving for at least 12 months unless the court finds that there are 'special reasons' for not disqualifying him or for disqualifying him for less than 12 months. A 'special reason' must be connected with the commission of the offence itself; mitigation which is personal to the offender is not a special reason (*Whittall v Kirby* [1947] KB 194). Other road traffic offences carry discretionary disqualification (see Sch 1 to the Road Traffic Offenders Act 1988). In such cases, the punishment of disqualification should generally be restricted to cases involving bad driving, persistent motoring offences, or the use of vehicles for the purposes of crime (per Morland J in *R v Callister* [1993] RTR 70).

Many road traffic offences carry a number of penalty points which have to be endorsed on the offender's driving licence in the event of conviction. The number of points to be endorsed is set out in Sch 1 to the Road Traffic Offenders Act 1988; sometimes, the number is fixed; sometimes, there is a range, with a minimum and a maximum number specified.

Under s 35 of the Road Traffic Offenders Act 1988, where a person is convicted of an offence which carries discretionary disqualification and mandatory endorsement and the number of penalty points on the offender's driving licence (including those imposed for the present offence) number 12 or more, the court must disqualify the offender from driving for at least six months (if it is his first disqualification) or 12 months (if it is his second) or two years (if he has already been disqualified twice) unless the court takes the view that there are grounds for not doing so or for disqualifying for a shorter period. Penalty points are taken into account if they were imposed within the last three years (s 29(2)). This is known as a 'totting up' disqualification.

When the court is deciding whether there is mitigation to justify not disqualifying the offender (or for shortening the disqualification), s 35(4) states that the court cannot take account of (a) any circumstances that are alleged to make the offence or any of the offences not a serious one, (b) hardship, other than exceptional hardship, or (c) any circumstances which, within the three years immediately preceding the conviction, have been taken into account under that subsection in ordering the offender to be disqualified for a shorter period or not ordering him to be disqualified.

Additionally, s 146 of the Powers of Criminal Courts (Sentencing) Act 2000 provides that, in addition to, or instead of, dealing with an offender in any other way, a court may disqualify the offender from holding or obtaining a driving licence for such period as it thinks fit. Thus, the penalty of disqualification from driving can be imposed for any offence, not just driving offences. In *R v Cliff* [2004] EWCA Crim 3139; [2005] 2 Cr App R (S) 22, the court said that it is not necessary for the offence to be connected to the use of the motor car: the section provides an additional punishment available to the court. However, the court added that there must be a sufficient reason for the disqualification.

15.9.4 Registration of sex offenders

Sections 80–92 of the Sexual Offences Act 2003 require those convicted of specified sexual offences (listed in Sch 3 to the Act) to notify certain personal details to the police. This process is commonly known as being put on the 'sex offenders' register'.

15.9.5 Confiscation under the Proceeds of Crime Act 2002

Section 6 of the Proceeds of Crime Act 2002 provides that, where an offender is being sentenced in the Crown Court (having been convicted there or committed sentence from a magistrates' court), the court may (at the request of the prosecution or of its own motion) proceed to decide whether the defendant has a criminal lifestyle and, if so, whether the offender has benefited from 'general criminal conduct' (if the court decides that the offender does not have a criminal lifestyle, it must decide whether the offender has benefited from 'particular criminal conduct', namely the offence(s) of which the offender has been convicted). An offender can have a criminal lifestyle in three ways:

(a) the offence of which the offender has been convicted is specified in Sch 2;
(b) the offence constitutes 'conduct forming part of a course of criminal activity' (ie the offender has been convicted of three or more other offences and has benefited from them, or the offender has two or more separate previous convictions during the last six years and has benefited from them); or
(c) the present offence was committed over a period of at least six months and the offender has benefited from it. For these purposes, an offence is disregarded unless the offender obtained benefit of more than £5,000 from it.

The next stage is for the court to decide the value of the benefit which the offender has derived from the criminal lifestyle. In deciding whether an offender has benefited from criminal conduct, the court is required to make certain assumptions (contained in s 10):

1. Any property transferred to the offender in the six years prior to the commencement of the present proceedings (ie property acquired during that period) was obtained as a result of general criminal conduct.
2. Any property held by the offender at any time after the date of conviction (in effect, property currently owned by the offender) was obtained as a result of general criminal conduct.
3. Any expenditure incurred by the offender in the previous six years was met from property obtained by the offender as a result of general criminal conduct.
4. The offender holds all property free of any other interests in it.

By virtue of s 10(6), the court must not make a required assumption in relation to particular property or expenditure if either: (a) the assumption is shown (on the balance of probabilities) to be incorrect, or (b) there would be a serious risk of injustice if the assumption were made. The practical effect is that the offender has to show (on the balance of probabilities) that the assets to which the assumptions apply are not the proceeds of crime.

Having quantified the value of the offender's benefit from criminal conduct (the 'recoverable amount'), the court must go on to decide the 'available amount' (ie the value of the offender's current assets). If the offender shows that the 'available amount' is less than the total benefit from criminal conduct, the confiscation order will be for the available amount. It should be noted, however, that if the value of the offender's assets subsequently increases (and the confiscation order was for less than the total value of the offender's benefit from criminal conduct), the prosecution can apply for an increase in the amount of the confiscation order. Under s 38 of the Act, the court will impose a term of imprisonment in default (which will not start to run until the offender has served any prison sentence imposed for offence(s) which led to the confiscation order being made); serving a sentence in default does 'not prevent the confiscation order from continuing to have effect so far as any other method of enforcement is concerned' (so the offender still owes the money).

The importance of proportionality in the context of confiscation orders was emphasised in *R v Waya* [2012] UKSC 51; [2013] 1 AC 294.

15.10 Bind overs

A magistrates' court can bind a person over 'to be of good behaviour and to keep the peace'. The effect of such an order is that the offender promises to pay a specified sum of money in the event of misbehaving during the period specified by the court. When exercising its power to bind over, the court must fix the period during which the bind over is to last (ie the period during which misbehaviour will result in forfeiture of the recognisance) and must also fix the amount to be forfeited if the person breaches the order. Generally, binding over to keep the peace is only warranted where there is evidence of likely personal danger to others involving violence or the threat of violence (see *Percy v DPP* (1995) 159 JP 337 and *Emohare v Thames Magistrates' Court* [2009] EWHC 689 (Admin); (2009) 173 JP 303).

16

Custodial sentences in the magistrates' court

16.1 Introduction

In this chapter, we examine the custodial powers of the magistrates' court. These powers differ according to whether, at the date of conviction, the offender is aged between 18 and 20 or has attained the age of 21.

16.2 Magistrates' powers of custodial sentencing

If a summary offence is an imprisonable offence, the maximum custodial sentence is six months or that prescribed by the statute which creates the offence, whichever is less (s 78(1) of the Powers of Criminal Courts (Sentencing) Act (PCC(S)A) 2000). If an offence is triable either way because it is listed in Sch 1 to the Magistrates' Courts Act (MCA) 1980, the maximum sentence is six months' imprisonment (s 32(1) of the MCA 1980); if the offence is triable either way because the statute creating it gives alternative penalties for summary conviction and conviction on indictment, the maximum penalty is six months' imprisonment or the term specified in the statute creating the offence, whichever is the less (s 78(1) of the Powers of Criminal Courts (Sentencing) Act 2000). Section 133(1) of the Magistrates' Courts Act 1980 empowers a magistrates' court to order custodial sentences to run consecutively. However, the maximum aggregate sentence which may be imposed is six months (s 133(1)) unless the court is dealing with the offender for two or more offences which are triable either way, in which case the maximum aggregate sentence is 12 months (s 133(2)).

16.3 Imprisonment

Before a custodial sentence can be imposed, the case has to be regarded as sufficiently serious to cross the custody threshold.

16.3.1 The custody threshold

Section 152(2) of the CJA 2003 provides that:

The court must not pass a custodial sentence unless it is of the opinion that the offence, or the combination of the offence and one or more offences associated with it, was so serious that neither a fine alone nor a community sentence can be justified for the offence.

The Sentencing Guidelines Council (SGC) guidance on seriousness (<http://www.sentencingcouncil.org.uk/wp-content/uploads/web_seriousness_guideline.pdf>) state that:

- Parliament's clear intention is to reserve imprisonment as a punishment for the most serious offences;

- passing the custody threshold does **not** mean that a custodial sentence should be regarded as inevitable: custody can still be avoided in light of personal mitigation or where there is a suitable community order which provides sufficient restriction (by way of punishment) while addressing the rehabilitation of the offender to prevent future crime.

The custody threshold under the legislation that preceded the CJA 2003 was considered in *R v Cox* [1993] 1 WLR 188, where it was held that an offence is 'so serious that only a custodial sentence can be justified' (the test then applicable) if it is such as to make all right-thinking members of the public, knowing all the facts, feel that justice would not be done by the passing of anything other than a custodial sentence. In *R v Howells* [1999] 1 WLR 307, the Court of Appeal expressed the view that this test was not particularly helpful. The court chose not to replace the test with a different form of words, but did set out some factors that could make the difference between a custodial or non-custodial sentence. Lord Bingham CJ said that:

> in approaching cases which are on or near the custody threshold courts will usually find it helpful to begin by considering the nature and extent of the defendant's criminal intention and the nature and extent of any injury or damage caused to the victim. Other things being equal, an offence which is deliberate and premeditated will usually be more serious than one which is spontaneous and unpremeditated or which involves an excessive response to provocation; an offence which inflicts personal injury or mental trauma, particularly if permanent, will usually be more serious than one which inflicts financial loss only. In considering the seriousness of any offence the court may take into account any previous convictions of the offender or any failure to respond to previous sentences . . . and must treat it as an aggravating factor if the offence was committed while the offender was on bail . . .

In deciding whether to impose a custodial sentence in borderline cases the sentencing court will ordinarily take account of matters relating to the offender.

(a) The court will have regard to an offender's admission of responsibility for the offence, particularly if reflected in a plea of guilty tendered at the earliest opportunity and accompanied by hard evidence of genuine remorse, as shown (for example) by an expression of regret to the victim and an offer of compensation . . .

(b) Where offending has been fuelled by addiction to drink or drugs, the court will be inclined to look more favourably on an offender who has already demonstrated (by taking practical steps to that end) a genuine, self-motivated determination to address his addiction.

(c) Youth and immaturity, while affording no defence, will often justify a less rigorous penalty than would be appropriate for an adult.

(d) Some measure of leniency will ordinarily be extended to offenders of previous good character, the more so if there is evidence of positive good character (such as a solid employment record or faithful discharge of family duties) as opposed to a mere absence of previous convictions. It will sometimes be appropriate to take account of family responsibilities, or physical or mental disability.

(e) While the court will never impose a custodial sentence unless satisfied that it is necessary to do so, there will be even greater reluctance to impose a custodial sentence on an offender who has never before served such a sentence.

One issue is the extent to which the prevalence of an offence can affect its seriousness. The SGC notes that the key factor in determining whether sentencing levels should be enhanced in response to the prevalence of the particular offence is the level of harm that is being caused in the locality. The guidance emphasises that 'enhanced' sentences should be exceptional and in response only to exceptional circumstances, and that sentencers must sentence within the sentencing guidelines once prevalence has been addressed (see also *R v Oosthuizen* [2005] EWCA Crim 1978).

The Court of Appeal has encouraged sentencers to consider sentences other than custody—for example, imposing a fine instead. See, for example, *R v Kefford* [2002] EWCA Crim 519;

[2002] 2 Cr App R (S) 106, and *R v Baldwin* [2002] EWCA Crim 2647. In *Attorney-General's Reference (No 11 of 2006)* [2006] EWCA Crim 856; [2006] 2 Cr App R (S) 108, the Court of Appeal commented that, when prisons are overcrowded, the result is to hinder or prevent the valuable work of rehabilitation that a prison should normally provide. The fact that prisons are overcrowded may, for this reason, be a relevant factor where the sentencer's decision is 'on the cusp', so that there is a real issue as to whether a community sentence can be justified rather than a custodial sentence (per Lord Phillips CJ, at para 20). This point was re-emphasised in *R v Seed* [2007] EWCA Crim 254; [2007] 2 Cr App R (S) 69, when the Court of Appeal revisited the question of the custody threshold because of prison overcrowding. Lord Phillips CJ said that judges were, once again, confronted with the fact that the prisons are full. When considering the length of a custodial sentence, the court should bear in mind that the prison regime is likely to be more punitive as a result of prison overcrowding (para 5). His Lordship added (at para 6) that:

> Unless imprisonment is necessary for the protection of the public the court should always give consideration to the question of whether the aims of rehabilitation and thus the reduction of crime cannot better be achieved by a fine or community sentence rather than by imprisonment and whether punishment cannot adequately be achieved by such a sentence. We believe that there may have been a reluctance to impose fines because fines were often not enforced. Enforcement of fines is now rigorous and effective and, where the offender has the means, a heavy fine can often be an adequate and appropriate punishment. If so, the 2003 Act requires a fine to be imposed rather than a community sentence.

Particular care should be exercised before imposing a custodial sentence for the first time. Association with seasoned criminals may make re-offending more likely rather than deter it, particularly where the offender is young. A clean record can be important personal mitigation and may make a custodial sentence inappropriate, notwithstanding that the custodial threshold is crossed (para 7).

16.3.2 Proviso to the custody threshold

Section 152(3) of the CJA 2003 contains a proviso to s 152(2), that:

> *Nothing in subsection (2) prevents the court from passing a custodial sentence on the offender if—*
>
> *(a) he fails to express his willingness to comply with a requirement which is proposed by the court to be included in a community order and which requires an expression of such willingness . . .*

Community order requirements which can be imposed only with the offender's consent include mental health treatment, drug rehabilitation or alcohol treatment.

16.3.3 Length of sentence

Section 153(2) of the CJA 2003 provides that (apart from mandatory minimum sentence cases (see **Chapter 19**)) the custodial sentence 'must be for the shortest term (not exceeding the permitted maximum) that in the opinion of the court is commensurate with the seriousness' of the offence(s).

In *R v Howells* [1999] 1 WLR 307 (following such cases as *R v Ollerenshaw* [1999] 1 Cr App R (S) 65), Lord Bingham said that 'the sentence imposed should be no longer than is necessary to meet the penal purpose which the court has in mind'.

This is particularly so in the case of the offender who has not previously served a custodial sentence. For that offender, the effect of the 'clang of the prison gates' is spent after a comparatively short time in custody.

Where the offender is being sentenced for two or more offences, the court can make the terms run concurrently or consecutively. Essentially, this will depend on whether the offences constitute a single series of incidents (in which case, concurrent terms would be appropriate) or unrelated offences (in which case, consecutive terms would be appropriate). The CJA 2003, s 166(3)(b), preserves the 'totality' principle, which requires that where consecutive sentences are imposed, the court must ensure that the total time to be served is commensurate with the seriousness of the overall course of offending that is being dealt with.

In calculating the time to be served, s 240ZA of the CJA 2003 requires account to be taken of any time spent on remand prior to conviction/sentence. Section 240ZA(3) provides that: 'The number of days for which the offender was remanded in custody in connection with the offence or a related offence is to count as time served by the offender as part of the sentence'.

Section 240A of the 2003 Act also makes provision, where the offender was on bail subject to a curfew condition and an electronic monitoring condition, for half of the number of days spent subject to those conditions to count as time served by the offender as part of the sentence.

16.3.4 Procedure

Section 156 of the CJA 2003 requires the court to obtain and consider a pre-sentence report in order to decide whether the case is sufficiently serious for a custodial sentence and, if so, what length of sentence would be commensurate with the seriousness of the offence. However, if the offender has attained the age of 18, the court may refrain from seeking a report on the basis that it is unnecessary to obtain one.

In *Armsaramah* (2000) 164 JP 709, the Court of Appeal accepted that there may be cases where it is open to court to pass a custodial sentence without seeking a pre-sentence report even where the offender has not served a custodial sentence before.

16.3.5 Release from custody

Section 243A of the CJA 2003 (as amended by the Offender Rehabilitation Act 2014) provides that offenders serving a fixed-term sentence of less than 12 months will be released on licence when they reach the halfway point in their sentence. By virtue of s 256AA of the CJA 2003, the offender is subject to supervision during the period beginning with the end of the sentence and ending on the expiry of 12 months from the date of automatic release (see **20.2**).

16.4 Suspended sentences

Suspended sentences of imprisonment are governed by ss 189–191 of the CJA 2003.

A custodial term of up to two years (in the Crown Court), or 12 months (in the magistrates' court, where the offender is being dealt with for two or more either-way offences) may be suspended. This means that the sentence of imprisonment does not take effect unless either (a) during the 'supervision period', the offender fails to comply with any requirement imposed under the order, or (b) during the 'operational period', the offender commits another offence (whether or not punishable with imprisonment): s 189(1).

Thus, where the court passes a suspended sentence it must specify an 'operational period' (the time for which the sentence is suspended) and, if any requirements are added to the order, a 'supervision period' (the time during which the offender has to comply with those requirements). The 'supervision period' and the 'operational period' both have to be between six months and two years (s 189(3)). The 'supervision period' must end not later than the operational period (s 189(4)).

During the supervision period, the offender can be required to comply with additional requirements which are the same as those which comprise a community order: s 190 of the CJA 2003.

Sections 191 and 192 provide for periodic reviews by the court of the offender's progress in complying with the requirements of the sentence.

It should be emphasised that a suspended sentence counts as a custodial sentence and so is appropriate only for an offence that passes the custody threshold and for which imprisonment is therefore the only option.

The SGC guidance on the imposition of requirements during the supervision period says that, in order to ensure that the overall terms of the sentence are commensurate with the seriousness of the offence, the requirements to be undertaken during the supervision period should usually be less onerous than if a community sentence had been imposed (because of the clear deterrent threat involved in a suspended sentence). A court wishing to impose onerous community requirements on an offender should therefore consider whether a community sentence might be more appropriate than a suspended sentence. Any community requirements should address those factors that are most likely to reduce the risk of re-offending.

16.4.1 Breach of suspended sentence requirements or re-offending during the operational period

This is governed by Sch 12 to the CJA 2003.

Where an offender has breached any of the requirements without reasonable excuse for the first time, the responsible officer must either give a warning or initiate breach proceedings (para 4). Where there is a further breach within a 12-month period, breach proceedings *must* be initiated (para 5).

Under para 8, if the offender is brought to court because he or she:

- has failed, without reasonable excuse, to comply with any of the community requirements of the suspended sentence order, or
- is convicted of an offence committed during the operational period of a suspended sentence,

then the court has four options:

1. order that the suspended sentence take effect with its original custodial period unaltered (this is sometimes known as 'activating' the suspended sentence); or
2. order that the sentence take effect but with a shorter period of custody (ie activating the suspended sentence only in part); or
3. impose of a fine of up £2,500; or
4. (where the suspended sentence order imposed one or more community requirements) amend the order by:
    - imposing more onerous community requirements,
    - extending the supervision period, or
    - extending the operational period.

There is a presumption (under para 8(3)) that the suspended prison sentence will be activated, either with its original custodial term or a lesser term, unless the court takes the view that this would, in all the circumstances, be 'unjust'. In reaching this decision, the court may take into account both the extent to which the offender has complied with the requirements and the facts of the new offence.

The SGC guidance on the action to be taken where the offender commits a further offence during the operational period of the suspended sentence says that:

- If the new offence is committed near the end of the operational period (the offender having complied with the requirements imposed), it may be more appropriate to amend the order rather than activate the custodial term.
- If the new offence is of a less serious nature than the offence for which the suspended sentence was passed, this may justify activating the suspended sentence with a reduced term or amending the terms of the order.
- It is expected that any activated suspended sentence will be consecutive to the sentence imposed for the new offence.
- If the new offence is non-imprisonable, the sentencer should consider whether it is appropriate to activate the suspended sentence at all (the implication being that it would generally not be appropriate).
- Where the court decides to amend a suspended sentence order rather than activate the custodial sentence, it should give serious consideration to extending the supervision or operational periods (within statutory limits) rather than making the requirements more onerous.

16.5 Offenders aged 18–20: detention in a young offender institution

Under s 96 of the PCC(S)A 2000, the custodial sentence applicable to an offender who is aged 18, 19 or 20 at the date of conviction is 'detention in a young offender institution'.

The maximum term of such detention is the same as the maximum term of imprisonment that the court may impose on an adult for that offence.

Under s 189(1) of the CJA 2003, a sentence of detention in a young offender institution may be suspended in the same way that a sentence of imprisonment can.

This sentence is due to be abolished (so that offenders aged between 18 and 20 would be sentenced to the custodial sentences that are currently available in the case of offenders who have attained the age of 21). However, the provision that repeals s 96 of the 2000 Act (s 61 of the Criminal Justice and Court Services Act 2000) has not yet been brought into force.

17

Non-custodial sentences in the youth court

17.1 Introduction

In this chapter, we look at the non-custodial sentences available where the offender is under the age of 18 at the date of conviction (see *R v Danga* [1992] QB 476, where the Court of Appeal confirmed that the date of conviction—not the date when sentence is passed—is the relevant date for these purposes). Offenders under the age of 18 are subject to a different range of non-custodial sentences to adult offenders.

Useful guidance is contained in the Sentencing Guidelines Council (SGC) document entitled *Overarching Principles—Sentencing Youths* available at <http://www.sentencingcouncil.org.uk/wp-content/uploads/web_overarching_principles_sentencing_youths.pdf>.

In *Attorney-General's Reference No 55 of 2012* [2012] EWCA Crim 2624, the Court of Appeal considered these Guidelines. Hughes LJ, at paras 21–23, said:

> The Sentencing Guidelines Council has also produced separate guidelines on the general approach to the sentencing of youths which is, it needs always to be remembered, a different exercise in some respects from the sentencing of adults who must be fixed with full responsibility for their actions. The statute itself makes a difference. The statutory aims for a court when sentencing an offender under the age of 18 involve two limbs. The principal aim must be to prevent offending by children and young persons, but secondly the court must also have regard to the welfare of the offender. That is not simply out of some indulgence to youths. It is because it is in the public interest that errant youths should be corrected, if possible.
>
> The same guidelines make it clear, in particular at paragraph 2.1 and onwards, that the approach to the sentence of youths needs to be more individualistic than it is often possible to be with the sentencing of adults. That has the corollary that in the case of youths more than in the case of adults it may well be necessary not simply to look at the acts constituting the offence and attribute to them what taken in the abstract they may be worth.
>
> At paragraph 3.2 and onwards, the same guidelines draw attention to some of the practical considerations which courts need to have in mind in giving effect to these overall principles. They include the clear proposition that offending in a young person may be a phase which will pass . . . Secondly, as is common sense, the impact of incarceration, necessary as it will be in a serious case like this, is felt more heavily by the young than by those who are older. Thirdly, the guidelines point out that young people may be more receptive to change than their older counterparts. In other words, a greater emphasis can properly be placed upon rehabilitation when sentencing the young as compared with sentencing adults. Courts do know that happily sometimes the lesson is learned and a sharp dose of punishment actually works. It does not always, but it may.

17.2 Fines and discharges

Young offenders may be dealt with by means of a fine or an absolute or conditional discharge.

17.2.1 Absolute discharge

See **15.1**.

17.2.2 Conditional discharge

See **15.2**. In the case of young offenders, it should be noted that s 66F of the Crime and Disorder Act 1998 provides that where a juvenile who has received a youth conditional caution is convicted of an offence committed within two years of the caution, the court is not permitted to order a conditional discharge in respect of the offence unless it is of the opinion that there are exceptional circumstances relating to the offence or the offender which justify its doing so.

17.2.3 Fines

Where the offender is aged between 14 and 17, the maximum fine that may be imposed is £1,000. Where the offender is aged between ten and 13, the maximum fine is £250.

Where the offender is under 16, the court *must* order that the fine is paid by the offender's parents (and so the means of the parents have to be taken into account in assessing the amount of the fine). If the offender is aged 16 or 17, the court *may* order the parents to pay the fine. See s 137 of the Powers of Criminal Courts (Sentencing) Act (PCC(S)A) 2000.

17.2.4 Binding over

Where the offender is under the age of 16, the court must consider binding over the parents to take proper care of, and exercise proper control over, the offender. See s 150 of the PCC(S)A 2000. In fact, such orders are comparatively rare.

17.3 Referral order

Provision for referral orders is made by ss 16–18 of the PCC(S)A 2000.

Under ss 16(2) and 17(1), the making of a referral order is *mandatory* (unless the court is considering either an absolute or conditional discharge, or the imposition of a custodial sentence) if the offender pleads guilty to an imprisonable offence (and to any connected offence) and has not previously been convicted of any offence.

Under ss 16(3) and 17(2), the making of a referral order is *discretionary* if the compulsory referral conditions are not satisfied but the offender pleaded guilty to the offence, or is being dealt with for two or more connected offences and pleaded guilty to at least one of them. It is important to note that the existence of previous findings of guilt does not preclude the court from making a discretionary referral order (even if the offender has already been subject to a referral order).

Under s 19(4), where the court makes a referral order, it cannot also impose a community sentence, a fine, a reparation order or a conditional discharge, nor can it bind the offender's parents over.

As part of complying with the referral order, the offender has to attend meetings with a 'youth offender panel', over a period of between three and 12 months.

In addition, the offender can be required to comply with additional requirements (see s 23), such as:

- making reparation;
- undergoing mediation;
- carrying out unpaid work;
- taking part in specified activities;
- refraining from taking part in specified activities;
- staying away from specified places and/or people.

Where a young offender has been referred back to the youth court, and it is proved to the satisfaction of the court that the offender has failed, without reasonable excuse, to comply with the terms of the referral order contract, the court may revoke the order, or else may order the offender to pay a fine of an amount not exceeding £2,500, or may extend the length of the period for which the contract has effect (but not so as to extend that period so that it becomes longer than 12 months).

17.4 Pre-sentence reports on young offenders

Section 156 of the Criminal Justice Act (CJA) 2003 requires the court to obtain a pre-sentence report before deciding that an offence is sufficiently serious to merit a community sentence and before deciding what restrictions on the offender's liberty are commensurate with the seriousness of the offence. Where the offender has attained the age of 18, the court can take the view that a report is unnecessary. However, under s 156(5), if the offender is under the age of 18, the court cannot dispense with a pre-sentence report unless there exists a previous pre-sentence report obtained in respect of the offender, and the court has had regard to the information contained in that report (or, if there is more than one such report, the most recent report). The statute is silent on how recent the earlier report must be in order for the court to choose to rely on that report instead of requiring the production of a new one; however, as a matter of practice, a report that is significantly out of date is unlikely to be much use.

17.5 Youth rehabilitation orders under the Criminal Justice and Immigration Act 2008

17.5.1 Youth rehabilitation orders

Section 1 of the Criminal Justice and Immigration Act 2008 creates a generic community sentence—the 'youth rehabilitation order'—for offenders under the age of 18 at the date of conviction, mirroring the generic community order for adults established by the CJA 2003.

A youth rehabilitation order may include any one or more of the following requirements (the detailed description of each being set out in Sch 1 to the Act):

(a) an 'activity requirement': this requires the offender to participate in specified activities for a total of up to 90 days;

(b) a 'supervision requirement': this requires the offender to attend appointments with their supervisor;

(c) where the offender is aged 16 or 17 at the date of the conviction, an 'unpaid work requirement': the number of hours must be between 40 and 240, and the work should be completed within 12 months;

(d) a 'programme requirement': this requires participation in a systematic set of activities (designed to allow juvenile offenders to engage in programmes that will address their offending behaviour, teach life-skills and engage in other positive interventions to prevent re-offending);

(e) an 'attendance centre requirement': up to a maximum of 12 hours for an offender aged under 14, between 12 and 24 hours for an offender aged 14 or 15, and between 12 and 36 hours if the offender is aged 16 or over (an offender cannot be required to attend at an attendance centre on more than one occasion on any day, or for more than three hours on any occasion; whilst at the attendance centre, the offender is required to engage in occupation, or receive instruction, under the supervision of and in accordance with instructions given by the officer in charge of the centre);

(f) a 'prohibited activity requirement': this requires the offender to refrain from participating in specified activities for a specified period;

(g) a 'curfew requirement': this requires the offender to remain, for specified periods, at a specified place for between two and 16 hours in any given day over a period of up to 12 months;

(h) an 'exclusion requirement': this prohibits the offender from entering a specified place for a specified period of up to three months;

(i) a 'residence requirement': this requires the offender to reside with a specified individual or, if the offender was aged 16 or over at the time of conviction, at a specified place;

(j) a 'local authority residence requirement': this requires the offender to reside, for up to six months, in accommodation provided by the local authority; this requirement can only be imposed if the court is satisfied that the behaviour which constituted the offence was due to a significant extent to the circumstances in which the offender was living, and that the imposition of the requirement will assist in the offender's rehabilitation;

(k) a 'mental health treatment requirement': this requires the offender to undergo mental health treatment, as an in-patient or out-patient, by a registered medical practitioner and/or chartered psychologist; such a requirement may be imposed only if the mental condition of the offender is such as requires and may be susceptible to treatment, but is not such as to warrant the making of a hospital order or guardianship order under the Mental Health Act 1983; the consent of the offender is also required;

(l) a 'drug treatment requirement': this requires the offender to undergo drug treatment, as an in-patient or out-patient, by a specified person with the necessary qualifications; this requirement may be imposed only if the court is satisfied that the offender is dependent on or has a propensity to misuse any drug, and requires and may be susceptible to treatment; the consent of the offender is also required;

(m) a 'drug testing requirement': this requires the offender to provide samples for drug-testing purposes; such a requirement may only be imposed with a drug treatment requirement and with the consent of the offender;

(n) an 'intoxicating substance treatment' requirement: this requires the offender to undergo treatment, as an in-patient or out-patient, but may only be imposed if the offender is dependent on, or has a propensity to misuse, intoxicating substances, and this dependency or propensity is such as requires and may be susceptible to treatment; the consent of the offender is also required; and

(o) an 'education requirement': this requires the offender to comply with approved education arrangements, namely those made by the offender's parent or guardian and approved by the local authority; such a requirement may be imposed only if the court is satisfied that it is necessary for the offender's future good conduct or prevention of further offending.

The Act enables the court to impose an electronic monitoring requirement as part of a youth rehabilitation order (s 1(2)).

Under s 1(3), a youth rehabilitation order may be a 'youth rehabilitation order with intensive supervision and surveillance' (this is an 'extended activity requirement' for between a total of 90 and 180 days, together with a supervision requirement, a curfew requirement and an electronic monitoring requirement) or a 'youth rehabilitation order with fostering' (this is a requirement that the offender must reside with a local authority foster parent for up to 12 months; such a requirement can only be imposed if the court is satisfied that the behaviour which constituted the offence was due to a significant extent to the circumstances in which the offender was living, and that the imposition of a fostering requirement would assist in the offender's rehabilitation). An order may only take one of these forms if the offence for which the juvenile is being sentenced is punishable with imprisonment in the case of an adult offender, and the court is of the opinion that the offence(s) are so serious that a custodial sentence would otherwise be appropriate. Moreover, if the offender was aged under 15 at the time of conviction, the court must also be of the opinion that he is a persistent offender.

Section 1(6) of the Act makes it clear that the power to impose a youth rehabilitation order is subject to ss 148 and 150 of the CJA 2003 (restrictions on community sentences), and so a youth rehabilitation order may be imposed only if the seriousness of the offence merits it, and the requirements imposed must be commensurate with the seriousness of the offence.

Para 10.21 of the Sentencing Guidelines Council guideline on sentencing young offenders says that:

In determining the length of an order, a court should allow sufficient time for the order as a whole to be complied with, recognising that the young person is at risk of further sanction throughout the whole of the period, but allowing sufficient flexibility should a sanction need to be imposed for breach of the order. Where appropriate, an application for early discharge may be made.

The approach to be taken when determining the requirements to be imposed in a youth rehabilitation order are summarised in para 10.22 of that guideline:

. . . Where a court is satisfied that an offence has crossed the community sentence threshold and that such a sentence is necessary or has crossed the custody threshold but is an offence for which a youth rehabilitation order is nonetheless considered to be appropriate, taking account of the assessment in the pre-sentence report, the consideration process that the court should follow is:

i) what requirements are most suitable for the offender?

ii) what overall period is necessary to ensure that all requirements may be satisfactorily completed?

iii) are the restrictions on liberty that result from those requirements commensurate with the seriousness of the offence?

Schedule 2 to the Act makes detailed provision about failures to comply with the requirements of youth rehabilitation orders and about the revocation or amendment of such orders. These provisions are very similar to those which apply in the case of adults who have breached community orders. The maximum fine for a breach of a youth rehabilitation order is £2,500.

17.6 Compensation orders

The youth court can also make ancillary orders, such as a compensation order. By virtue of s 131(1) of the PCC(S)A 2000, the maximum amount of compensation that can be ordered in respect of an offence where the offender is under the age of 18 is £5,000. Where such an offender is convicted of several offences there is no restriction on the aggregate sum of compensation (ie he may be ordered to pay £5,000 for each offence). Where a juvenile asks for offences to be taken into consideration, compensation may be ordered in respect of those offences, but the total amount ordered must not exceed the maximum which could be ordered for the offence(s) of which he has actually been convicted (s 131(2)).

18

Custodial sentences in the youth court

18.1 Introduction

In this chapter, we look at the detention and training order, which is the custodial sentence applicable to offenders who fall within the jurisdiction of the youth court.

18.2 Detention and training orders

Under the Powers of Criminal Courts (Sentencing) Act (PCC(S)A) 2000, s 100, an offender aged under 18 at the date of conviction may be sentenced to a detention and training order (DTO).

The minimum age for such a sentence is 12 (although the Secretary of State has power under the Act to include 10- and 11-year-olds).

If the offender was under 15 at the date of conviction, a DTO may be imposed only if the juvenile is a 'persistent offender'. Surprisingly, this term is not defined in the legislation. Normally, a juvenile will be regarded as a persistent offender because of the number of previous findings of guilt. However, a juvenile may also be regarded as a persistent offender on the basis that he or she is currently being dealt with for several offences (see *R v Charlton* (2000) 164 JP 685). Paragraph 6.5(ii) of the Sentencing Guidelines Council document entitled 'Overarching Principles: Sentencing Youths' (<http://www.sentencingcouncil.org.uk/wp-content/uploads/web_overarching_principles_sentencing_youths.pdf>) says that a young offender is likely to be found to be 'persistent' where he or she 'has been convicted of, or made subject to a pre-court disposal that involves an admission or finding of guilt in relation to, imprisonable offences on at least three occasions in the past 12 months'. In *R v L* [2012] EWCA Crim 1336, the court again had to consider the meaning of the phrase 'persistent offender'. The court cited with approval *R v G (TT)* [2004] EWCA Crim 3086, where McCombe J (at para 10) had said:

> It has been held . . . that formal cautions can be considered along with convictions in deciding whether or not an offender is persistent in his offending . . . Indeed, it is not necessary that there should be previous convictions or cautions at all. The provisions can apply in the case of a previously unconvicted offender who embarks on a brief, but nevertheless persistent, spree of offending . . . However . . . the term 'persistent offender' is an ordinary term of the English language and falls to be applied in its clearly understood meaning.

A sentence of DTO is a custodial sentence (and so the custody 'threshold' criteria have to be met). The SGC guidance (at para 11.11) says that, before deciding to impose a custodial sentence on a young offender, the court must be satisfied that the offender cannot properly be dealt with by a fine alone or by a youth rehabilitation order, and that a youth rehabilitation order with intensive supervision and surveillance or with fostering cannot be justified; the court must also bear in mind that 'custody is the last resort' and should 'take account of the circumstances, age and maturity of the young offender'. Paragraph 11.12 goes on to emphasise that:

Where the offence(s) has crossed the custody threshold, the statutory tests are likely to be satisfied only where a custodial sentence will be more effective in preventing offending by children and young persons. The obligation to have regard to the welfare of the offender will require a court to take account of a wide range of issues including those relating to mental health, capability and maturity.

The total length of the DTO has to be 4, 6, 8, 10, 12, 18 or 24 months (s 101(1)). It follows that a DTO cannot be imposed where the maximum sentence in the case of an adult offender is less than four months. Accordingly, it is unlawful for a youth court to impose a DTO for an offence of criminal damage in respect of an offender under the age of 18 where the value of the damage is less than £5,000, since the maximum sentence for an adult in such a case is currently three months but the minimum DTO is four (*Pye v Leeds Youth Court* [2006] EWHC 2527 (Admin)). For summary offences, the length of the DTO must not exceed six months (s 101(2A)).

An offender who receives a DTO is placed in detention for half of the term of the order. On release, the juvenile is then placed under supervision for the rest of the order (supervision being provided by a probation officer, social worker or member of youth offending team).

It should be noted that, as regards the DTOs, the powers of the youth court and the Crown Court are identical, as neither court can exceed the maximum duration of 24 months.

If the juvenile fails to comply with the supervision requirement under the DTO, the court may (under s 104(3)):

- order that the offender must return to custody (for three months or the period beginning with the date of the failure to comply with the requirement and the last day of the term of the DTO, whichever is shorter); or
- extend the period of supervision under the order (again, for three months or the period beginning with the date of the failure to comply with the requirement and the last day of the term of the DTO, whichever is shorter); or
- impose a fine of up to £1,000.

By virtue of s 104(3C), the court may order a period of detention or supervision, or impose a fine, even if the DTO has expired.

If the juvenile re-offends during the supervision period of the DTO, the court may (as well as dealing with the offender for the later offence) order that the offender return to custody for the length of time between the date of the offence and the expiry of the original order (s 105).

18.3 More serious offences

If the juvenile is charged with an offence which falls within the scope of s 91 of the PCC(S)A 2000 (long-term detention; see **Chapter 20**) the youth court has to decide whether to try the case itself or to send the juvenile to the Crown Court (bearing in mind the limitations on both the length of the DTO and the offenders who can be made subject to a DTO) so that the Crown Court may pass a sentence under s 91 if the juvenile either pleads guilty or is found guilty there.

18.4 Summary: custodial sentences available according to age

- 10–11 years: the only custodial sentence available is detention under s 91 of the PCC(S)A 2000 (and only the Crown Court can impose such a sentence);
- 12, 13 or 14 years: a 'DTO' is available, provided that the juvenile is a 'persistent offender'; detention under s 91 of the 2000 Act is also available (in the Crown Court) in appropriate cases;
- 15, 16 or 17 years: a 'DTO' is available; detention under s 91 is also available (in the Crown Court) in appropriate cases.

19

Non-custodial sentences in the Crown Court

Apart from the amount of any fine, the powers of the Crown Court to impose non-custodial sentences are identical to those of the magistrates' court, set out in **Chapter 15**. This chapter will therefore simply summarise some of the key points relevant to such sentences.

19.1 Fines

The Crown Court is empowered to impose a fine instead of, or in addition to, dealing with the offender in any other way (the Criminal Justice Act (CJA) 2003, s 163). This is so whether the offender was convicted in the Crown Court or was committed to the Crown Court for sentence under the Powers of Criminal Courts (Sentencing) Act (PCC(S)A) 2000, s 3.

There is no statutory limit on the amount of a fine imposed by the Crown Court.

Where the Crown Court imposes a fine it *must* fix a term of imprisonment (if the offender is aged 21 or over) or detention in a young offenders institution (if the offender is aged between 18 and 20) in default. The maximum term set in default depends on the amount of the fine (see PCC(S)A 2000, s 139(4)) and is summarised in **Table 19.1**.

Table 19.1 **Crown Court default sentencing**

Fine (£)	Term (maximum)
1–200	7 days
201–500	14 days
501–1,000	28 days
1,001–2,500	45 days
2,501–5,000	3 months
5,001–10,000	6 months
10,001–20,000	12 months
20,001–50,000	18 months
50,001–100,000	2 years
100,001–250,000	3 years
250,001–1,000,000	5 years
over 1,000,000	10 years

19.2 Other non-custodial sentences

Like a magistrates' court, the Crown Court is empowered to impose any of the following:

- absolute discharge;
- conditional discharge (one to three years);
- community order.

Where the Crown Court is dealing with a juvenile (eg where the juvenile was charged alongside an adult and the magistrates decided that it was necessary in the interests of justice for the juvenile to be sent to the Crown Court to be tried with the adult), there is a statutory presumption that the Crown Court should remit the juvenile to the youth court for sentence. Section 8(2) of the PCC(S)A 2000 provides that in such a case the court shall, unless satisfied that it would be undesirable to do so, remit the case to the youth court. However, in *R v Lewis* (1984) 79 Cr App R 94, Lord Lane CJ pointed out that a decision not to remit to the youth court could be justified for a number of reasons (eg the Crown Court judge will, after the trial, be better informed about the facts of the offence and general nature of the case than the youth court could hope to be; sentencing the juvenile in the Crown Court will avoid the risk of unjustifiable disparity in sentencing that could otherwise arise if the juvenile and adult are sentenced by separate courts; and remitting the case would cause delay, unnecessary duplication of proceedings and extra expense). Where the Crown Court does pass sentence on the juvenile, all the non-custodial options available to a youth court are equally available to the Crown Court (see **Chapter 17**).

19.3 Breach of community order imposed by the Crown Court

Where the Crown Court imposes a community order, it can include in the order a direction that any failure to comply with the requirements of the order is to be dealt with by a magistrates' court. Where the order does not contain such a stipulation and the offender breaches the order, he or she will be brought before the Crown Court pursuant to para 8(2) of Sch 8 to the CJA 2003; if it appears to the Crown Court that the offender has failed to comply with any of the requirements of the order, it may issue a summons (or an arrest warrant) to secure the offender's attendance. Under para 8(4), if a summons is issued but the offender fails to appear before the Crown Court, an arrest warrant may be issued.

Under para 9(6), where a community order was made by the Crown Court and the order provided that any failure to comply could be dealt with by a magistrates' court, and the offender is brought before the magistrates for non-compliance with the order, the magistrates have a discretion to commit the offender (in custody or on bail) to the Crown Court to be dealt with for the breach.

Paragraph 10(1) sets out the powers of the Crown Court where it is dealing with an offender for breach of a community order. If it is proved to the satisfaction of the court that the offender has failed, without reasonable excuse, to comply with any of the requirements of the community order, the Crown Court may deal with the offender in one of the following ways:

(a) by amending the terms of the community order so as to impose more onerous requirements which the Crown Court could impose if it were then making the order;

(aa) by ordering the offender to pay a fine of an amount not exceeding £2,500;

(b) by dealing with him, for the offence in respect of which the order was made, in any way in which he could have been dealt with for that offence by the court which made the order if the order had not been made;

(c) where—

(i) the offence in respect of which the order was made was not an offence punishable by imprisonment,

(ii) the offender is aged 18 or over,

(iii) the offender has wilfully and persistently failed to comply with the requirements of the order, by dealing with him, in respect of that offence, by imposing a sentence of imprisonment . . . for a term not exceeding 6 months.

Paragraph 10(2) requires the Crown Court to take account of the extent to which the offender has complied with the requirements of the community order.

Paragraph 10(3) makes it clear that, if the Crown Court adopts the option set out in para 10(1)(a), it may extend the duration of particular requirements under the community order, but not beyond the three-year maximum duration of community order fixed by s 177(5) of the Act.

Paragraph 10(4) goes on to provide that where the Crown Court adopts the option set out in para 10(1)(b) in the case of an offender who has wilfully and persistently failed to comply with the requirements of the community order, it may impose a custodial sentence (provided the offence for which the community order was imposed was an imprisonable offence) whether or not the original offence crossed the custody threshold contained in s 152(2) of the Act.

Under para 10(5), if the Crown Court chooses either of the options set out in para 10(1)(b) or (c), it must also revoke the community order if it is still in force.

Finally, para 10(6) makes it clear that the question whether the offender has complied with the requirements of the community order is to be determined by a Crown Court judge sitting alone (without a jury).

19.4 Commission of subsequent offences

Paragraph 22(1) of Sch 8 to the CJA 2003 provides that where an offender is subject to a community order made by the Crown Court and is convicted of an offence by a magistrates' court, the magistrates' court may commit the offender (in custody or on bail) to the Crown Court.

Under para 23(1) and (2), where an offender in respect of whom a community order is in force is either convicted of an offence by the Crown Court, or sent to the Crown Court under para 22, the Crown Court may either revoke the order or else both revoke the order and re-sentence the offender for the original offence.

Paragraph 23(1)(b) stipulates that the Crown Court may only exercise the power conferred by para 23 if it would be in the interests of justice to do so, having regard to circumstances which have arisen since the community order was made.

If the court re-sentences the offender for the original offence, it must take into account the extent to which the offender has complied with the requirements of the community order (para 23(3)).

20

Custodial sentences in the Crown Court

20.1 Introduction

In this chapter we consider the custodial sentences that can be imposed by the Crown Court on offenders who have attained the age of 18; and, at **20.6**, the sentence of long-term detention that the Crown Court can impose on juvenile offenders.

Where the offender is aged 18 to 20 (inclusive) the appropriate custodial sentence is 'detention in a young offender institution' (see **Chapter 16**). The maximum sentence is the same as that applicable to offenders who have attained the age of 21.

Where the offender has attained the age of 21, a custodial sentence takes the form of imprisonment.

20.2 Sentences over 12 months—release on licence

Prisoners serving sentences of 12 months or more (apart from dangerous offenders and life sentence prisoners, for whom there is separate provision) must be released on licence after serving half of their sentence. This release is subject to 'standard' and 'prescribed' conditions (and so, in effect, the second half of the sentence is 'served in the community').

The Criminal Justice (Sentencing) (Licence Conditions) Order 2015 (SI 2015/337) sets out conditions of licences upon release from prison under s 250 of the Criminal Justice Act 2003: there are standard conditions and additional conditions that may be imposed. The standard conditions of licence (under para 3) include requirements that the offender must: be of good behaviour and not behave in a way which undermines the purpose of the licence period; not commit any offence; keep in touch with the supervising officer and receive visits from the supervising officer; permanently reside at an address approved by the supervising officer (and obtain prior permission for any stay of one or more nights at a different address); not undertake work without the prior approval of the supervising officer; not travel outside the UK without prior permission. Other conditions of licence that may be imposed on a prisoner (eg under para 7) include ones relating to residence at a specified place; making or maintaining contact with a person; participation in, or cooperation with, a programme or set of activities; possession of specified items or documents; disclosure of information; a curfew arrangement; freedom of movement; supervision in the community by the supervising officer.

The Offender Rehabilitation Act 2014 also inserts a new section, s 256AA, into the Criminal Justice Act 2003. This creates a new period of supervision for offenders serving custodial sentences of less than two years. The supervision period begins at the end of the sentence and ends on the expiry of 12 months from the date of automatic release (s 256AA(4)). This means that an offender serves half of their custodial sentence in custody, the second half under licence in the community, with the post-sentence supervision period then applying until the offender has spent 12 months in the community since their automatic release date. The purpose of such supervision is the rehabilitation of the offender (s 256AA(5)).

The 2014 Act also inserts a new section, s 256AB, into the 2003 Act. This sets out requirements that may be specified during the supervision period, including: to be of good behaviour and not behave in a way that undermines the rehabilitative purpose of the supervision period; not to commit any offences; to keep in touch with the supervisor; to receive visits from the supervisor; to reside permanently at an address approved by the supervisor and to obtain prior permission for any stay of one or more nights a different address; not to undertake work, or a particular type of work, unless it is approved by the supervisor, and to notify the supervisor of any proposal to undertake work; not to travel outside the British Islands except with prior permission of the supervisor; to participate in activities in accordance with instructions given by the supervisor (including a rehabilitation activity requirement under s 200A).

20.3 Life sentences—murder

An offender aged 21 or over who is convicted of murder must be sentenced to imprisonment for life. In fact, as is well known, life generally does not mean life. The offender will be eligible for release after serving a specified minimum period of detention. The setting of the 'tariff' for such cases is governed in part by Sch 21 to the CJA 2003. However, in *R v Last* [2005] EWCA Crim 106; [2005] 2 Cr App R (S) 64, the Court of Appeal said that judges are free to depart from the guidelines contained in Sch 21 (and guidance issued by the SGC), provided that valid reasons are given for doing so.

Where the offender was under the age of 18 at the time of the offence, the sentence is one of 'detention at Her Majesty's Pleasure' (Powers of Criminal Courts (Sentencing) Act (PCC(S)A) 2000, s 90).

20.4 Mandatory minimum sentences

Under the PCC(S)A 2000, s 110, the court must impose a mandatory minimum sentence of at least seven years' custody where the offender is convicted for the third time of trafficking in Class A drugs unless 'particular circumstances' (relating to the offences or the offender) make this 'unjust'. Similarly, under s 111 of the 2000 Act, the court must impose a sentence of at least three years' custody where the offender is convicted for the third time of domestic burglary unless 'particular circumstances' (relating to the offences or the offender) make this 'unjust'. Under s 144(2) of the CJA 2003, discount for a guilty plea cannot result in a sentence of less than 80 per cent of the prescribed minimum sentence under s 110 or s 111.

An example of a case where it was held to be 'unjust' to impose the mandatory minimum sentence is *R v Stone* [2011] EWCA Crim 2823. The defendant had put his arm through an open window and removed a box containing items worth £60 and then walked off. This was his third offence of dwelling-house burglary and so s 111 of the 2000 Act applied. The Court of Appeal said that, in light of the nature of the offence and strong personal mitigation, it would be unjust to impose a sentence of three years.

Section 51A of the Firearms Act 1968 lays down mandatory minimum sentences for certain firearms offences: a minimum term of five years in the case of an offender who was aged 18 or over when he committed the offence or three years in the case of an offender who was under 18 at that time. The court has to impose a sentence of not less than this minimum term unless it is of the opinion that there are exceptional circumstances relating to the offence or to the offender which justify not doing so. In *R v Redfern* [2004] EWCA Crim 3291; [2005] 2 Cr App R (S) 44, the Court of Appeal expressed the view that cases where there are exceptional circumstances will be rare.

20.5 Dangerous offenders

There are three types of sentence that are specific to dangerous offenders.

20.5.1 Life sentences for dangerous offenders

Section 225 of the CJA 2003 applies where:

- a person aged 18 or over is convicted of a serious offence (ie a specified violent offence or a specified sexual offence, listed in Sch 15); and
- the offence is punishable with imprisonment for life; and
- the court 'is of the opinion that there is a significant risk to members of the public of serious harm occasioned by the commission by him of further specified offences'; and
- the court considers that the seriousness of the offence is such as to justify the imposition of a sentence of imprisonment for life.

In those circumstances, the court must impose a sentence of life imprisonment ('custody for life' where the offender is aged between 18 and 20).

Section 226 makes similar provision ('detention for life') for offenders under the age of 18.

20.5.2 Life sentence for 'second listed offence'

Section 224A of the CJA 2003 makes provision for a life sentence for a 'second listed offence'. A number of conditions have to be satisfied:

(a) A person aged 18 or over is convicted of an offence listed in Part 1 of Sch 15B.

(b) The court would otherwise impose a sentence of imprisonment for ten years or more (the 'sentence condition').

(c) At the time the present offence was committed, the offender had been convicted of an offence listed in Sch 15B and, for that previous offence, either a life sentence where the offender was not eligible for release during the first five years of the sentence, or a sentence of imprisonment for ten years or more, had been imposed on the offender (the 'previous offence condition').

Where those conditions are met, the court must impose a sentence of imprisonment for life unless it is of the opinion that there are particular circumstances which relate to the offence, to the previous offence or to the offender, and which would make it unjust to do so in all the circumstances.

20.5.3 Extended sentences

Section 226A of the CJA 2003 makes provision for extended sentences for offenders who have attained the age of 18 and who have been convicted of certain violent or sexual offences. It applies where a number of conditions are met:

(a) A person aged 18 or over is convicted of a specified offence.

(b) The court considers that there is a significant risk to members of the public of serious harm occasioned by the commission by the offender of further specified offences.

(c) The court is not required by s 224A or 225 (see earlier) to impose a sentence of imprisonment for life.

(d) Either:

  (i) at the time the offence was committed, the offender had been convicted of an offence listed in Sch 15B, or

  (ii) if the court were to impose an extended sentence of imprisonment, the term that it would specify as the appropriate custodial term would be at least four years.

Where these conditions are met, the court may impose an extended sentence of imprisonment on the offender.

An extended sentence comprises (a) the appropriate custodial term (ie the term of imprisonment which would otherwise have been imposed), and (b) a further period (the 'extension period') for which the offender is to be subject to licence.

The extension period must be a period of such length as the court considers necessary for the purpose of protecting members of the public from serious harm occasioned by the commission by the offender of further specified offences, but cannot exceed five years in the case of a specified violent offence or eight years in the case of a specified sexual offence (CJA 2003, s 226A(7) and (8)). Under s 226A(7A), the extension period must be at least one year.

Section 226B makes similar provision for offenders under the age of 18.

Under s 246A of the 2003 Act (as amended by the Criminal Justice and Courts Act 2015), where a prisoner is serving an extended sentence under s 226A or 226B, the Parole Board is able to direct release after the requisite custodial period (ie two-thirds of the appropriate custodial term), but there is no automatic release until the appropriate custodial term has been served. The Secretary of State must refer the case to the Parole Board when the two-thirds point of the appropriate custodial term has been reached; however, the Board can only direct the release of the prisoner if satisfied that it is no longer necessary for the protection of the public that he should be confined. The prisoner is released automatically at the end of the appropriate custodial term if he has not already been released.

20.5.4 Assessing dangerousness

In *R v Lang* [2005] EWCA Crim 2864; [2006] 2 Cr App R (S) 3, the Court of Appeal (considering earlier legislation on dangerous offenders) ruled that:

(a) 'Significant risk to members of the public' requires significant risk to be shown in relation to two matters: the commission of further specified offences; and the causing thereby of serious harm to members of the public. The risk must be significant, meaning 'noteworthy, of considerable amount or importance'.

(b) In assessing the risk of further offences being committed, the court must take into account the nature and circumstances of the present offence, the defendant's history of offending (including the kind of offence, its circumstances and the sentence passed, and whether the defendant demonstrated any pattern), social and economic factors in relation to the defendant (including accommodation, employability, education, associates, relationships and drug or alcohol abuse) and the defendant's attitude towards offending.

(c) A pre-sentence report should usually be obtained before any sentence is passed which is based upon significant risk of harm. The court will be guided, but not bound by, the assessment of risk in such reports; if the judge contemplates differing from the assessment in the report, counsel should be given the opportunity of addressing the judge on the point.

(d) The court should guard against assuming that there is a significant risk of serious harm merely because the foreseen specified offence is serious. Where the foreseen specified offence is not serious, there will be comparatively few cases in which a risk of serious harm can properly be regarded as significant.

In *R v Johnson* [2006] EWCA Crim 2486; [2007] 1 WLR 585, the Court of Appeal observed that previous convictions for offences which are not specified offences may be relevant (since a pattern of minor previous offences of gradually escalating seriousness may be significant).

20.5.5 Special custodial sentences for certain offenders of particular concern

Section 236A of the CJA 2003 (inserted by the Criminal Justice and Courts Act 2015) makes provision for 'special custodial sentences for certain offenders of particular concern'. Section 236A applies where (a) a person is convicted of an offence listed in Sch 18A to the CJA

2003; (b) the offender was aged 18 or over when the offence was committed; and (c) the court does not impose a sentence of life imprisonment for life or an extended sentence under s 226A. Where those conditions are satisfied, if the court imposes a sentence of imprisonment for the offence, the term of the sentence must be equal to the aggregate of the appropriate custodial term and a further period of one year for which the offender is to be subject to a licence. By virtue of subs (4), the term of a sentence of imprisonment imposed under s 236A must not exceed the maximum term permitted for the offence. The offender is eligible for release by the Parole Board after serving half the custodial term (and must be released at the end of the custodial term).

20.6 Young offenders—long-term detention under PCC(S)A 2000, s 91

Under s 91 of the PCC(S)A 2000, the Crown Court may impose a sentence of long-term detention (the maximum length of the sentence being the same as for an adult offender) where an offender under the age of 18 is being dealt with for an offence which is punishable (in the case of an adult offender) with 14 years' imprisonment or more (or where the offence is one of those specified in s 91 itself, eg sexual assault). This power may be exercised where the juvenile is sent to the Crown Court for trial and is convicted at that trial, or where the juvenile indicates an intention to plead guilty at a 'plea before venue' hearing in the youth court or is convicted following summary trial and is then committed to the Crown Court for sentence under s 3B of the PCC(S)A 2000.

Section 91 has two important effects:

(a) it enables the Crown Court to impose a sentence of detention that is longer than a detention and training order (the DTO being limited to a maximum of 24 months: see **Chapter 18**); and

(b) it enables the Crown Court to impose a custodial sentence on young offenders for whom a detention and training order is not available (namely (i) those aged 10 and 11, and (ii) those aged 12 to 14 and who are not 'persistent offenders').

In *R (C) v Balham Youth Court* [2003] EWHC (Admin) 1332; [2004] 1 Cr App R (S) 22, Scott Baker LJ (at para 33) said that 'the fact that an offender . . . does not qualify for a detention and training order because he is only 14 and not a persistent offender is not an exceptional circumstance to justify passing a sentence of less than two years under s 91 of the 2000 Act'. At para 34, his Lordship said that the relevant question in that case was whether it was such a serious case that detention above two years would or might realistically be required. In *R (M and W) v West London Youth Court* [2004] EWHC (Admin) 1144, Leveson J (at para 16) put the same question in slightly different terms:

> Whether there is a real prospect that a custodial sentence of, or in excess of, two years might be required, or is there any unusual feature of this case which might justify a sentence of less than two years, pursuant to s 91(3), for which purpose the absence of a power to impose a detention and training order because the offender is under the age of 15 is not an unusual feature.

In *R (H) v Southampton Youth Court* [2004] EWHC 2912 (Admin); [2005] 2 Cr App R (S) 30, it was emphasised that offenders under 18, and in particular those under 15, should be tried in the youth court, with Crown Court jurisdiction being reserved for the most serious crimes. It would, said the court, only be in exceptional cases that an accused aged 12 to 14 should be sent for trial to the Crown Court. Leveson J summarised the relevant principles as follows (paras 33–35):

> 33. The general policy of the legislature is that those who are under 18 years of age, and in particular children of under 15 years of age, should, wherever possible, be tried in the youth court. It is that court which is best designed to meet their specific needs. A trial in the Crown Court with the inevitably greater formality and greatly increased number of people involved (including a jury and the public) should be reserved for the most serious cases.

34. It is a further policy of the legislature that, generally speaking, first-time offenders aged 12 to 14 and all offenders under 12 should not be detained in custody and decisions as to jurisdiction should have regard to the fact that the exceptional power to detain for grave offences should not be used to water down the general principle. Those under 15 will rarely attract a period of detention and, even more rarely, those who are under 12.

35. In each case the court should ask itself whether there is a real prospect, having regard to his or her age, that this defendant whose case they are considering might require a sentence of, or in excess of, two years or, alternatively, whether although the sentence might be less than two years, there is some unusual feature of the case which justifies declining jurisdiction, bearing in mind that the absence of a power to impose a detention and training order because the defendant is under 15 is not an unusual feature.

A useful summary of the approach to be taken in cases which fall within the ambit of s 91 may be found in *R (CPS) v Redbridge Youth Court* [2005] EWHC 1390 (Admin); (2005) 169 JP 393, at para 11. Detailed guidance can also be found in the Sentencing Guidelines Council publication *Overarching Principles—Sentencing Youths* (<http://www.sentencingcouncil.org.uk/wp-content/uploads/web_overarching_principles_sentencing_youths.pdf>).

Where an offender under the age of 18 is convicted of an offence which carries life imprisonment in the case of an adult, the court may order detention for life under the PCC(S)A 2000, s 91.

Where an offender aged between 18 and 20 is convicted of an offence which carries life imprisonment in the case of an adult, the court may impose 'custody for life' under the PCC(S)A 2000, s 94.

APPENDIX 1
PLEA AND CASE MANAGEMENT HEARING: ADVOCATES' QUESTIONNAIRE

The Crown Court

CC Case Number D1

Date of trial

Fixed ☐
Warned ☐

Plea and Case Management Hearing

Advocates' Questionnaire

- Parties must complete this form.
- This form is to be used at all Crown Court Centres, without local variation.

There is an electronic version of the form on the Ministry of Justice website, at:
www.justice.gov.uk/courts/procedure-rules/criminal/formspage

PART ONE
(Questions 1 to 15 are to be completed in all cases, together with question 37 'Witness List')

1 Date of trial and custody time limits

1.1 Date of PCMH

PTI URN

Judge

Estimated length of trial

1.2 What are the custody time limit expiry dates as agreed between the parties? *(If different custody time limits attach to different offences or defendants, please give details.)*

1.3 Can an application to extend any custody time limit be made today? ☐ No ☐ Yes

2 Parties

	Prosecuting authority		Advocate
P			

	Defendant's name	Age	Remand status	Trial Advocate	PCMH Advocate (if different)
D1			C ☐ B ☐		

3 Contact details

3.1 Parties

P Office

Name	Phone
Email	

Advocate

Name	Phone
Email	

D1 Solicitor

Name	Phone
Email	

Advocate

Name	Phone
Email	

3.2 Case progression officers

P

Name	Phone
Email	

D1

Name	Phone
Email	

Court

Name	Phone
Email	

4 Readiness for PCMH

4.1 Which, if any, of the orders made at the magistrates' court have not been complied with?

P

D1

4.2 Are the parties ready for the PCMH? If not, why not?

P

D1

5 Has the defendant been advised that he or she will receive credit for a guilty plea?

D1 ☐ No ☐ Yes

6 Has the defendant been warned that the case may proceed in his or her absence?

D1 ☐ No ☐ Yes

7 What guilty plea(s) (if any) is the defendant offering?

D1

8 Should the case be referred to the Resident Judge for a trial judge to be allocated? ☐ No ☐ Yes

9 Give details of any issues relating to the defendant's fitness to plead or to stand trial.

D1

10 Prosecution evidence

10.1 Has the prosecution served the principal evidence on which the prosecution case relies, and if so when (give the date)? If not, why not?

P

10.2 What further evidence (if any) does the prosecution expect to serve? By when is it reasonably practicable to serve it (g ive the date)?

P

10.3 Defence comments (if any) on the prosecution replies to 10.1 and 10.2:

D1

11 Disclosure, defence statement and defence witness notice

11.1 Has the prosecution made statutory disclosure and if so when (give the date)? If not, why not?

P

11.2 When does / did the time expire for service of a defence statement and witness notice (give the date)?

P

11.3 Defence comments (if any) on the prosecution replies to 11.1 and 11.2:

D1

11.4 Has the defence served (a) a defence statement and (b) a witness notice, and if so when (give the date(s))? If not, why not?

D1

11.5 Do the defence statement and witness notice comply with the statutory requirements?

P *Prosecution comments (if any):*

11.6 Has the defendant been warned of the consequences of any failure to serve a defence statement and witness notice (a) within the time prescribed and (b) complying with the statutory requirements? ☐ No ☐ Yes

11.7 If the defendant has served a defence statement, does the defendant expect to apply for further prosecution disclosure? ☐ No ☐ Yes

11.8 If not clear from the defence statement, what are the real issues?

D1

P *Prosecution comments (if any):*

12 Expert evidence

12.1 Give details of any expert evidence likely to be relied upon, including why it is required and by when it is reasonably practicable to serve this.

P

D1

12.2 Is a note of agreement / disagreement required?

13 Witnesses

13.1 Have the parties completed the Witness List (see **37**)? ☐ No ☐ Yes

13.2 Are the parties satisfied that all the listed witnesses are needed (see **37**)? ☐ No ☐ Yes
If 'no', give details.

13.3 Are the parties satisfied that the time estimates for questioning witnesses are realistic (see **37**)? ☐ No ☐ Yes
If 'no', give details.

13.4 Is any witness summons necessary? ☐ No ☐ Yes
If 'yes', give particulars:

13.5 Can a timetable be fixed now for the calling of witnesses? ☐ No ☐ Yes
If 'no', why not?

14 Timetabling of the trial

14.1 Are there matters which need to be determined at the start of the trial, which may affect the timetable? ☐ No ☐ Yes
If so, when will (1) the jury and (2) the witnesses be required?

14.2 What timetable can now be set for the conduct of the trial (see rule 3.10)?

15 The indictment

15.1 Has the indictment been signed and dated as required by Part 14 of the CrimPR? ☐ No ☐ Yes

15.2 Is any amendment of the indictment required? ☐ No ☐ Yes

PART TWO
Question 37 (Witness list) is to be completed in every case
Answer the remaining questions only where relevant

16 Admissions and agreed facts

What matters can usefully be admitted or put into schedules, diagrams, visual aids etc.?

17 Case summary

P Is it proposed to serve a case summary or note of opening? ☐ No ☐ Yes

18 Measures to assist witnesses and defendants in giving evidence

18A Measures to assist a witness in giving evidence.

Each of these issues must be addressed separately in respect of each young vulnerable or intimidated witness who is or may be required to give evidence in person. (If completed electronically, the form will expand to deal with each separate witness separately. If completed manually, attach separate sheets if necessary.)

Name and age of witness:

Name: Age:

What arrangements have been made for a pre-trial visit?

What arrangements have been made to ensure that the witness sees the video of their evidence BEFORE the trial (i.e. not immediately before giving their evidence over the live link)?

Has the witness been offered a 'supporter'? ☐ No ☐ Yes
If 'yes', give particulars:

Does the witness need an intermediary? ☐ No ☐ Yes
If 'yes', give particulars:

What arrangements have been made for the witness to access the court building other than by the main public entrance?

What are the arrangements to ensure that this witness can give evidence without waiting or at least by reducing waiting to a minimum *(e.g. by ensuring that the opening and any preliminary points will be finished before the time appointed for the witness to attend or by agreeing and fixing a timed witness order in advance)* ?

Have the views of the witness been sought and, if so, has s/he expressed any particular view or concerns? ☐ No ☐ Yes

If 'yes', give particulars:

If views not sought, why not?

What material (if any) needs to be available to the witness in the video suite?

18B Defendant's evidence direction

Is any defendant's evidence direction to be sought?	☐ No	☐ Yes
If so, has the necessary application been made, complying with Section 4 of CrimPR Part 29?	☐ No	☐ Yes

If so, give details

18C **Witness anonymity order**

Is any witness anonymity order sought / to be made? ☐ No ☐ Yes

If so, has an application been made, complying with Section 5 of CrimPR Part 29? ☐ No ☐ Yes

If so give details (subject to the restrictions in Section 5 of CrimPR Part 29).

19 Young or vulnerable defendants

Are any other arrangements needed for any young or vulnerable defendants?

D1

20 Reporting restrictions

State type and grounds of any reporting restriction sought.

P

D1

21 Third party material

Is any application to be made for the production of third party material? ☐ No ☐ Yes

22 Defendant's interview(s)

22.1 Specify any issue relating to the admissibility of all or any part of the defendant's interview(s). Can the issue be res olved now ? If not, when ? Are skeleton arguments needed and, if so, when ?

22.2 By how much can the interview(s) be shortened by editing / summary for trial ? Give a timetable for the service of any proposed summary by the prosecution and agreement / counter-proposal by the defence.

22.3 Specify any other issues concerning the defendant's interview(s).

23 Witnesses giving evidence by video or DVD interview

23.1 Is there video or DVD evidence of any young / vulnerable / intimidated witness yet to be served?

23.2 Has each video been transcribed?

23.3 Is there an issue in relation to the accuracy / admissi bility / quality / length of any video or transcript?

24 Witness interview(s)

24.1 Are there any videos / audio tapes of witness interviews which, if they meet the disclosure test, are yet to be discl osed as unused material?

24.2 If so, is any application made for that video / audio tape to be transcribed and, if so, why?

25 CCTV evidence

25.1 Are there any outstanding issues in relation to service or disclosure of CCTV footage? *If the material is in the possession of a third party, complete **21** instead.*

25.2 Is an edited version to be served / used?

26 Electronic equipment

26.1 Give details of any special equipment (e.g. CCTV, live link, audio recordings, DVD) required in the trial courtroom.

P

D1

26.2 Is the evidence in its present form compatible with the equipment in court?

27 Cross-examination on sexual history

If an application has not already been made, does the defence intend to make an application under section 41 of the Youth Justice and Criminal Evidence Act 1999 to cross-examine a witness about his or her sexual history?

D1

28 Bad character

Are any directions necessary in relation to bad character applications? Are there to be any further applications?

P

D1

29 Hearsay

Are any directions necessary in relation to hearsay applications? Are there to be any further applications?

P

D1

30 Admissibility and legal issues

What points on admissibility / other legal issues are to be taken? Is it necessary for any to be resolved before trial?

P

D1

31 Public interest immunity

Is any 'on notice' public interest immunity application to be made?

P

32 Jury bundle

What proposals do the prosecution make for a jury bundle?

P

33 Concurrent family proceedings

Give details of any concurrent family proceedings.

34 Other special arrangements

Give details of any special arrangements (e.g., interpreter, intermediary, wheelchair access, hearing loop system, breaks) needed for anyone attending the trial.

35 Linked criminal proceedings

Are there other criminal proceedings against the defendant or otherwise linked?

36 Additional orders

Are any additional orders required?

37 Witness List (see table for completion, over page)

37 Witness List

The parties should indicate here which prosecution witnesses are required to give evidence at trial. The attendance of any witness is subject to the judge's direction.

Name of witness	Page No.	Required by	What is the relevant, disputed issue?	Estimated time for questioning	
				Chief	X - exam

APPENDIX 2
PREPARATION FOR EFFECTIVE TRIAL: CRIMINAL PROCEDURE RULES PARTS 1 & 3

.... Magistrates' Court

Preparation for effective trial
Criminal Procedure Rules Parts 1 & 3

- This form:
  - collects information about the case that the court will need to arrange for an effective trial: CrimPR rules 3.2 and 3.3
  - records the court's directions: CrimPR rule 3.5.
- After the court gives directions for trial, if:
  - information about the case changes, or
  - you think another direction is needed

  you must tell the court at once: CrimPR 1.2(1) & 3.9.

- If the defendant pleads not guilty, and the court requires:
  - the prosecutor must complete Parts 1, 2 and 4
  - the defendant must complete Parts 1, 3 and 4
  - the court will record directions in Parts 4 and 5.

See the separate notes for guidance on the use of this form.

There is extra space on page 4, or attach extra sheets if required. The electronic version of this form will expand.*

A list of standard trial preparation time limits is at page 7.

Part 1: to be completed by the prosecutor and the defendant (or defendant's representative)

Defendant

	Date of birth: Age: years

☐ Summons ☐ Requisition ☐ Charge ☐ Bail ☐ Custody Time limit expires:

Offence(s)

Police / CPS URN **Date of first hearing**

1 **Prosecution contact details**

Prosecuting authority		Phone Fax
	Email	

2 **Defendant's contact details**

Defendant	Address	Phone Mobile
	Email	

3 **Defendant's representative** *(if applicable)*

Solicitor		Phone Fax Ref
	Address	
	Email	

Representation is:
Defendant's representative to complete

legal aid granted ☐
legal aid applied for ☐
privately funded ☐

*Forms for use with the Rules are at: http://www.justice.gov.uk/courts/procedure-rules/criminal/formspage.

Part 2: to be completed by the prosecutor

4 Case management information

4.1 Are there any pending enquiries or lines of investigation? ☐ Yes ☐ No
If yes, give brief details:

4.2 Does the prosecutor intend to serve more evidence? ☐ Yes ☐ No
If yes, give brief details:

4.3 Does the prosecutor intend to serve a diagram, sketch map or photos? ☐ Yes ☐ No
If yes, give brief details:

4.4 The prosecution will rely on:
Tick / delete as appropriate

- defendant's admissions in interview ☐
- defendant's failure to mention facts in interview ☐
- [a summary] [a record] of the defendant's interview ☐
- [expert] [hearsay] [bad character] evidence ☐
- [CCTV] [electronically recorded] evidence ☐

4.5 What equipment (tape / DVD player, etc.) will the prosecutor need in the trial courtroom?
The prosecutor must make sure that the tape / DVD can be played in the courtroom.

4.6 Does the prosecutor presently expect the case to involve a complex, novel or unusual point of law and / or fact? *This information will help the court officer to list the case effectively.* ☐ Yes ☐ No
If so what?

5 Applications for directions

5.1 Does the prosecutor want the court to vary a standard trial preparation time limit? ☐ Yes ☐ No
If yes, give details:

5.2 Does the prosecutor want the court to arrange a discussion of ground rules for questioning? ☐ Yes ☐ No
If an intermediary is appointed, the court must discuss ground rules with the intermediary and advocates. A discussion may be helpful in other cases.

5.3 Does the prosecutor want the court to make any other direction? ☐ Yes ☐ No
If yes, give details:

Part 3: to be completed by the defendant (or defendant's representative)

6 Advice on plea and absence

Does the defendant understand that:

(a) he or she will receive credit for a guilty plea? ☐ Yes ☐ No
A guilty plea may affect the sentence and any order for costs

(b) the trial can go ahead even if he or she does not attend? ☐ Yes ☐ No
CrimPR rule 37.11

7 Partial or different guilty plea

7.1 If more than one offence is alleged, does the defendant want to plead guilty to any of them? ☐ Yes ☐ No ☐ N/A
If yes, which offence(s)?

7.2 Does the defendant want to plead guilty, but not on the facts alleged? ☐ Yes ☐ No
If yes, the court must be given a written note of the facts on which the defendant wants to plead guilty.

7.3 Does the defendant want to plead guilty, but to a different offence? ☐ Yes ☐ No
If yes, what offence?

8 Case management information

8.1 *Initial details of the prosecution case should have been served: CrimPR rule 10.2. The following statements are to help the court find out what is in dispute and give appropriate directions for trial. Tick as appropriate.*

The defendant [carried out] [took part in] the conduct alleged ☐ Yes ☐ No ☐ N/A

The defendant was present at the scene of the offence alleged ☐ Yes ☐ No ☐ N/A

The defendant was correctly identified ☐ Yes ☐ No ☐ N/A

The defendant was arrested lawfully ☐ Yes ☐ No ☐ N/A

[Nature of injury] [extent of loss or damage] ☐ Yes ☐ No ☐ N/A
If not agreed, explain what is in dispute:

[Fingerprint] [DNA] evidence ☐ Yes ☐ No ☐ N/A
If not agreed, explain what is in dispute:

[Medical] [identification of drug] [other scientific] evidence ☐ Yes ☐ No ☐ N/A
If not agreed, explain what is in dispute:

The [alcohol] [drug] testing procedure was carried out correctly ☐ Yes ☐ No ☐ N/A
If not agreed, explain what is in dispute:

Exhibits and samples were collected and delivered as stated (i.e. continuity) ☐ Yes ☐ No ☐ N/A
If not agreed, explain what is in dispute:

Defendant's interview [summary] [record] is accurate ☐ Yes ☐ No ☐ N/A
If not agreed, explain what is in dispute:

The defendant was [disqualified from driving] [subject to the alleged court order] at the time of the offence alleged ☐ Yes ☐ No ☐ N/A

The list of the defendant's previous convictions is accurate ☐ Yes ☐ No ☐ N/A
If not agreed, explain what is in dispute:

8.2 What are the **DISPUTED** issues of fact or law for trial, in addition to any identified in paragraph 8.1? *Give details. This question is to help the court find out what is in dispute and give appropriate directions for trial.* *CrimPR rules 3.2(2)(a), 3.3(a)*

8.3 Will the defendant give a defence statement? *Giving a defence statement is voluntary, but if one is given it must include the information collected in paragraphs 8.1 and 8.2 and must include particulars of facts relied on by the defence.* ☐ Yes ☐ No

8.4 Will the defendant need any tape or DVD player, etc. in the trial courtroom?
The defendant must make sure that any tape / DVD can be played in the courtroom.

8.5 Does the defendant presently expect the case to involve a complex, novel or unusual point of law and / or fact? *This information will help the court officer to list the case effectively.* ☐ Yes ☐ No
If so what?

9 Admissions

Can any facts which are not in dispute be recorded in a written admission? ☐ Yes ☐ No
Undisputed facts might include any statement accepted in paragraph 8.1.

If yes, a written admission [is set out here] [is attached] [will be served later].
Facts which are admitted are evidence: CrimPR rule 37.6 & Criminal Justice Act 1967, s.10.

If no, explain why:

10 Applications for directions

10.1 Does the defendant want the court to vary a standard trial preparation time limit? ☐ Yes ☐ No
If yes, give details:

10.2 Does the defendant want the court to arrange a ground rules discussion? ☐ Yes ☐ No
If an intermediary is appointed, the court must discuss ground rules with the intermediary and advocates. A discussion may be helpful in other cases.

10.3 Does the defendant want the court to make any other direction? ☐ Yes ☐ No
If yes, give details:

Parts 2 & 3 continued: additional information

Use this space to record any additional information, or to continue an answer started above:

Defendant's name:

Part 4: to be completed by the prosecutor, the defendant (or the defendant's representative) and the court

11 Prosecution witnesses. *If this information changes,* ***you must tell the court at once****: CrimPR rule 1.2(1) & 3.9.*

Name of witness	Tick if under 18 (*Prosecutor to complete*)	Interpreter needed? If so, specify language and dialect. (*Prosecutor to complete*)	Special or other measures needed? If so, specify.** (*Prosecutor to complete*)	What disputed issue in the case makes it necessary for the witness to give evidence in person? (*Defendant to complete*)	Tick if attendance proposed P (*Both parties to complete*)	D	Evidence to be read ('R') or time required per witness (*For the court*)
1)	☐				☐	☐	
2)	☐				☐	☐	
3)	☐				☐	☐	
4)	☐				☐	☐	
5)	☐				☐	☐	
6)	☐				☐	☐	

12 Expected defence witnesses. *If this information changes,* ***you must tell the court at once****: CrimPR rule 1.2(1) & 3.9.*

Name of witness	Tick if under 18 (*Defendant to complete*)	Interpreter needed? If so, specify language and dialect. (*Defendant to complete*)	Special or other measures needed? If so, specify.** (*Defendant to complete*)	What disputed issue in the case makes it necessary for the witness to give evidence in person? (*Prosecutor to complete*)	Tick if attendance proposed D (*Both parties to complete*)	P	Evidence to be read ('R') or time required per witness (*For the court*)
1)*	☐				☐	☐	
2)	☐				☐	☐	
3)	☐				☐	☐	

*If the defendant is likely to give evidence, list him or her as the first expected defence witness. **Special or other measures may include screens, evidence by live link or in private, video recorded interview as evidence, intermediary, breaks in examination or other measures to accommodate disability. They may increase the time needed for the witness. In some cases, the defendant may not be allowed to cross-examine a prosecution witness.

Defendant's name:

Part 5: record of court's decisions and directions for effective trial

13 Directions for trial *The court must actively manage the case by giving any direction appropriate to the needs of that case as early as possible: CrimPR rule 3.2(3). Complete or delete the following as appropriate*

13.1 The prosecutor must serve any further evidence by: *(date)*

13.2 The prosecutor must comply with the initial duty of disclosure by: *(date)*

13.3 A party who wants to use a tape / DVD player, etc. must check before the trial that it can be played in the courtroom.

13.4 The court expects only the witnesses listed as attending in Part 4 to give evidence in person and the evidence of other witnesses to be read.

13.5 [Witness summons / warrant] [other steps to secure attendance] for witness(es): *insert name(s)* *CrimPR Part 28; rule 3.8(4)*

13.6 Interpretation in the language(s) specified in Part 4 is required for: To be arranged by:

(defendant) Court staff *CrimPR rule 3.8(6)*

(witness) Prosecutor ☐ Defendant ☐

13.7 Special or other measures are directed for: As specified in:

(defendant) Part 4 ☐ paragraph 13.11 ☐

(witness) Part 4 ☐ paragraph 13.11 ☐

(witness) Part 4 ☐ paragraph 13.11 ☐

13.8 The court will discuss ground rules for questioning on: *(date)*
If an intermediary is appointed for a witness or for the defendant, the court must discuss the ground rules for questioning wit h the intermediary and the advocates before the witness or defendant gives evidence. Sufficient time must be allowed for this.

13.9 The defendant in person may not cross-examine witness(es): *insert name(s)* *CrimPR Part 31*
and the court directs cross-examination for that purpose by: *name representative*

13.10 Standard trial preparation time limits apply [except] [with these variations]:

13.11 Other directions:

14 Arrangements for trial

Date:		
Time:		
Court:		Court category:
Estimated trial length. *Include time for the court's deliberations and decision.*	.... hours *A detailed trial timetable must be considered and attached if necessary: CrimPR rules 3.8 & 3.10*	

After the court gives directions for trial, if information about the case changes, or you think another direction is needed, **you must tell the court at once**: CrimPR rules 1.2(1) & 3.9.

Signatures .... [on the direction of] [court]

Signed: .... for prosecution

Signed: .... [defendant] [defendant's solicitor]

Date: ....

Standard trial preparation time limits

The court can vary any of these time limits. Time limits marked * are not prescribed by rules or other legislation.

The total time needed to comply with all these time limits is 6 weeks (9 weeks if paragraph m applies).

Written admissions (Criminal Procedure Rules, r.37.6; Criminal Justice Act 1967, s.10)

a. The parties must serve any written admissions of agreed facts within **14 days.***

Defence statement (Criminal Procedure Rules, r.22.4; Criminal Procedure and Investigations Act 1996, s.6)

b. Any defence statement must be served within **14 days** of the prosecutor complying with the initial duty of disclosure.

Defence witnesses (Criminal Procedure and Investigations Act 1996, s.6C)

c. Defence witness names, etc. must be notified within **14 days** of the prosecutor complying with the initial duty of disclosure.

Application for disclosure (Criminal Procedure Rules, rr.22.2 & 22.5; Criminal Procedure and Investigations Act 1996, s.8)

d. The defendant must serve any application for an order for prosecution disclosure as soon as reasonably practicable after the prosecutor complies with the initial duty of disclosure.* *Under s.8 of the Criminal Procedure and Investigations Act 1996, no such application may be made unless a defence statement has been served.*

e. The prosecutor must serve any representations in response within **14 days after that**.

Witness statements (Criminal Procedure Rules, r.27.4; Criminal Justice Act 1967, s.9)

f. The defendant must serve any defence witness statement to be read at trial at least **14 days before the trial**.*

g. Any objection to a witness statement being read at trial must be made within **7 days of service of the statement.** *This does not apply to the statements listed in Part 4.*

Measures to assist a witness or defendant to give evidence (Criminal Procedure Rules, rr.29.3, 29.13, 29.17, 29.22, 29.26)

h. Any [further] application for special or other measures must be served within **28 days.**

i. Any representations in response must be served within **14 days after that**.

Cross-examination where defendant not represented (Criminal Procedure Rules, rr.31.1, 31.4)

j. The defendant must serve notice of any representative appointed to cross-examine within **7 days**.

k. The prosecutor must serve any application to prohibit cross-examination by the defendant in person as soon as reasonably practicable.

l. Any representations in response must be served within **14 days after that**.

Expert evidence (Criminal Procedure Rules, rr.33.4, 33.6)

m. If either party relies on expert evidence, the directions below apply.

- (i) The expert's report must be served within **28 days**.*
- (ii) A party who wants that expert to attend the trial must give notice within **7 days after (i)**.*
- (iii) A party who relies on expert evidence in response must serve it within **14 days after (ii)**.*
- (iv) There must be a meeting of experts under rule 33.6 within **14 days after (iii)**.*
- (v) The parties must notify the court **immediately after (iv)** if the length of the trial is affected by the outcome of the meeting.*

Hearsay evidence (Criminal Procedure Rules, rr.34.2, 34.3)

n. The prosecutor must serve any notice to introduce hearsay evidence within **28 days**.

o. The defendant must serve any notice to introduce hearsay evidence as soon as reasonably practicable.

p. Any application to determine an objection to hearsay evidence must be served within **14 days of service** of the notice or evidence.

Bad character evidence (Criminal Procedure Rules, rr.35.2, 35.3, 35.4)

q. The prosecutor must serve any notice to introduce evidence of the defendant's bad character within **28 days**.

r. Any application to determine an objection to that notice must be served within **14 days after that**.

s. Any application to introduce evidence of a non-defendant's bad character must be served within **14 days** of prosecution disclosure.

t. Any notice of objection to that evidence must be served within **14 days after that**.

Previous sexual behaviour evidence (Criminal Procedure Rules, rr.36.2, 36.3, 36.4. 36.5)

u. The defendant must serve any application for permission to introduce evidence of a complainant's previous sexual behaviour within **28 days** of prosecution disclosure.

v. The prosecutor must serve any representations in response within **14 days after that**.

Point of law, including abuse of process etc. (Criminal Procedure Rules, rr.3.3, 3.9)

w. Any skeleton argument must be served at least **14 days before the trial**.*

x. Any skeleton argument in reply must be served within **7 days after that**.*

Trial readiness (Criminal Procedure Rules, rr.3.3, 3.9)

y. The parties must certify readiness for trial at least **14 days before the trial**,* confirming which witnesses will give evidence in person and the trial time estimate.

November 2014

INDEX

P

Q

R

S